European Russia in 1773

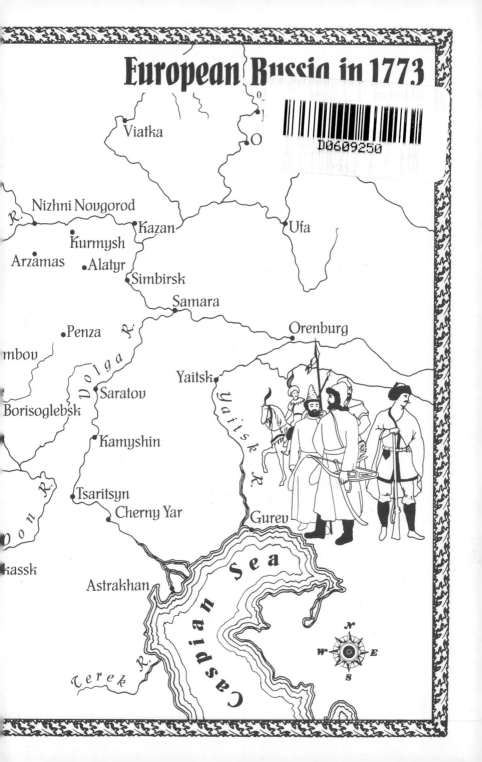

Viatka

O

O

Nizhni Novgorod

R.

Kurmysh

Kazan

Ufa

Arzamas

Alatyr

Simbirsk

Samara

Penza

Orenburg

mbov

Volga R.

Yaitsk

Borisoglebsk

Saratov

Yaitsk R.

Kamyshin

Tsaritsyn

Cherny Yar

Gurev

Don R.

kassk

Astrakhan

Caspian Sea

Terek R.

N W E S

Russian Rebels, 1600–1800

Russian Rebels

1600–1800

PAUL AVRICH

SCHOCKEN BOOKS · NEW YORK

ACKNOWLEDGMENTS. The bulk of the research for this volume was carried out during 1967 and 1968, while I was a Senior Fellow at the Russian Institute of Columbia University. I am grateful to the Institute's director, Professor Marshall Shulman, for his hospitality and encouragement, and to Professor Marc Raeff, who read the manuscript and offered his valuable advice. My thanks are due also to the staffs of the Columbia and New York Public libraries for their courteous assistance, and to the John Simon Guggenheim Memorial Foundation for supporting my research on Russian anarchism and peasant revolts.

P. H. A.

New York
January 1972

Contents

I. Bolotnikov, 1606–1607

II. Razin, 1670–1671

III. Bulavin, 1707–1708

IV. Pugachev, 1773–1774

V. The Legacy

Illustrations

SOURCES: (1) Isaac Massa, *Album Amicorum*, in *Archief voor Nederlandsche Kunstgeschiedenis*, Rotterdam, 1881–1882, Vol. IV. (2) E. S. Ovchinnikova, *Portret v russkom iskusstve XVII veka*, Moscow, 1955. (3) Adam Olearius, *Ausführliche Beschreibung*, Schleswig, 1663. (4) *Istoricheskii Vestnik*, LXII, 1895. (5) Jan Struys, *Voyages and Travels*, 1676 edn. (6) *A Relation Concerning . . . the Rebellion Lately Raised in Muscovy by Stenko Razin*, London, 1672. (7) D. A. Rovinskii, *Russkie narodnye kartinki*, St. Petersburg, 1881, Vol. I, part 3. (8) *Krest'ianskie i natsional'nye dvizheniia . . . Bulavinskoe vosstanie*, Moscow, 1935. (9) *Pamiatniki Kul'tury*, No. 32, 1961. (10) *Russkaia Starina*, 1876, book 1. (11) A. I. Dmitriev-Mamonov, *Pugachevskii bunt v Zaurale i v Sibiri*, St. Petersburg, 1907.

NOTE: In transliterating Russian words and proper names, I have followed the Library of Congress system in the footnotes and bibliography but have modified this in the text for the sake of readability. Similarly, I have modernized the spelling of quotations from early English sources, and have adopted the common short forms of the names of Cossack towns: for example, Yaitsk for Yaitskii Gorodok and Panshin for Panshinskii Gorodok, or Panshinskaia Stanitsa.

Introduction

"RUSSIAN REVOLTS, senseless and merciless." Such was Pushkin's description of the four great rebellions, led by Bolotnikov, Razin, Bulavin, and Pugachev, which shook the Russian state in the seventeenth and eighteenth centuries. Whirlwinds of death and destruction, they originated in the southern borderlands and swept across the open steppe into the Russian heartland, sending a thrill of terror through the landlords and officials in Moscow. Each time the violence spread with appalling swiftness, as tens of thousands of Russian peasants and townsfolk, joined by native tribesmen from the Volga and the Urals, rallied to the rebel standard, only to be crushed by government troops as they approached the centers of state power.

The four revolts, spread out over two centuries, were extremely complicated episodes with many disparate features that cut across social and political lines. They combined Cossack insurrections with urban risings, peasant jacqueries, anticolonial resistance, religious and sectional conflict, and political intrigue. Yet they all had much in common. In each case it was a Cossack from the Don who took the lead. In each case the line between banditry and rebellion was exceedingly thin. In each case the rising was directed not against the tsar but against the nobility and bureaucrats and the innovating state which they administered. Each originated in the southern frontier. Each occurred during or soon after a major war, when the burden of taxes and recruitment was heaviest and social dislocation most severe. Each was marked by savage violence and immense human suffering. In each, moreover, religious and social myths played a key part in inciting the rebellion. The lower classes were hungry for a messiah, and the ground swell of popular support that arose about the rebel leaders owed much to the belief that the promised savior had arrived to punish the wicked and purge the land of sin and suffering. All the leaders appreciated the power of propaganda, and they spread their "seditious letters" as far and wide as circumstances allowed. But the revolts were diffuse, elemental, and destructive. They lacked a coherent program and a coherent organization and, faced with regular military formations, were suppressed with great bloodshed. The leaders, in every case, were victims of betrayal. And similar legends grew up around them after their death.

Given the immense scope of the four rebellions and their jarring impact on Muscovite society, it is not surprising that they should have inspired an extensive body of literature, in Russia if not in the West. No less a writer than Pushkin thought Stenka Razin "the one poetic figure in Russian history" and collected poem cycles dealing with his exploits. Pushkin became interested in Pugachev as well, so much so that he made him the subject of a famous novel *(The Captain's Daughter)* and journeyed to the Urals to gather material for a history of his rebellion. In 1834, when Pushkin's history was finished, Tsar Nicholas I personally acted as censor and ordered the title changed from *A History of Pugachev* to *A History of the Pugachev Rising* on grounds that "a criminal like Pugachev can have no history," [1] but the work, in somewhat truncated form, was allowed to appear in print, and it became the starting point for all subsequent explorations of the subject.

Since Pushkin's time there has been a steady stream of literature on the four risings. Yet there are still important areas about which little is known, so that the historian who undertakes to investigate them today is faced with a difficult task. Even the most fundamental questions, such as the motives and social composition of the rebels, remain in dispute. The label "peasant wars," appropriated from Friedrich Engels' study of the great jacquerie in sixteenth-century Germany, did not come into vogue until after the Bolshevik Revolution. Before then, scholars were sharply divided over which social group constituted the driving force of the rebellions. A number of nineteenth-century historians, including Sergei Soloviev, assigned a dominant place to the Cossack legions of the southern frontier who, deprived of their traditional areas of plunder when the Turks sealed off the Black Sea, shifted the direction of their predatory attacks to the east and north, with Moscow as the ultimate target. The peasants, in Soloviev's estimation, played a significant but secondary role. For Soloviev, indeed, these were not "revolts" at all, but "raids" or "mutinies" launched by marauding freebooters in search of new territories for pillage and adventure.

Like Soloviev, Nikolai Kostomarov emphasized the role of the Cossacks in his history of Razin's rebellion, which, for all its romanticism, remains the most readable and imaginative treatment of the subject. But where Soloviev's sympathies clearly lay with the government and with the victims of rebel fury, Kostomarov sided with the Cossacks, who, it seemed to him, were far less interested in booty than in staving off Muscovite encroachments upon their cherished "liberties." The son of a serf-girl from the Ukraine who became a professor at Kiev University (rather than Moscow where Soloviev taught), Kostomarov was an ardent champion of Ukrainian autonomy and a member of the "federalist" school of historians, for whom Soloviev's exaltation of the centralized Russian state was anathema.[2]

Another prominent member of the federalist school whose background may have disposed him to favor the rebels was A. P. Shchapov, a native of Siberia and a professor in the Volga city of Kazan, the heart of an ethnically diversified region that saw some of the worst rioting in the days of Razin and Pugachev. Just as Kostomarov viewed Razin's uprising as a chapter in the age-old struggle in Russia between the decentralist and centralist traditions, Shchapov saw the *Pugachevshchina* as a conflict between the "antistatist, democratic, regional spirit of the masses," on the one side, and the ever-expanding power of the central government, on the other.[3] On the question of who revolted, however, Shchapov parted company with his fellow federalists and joined a group of eminent scholars—Platonov and Kliuchevsky among them—whose interpretation of the risings was tinged with populist sympathies. For these historians the outbreaks of Bolotnikov, Razin, Bulavin, and Pugachev were not mere Cossack mutinies but broad and shapeless revolts of all the have-nots in Russia, embracing Cossacks and impoverished noblemen as well as primitive peasants, brigands, vagabonds, and the flotsam thrown up from the lower depths of the towns, all of them pitted against the landlords and officials who throve on their misery and enslavement. "Bolotnikov," as Kliuchevsky put it in his tantalizingly brief account of the first great rebellion, "summoned to his standard all who desired to attain freedom, distinction, and wealth. For such folk the Pretender was the real tsar, although in the eyes of the more respectable citizens he was only the embodiment of lawlessness and disorder." [4]

Broadly speaking, then, Russian historians before 1917 treated the mass revolts either as Cossack outbursts which happened to touch off sporadic and uncoordinated peasant disturbances, or as all-encompassing, elemental risings of the downtrodden and dispossessed—"social discord between the depths and heights of society," as one writer expressed it in 1906, when Russia was undergoing an upheaval of even greater proportions.[5] Soviet scholars, however, have rejected both interpretations as "pseudo-scientific." Since 1917, as a leading Soviet authority on Pugachev has observed, "the young Soviet historical science has waged a relentless struggle with the landlord and bourgeois historical science. Soviet historians have deeply studied the works of Marx, Engels, and Lenin, and have striven to build their research on the foundations of historical materialism." [6]

The first fruit of these efforts was the new label "'peasant wars," derived, as we have noted, from Engels' famous work on sixteenth-century Germany. For Soviet specialists Russian history was more or less a recapitulation of what had already taken place in central and western Europe a century or two earlier. Accordingly, in the seventeenth and eighteenth centuries Russia, like Germany before it, was passing through the feudal epoch of history, and the risings of Bolotnikov and his successors, far from being mere "adventures of brigands," as Soloviev and Kostomarov portrayed them, were class struggles of the peasants to throw off the "yoke of feudalism."

Though the doctrinaire approach of these Soviet scholars leaves something to be desired (terms like "merchant capital" and "feudal mode of production" are freely applied to historical settings in which their relevance is dubious), their mastery of primary sources is matched only by the very greatest of their nineteenth-century forebears, and they provide a wealth of information without which it would be impossible to analyze the social composition of the rebellions. Who then were the insurgents? First place, in initiative if not in numbers, must be assigned to the Cossacks, who in every case provided leadership, organization, and a military ability which the other rebels lacked. Skilled horsemen and sailors, masters of sword and rifle, they combined an indomitable energy with a resourcefulness and love of adventure that was rare among the inhabitants to the north. Moreover, less dependent on the seasons which governed the rhythms of peasant life, they could plunge into action when the villagers were busy with planting, harvesting, or marketing their crops. And if many of the Cossack insurgents were themselves runaway serfs, Razin, Bulavin, and Pugachev all came from established families of several generations' residence, as did most of their lieutenants.

The Cossacks provided not only military leadership but a spirit of equality and justice and a model of independence, of a free and untrammeled life, that posed a serious challenge to the centralizing autocracy. But as they swept north their preponderance dwindled as a mass of new adherents streamed to their flag. Serfs, tribesmen, and urban poor "went Cossack" by the thousands— but Cossack in name only, with self-styled *atamans* to lead them. Of these recruits, of course, the peasants were the most numerous. Razin's revolt, in fact, was the largest jacquerie in Europe in the seventeenth century, just as Pugachev's was the largest in the eighteenth before the French Revolution, so that the label "peasant wars," however imprecise, does in fact convey something of the nature of the risings. More than that, many of the other participants—the lesser Cossacks, the lower clergy, the traders and craftsmen of the towns, the Volga boatmen and Urals foundry workers—were themselves essentially peasants, only recently uprooted from the soil, who retained their rural habits and grew much of their own food. Moreover, the majority of tribal adherents—the Mordva, Mari, and Chuvash, if not the Bashkirs— were also agriculturalists, in contrast to the nomadic Tatars and Kalmyks who often opposed them. On the other hand, the differences among the insurgents, religious, national, and social, must not be overlooked. Nor must the fact that in two of the revolts the peasant component was small: in Bolotnikov's only the Komaritskaya peasants were involved in large numbers, and in Bulavin's the jacquerie encompassed only the districts of Kozlov and Tambov, which were adjacent to Cossack territory. More important, in none of the risings did the peasants themselves take the initiative. The spark was provided, rather, by rebellious Cossacks or townsmen or by a pretender or other "outside agitator" who promised liberation.

But to call the risings either Cossack mutinies or peasant jacqueries, to the exclusion of other important elements, would be misleading. A contemporary Soviet scholar is on the right track when he notes in all the rebellions a "confusion of the interests of various classes." [7] The point is well illustrated by Stenka Razin's ecumenical battle cry, "For God and the Prophet, for the Sovereign and the Cossack Host!" The four revolts, as this slogan suggests, were phenomena of such bewildering complexity that no single formula can apply with any precision. The populist historians who saw the risings as amorphous struggles between the have-nots and the haves perhaps came closest to the true picture. One is confronted by a jumble of economic, political, social, religious, cultural, and sectional conflicts, compounded by simultaneous foreign wars and by an endless series of adventurers and intriguers lurking in the background. Cossacks of the steppe fought against the central government, poor Cossacks fought rich Cossacks, rising gentry clashed with declining boyar aristocracy, national minorities attacked Russian colonizers, Old Believers resisted the new faith, serfs rose against landlords, village went against town, periphery against center. Symbolic of the confusion was the bizarre spectacle of the runaway slave Bolotnikov fighting side by side with his former master, a prince and boyar, against the Muscovite government.

The aim of this book is to unravel the tangled story of the four revolts, to examine their nature, course, and outcome, and to analyze their ultimate historical significance. Who were the rebels? What were their motives, social origins, and modes of behavior? What did they want and what did they achieve? Such are the questions this work will try to answer. Comparisons between the revolts will be made throughout the text, and especially in the concluding section of each chapter, while a final chapter will evaluate the overall significance of the revolts and their impact on the subsequent history of Russia. In particular, an effort will be made to determine the extent to which they foreshadowed the revolutions of 1905 and 1917, which so profoundly affected the course of contemporary history.

This volume, however, is a general history of a very complex phenomenon. It makes no claim to be definitive. On the contrary, there is much work for future scholars to do—indeed each of the four revolts, to say nothing of the sporadic urban risings of the seventeenth and eighteenth centuries, deserves an independent study of its own, and it is hoped that this book will stimulate further research into the subject. For Western scholarship of early modern Russia, particularly of its social history, is still in a rudimentary stage. And those who have examined the Russian revolutionary tradition have tended to focus upon the political and intellectual movements of the nineteenth and twentieth centuries, on the revolutionary groups and parties, to the neglect of the peasantry and urban poor, one anonymous generation after another, "plundered, profaned, and disinherited," in Edwin Markham's phrase, who grew up, suffered, and died, then sank into oblivion, forgotten by posterity.

There are a number of reasons for this neglect. For one thing, peasants and artisans, "the poorest and most numerous class," as Saint-Simon described them, have left few records behind for scholars to examine. Even when literate, which was rare, they kept no diaries but have remained nameless, undocumented, and obscure, so that their aims and attitudes must be gleaned from sketchy government reports and other, often biased, fragments of evidence. Moreover, as Eric Hobsbawm has pointed out, most professional historians are educated townsmen with a strong rationalist bias who have made insufficient efforts to understand people so unlike themselves.[8] In recent years, however, a number of outstanding scholars, Hobsbawm himself among them, have shown a proper appreciation of the role of spontaneous mass movements in shaping history. From the work of Hobsbawm, George Rudé, E. P. Thompson, and also of Barrington Moore, who recently investigated the relationship between modernization and agrarian revolt, we are coming to understand that modern revolutions, like those of the past, have been largely spontaneous, driven by mass movements of urban and rural laborers, and in spirit predominantly anarchistic. No longer can these primitive, inarticulate, and often irrational groups be written off as fringe elements to be ignored by the historian. They lie, rather, at the very root of social change.

BOLOTNIKOV is, with the possible exception of Bulavin, the least well known of the four rebel leaders whose activities make up the contents of this book. Yet from the little we know of him he was an impressive figure, endowed with considerable personal magnetism, as well as a gift for military leadership and an extraordinary ability to command the devotion of the lower classes. He was the first of Russia's great social rebels; the first, that is to say, whose rising was not only a political rebellion against the Muscovite government but also a social rebellion against the system of bondage and exploitation. His was the first mass movement to combine a peasant uprising with widespread urban insurrection, the first movement from below bent on overturning the existing social order, even if it was not at all clear what was to take its place. Moreover, his rising in many ways set the pattern for future mass upheavals in the tsarist empire. The object of this chapter is to examine this first of Russia's "peasant wars," its origins, its rise and fall, and its ultimate significance in Russian history.

1. The Time of Troubles

"God hath a great plague in store for this people." Such was the gloomy prediction which Jerome Horsey, England's chief commercial agent in Moscow, entered into his notebook near the close of the sixteenth century.[1] A few years later, Tsar Fyodor, the last scion of the Rurik clan, was dead, and Muscovy was plunged into a chaos of famine, rebellion, and war known in history as the "Time of Troubles." Horsey, a seasoned observer of Russian affairs, blamed the gathering crisis on the misdeeds of Fyodor's infamous father, Ivan the Terrible, whose cruelty had bred "a general hatred, distraction, fear, and discontentment throughout his kingdom." [2] Nor is there any reason to challenge this indictment. During a long and brutal reign ending in 1584, Ivan had undermined the traditional order of the Muscovite state, leaving his subjects restless and disaffected. By the turn of the century Russia was ripe for a major upheaval. Ivan's "tyrannous practice," to quote the prophetic words of Giles Fletcher, "hath so troubled that country, and filled it so full of grudge and mortal hatred ever since, that it will not be quenched (as it seemeth now) till it burn again into a civil flame." [3]

The chief victims of Ivan's tyranny were the aristocratic boyars, the hereditary princes of the land, who had been waging a long but unsuccessful struggle to maintain their ancient privileges against the expanding claims of the throne. Assisted by the *oprichniki*, his agents of death and destruction, Ivan subjected the boyars and all others whom he considered disloyal to a campaign of terror. Thousands of his enemies, both real and imaginary, were flogged, tortured, and executed. Princely families were evicted from their ancestral estates in the Muscovite heartland and scattered along the southern frontier, where, Ivan believed, they would present no further obstacle to his autocratic ambitions. Boyar lands were confiscated and parceled out among the rising class of service gentry, who allied themselves with the tsar in his struggle against the entrenched power of the aristocracy.

In this way Ivan created a lasting foundation for the growth of Russian absolutism. The old society of semi-independent principalities, on the wane for more than a century, was dealt a blow from which it was never fully to recover. In its place there arose a centralized autocracy buttressed by a growing class of military landholders whose tenure depended on their loyal service to the crown. Yet it would be wrong to conclude that the once awesome power of the aristocracy had been completely eliminated. The boyars, though fatally weakened, retained a sense of pride in their exalted lineage and clung to the hope that their ancient privileges and independence would ultimately be restored.

The landed magnates were by no means the only victims of Ivan's violent reign. On the shoulders of the ordinary citizens fell the heavy burdens of taxation and troop levies to sustain the Livonian War, which dragged on for twenty-five years without securing Ivan's coveted foothold on the Baltic. Reduced to privation and despair, large segments of the population abandoned their native districts and fled across the Oka River to the sparsely occupied steppe in the south or else made for the fertile lands of the Volga basin, which had been opened to colonization by Ivan's conquest of Kazan and Astrakhan. By the end of Ivan's reign the stream of uprooted humanity, swelled by homeless victims of the *oprichnina* and of periodic invasions by the Crimean Tatars, had reached alarming proportions. The old settled regions in the center and northwest were rapidly being depopulated. "Many villages and towns," noted Fletcher in 1590, "stand all unhabited: the people being fled all into other places by reason of the extreme usage and exactions done upon them." [4]

The rising tide of fugitive peasants and townsmen at length drove the government to act. Although colonists were needed to strengthen Muscovy's hold on its newly acquired territories in the south and east, the depopulation of the heartland was depriving the state of its taxpayers and, worse still, was creating a shortage of agricultural labor which threatened the new class of service landowners with ruin. Thus crown and gentry worked hand in hand to curb internal migration. Desperate expedients were introduced in an effort to bind the peasant to the land and to his master. A notorious example was the so-called forbidden years, during which the right of departure was suspended. Such measures, however, were never completely successful. The dream of land and liberty continued to draw swarms of refugees to the open frontier, beyond the reach of landlords and government officials, where they hoped to live out their lives in justice and tranquillity as they imagined their ancestors had done in an earlier age.

The wholesale depletion of the center augured ill for the future stability of the Russian empire. Deprived of much of their labor force, the service gentry were left in an extremely precarious condition. As a result, they squeezed everything they could from their remaining serfs, which only drove an ever-increasing number to flight. For the villagers who stayed behind, the burdens of labor, taxation, and recruitment soon reached the breaking point. In the last decades of Ivan's rule serious rioting erupted in central Russia, where bands of peasants and highwaymen attacked monasteries and private estates in search of grain, booty, and revenge.[5] Even more alarming, however, was the situation in the borderlands. Here the way had been cleared for a full-scale civil war against the Muscovite center. Ivan's expulsion of the boyars, together with the swelling exodus of peasants and townsfolk, had concentrated along the southern frontier a throng of desperate men nursing sundry grievances against the crown and its supporters. "All the state hath he sundered in twain, as it were with an axe," wrote one of Ivan's contemporaries, "and this division, methinks, was the forerunner of all the dissensions by which the land is vexed to this day." [6]

Only a single spark was needed to set off a general conflagration. Yet it was not until the turn of the century, some fifteen years after Ivan's death, that the spark occurred, ironically at a time when the decline of the center seems to have been reversed and Muscovy was beginning to show signs of economic recovery.[7] In 1598 Tsar Fyodor, Ivan's last surviving son, died without heirs, bringing to an end the Muscovite branch of the Rurik dynasty. The nation was at once plunged into confusion. Throughout the realm men felt a sense of loss, for in the popular mind the tsar was the personification of the state, the protector of the people, the anointed mediator between man and God. "Without the tsar the land is a widow," went an old Russian proverb. "Without the tsar the people is an orphan." [8] In the eyes of his subjects the sovereign was the sole embodiment of law and justice, the "central knot" of the kingdom, as the historian Kliuchevsky put it, without whom all order must fall apart. Nor could the new ruler, Boris Godunov, fill the gap, however able and conscientious he might be. To the mass of ordinary citizens an "elected tsar" like Boris (or like Vasili Shuisky after him) must have seemed "something akin to an infringement of the laws of nature." [9]

Before the nation could recover from this unprecedented shock, a new catastrophe struck, causing fresh ferment in every corner. In the autumn of 1601, severe frosts and heavy snows caused disastrous crop failures throughout the land. During the next three years Russia lay in the grip of famine and pestilence. Godunov provided what relief there was, but grain hoarding and profiteering by landlords and merchants went largely unchecked, provoking much bitterness among the hungry and destitute, who attributed their plight to the absence of their legitimate tsar–protector. According to foreign witnesses, Muscovites were reduced to eating grass, birch bark, dogs and cats, and, when there was nothing else, even the corpses of their relatives and friends.[10] Some say that more than 100,000 were buried in the capital alone. Starvation and plague wiped out whole villages, and countless peasants, cast adrift by masters who were unable to feed them, flocked to the towns or roamed the countryside in search of food. The population, in the words of a contemporary chronicle, "threw itself from fear and horror into woods and swamps." [11] Fugitives in greater numbers than ever streamed to the southern frontier. Everywhere the roads were strewn with corpses.

The Time of Troubles had begun. In the absence of their natural sovereign, what the Russian people had endured for so long became unbearable, and they lashed out in a destructive fury against the emerging social order. There ensued a dozen years of chaos during which the very survival of the state seemed in doubt. In the early stages, social opposition took the relatively mild form of brigandage. With the authority of the state disrupted, bands of marauders sprang up in every quarter, playing havoc with the lives and property of the rich and powerful. Pleasant woodlands became the haunts of desperate men ready to swoop down on the granaries of monasteries and estates whenever the opportunity presented itself. Banditry of this sort, rooted as it was in social and economic discontent, constituted a distinct species of revolt. An indefinable borderland existed between criminal activity and rebellion, and the label "brigand," which the Russian government attached to dangerous rebels from Bolotnikov to Pugachev, was as much a reflection of this fact as it was a term of abuse.

The first important social rebel during the Time of Troubles to earn the title "brigand" was a certain Khlopko, about whom little is known other than that he bore the nickname "pigeon-toed" (Kosolap). In September 1603, during the height of the famine, Khlopko collected a band of slaves and peasants and headed for Moscow with the object of murdering the wealthy and seizing their food and possessions. As he approached the capital, however, he was met by a large government force commanded by Ivan Basmanov, one of Godunov's ablest officers. A fierce struggle took place, with heavy losses on both sides. Basmanov was killed and Khlopko, himself gravely wounded, was taken prisoner and carried off to Moscow, where he either died from his injuries or was executed. At the tsar's orders Basmanov was buried "with honor" in the great Trinity Monastery of St. Sergei.[12]

This fleeting episode, while interesting in its own right, takes on added significance when seen as the first of a series of rebel assaults on the Russian capital. Khlopko's movement, as a number of Soviet scholars have suggested,[13] represents the beginning of a great wave of social protest which did not recede till 1613, with the accession of Tsar Michael, the first ruler of the Romanov dynasty. Khlopko, in other words, claims our attention primarily as the forerunner of the two pseudo-Dmitris and of Bolotnikov, figures who also rose from obscurity to challenge the occupant of the throne. In fact, there is reason to believe that after their defeat by the government the survivors of Khlopko's band fled to the southern frontier and became eager recruits for these more formidable "brigands" who took up the standard of rebellion soon after.

Khlopko's successor, the False Dmitri, made his appearance the following year. Dmitri enjoyed enormous advantages over his hapless predecessor. He was not only very able and intelligent but also received extensive support from the Poles, who sought to exploit the distress and confusion in which Russia found herself. More than that, by calling himself the "Tsarevich Dmitri" he was able to capitalize on the longing of the Russian people for a "born tsar" to rescue them from their misery. The populace yearned for a messiah to restore a lost era of freedom and happiness. Ever since the famine had struck three years before, rumors had been afloat that a legitimate sovereign, with unbroken links to the Rurik clan, was still alive. Now, in the autumn of 1604, the rumors assumed tangible shape. The Tsarevich Dmitri, it was said, son of Ivan the Terrible and rightful heir to Muscovy, was on his way from Poland to reclaim the throne of his forefathers.

Actually the real Dmitri had died as a child in 1591, perhaps by stabbing himself while in the throes of epilepsy.[14] It was widely believed, however, that he had been murdered by the henchmen of Boris Godunov, who was hungry for the throne. According to the new rumors, Dmitri had miraculously escaped the assassin's knife and was returning to Moscow to deliver his subjects from their afflictions. The story at once gained widespread acceptance. This was partly because of the mystery which surrounded Dmitri's violent and untimely death; but the main reason was that the people wanted desperately to believe it—so desperately, in fact, that Muscovy during the Time of Troubles spawned at least a score of impostors. When men are miserable, Kliuchevsky observed, the way opens up for a pretender. And from the time of the first pseudo-Dmitri, pretendership became a "chronic malady" of the Russian state.[15]

The False Dmitri's campaign against Moscow originated in October 1604 in the inflammable borderlands of the southwest. The effects of the great famine had not yet worn off. In the town of Putivl, later to serve as Bolotnikov's base as well, a ragtag army of malcontents—political exiles, runaway peasants and slaves, Cossacks, petty service men, vagrants, urban poor—flocked to the Pretender's banner. Though their goals were disparate, Dmitri's followers made common cause against the emerging order of autocracy and serfdom, the untamed frontier rising in a fury of revolt against the centralized power of the Muscovite heartland. As the Pretender advanced toward the capital, gathering fresh adherents as he went, Godunov's forces deserted in droves, unwilling to oppose the "true sovereign," who promised to free his supporters of "all taxes and impositions" for ten years.[16] Such promises proved enormously effective. Dmitri's agents galloped from village to village and town to town as far as Moscow itself, disseminating their "seditious leaflets" over vast stretches of the country. A wave of rebellion and mass hysteria engulfed the whole area from Putivl to the Oka River at the very edge of the Muscovite center.

In April 1605, at the height of the crisis, Tsar Boris suddenly died, his spirit perhaps broken by the impostor's astonishing success. By June his young son Fyodor had been deposed and murdered at the instigation of the boyars, who had never reconciled themselves to the rule of the upstart Godunovs. Tsarevich Dmitri was then installed on the throne, while the old nobility awaited the moment to reassert their vanishing authority. Dmitri's rule was brief. In May 1606, barely eleven months after his triumphant coronation, the Pretender fell victim to a plot hatched by a prominent and ambitious boyar named Vasili Shuisky. Shuisky and his accomplices, at the head of an unruly mob, forced their way into the Kremlin on the pretext of preventing the Poles from "killing the boyars and our tsar." [17] In the melee Dmitri was hacked to pieces. His remains were then burned and the ashes fired from a cannon in the direction of Poland from which he had come. Then, in a noisy demonstration organized by the plotters, the mob proclaimed Shuisky tsar, the fourth ruler to occupy the Russian throne in little more than a year. It seemed, for the moment at least, that the aristocracy's dream of restoring their ancient rights and influence had been realized. But the boyars, as a modern historian has remarked, soon discovered that "it was easier to conjure a ghost than to get rid of one." [18]

2. Bolotnikov

No sooner had Tsar Vasili ascended the throne than fresh rumors began to circulate that the "Tsarevich" was still alive. Dmitri, it was said, had been spirited away to safety and another man butchered in his place. Sophisticated observers of the Muscovite scene "did not believe" this tale, noted a Polish visitor in his diary.[19] But the ordinary citizen, whose hopes had been stirred by the Pretender, was convinced it was true and yearned for Dmitri's speedy return. Shuisky took immediate steps to scotch the rumors before they could touch off a renewed crisis. A barrage of government charters was launched into every corner proclaiming that the Pretender and the real Tsarevich were both dead and that Vasili Shuisky was now the legitimate ruler of Muscovy. When this failed to halt the whispering, Shuisky persuaded the church to canonize the child Dmitri as a martyr and thus block any further attempts to invoke his identity. In June 1606 his body (rumored to be in a marvelous state of preservation, as befits the corpse of a saint) was disinterred from its resting place in Uglich and brought to Moscow for all to see. From the gates of the capital a solemn procession, headed by Shuisky and his boyar associates together with church dignitaries bearing icons and crosses, escorted the coffin to the Kremlin, where, at the conclusion of an elaborate ceremony, everyone repeated the oath of loyalty to the new tsar.[20]

As an added precaution, Shuisky adopted the tactic earlier employed by Ivan and Boris of banishing potential opponents to the frontier, entrusting some with responsible positions in local government. This, as it turned out, was a shortsighted expedient. True, there was little else one could do with unreliable persons at such a dangerous moment, short of exterminating them. But to pack them off to the incendiary borderlands spelled trouble of the worst sort. Indeed, it was Grigori Shakhovskoi, one of the first to be exiled by Shuisky, who triggered the rebellion of which Bolotnikov was shortly to assume leadership.

Shakhovskoi, though he bore the title of prince, was in fact a minor nobleman who had cast his lot with the False Dmitri in hopes of achieving the prominence which his undistinguished birth had denied him. Eventually he became one of the Pretender's closest associates. Yet Shuisky now appointed him military governor (*voevoda*) of Putivl, the very town from which Dmitri had launched his revolt against Moscow. Whether Shakhovskoi had won Shuisky's confidence or whether Shuisky simply wanted to get rid of him is not clear, though the latter seems more likely. At all events, from the moment he arrived in Putivl, Shakhovskoi began to incite the populace against the tsar, whom he denounced as a traitor and an assassin responsible for the taking of Dmitri's life. Shakhovskoi's words had a profound effect. Putivl, an ancient town famous for its historic role in Prince Igor's twelfth-century campaign against the Kumans,[21] cherished its glorious past and deeply resented its new role as a mere frontier outpost of Muscovite expansion. Its population, swollen by fugitives from central Russia, had been among the first to rally to Dmitri's flag in 1604, and many regarded him with lingering affection. Thus, when Shakhovskoi told them that Shuisky's plot had failed, that the tsarevich was safe in his former Polish sanctuary and would soon reclaim his throne from the boyar assassins, they "listened to this news with great rejoicing." [22] Refusing to swear allegiance to Shuisky, they took a new oath to Dmitri instead. Other towns in the neighborhood quickly followed suit. Before long the tidings of Dmitri's miraculous escape spread throughout the entire Slobodskaya Ukraina (as southwestern Russia was then called) and once more the area flared up in revolt against Moscow. In Putivl, the base of the new rising as of the old, Shakhovskoi set up a "great council" to supervise rebel operations. Local officials who remained faithful to Moscow, and government emissaries who had recently arrived to administer an oath of loyalty to Shuisky,

were put to the sword. In the words of a contemporary chronicle, the "spilling of Christian blood" had begun.[23]

Meanwhile, as Shakhovskoi promoted insurrection in Slobodskaya Ukraina, his principal confederate, Mikhail Molchanov, was
on his way to Galicia to drum up Polish support for a new march
on Moscow. Molchanov was a clever adventurer of gentry background, who shared his comrade's ambition and taste for political
intrigue. Well-educated and fluent in Polish and Latin, he had
hoped to win a place of influence in the court of Boris Godunov.
For unknown reasons, however, he fell out with the tsar and was
imprisoned on charges of practicing witchcraft. In revenge, he
took part in the murder of Godunov's son Fyodor, and afterward, like Shakhovskoi, joined the entourage of the Pretender.
But when Dmitri was slain and Shuisky installed in his place,
Molchanov fled the capital and made for Putivl and the Polish
frontier. As he went, he spread the word that the tsarevich had
been spared by the grace of God, and he urged his listeners to
help oust the boyar usurpers who had tried "to murder their
prince and then to choose a new king without making them acquainted with the causes of deposing the first nor asking their
consent in the choice of the latter." [24]

No sooner had he arrived in Sambor, Galicia, at the castle of
the pseudo-Dmitri's patron, George Mniszek, than Molchanov
received an urgent appeal from Shakhovskoi to return to Putivl
in the guise of the slain tsarevich. The rebellion, it seems, had
gathered momentum more rapidly than had been expected, and the
time was already ripe for a new pretender to appear at the lead.
Molchanov, however, was no more eager to assume the role than
Shakhovskoi himself appeared to be. He protested that he was
too well known in Moscow to pass himself off as Dmitri and that
he did not look at all like the slain impostor. Indeed, when he
halfheartedly tried out the part in Sambor, nobody would believe
him. A poor likeness, however, was seldom enough to deter a
would-be pretender, and one may safely assume that Molchanov,
mindful of Dmitri's fate, feared the consequences of failure.
In any event, matters took a new turn when a stranger named
Bolotnikov appeared in Sambor and accepted Molchanov's claim
to be the "Tsar Dmitri."

Though information about Bolotnikov's past is scanty, we

know enough to gain a fairly vivid impression of his character. A slave of Prince Andrei Teliatevsky, who will himself figure prominently in our story, Ivan Isaevich Bolotnikov ran away as a youth to the bands of Cossacks that roved the open frontier between Muscovy and the Crimean khanate. John Merick's narrative of the rebellion refers to Bolotnikov as "an old robber or borderer of the Volga." [25]

It hardly seems a mere coincidence that Bolotnikov and his successors—Razin, Bulavin, and Pugachev—should all have spent their formative years in the untamed steppe of the south, with its long tradition of rough-and-ready democracy and heroic adventure. As a haven for the dispossessed, the steppe posed a continual challenge to the unfolding Muscovite order of serfdom and autocracy. In this no-man's-land between the Dnieper and the Urals, Bolotnikov and his heirs nurtured their taste for an untrammeled life and the restlessness which drove them to seek adventure wherever they might find it. The Cossacks, moreover, had a military capacity and fighting spirit which the mass of peasants and townspeople lacked, and so they often took the lead in the risings, of the seventeenth and eighteenth centuries.

At some point in his Cossack career, Bolotnikov fell into the hands of one of the raiding bands of Crimean Tatars that periodically swept across the steppe "as wild geese fly, invading and retiring where they see advantage." [26] Sold into slavery, he worked for some years as a helmsman on a Turkish galley. Then, in the midst of a sea battle, he was liberated by German ships and taken to Venice, where he began the long journey back to Muscovy. Passing through Poland, he learned of the ferment in his homeland and apparently was attracted to Sambor by rumors that the deposed Tsar Dmitri had found sanctuary there. Thus the stranger who now confronted Molchanov was a seasoned warrior who had tasted both the abject servility of the bondsman and the unbridled freedom of the open steppe. Contemporaries depict him as tall and powerfully built and as an intelligent and energetic leader. His years as a Cossack and a galley slave had made him a skilled and courageous fighter, qualities for which he was to be praised by friend and foe alike.[27]

Molchanov must have recognized in Bolotnikov a remarkable

and useful man. Identifying himself as Tsar Dmitri, Molchanov presented his visitor with a saber, a fur coat, and a small sum of money and directed him to proceed immediately to Muscovy and open the way for his return to the throne. Whether Bolotnikov believed that he had actually spoken with the real tsar or whether he wished to satisfy his own lust for high adventure is not clear. Perhaps the quest for adventure led him to dismiss any doubts he might otherwise have entertained as to "Dmitri's" true identity. At any rate, during the ensuing years of rebellion, Bolotnikov consistently acted in Dmitri's name and, until the end, behaved as though he firmly believed that he was serving the rightful sovereign of Russia. On the other hand, Shakhovskoi and Molchanov plainly intended to treat Bolotnikov in the same way that Shuisky and the boyars had treated the False Dmitri —as an instrument to launch themselves into power and then to cast aside once he had outlived his usefulness.

In June or July of 1606 Bolotnikov arrived in Putivl armed with a letter from Molchanov identifying him as a faithful servant of Tsar Dmitri. The letter asked that he be furnished with every means of support. Shakhovskoi, eager for a commander to lead the march on Moscow, gave Bolotnikov a warm reception. He evidently agreed with Molchanov's high opinion of the newcomer, for according to a German observer named Conrad Bussow, he appointed Bolotnikov commander-in-chief (*Bolschoi Woywoden*) of the insurgent army and entrusted him with an initial force of 12,000 men.[28] These included a large part of the local garrison, of which Shakhovskoi, as *voevoda* of Putivl, was in command, augmented by fugitive peasants, impoverished townsmen, Cossacks, slaves, brigands, and drifters of every description who had flocked to Putivl to join the rebellion. Yet for all its motley character the rebel army was a force to be reckoned with. Its ranks were filled with desperate men who had nothing to lose. More than a few were veterans of Khlopko's and the False Dmitri's earlier campaigns against Moscow, and their fighting spirit was now revived by the news that the "true sovereign" was alive, and by the appearance of the remarkable stranger who had come to lead them in his name. Muscovy seemed to be witnessing a repetition of the popular ground swell which nearly two years before had carried the False Dmitri to the capital and deposited him on the throne. With Dmitri dead, however, it was his phantom that rode at the head of the new rebellion.

Once Bolotnikov arrived on the scene, the flames of revolt spread swiftly. By midsummer at least a dozen towns of the south-western frontier had gone over to the insurgents, and bloodletting and destruction devastated the area. The local residents, according to a contemporary chronicle, began to "seize the *voevodas* and throw them into the dungeons; they destroyed the houses of the boyars and robbed them of their possessions, and their wives and children they took for themselves." [29] In the midst of this violence Bolotnikov began his march to the north. Following the trail of Dmitri the Pretender, he led his army through the Komaritskaya district, a densely populated agricultural region situated on the divide between the Desna–Dnieper and Oka–Volga basins, across which lay the quickest route to the capital. His initial object was Kromy, an ancient town (mentioned in the chronicles as early as 1147, the same year that Moscow itself first appears) which, having fallen into obscurity with the decline of Kiev, had recently regained a certain measure of importance when a fort was constructed there to guard against invasions by the Crimean Tatars. This town, one of the first to go over to the rebels, formed a strategic gateway between Slobodskaya Ukraina and central Russia.

In an effort to stop the revolt before it ignited the heartland, Shuisky dispatched to Kromy a large force commanded by Prince Yuri Trubetskoi. Trubetskoi, driving back a column of insurgents who came out to meet him, placed the town under siege. For a moment it appeared that the rising might be nipped in the bud, but the situation changed when Bolotnikov arrived with his main army. Though they outnumbered the rebels by a wide margin, Trubetskoi's soldiers showed little inclination to fight. Petty servitors, they were unwilling to risk their necks for the "boyar tsar," and when the enemy approached they broke ranks and headed for home. News of their defection traveled quickly and shattered the morale of a second government force under Shuisky's brother-in-law, Prince Ivan Vorotynsky, who had meanwhile invested the nearby town of Elets, where the False Dmitri had left a cache of weapons and supplies the year before.

On first contact with the enemy, Vorotynsky's regiment melted away, and he himself, according to a contemporary source, "barely managed to flee to Moscow." [30]

From that moment the rebellion spread like wildfire. As Shuisky's forces distintegrated through mass desertion, the rebel army was swollen by a flood of new adherents anxious to serve the "true tsar." Between Kromy and Tula the unexpected appearance of retreating government troops set off a chain of local uprisings. Town after town throughout south-central Muscovy, spurred by the news of Bolotnikov's early success, "kissed the cross" for Tsar Dmitri.[31] It was as though the defeats of Trubetskoi and Vorotynsky were a signal awaited by every disaffected group to rally to the rebel standard.

3. The Towns

Although Bolotnikov's movement is often described as a "peasant war," in fact relatively few of his followers came from the countryside. Information is rather sketchy, but it seems clear that the rural population in Russia was not to play a major insurrectionary role until the revolts of Razin and Pugachev. It is also worth noting that those peasants who did join Bolotnikov did not as a rule come from the central regions, where serfdom was already well established and where the villagers lived in the deepest misery and oppression. They came, rather, from the Komaritskaya district in the southwest, a black-soil area rich in grain, beeswax, honey, flax, and hemp, where the peasants, though hard hit by the great famine, were comparatively well-off and still strong enough to array themselves against the approaching menace of bondage. In 1604 the Komaritskaya peasants had fought savagely for the False Dmitri, who had promised them a remission of their dues and of their recruitment quotas. In reprisal, Tsar Boris's armies had laid waste the countryside, leaving behind a smoldering desire for vengeance against the central government. Thus when Bolotnikov, flourishing the banner of Dmitri, launched his drive on the capital, the Komaritskaya populace flocked to him in considerable numbers.

But it was the towns that supplied the bulk of Bolotnikov's supporters and constituted the main theater of rebel activity. From available tabulations it appears that at least fifty cities of varying size and strategic importance went over to Bolotnikov's side, while dozens more remained in a state of unrest bordering on open insurrection.[32] The reasons for this are not hard to discover. As we have seen, Ivan the Terrible's wars and reign of terror had left the towns of Muscovy in a condition of acute and unprecedented distress. In the central and northwestern regions, where the development of handicrafts and trade had been seriously disrupted, the number of taxable households had fallen drastically, and in some cases whole cities were desolated, their inhabitants having run off to the frontier.[33] Beyond the Oka, however, the situation was becoming as desperate as that farther north. During the famine of 1601–1603, the sudden influx of hungry fugitives from the central districts had transformed such towns as Tula, Orel, Kromy, and Putivl into tinderboxes. A mass of destitute peasants, slaves, beggars, thieves, and other human debris crowded into the *posads* (taxpayers' quarters), aggravating the plight of the local artisans and small traders, who were already near the brink of starvation.[34]

The whole urban population was in constant flux. Each week saw the arrival and departure of rootless and destitute men who could find no secure place in a society where traditional ties were disintegrating. Anxiety and despair were endemic. To complicate matters, a large segment of the townspeople, particularly in the borderlands, consisted of petty service men—Cossacks, cannoneers, watchmen, gatekeepers, musketeers—whose reliability in times of stress was dubious. These men were recruited largely from the *posad* and shared its dissidence and propensity for violent outbursts. Thus it is small wonder that during Bolotnikov's march on Moscow, "many cities were taken." [35] As hotbeds of disaffection and as military, administrative, and financial outposts of the central government, the towns presented logical targets for frontal assaults by the insurgent forces. The rebels, often with the aid of the local inhabitants, would breach the citadels, throw open the jails, plunder the arsenals and treasuries, burn the tax rolls and title deeds, ransack the houses of the wealthy, and murder all who stood in their way.

Amid all this devastation, Bolotnikov had remarkable success in winning the loyalty and devotion of his ragged army. No doubt his courage and resourcefulness inspired confidence, but more important, he had sprung from the same social depths as his adherents and was able to articulate their grievances and aspirations. As "Dmitri's" commander-in-chief, he promised his followers freedom and land, honor and riches. All their woes he blamed on the landlords and officials who, he said, sucked the blood of the poor. In the words of Patriarch Hermogen, Bolotnikov's agents "disseminated their thievish letters in the towns . . . ordering the brigands to commit every wicked act from murder to plunder and to kiss the cross to that dead scoundrel and impostor, the unfrocked monk [pseudo-Dmitri], proclaiming the cursed one to be alive." [36] Under Dmitri's banner, Bolotnikov transformed the Time of Troubles into a social rebellion of the poor against the rich. His was a cry of vengeance for the have-nots—slaves, vagabonds, Cossacks, peasants, and the flotsam thrown up from the lower depths of the Russian towns—against those that thrived on their misery and enslavement.

Yet, for all its social content, the revolt did not divide Muscovite society strictly along class lines. On the contrary, a very complex struggle was unleashed, pitting men of the same class against each other and bringing men of different social position together to attain a common goal. Thus, while the lower classes predominated, a substantial part of the rebel army consisted of lesser noblemen bent on unseating the boyars and elevating their own rank and station. Like the common folk, the service gentry had fallen on hard times, and they too attributed their plight to the machinations of the boyars. In the scramble for labor caused by the mass flight of peasants to the frontier, the gentry found themselves losing out to the surviving boyar magnates, who were able to offer their tenants greater security and better conditions. As a result, more than a few impoverished landowners sank into the ranks of the peasantry, while others eked out a precarious existence by borrowing heavily and increasing the obligations of their serfs. Many were ruined outright during the great famine at the beginning of the century.

With Shuisky's rise to power, the minor nobility, who were striving to maintain their recently won social status against the

resurgent claims of the boyars, saw their worst fears realized.
For them the rule of Vasili Shuisky and his aristocratic clique
represented a disastrous throwback to the old landed oligarchy,
a radical departure from the pattern set by Ivan the Terrible and
his predecessors, of which they, the service gentry, had been the
chief beneficiaries. The "boyar reaction," they feared, meant
nothing else but the triumph of the genealogical principle over
the principle of merit; it would bar from advancement in the
civil and military hierarchies everyone whom Shuisky and his
coadjutors took to be of lowly birth.

It is not surprising, therefore, that the guiding spirits behind
Bolotnikov's revolt, Shakhovskoi and Molchanov, should have
been service noblemen. Nor is it surprising that among the first
to join them were the gentry of Tula, Riazan, Putivl, and other
towns beyond the Oka River, where the peril of Tatar raids had
bred a truculence like that of the Cossacks who roamed the
neighboring steppes. It was a squire from Tula, Istoma Pashkov,
who seems to have led the rebel detachment that put Prince
Vorotynsky to flight at Elets in one of the earliest engagements
of the uprising.[37] And no less important to the rebel cause was
the militia of Riazan commanded by Prokopi Liapunov, the
descendant of a line of boyars who had sunk to the level of
service gentry.

So it happened that gentry and rabble, for all their divergence
of outlook and aims, were thrown together by their common
determination to dislodge Tsar Vasili and his princely regime.
Landowners rubbed shoulders with bondsmen—or, to be more
precise, landowners and bondsmen marched in parallel columns
as two distinct but synchronized movements, intending to strike
in unison at the gates of the capital. The alliance, however, was
founded on shifting sand; where the gentry were bent on pre-
serving the new order of serfdom and autocracy from a boyar
restoration, the commoners, like the boyars themselves, were
struggling to recover the ancient liberties of which they had
been deprived by the rise of the service nobility and the centralized state. The gentry, as Platonov remarked, had entered
into an agreement with "their social adversaries."[38] And such an
agreement could not be of long duration.

4. Moscow

The rebels marched on Moscow as two separate armies, reflecting the broad social gulf which divided them. Yet they marched under the common banner of Tsar Dmitri, who had entered the capital in a blaze of triumph little more than a year before. Within both insurgent groups, hopes were high that Dmitri's success could be repeated. The left wing (both geographically and socially), led by Bolotnikov himself, followed the road from Kromy to Kaluga, intending to proceed from there to Serpukhov and Moscow. The right wing, under Istoma Pashkov and joined later by Liapunov and his Riazan militia, advanced on the capital by way of Tula (Pashkov's native city) and Kolomna. Numbering between 50,000 and 100,000 men, of whom the gentry constituted a small but powerful and well-equipped minority, the two forces expected to converge on the city and, in a joint assault, overwhelm the defenders, whose ranks had been depleted by mass desertion.

Meanwhile, Shuisky made a desperate effort to mobilize fresh troops to meet the impending onslaught. In a widely distributed charter the tsar appealed to his subjects to rally against the evil brigands who had "troubled many towns, wrecked and plundered churches, torn out icons and altars and gospels, smashed holy images of the Lord and trampled them under foot, murdered noblemen and merchants and townsfolk and taken their wives and daughters for their pleasure." [39] Though these words would seem better calculated to inspire terror than loyalty, Shuisky succeeded in collecting a new army to do battle with the advancing rebel columns. As the staging area for the government's forces the tsar chose the town of Kaluga, the hub of a defensive system along the upper Oka, and he appointed his brother Ivan Shuisky commander-in-chief. The appointment, however, was not a wise one. A man of mediocre gifts of mind and character, Ivan Shuisky lacked his brother's shrewdness and tenacity. Though his staff included Princes Yuri Trubetskoi and Ivan Vorotynsky, who were experienced in combat with the rebels, their regiments had been vanquished the previous month at Kromy and Elets, and this time they would fare no better.

On September 23, 1606, Bolotnikov's army reached the confluence of the Oka and Ugra rivers, a few miles below Kaluga. At this spot Ivan Shuisky chose to make his stand. The two armies joined in combat, but after a long and bloody battle Shuisky's men broke ranks and fled in disorder, while Bolotnikov's forces emerged intact and were able to continue their northward trek virtually unopposed. "The boyars who were defeated on the banks of the Oka," wrote a visiting merchant from Augsburg, "were compelled to fall back on the capital, in which there arrived each day thousands of wounded, slaughtered, and maimed." [40] Bolotnikov hurried on to Serpukhov, the last important town on his route to Moscow, and occupied it without a struggle. The capital, only twenty miles away, was seized with panic and confusion. For Vasili the end seemed near. As a final expedient, he ordered his brilliant young nephew, Mikhail Skopin-Shuisky, to head off the retreating remnant of his brother's army and take effective command. Skopin-Shuisky managed to rally the demoralized troops at the Pakhra River, twelve miles south of Moscow, and in the government's first major victory stalled Bolotnikov's' advance for a full three weeks, preventing him from linking up with Pashkov and mounting a concerted attack on the capital. Through this delay Shuisky's government won a desperately needed respite in which to regroup its battered forces.

In the meantime, Pashkov's column had made steady progress along its easterly route, encountering no serious resistance until Kolomna, the last government stronghold before Moscow. After a fierce struggle Kolomna was taken, and in reprisal the town was subjected to an orgy of looting, burning, and killing. When the rebels had satisfied their thirst for vengeance, they moved on to the village of Troitskoe, where government troops under Prince Fyodor Mstislavsky and Dmitri Shuisky (a second brother of the tsar) tried to block their advance. By now, however, Pashkov's army had been strengthened by the arrival of the Riazan militia, and an unequal contest took place in which "the brigands slaughtered and dispersed the boyars." [41] Mstislavsky and Dmitri Shuisky turned tail and fled, allowing the insurgents to advance to the very outskirts of Moscow. In early October Pashkov made camp at the village of Kolomenskoe, within easy striking distance of the capital. While awaiting Bolotnikov's arrival, he began the long siege (October 7–December 2, 1606) during which the fate of the rebellion was decided.

Shuisky's most serious problem during this critical period was the unreliability of his military personnel, from infantry and cannoneers to their gentry and boyar commanders. Men of every rank fled with their families to safer locations outside the capital. Owing to combat losses and mass desertion, in the succinct words of the chronicle, "Tsar Vasili in Moscow was left with few men." [42] Undaunted, Shuisky mobilized whatever resources he could find. "Shuisky," writes Kliuchevsky, "though small of stature, plain of exterior, and short of sight, was nevertheless no fool." [43] Under his capable supervision Moscow girded itself for the coming attack. Improvised fortifications were hastily thrown up around the city. A new oath of loyalty was administered to the populace. Men and boys were conscripted for immediate service. To Shuisky's brother Ivan fell the task of raising fresh troops from the towns, monasteries, and estates remaining outside the orbit of rebel control. And although Ivan's emissaries got a cool reception, enough men were mustered to offer the besiegers serious resistance.

The tsar divided these forces into two separate units. The main body entrenched itself at the southern end of the city, behind the wooden walls built by Ivan the Terrible to withstand the recurrent raids of the Crimean Tatars. Meanwhile, a mobile detachment of picked troops under young Skopin-Shuisky launched hit-and-run attacks against the rebel bases at Kolomenskoe and Zaborie. By this strategy Bolotnikov and Pashkov were held at bay for several weeks, during which they prepared their forces for a major assault on the capital.

The key to Moscow's fate lay in the hands of its lower-class inhabitants. For several months the city's poor had been greatly agitated by rumors of Tsar Dmitri's return. Now, as the siege wore on and food supplies dwindled to precarious levels, their patience was running out. Everywhere, noted a Polish observer, "there was hunger, alarm, and great disquiet," as Muscovites witnessed a grim repetition of scenes from the famine of 1601–1603. Many dropped in the streets from lack of food; others, afflicted with headaches, coughing fits, and cracking limbs, "died from these ailments, while the living bore their suffering with patience, awaiting their salvation from God." [44] At any moment, it seemed, the growing unrest might erupt into open rebellion. For who, asked the historian Soloviev, would go hungry for Shuisky? [45]

Throughout the siege Bolotnikov and Shuisky competed for the allegiance of the Muscovite mob. Bolotnikov's most effective weapons were the "thievish letters" which his fifth column smuggled into the capital and distributed in the lower-class districts with telling effect. Although the actual leaflets have not been preserved, something of their contents is known from references in contemporary chronicles, as well as in John Merick's narrative and in the charters of Patriarch Hermogen. Issued in the name of Tsar Dmitri, they called on the people to "seize Moscow, destroy the houses of the magnates, the powerful, and the well-born, and take their wives and daughters for yourselves." [46] The fullest description is given by the Patriarch in a letter to Metropolitan Filaret written in November 1606: "The rebels stay in Kolomenskoe near Moscow and write their cursed leaflets, ordering the boyars' slaves to kill their masters, promising them their wives and estates, urging them to massacre all the merchants and to seize their goods, and summoning them to the rebel camp to be given the rank of boyar, *voevoda*, chamberlain, or state secretary." [47]

In October and November 1606, manifestoes of this sort aroused new hope among the Muscovite poor and fanned their hatred of the wealthy and powerful. So alarmed was Shuisky that he had all the scribes of the Moscow area rounded up and their handwriting compared with the handwriting on the leaflets, but to no avail. Failing in this, he spared no effort to counteract the effects of the propaganda on the uneasy populace, calling on the church to assist him. "The grand princes," wrote a Polish visitor, "ordered the people to visit the churches and pray before the Blessed Virgin and the Archangel Gabriel and beg with tears for their assistance against the enemy." Special services were conducted in which bishops and priests admonished their parishioners not to "betray themselves into the hands of the wicked brigands and blood-poisoners," and on one such occasion Archpriest Terenti of the Annunciation Cathedral in the Kremlin described a dream in which the Holy Spirit appeared to him and damned the rebels as heretics, while promising salvation for Tsar Vasili's loyal supporters.[48]

Shuisky's chief ally in these endeavors was Patriarch Hermogen, an old man of eighty and former Metropolitan of Kazan, whom the tsar had raised to his exalted position only a few months before. Despite his advanced age, Hermogen proved himself one of the most energetic figures on the government's side during these troubled times. Several years later, in 1612, he was to die a martyr's death in prison at the hands of the Polish invaders. Now, describing the rebellion as the work of "Satan and his demons," he appealed to the Orthodox to rally behind the tsar. Vasili, he declared, was "'in truth the holy and legitimate and genuine Christian tsar." [49] Rumors persisted, however, of the imminent return of the "real sovereign" to his rightful place on the throne. According to Conrad Bussow, a delegation of ordinary Muscovites even went to the rebel camp in Kolomenskoe and asked to see Tsar Dmitri "with their own eyes." Bolotnikov dispatched an urgent message to Shakhovskoi to send "Dmitri" to the capital without delay, since the people were ready to swear allegiance to him if he appeared in the flesh.[50]

By the middle of November the mob, which had adopted a wait-and-see attitude, was ready to cast its lot with the rebels. Angry crowds gathered before the Kremlin to shout their disapproval of Shuisky's government. According to a German witness, a full-scale insurrection would surely have broken out within the capital but for the unexpected news on November 15 that Liapunov and his Riazan militia had forsaken their allies and gone over to the tsar.[51] This windfall, together with the arrival of badly needed reinforcements from the Smolensk area and from the towns of the Northern Dvina, ended all further prospects of rebellion in Moscow and marked a sharp turning point in Shuisky's fortunes.

What had prompted Liapunov to defect? The underlying reason, it appears, was the incompatibility between the service nobles and their plebeian confederates. Through the adherence of the gentry the rising lost whatever lower-class homogeneity it had originally possessed. It was under the walls of Moscow that Liapunov and his fellow squires realized that an unbridgeable gulf

separated their own rebellion from that of the common folk. Bolotnikov's manifestoes bore eloquent testimony to the social character
of his movement, and the gentry began to fear for their own lives
and property. However jealous they might be of the aristocracy,
they now felt their common links as landowners and noblemen
and desperately strove to stem the popular tide that they had
helped to set loose. As Merick noted, "the nobles and better sort
of citizens, perceiving in what extremity they were, employed all
their credit and means to assist the emperor." [52] Shuisky, for his
part, was ready to meet the lesser nobility halfway. To Liapunov,
for example, he offered higher rank, a seat in the boyar council,
and a large purse of silver. In effect, the "boyar tsar" had been
compelled to modify the aristocratic nature of his regime and
to restore, at least in part, the alliance between gentry and crown
forged by Ivan the Terrible and his predecessors. The result, in
Platonov's words, was a "breakup of the rebel mass into the social
elements of which it was composed." [53]

Liapunov's desertion had immediate and profound repercus-
sions. Not only did it deprive the insurrection of its most formidable warriors, but it also aroused wide dissension in the rebel
camp, thereby preparing the way for further defections. As a
result, the balance of strength rapidly shifted in Shuisky's favor.
Reinforcements continued to pour in from Smolensk, Rzhev,
Volokolamsk, Mozhaisk, Viazma, and Dorogobuzh, and from the
commercial settlements along the Northern Dvina. Moreover,
many towns which earlier had turned a deaf ear to Ivan Shuisky's
recruiting sergeants eagerly sent additional troops to the capital.

A glance at the map (see endpapers) reveals the sectional character of the conflict. Roughly half the territory of the realm refused to accept Shuisky's rule. Opposition was concentrated in
the south and along the middle and lower Volga from Nizhni
Novgorod to the river's mouth at Astrakhan. The center and
north, by and large, continued to support Moscow. In a rough
way this corresponds to Ivan the Terrible's division of the land
into the *oprichnina*, in which he settled his loyal supporters, and
the outlying *zemshchina*, to which he banished his opponents.
Toward the end of Ivan's reign, when the center fell into decline,
the balance of strength began to tip to the peripheries, which,

thronged with fugitives and malcontents of every type, rose to challenge Moscow's authority.

Bolotnikov's revolt, like Dmitri's before it, was a major episode in this sectional war of the frontier against the heartland. The inhabitants of the steppe, with their rough-and-tumble independence, lashed out against Moscow's efforts to bring them to heel. In the ensuing struggle the trading communities along the Northern Dvina and upper Volga rushed to defend the capital, with which they had strong regional and commercial ties. It seems likely, moreover, that a nationalist element was also involved, for the population of these northern regions was of the same Great Russian stock as Moscow, in contrast to the mixed Cossack, Tatar, Ukrainian, Polish, and tribal inhabitants of the southern borderlands. Significantly, the same towns of the north were to form the backbone of the national army which expelled the Poles from Moscow a few years later, bringing the Time of Troubles to an end. By the same token, it was the strong hostility of Smolensk and its neighbors toward the Poles that brought them in against Bolotnikov, whose imaginary "Tsar Dmitri" was tainted with Polish support.

If the rebellion was to have any chance of success, then, Bolotnikov had to stop the flow of men and supplies through Moscow's northern gates, which opened onto the region furnishing Shuisky with his strongest support. So far, as Merick noted, Moscow was only half besieged, "the other part of town I know not through what blindness left open to take in forces and victuals." On November 26, Bolotnikov attempted to "block it up." [54] With a large force he set out along the banks of the Moscow River to the northern end of the city, intending to seal it off from the outside. Shuisky marshaled every available unit to head the rebels off. By now the government could again boast a formidable army. In addition to Skopin-Shuisky and his crack cavalry, there were also Liapunov's militia, a contingent of musketeers (*streltsy*) from the commercial towns linking central Muscovy with the White Sea, and a powerful regiment from the Smolensk area under the able command of Ivan Kolychev, who, fresh from lifting a rebel siege at Volokolamsk, had raced to Moscow when he heard that the besiegers intended to "kill the tsar and boyars." [55]

Shuisky's impressive army assembled in Red Square to hear Patriarch Hermogen intone a prayer for victory. Then its helmeted horsemen rode off to the clanging of bells in the towers and cathedrals of the Kremlin. That evening—it was November 26—the rebels were intercepted at the northern suburb of Krasnoe Selo. A fierce battle began which continued through the night and into the next morning. Blood flowed freely, and the battlefield was thick with dead and wounded from both sides. Then, by an act of treachery, Bolotnikov's fate was sealed. At the height of the struggle Istoma Pashkov "went over with all his service gentry to Tsar Vasili." [56] Pashkov, like Liapunov before him, apparently experienced a moment of truth in which Shuisky seemed a lesser evil than Bolotnikov. His decision no doubt was strengthened by a handsome reward of rank and riches held out to him by the tsar. Perhaps, too, as Bussow suggests, he was jealous of Bolotnikov's title of "great *voevoda*," which Shakhovskoi had bestowed on the former slave back in Putivl.[57] But more important, Pashkov had come to realize that his plebeian comrade-in-arms was a graver menace to his class and to the social order which had evolved over the last two centuries than was the boyar oligarchy headed by Shuisky.

Pashkov's defection dealt a severe blow to the rebel cause. "The enemy," reported Merick, "being abashed at the departure of one of their chief leaders [were] all divided amongst themselves." [58] Aside from a battered collection of townsfolk, slaves, and peasants, only a hard core of serving men remained loyal to Bolotnikov,[59] and Shuisky's forces had little difficulty in putting them to flight. At a single stroke the initiative had passed to the government. Seizing the offensive, Skopin-Shuisky, on December 2, led a confident army against the rebel strongholds of Kolomenskoe and Zaborie. Bolotnikov mustered his weary followers and advanced to meet them. At the village of Kotly, midway between Kolomenskoe and Moscow, the two forces locked horns in a terrible struggle which cost the insurgents 1000 dead and more than 20,000 prisoners. With Skopin-Shuisky hot on his heels, Bolotnikov beat a retreat to Kolomenskoe and hastily dug in against his pursuers. Rather than storm the rebel bastion and risk heavy casualties, Skopin-Shuisky launched a merciless cannonade which lasted three days without letup. Finally Bolotnikov's redoubt was set ablaze, forcing him and a tattered remnant of his once enormous army to flee toward the south, the direction from which they had come. Skopin-Shuisky then made directly for the second rebel camp at Zaborie, a few miles away, where the demoralized defenders surrendered without a fight. Eventually they were given as slaves to the boyars and gentry who had proved in combat their loyalty to the tsar. A different fate, however, awaited those who had been captured in battle. Each night they were taken out by the hundreds and slaughtered "like oxen" and their bodies shoved beneath the ice of the Yauza River.[60]

Thus the siege of Moscow was lifted, and—among the upper classes at least—there was great rejoicing. In every church, recorded a Polish witness, thanksgiving prayers were recited and bells pealed forth their triumphant message, "for such was the custom." [61] For valor in battle Skopin-Shuisky and Ivan Kolychev were elevated to the coveted rank of boyar. Tsar Vasili at once issued charters proclaiming that the revolt had been crushed and the country saved from disaster. Yet, for all the jubilation and excitement, the situation remained precarious. Vast stretches of the south remained in rebel hands, and each week brought news of fresh risings along the Volga. Moreover, Bolotnikov himself was still at large. And the ghost of Dmitri continued to haunt the land.

5. Kaluga and Tula

Bolotnikov's defeat at Moscow had shattered the backbone of his movement. Nevertheless, in widely scattered areas outside the main orbit of the revolt, disturbances occurred long after the siege of the capital had been lifted. In early December the northeastern towns of Viatka and Perm, in the foothills of the Urals, rose against the central government on the premature news that Tsar Dmitri had "arrived at Moscow with a great quantity of men and taken it." In the northwest, at the medieval city of Pskov, "much blood was spilled" as a result of false rumors that Shuisky planned to make a deal with the hated Swedes.[62] More serious still was the situation on the Volga. Conquered by Ivan the Terrible in the middle of the sixteenth century, the Volga basin had been opened to a tide of Muscovite colonization, to which the local tribes had never reconciled themselves. For a whole year following Shuisky's accession to the throne, violence raged unchecked over a large swath of territory from the bend of the river to its mouth at the Caspian. During the winter months Mordva beekeepers and peasants joined dissident Russians in besieging Nizhni Novgorod, the main administrative center of the middle Volga. Serious rioting, in which Russian peasants fought side by side with Mordva, Mari, Chuvash, and Tatars, spread to Arzamas and Alatyr, and the inhabitants of nearby Sviiazhsk swore an oath of fealty to Tsar Dmitri, which they renounced only when the Metropolitan threatened to place the town under interdiction. Finally, at the mouth of the Volga the *voevoda* of Astrakhan, Prince Ivan Khvorostinin, playing a role analogous to that of Shakhovskoi in Putivl, incited a rebellion in Dmitri's name which took the government several months to put down.[63]

These risings were in every case spontaneous affairs without direct links to Bolotnikov and his movement. Yet the participants undoubtedly knew of Bolotnikov's activities, and they shared his hatred of the Muscovite government, as well as a common desire for local autonomy as against the autocratic system that threatened to engulf them. Shuisky faced a very difficult task in bringing these far-flung eruptions under control. To meet his pressing need for funds, the tsar extracted large sums from merchants and monasteries—the rich Trinity Monastery was tapped no less than three times in a six-month period—as well as from his boyar associates. In an effort to preserve the allegiance of his troops, he compensated them for injuries suffered on the battlefield and promised a bounty for every rebel killed or captured. Officers who distinguished themselves in combat were rewarded with land and money and were allowed to claim for their own the rebel slaves and peasants whom they took prisoner, a practice which sometimes embroiled them in disputes with the legal owners.[64]

Beyond this, Shuisky took steps to curb the flight of peasants and townsmen, which continued to deprive the state of taxes and recruits while serving to perpetuate social unrest. By a decree of March 9, 1607, he extended the period for recovering runaway peasants from five to fifteen years. Local officials were directed to carry out periodic searches for fugitives, and landlords caught harboring them were fined and subjected to public flogging. This measure was intended as a sop to the service gentry, who suffered most from peasant flight and whose support, so crucial during the Moscow siege, the government was bent on consolidating. A genuine aristocratic reaction had proved impossible to achieve. Irresistibly, Russia was carried along by the powerful tides of absolutism, state service, and peasant bondage. The old order of decentralization and boyar independence was lost forever. Distinctions between noblemen of birth and noblemen of service were gradually becoming blurred, as both groups were bound together in a mutual alliance with the crown for the purpose of keeping the lower orders in check.

The immediate task before Shuisky was to track down and annihilate Bolotnikov's bedraggled forces, who meanwhile had retreated to Serpukhov, some twenty miles southwest of the capital. Finding the town short of food and supplies and its citizens none too happy at the appearance of his hungry army, Bolotnikov continued to retrace his steps, hoping to meet a friendlier reception farther south. This, at last, he found on the Oka River at Kaluga, whose inhabitants eagerly accepted him as the authentic representative of Tsar Dmitri. And just in time, for a few days later his pursuers, led by Dmitri Shuisky, arrived in force and mounted a savage attack on the city. Bolotnikov was ready for them, and after a furious battle Shuisky was forced to withdraw with heavy casualties to await reinforcements. These arrived in due course, equipped with battering rams and siege guns. Yet the rebels fought back with reckless courage and, despite a murderous bombardment, the walls could not be breached. "Much blood was spilled," says the chronicle, "but Kaluga was not taken." [65]

In Moscow, Bolotnikov's stubborn resistance provoked renewed alarm. Shuisky, though still confident of victory, grew anxious and impatient; and when a Baltic adventurer named Friedrich Fiedler offered to go to Kaluga and murder the rebel chieftain, the tsar eagerly accepted, furnishing him with money, a horse, and the promise of a large estate with an annual subsidy once the deed had been accomplished. But when Fiedler arrived, says Conrad Bussow, who happened to be in Kaluga during the siege, he at once revealed the whole plot and was handsomely rewarded by a grateful Bolotnikov.[66] Meanwhile the besiegers tried a new tactic. Next to Kaluga's walls they constructed a high tower from wood that neighboring peasants had been ordered to cut. Their plan was to set the tower ablaze when the wind was blowing in the direction of the town and thereby produce a general conflagration. During the night, however, in a daring maneuver, the defenders tunneled under the walls and planted kegs of powder at the base of the tower. When these were ignited there was a great explosion, and the tower burst into flames and collapsed, killing everyone on it. This new setback convinced the Muscovites that there was no easy way to capture the town, so they proceeded to impose a total blockade in the hope of starving its population into submission. Before long Kaluga lay in the grip of hunger, and its inhabitants were reduced to eating their horses and oxen. Yet Bolotnikov and his followers, for all their anxiety over dwindling food and munitions, showed remarkable fortitude, and the siege was to take nearly six months to run its course.[67]

At this point a new pretender enters our already overpopulated story, a certain Ileika (or Ilya) Gorchakov from the town of Murom. By an interesting coincidence, his name carried heroic associations, for Ilya of Murom, according to ancient epic, was a warrior who served "the Christian faith, the Russian land, the city of Kiev, the widows, the orphans, and the poor." The present Ilya of Murom, however, was of a different stamp. The illegitimate son of a cobbler, he was no less typical than Bolotnikov himself of the bandit-Cossack element in the revolt, the restless drifters cut loose from insecure social moorings to seek their fortune in brigandage and adventure. As a youth Gorchakov had left his native town to find work in the busy *posad* of Nizhni Novgorod. But he soon tired of the humdrum life of a shop assistant and signed on as cook of a merchant vessel plying the Volga route between Nizhni and Astrakhan. Once in Astrakhan he jumped ship and fled to the Cossack community on the Terek River, where he sold himself into slavery to a service nobleman named Grigori Elagin. It was on the Terek that Gorchakov began to call himself "Tsarevich Peter," the nonexistent son of Fyodor Ivanovich, last tsar of the Rurik line, whose death in 1598 had precipitated the troubles in which Russia now floundered. "Petrushka" (a diminutive of Peter) attracted a band of

300 Cossacks, slaves, and *streltsy*, pillaged the bazaars and palaces of Astrakhan, then made his way up the Volga and across the steppe to Putivl, where Shakhovskoi had sent for him.[68]

During the long and fruitless siege of Moscow, Shakhovskoi had begun to cast about for a new instrument with which to realize his ambitions. Bolotnikov's campaign had been losing momentum, and no new Dmitri had appeared to give it a boost. Thus, hearing of Gorchakov's exploits in Astrakhan, Shakhovskoi summoned him to his headquarters, spreading the word meanwhile that the dead daughter of Tsar Fyodor was really a boy named Peter, who had miraculously survived and would soon be in Putivl to ride with him against the boyars. Fantastic though this story was, it nevertheless secured Tsarevich Peter a considerable following. By the time he reached Putivl his band of desperadoes had swelled into a small army some 4000 strong, which might have been even larger had the new impostor been more amply endowed with personal magnetism. But Petrushka lacked Bolotnikov's sympathetic qualities and gifts of character. He was a coarse and bloodthirsty brigand with a virulent hatred of the upper classes. On his way through the Slobodskaya Ukraina he put the nobility and officials through excruciating tortures, dangling them by their heels or nailing them up by their hands and feet before they were shot to death or thrown from bridges and watchtowers into the moats below. When he arrived in Putivl he murdered the former *voevoda*, a supporter of Shuisky, and "shamefully took his daughter to bed." [69]

Petrushka and Shakhovskoi, having collected a force of 30,000, set out to the north to combine with Bolotnikov in a fresh campaign against Moscow. Alarmed at the appearance of a new pretender, Vasili issued a charter proclaiming that

> the Great Sovereign and Tsar and Grand Prince Fyodor Ivanovich, of blessed memory, autocrat of all Russia, had no sons (there was one daughter, the Tsarevna and Grand Princess Feodosia, who by God's wish did not survive her childhood, but aside from the one daughter Tsar and Grand Prince Fyodor Ivanovich of all Russia had no other offspring). The bandit Cossack Ileika, who calls himself Tsarevich Peter, is the slave of the service nobleman Grigori Elagin, and his mother and wife and sister, all of lowly stock, are still alive.[70]

At the same time Shuisky ordered reinforcements to Kaluga to prevent Bolotnikov's allies from liberating his beleaguered army.

This, of course, was exactly what Shakhovskoi intended to do. While proceeding to Tula, which now replaced Putivl as headquarters of the revolt, he detailed a dissident boyar and fellow supporter of the False Dmitri, Prince Vasili Masalsky, to relieve Bolotnikov. On February 11, 1607, Masalsky was just a few miles from Kaluga when catastrophe overtook him. On the banks of the Vyrka River, a tributary of the Oka, his detachment was caught off guard by a fierce onslaught by government troops. What followed was a massacre rather than a battle. The rebels lost most of their men and all their standards and supply wagons. In despair, a group of survivors sat down on some powder kegs, set them alight and blew themselves sky high. Masalsky himself fell mortally wounded on the battlefield and was carried off to Moscow, where he died. According to Isaac Massa, a Dutch merchant in Moscow who left a valuable account of the rebellion, the victors raced back to Kaluga and shouted the news of their triumph to the rebels inside, demanding that they now surrender, but Bolotnikov laughed defiantly and swore to remain loyal to the true sovereign, Dmitri.[71]

It was nearly three months before a second relief force was dispatched to Kaluga. Ironically enough, it was headed by Bolotnikov's former master, Prince Andrei Teliatevsky, an able officer of boyar rank who, like so many of Bolotnikov's noble supporters, including Shakhovskoi, Molchanov, and Liapunov, had sided with the False Dmitri two years before; indeed, it was he who brought Dmitri the invitation to take the throne after Fyodor Godunov's murder. Thus it is not surprising that he should now oppose the man responsible for Dmitri's downfall. Shuisky, moreover, had banished him to the southwest to serve as *voevoda* of Chernigov, just as his confederate Shakhovskoi had been banished to nearby Putivl.[72]

In early May Teliatevsky reached the village of Pchelnia, just south of Kaluga, where a large government force attempted to block his path. After a savage struggle the Muscovites were driven off, leaving thousands dead on the battlefield, among them their commander, Prince Andrei Cherkassky, as though in payment for Masalsky's death on the Vyrka. After six terrible months

the siege of Kaluga had been raised, and Bolotnikov was able
to join his associates in Tula.

With memories of Bolotnikov's siege still fresh, Moscow was
seized with panic at the thought of a new attack. To forestall
this, Shuisky laid plans for an immediate march on the rebel
bastion of Tula. At Serpukhov fresh regiments were collected
from every corner, and the town soon echoed to the sounds of
wagons and hooves, drums and trumpets. The size of Shuisky's
army was awe-inspiring, contemporary estimates being as high as
150,000 men.[73] The tsar himself was nominal commander-in-chief,
but he had enough sense to place his gifted nephew, Skopin-
Shuisky, in effective charge. In early June, as the troops made
ready to depart, Patriarch Hermogen prayed for God's assistance

> against the enemies of Christ's cross, the traitors, brigands, robbers,
> thieves, boyars' slaves, and Don and Volga Cossacks, who, having
> forsaken God and the Orthodox Christian faith and forsworn their
> oaths of loyalty, are defiling the churches of God and spilling
> Christian blood without stop and plundering estates and violating
> women and children. Aiming to destroy forever our Orthodox
> Christian faith and holy churches of God, they draw to themselves
> faint-hearted men, declaring that the dead scoundrel and unfrocked
> monk is still alive and calling him Tsarevich Dmitri.[74]

As Shuisky's army rumbled toward Tula, Bolotnikov and Teliatevsky assembled some 30,000 men and hurried north to intercept it. The bizarre spectacle of the runaway slave riding side
by side with his former master, a prince and boyar, is symbolic
of the complexity of the rebellion and of the general confusion
of the times. When they reached the Vosma River, below the
town of Kashira, the rebels ran into a large advance body of
Muscovites, and they joined in furious combat. Men flung themselves at one another, and the dead began to pile up. The climax
came when a contingent of 1700 insurgents dug themselves into
a narrow ravine and fired with murderous accuracy at the government troops. In an effort to dislodge them, Bolotnikov's former
allies from Riazan mounted their horses and charged the ravine.
At great cost they scattered the enemy, whose powder gave out
during their frantic resistance. The rebels were rounded up and
cut to pieces on the spot. Everything now went badly for the remainder of the insurgents, whose morale had been shaken by the

disaster that had befallen their comrades. After a day of carnage, in which Bolotnikov and Teliatevsky lost half their men and an immense quantity of equipment, the rebels fell back in disorder toward Tula. Four miles above the town, on the banks of the Voroniia River, Bolotnikov and Teliatevsky rallied their forces for another stand. But, following an unequal trial of strength with their pursuers, they abandoned the field and withdrew, utterly disheartened, to the shelter of the city.

At the end of June Tsar Vasili arrived at the gates of Tula with the main body of his huge army. Although he outnumbered the rebels by five to one, the reduction of the city was not an easy task. Tula boasted a fortified citadel of stone surrounded by an outer ring of wooden walls, which afforded its inhabitants considerable protection from intruders. At Shuisky's approach alarm bells sounded in every quarter, putting the defenders on the alert. Deploying his artillery on two sides of the city, the tsar's nephew, Skopin-Shuisky, opened the attack with a prolonged bombardment followed by an infantry assault in mass formation. Behind the walls, the rebels fought with everything they had to repulse the enemy, while working feverishly between assaults to repair their damaged defenses. Through it all, noted a Dutch merchant named Elias Herckman, Bolotnikov proved himself a brave and worthy commander.[75] For six weeks the pattern of bombardment and attack continued with ceaseless monotony, yet Shuisky's army achieved very little, and an increasing number began to desert for home.

At this point a petty nobleman from Murom named Ivan Krovkov came forward with a bold plan. His idea was to dam the Upa River, which flows through the city, and flood Tula's stubborn inhabitants into capitulation. Shuisky at first was skeptical, but when Krovkov persisted, offering his life if the plan should fail, the tsar gave his assent. Thus, in early August, a dam was built from sacks of earth on the Upa just west of Tula, and Krovkov's expectations were fulfilled. Much of the city was quickly inundated. Townsfolk had to get around on rafts or in small boats. Supplies of arms and powder fell to dangerous levels. Food became scarcer than ever. According to contemporary observers, men ate dogs and cats and carrion in the streets, and many died from hunger and exhaustion.[76] The strain began to tell on the defenders' nerves, occasionally breaking out into open quarrels and mutual accusations. For a growing segment of the population surrender appeared to be the only course.

In desperation Shakhovskoi sent message after message to Poland, begging George Mniszek to send a new tsarevich "from his pretender factory" without delay.[77] To the surprise of many, in July 1607 a second Dmitri did in fact make his long-awaited appearance near the Polish border. And two months later, having attracted a swarm of enthusiastic supporters, he began to march on the town of Briansk, intending to proceed from there to Tula and Moscow. Had the new pretender succeeded in joining forces with Bolotnikov and Shakhovskoi, their repeated promises of his arrival would have been realized, and this in turn might have produced a ground swell of support that could have altered the destiny of the rebellion. Thus Shuisky had to act quickly to end the stalemate at Tula. Rejecting an offer of help from the Swedes, the tsar, it appears, entered into direct negotiations with the rebel leaders. According to a number of sources, he offered to spare them and grant them "full liberty" if they surrendered immediately.[78] Other accounts deny that such overtures were made and insist that the weary townspeople themselves handed over the ringleaders. In any case, on October 10, 1607, after four months of hardship, Tula opened its gates to Shuisky's army, thus terminating the last siege of the rebellion.

Shuisky, exulting in his hard-won victory, issued a triumphant proclamation to his subjects: "By the grace of God, the treasonous men in Tula, Prince Andrei Teliatevsky and Prince Grigori Shakhovskoi and Ivashko Bolotnikov and all the Tula folk, have taken the oath to the Great Sovereign and Tsar and Grand Prince, Vasili Ivanovich. Acknowledging their misdeeds, they have kissed the cross, and the same is true of the slave of Grigori Elagin who calls himself Petrushka." [79] That same day Bolotnikov and Petrushka were brought to Shuisky's headquarters, where the angry soldiers cursed them for the death of their comrades, brothers, and sons. Then, if Bussow and Herckman are to be believed, the following exchange took place between the tsar and his adversary:

Shuisky: Are you the bandit and traitor who rose against his Sovereign and tried to defeat him, believing that you yourself could thus attain the heights of state power?

Bolotnikov: I have been true to the oath which I gave in Poland to the one who called himself Dmitri. Whether or not he was Dmitri I cannot tell, as I had never before set eyes on him. I served him faithfully, but he abandoned me, and now I am here at your mercy and under your power. If you wish to kill me, here is my own saber. If you wish, on the other hand, to show me clemency, according to your promise and oath, then I shall serve you as truly as I have served till now him who has forsaken me.[80]

Those, however, who had put any faith in Shuisky's clemency were doomed to be disappointed. From the tsar's camp at Tula Bolotnikov and "Tsarevich Peter" were conveyed under heavy guard to Moscow, where they underwent the grueling interrogations and tortures to which rebels and serious criminals were invariably subjected. In February 1608 Petrushka was taken to the Danilov Monastery outside the capital and hanged. The following month Bolotnikov was exiled to Kargopol, a small town in northern Russia some thirty miles beyond Beloozero. On his way he passed through the Volga city of Yaroslavl, where, according to a Polish eyewitness, the local nobility were indignant because he was traveling without chains. "Soon I shall put you yourselves in chains," he scowled, "and sew you into bearskins." [81]

It was an idle threat, however, for when he reached his destination his eyes were put out, and then he was drowned. Much more fortunate was his former master, Prince Teliatevsky. It seems that he died a peaceful death a few years later, having been neither punished nor deprived of his rank or property, which lends support to the theory that he had made some sort of deal with Shuisky.[82] As for Grigori Shakhovskoi, whom Bussow calls "the instigator of this whole war," he was banished to a hermitage in the frozen north, from which he soon escaped to try his luck with the new pretender.[83] The Second Dmitri had in the meantime collected a large army (which included many survivors of Bolotnikov's ill-starred campaign) and was threatening the capital from the western suburb of Tushino. After another long and difficult struggle, Skopin-Shuisky, aided by the same northern towns which had earlier defeated Bolotnikov, dispersed the new insurgents, whose leader was afterward murdered. The people of Muscovy now set their hopes on the gifted young hero to succeed his aging and childless uncle and bring an end to the chaos that for a decade had afflicted the land. But suddenly Skopin-Shuisky died, and there followed two more years of suffering and confusion, during which Tsar Vasili was dethroned and the Poles occupied the Kremlin. Only in 1612, when the invaders were driven out and a "true tsar," Michael Romanov, was found, whose birth could be linked with the extinct line of sovereigns, was a measure of tranquillity finally restored to the troubled realm.

6. Conclusion

The revolt of Bolotnikov thus passed into history. But it had set the pattern for a series of mass risings that convulsed the Russian state during the seventeenth and eighteenth centuries. Bolotnikov himself never enjoyed the hero worship that Razin and Pugachev were to enjoy, and his revolt left a shallower imprint on popular memory than those of his successors. Yet he was an impressive figure in his own right. He had a sincerity and simplicity of character that, while exposing him to the machinations of men far shrewder than himself, won him a widespread following. Moreover, with his Cossack upbringing, his gifts of military leadership, his personal magnetism, and his ultimate martyrdom, he was the original prototype of the Russian rebel-hero.

Bolotnikov's revolt, like those that followed, was an extremely complicated affair which, for all its class savagery, cut across recognizable social categories. It combined a peasant jacquerie with urban insurrection, sectional warfare, Cossack adventurism, anticolonial resistance, status rivalry, political intrigue, and sheer banditry. So far as one can generalize, the rising was a shapeless outburst of the have-nots in Russia, embracing Cossacks and impoverished noblemen as well as peasants, slaves, brigands, and townsfolk, against the Muscovite order. Its immediate causes—

the extinction of the ruling dynasty and the famine which followed—differed from those of later upheavals. But the long-
range causes were much the same: the growth of an oppressive
centralized autocracy; the ceaseless wars, with their attendant
burdens of taxation and recruitment; the progressive loss of land
and personal freedom; the notorious venality of public officials;
and, the result of all these, a vast floating population, rootless,
disoriented, and desperate, bereft of its traditional anchors of
family, village, and occupation, yet without any new anchors to
take their place.

In such times of social dislocation the Russian people lived
in a state of high emotion bordering on mass hysteria. Credulous
townsmen and villagers were more receptive than ever to myths,
rumors, and seditious propaganda. They listened eagerly to the
firebrands and missionaries who were able to translate their inarticulate hatreds and hopes into a more or less coherent vision.
During the Time of Troubles a number of myths arose that were
to live on for centuries to come, kindling mass rebellion when
social tensions became unbearable. Such, for instance, was the myth
of a conspiracy of the boyars to remove the sovereign so they
might suck the blood of the common folk without his interference.
To the poor the wealthy aristocrats were the authors of all the
miseries with which they were afflicted. The boyars, in their eyes,
had ceased to be human beings and had become the incarnation
of evil, monsters endowed with infernal powers, onto whom the
downtrodden projected all that they feared and hated. If Russia
was to be purged of suffering, then these malevolent interlopers
who disrupted the ancient bond between the people and their
sovereign had to be stamped out. A related myth was that of the
"true tsar," born of the Rurik line, whom the wicked boyars had
plotted to eliminate. Somewhere, it was rumored, he lay in
hiding, awaiting the proper moment to exterminate his enemies
and restore a golden past in which the common folk were justly
treated and lived as free townsmen and peasants. These myths
were widely and persistently believed, opening the way to fantastic intrigues and impersonations. The plethora of pretenders
spawned during the Time of Troubles attests to the unshakable
faith of the people in a messianic tsar who would someday
deliver them from their tormentors.

Once stirred to act by rumor or calculated propaganda, the lower classes revealed the full extent of their destructive capabilities. Bolotnikov's revolt served as a grim warning that the passivity of the masses could, by the right kind of agitation, be swiftly transformed into a paroxysm of burning, pillage, and slaughter. But in the end his rising was doomed to fail, for the vague myths which united its adherents in a loose coalition were no substitute for an effective organization and a coherent revolutionary program. What is more, the motley rebel army, for all its destructive fury, was an unequal match for the better organized and equipped—if not always reliable—regiments of the government. The rebellion, as a result, ended in bickering and treachery followed by merciless repression.

Ironically, it was partly because of Bolotnikov that the main thrust of Russian history during the preceding centuries—the thrust toward serfdom and autocracy—was able to reassert itself. Faced by a common danger from the lower classes, Shuisky and his gentry opponents were driven into an unforeseen alliance, thus hastening the process by which the boyars and petty landholders were eventually fused into a single class of service noblemen. As a result, the Muscovite order, though it had nearly fallen apart during the Time of Troubles, managed not merely to survive but to emerge with greater vitality than ever. The development of serfdom proceeded apace. The autocracy resumed its insatiable accumulation of power. The middling elements of society, most notably the service landowners, emerged victorious over both the lower orders and the old aristocracy. The boyar renaissance had been nipped in the bud, while the peasants, Cossacks, and urban poor were to see their remaining liberties whittled away by the expanding state and its gentry supporters. The sacrifices of Bolotnikov and his followers had been in vain. But they had left behind an example to inspire others.

1. Days of Shaking

The advent in 1613 of Tsar Michael, the first of the Romanov line, marked the end of the Time of Troubles. Russia had weathered one of the worst crises in its history and was not to experience another of comparable magnitude till war and revolution brought the monarchy to dust three hundred years later. But the violence which had plagued the country since the extinction of the Rurik dynasty was by no means over, for the Time of Troubles had rocked the Muscovite order to its foundations. The scars of war and insurrection were visible everywhere. Vast stretches of fertile land, left untilled for years, had reverted to wilderness and waste. In hundreds of towns, once-flourishing markets had closed down, and handicrafts and commerce were at a near standstill. Whole districts were deserted, their inhabitants having perished or fled to safer locations in the southern steppes or along the Volga. Foreign troops still occupied a broad swath of territory on Muscovy's western frontier. The empire's treasury was empty and its administrative machinery a shambles.

Small wonder that the country remained in the grip of insecurity and discontent, for the Time of Troubles had bred a spirit of lawlessness that was difficult to extinguish. In the south unruly Cossacks flouted the authority of the new government, and elsewhere, too, bands of armed marauders continued to roam the countryside, looting and burning whenever the occasion offered. These highwaymen, organized in Cossack style with an elected *ataman* at their head, ambushed traveling merchants or swooped down on defenseless estates and towns, often with the connivance of the local poor, who gave them shelter and alerted them to approaching danger.[1] Their ranks were replenished by desperate men cut adrift from their native habitats during the decade of troubles, men whose lawless escapades were deeply rooted in social and economic discontent and who, like the followers of Khlopko and Bolotnikov, refused to consider themselves criminals. "Neither thieves nor brigands we," they sang, "but brave and stalwart men." [2]

So long as the disorders persisted, the recovery of the country, on which depended the fate of the new dynasty, was inconceivable. At times, indeed, the operations of these Cossacks and outlaws—in seventeenth-century Russia the terms were virtually synonymous—assumed the proportions of a full-fledged rebellion against the local *voevoda* or against the crown itself. Accordingly, the authorities bent their efforts to subdue the brigands; and after a decade of sporadic but serious fighting, Muscovy at last settled down to a more tranquil existence in which the wounds of the past could begin to heal. Markets reopened for business; workshops again hummed with activity; more and more land was returned to cultivation; and for the first time in a generation the population showed signs of a slow but steady increase. At the same time, the state administration was renovated and strengthened, so that by the end of Michael's reign (1645) Muscovy had regained a measure of political stability.

Yet beneath the surface the effects of the troubles still made themselves felt. For the government took no steps to eliminate the underlying causes of the crisis with which the century had begun. Punitive measures merely drove the opposition underground, where discontent continued to rankle, while on the lower Volga and in the "wild fields" of the southern frontier banditry remained endemic, threatening to flare up at any moment into open revolt. Stability, moreover, was purchased at the expense of popular freedom. Following the lines laid down by Ivan the Terrible, Michael and his heir Alexis (1645–1676) strove to concentrate administrative and military authority in their own hands, or in the hands of their appointed officials. After the chaos that had plagued their predecessors, a centralized autocracy seemed to them the sole guarantee of order, on which depended the state's very survival. Only a strong monarchy, they insisted, could furnish adequate defense and administrative efficiency for the vast Russian empire, with its flat open plains and disparate and far-flung population. Thus bit by bit the Romanovs strengthened their power. The ancient boyar council gradually slipped into oblivion, a fate shared by the Zemski Sobor, the rudimentary national assembly which had chosen Michael as sovereign. At the same time, local initiative was everywhere stifled. Organs of self-government succumbed to the authority of the *voevoda*, whose rule bore down heavily on the local inhabitants. "The horse loves oats," went a popular saying, "the earth manure, and the governor tribute." [3]

The result was that a century which had opened with a decade of near anarchy saw the progressive subjugation of the Russian population. The government, determined to prevent its restless citizens from escaping the burdens of taxation and military service, evolved a rigidly stratified social system which fettered every man to his place of residence and inherited occupation. At the same time, an impassable barrier was created between the nobility, who owned the land in return for rendering service, and the lower classes, who cultivated the soil, furnished recruits, and replenished the coffers of the government. These arrangements were systematized by the Law Code of 1649, which divided the Russian population into fixed hereditary categories whose interests were subordinated to the military and fiscal needs of the state. Peasants were tied to the land, and townsmen were frozen into the occupations of their fathers and forbidden on penalty of death to move to new locations. This was done not only to insure an uninterrupted flow of tax revenue into the treasury but also to halt the perpetual wandering of the people, which grievously undermined social stability. For the same reasons, the state removed any time limit for the recovery of runaway peasants and imposed heavy penalties on landlords found guilty of harboring them. By this action the institution of serfdom was consecrated in the highest law of the land. At the same time, peasants and other citizens were prohibited from selling themselves into slavery, for the government needed the taxes from which slaves were exempt. As the century advanced, more and more slaves were entered on the tax rolls, so that the distinction between slave and serf, like that between boyar and service nobleman, was gradually obliterated.

The chief beneficiaries of the Code of 1649 were the service noblemen, on whom the crown relied both for its own protection and for the defense of the realm. By shouldering the burden of military and civil service in an age of continuous warfare and expansion, the small and middling landowners acquired a dominant position in Russian society. A growing proportion of the tsar's edicts was designed to satisfy their needs and interests. In particular, the service gentry gained increasing administrative powers on their local estates, where they gradually reduced their peasants to chattel. And as the gentry's ambitions were realized, such grievances as they may once have harbored against the throne evaporated. Hereafter they were to remain the bulwark of the Romanov regime. Even during the most critical periods their loyalty seldom wavered. Accordingly, though they had played a prominent role in Bolotnikov's rebellion, only a small number were to join forces with Razin, and fewer still with Bulavin and Pugachev, so that over the next hundred years mass upheavals in Russia took on a progressively sharper class character.

The peasants meanwhile resisted enserfment as best they could. Since land was abundant and labor scarce, their natural tendency was to run off to the steppe or to the fertile Volga valley, or across the Urals into Siberia, where colonization had begun toward the end of the sixteenth century. Under Michael and Alexis, in spite of severe punishment, flight remained their chief means of protest. To escape the tax collector and the recruiting sergeant, whose visits were becoming more and more frequent, peasants in growing numbers abandoned their villages and took to the road, often making their way to the Cossacks or to the bands of armed marauders who continued to rove the countryside. "Don't pay your dues," went a peasant saying. "Run off to the Volga, to the brigands or the boatmen." [4]

Peasant migration received a strong impetus in 1654 with the outbreak of war with Poland, and soon after with Sweden, which dragged on a dozen years and took a very heavy toll. Tax levies and military call-ups rose sharply, disrupting economic recovery in mid-course and greatly intensifying popular unrest. The exodus of peasants to the frontier swelled to flood tide. Often the runaways absconded with the grain, livestock, and personal belongings of their masters, many of whom had been summoned to the Polish front. Title deeds were destroyed, and nobles who had not gone to war sometimes found life more hazardous on their own estates than in combat with the enemy. Cases of serfs murdering their masters, though still rare, were on the rise, the victims being predominantly small proprietors who were notorious for their brutality.[5] Meanwhile, the large secular and ecclesiastical lords continued to entice and even abduct peasants from the estates of the petty landowners, who petitioned the tsar to assist them in recovering the fugitives.

Anxious to placate its servitors and in critical need of men and revenue to prosecute the war, the crown launched a series of organized manhunts into the black-soil regions adjoining the Volga and the southern prairie, which attracted the bulk of the runaways. In 1658 special officials were appointed to conduct search operations. Landlords who sheltered runaways risked floggings and heavy fines and were made to surrender four peasants of their own for every fugitive found in their possession. The recovery of serfs thus became a function of the state rather than a private concern of the masters. During the first half of 1662, search parties in the middle Volga districts of Arzamas, Alatyr, and Kurmysh, areas which in Razin's time were to become hotbeds of rebellion, netted no less than 5000 fugitive serfs. Some 3000 more were rounded up three years later in the Tambov region, another future Razin stronghold.[6] Government posses encountered fierce resistance, in reprisal for which new settlements were put to the torch and runaways were beaten with the knout and then put in irons and taken back to their legal owners. Nevertheless, the flight of the villagers showed no signs of slackening. For punitive policies alone offered no solution; they merely drove a large segment of the population outside the pale of law and order, creating an eager reserve for future rebellions. Recovery expeditions were to continue for the next hundred years, figuring prominently in the risings of both Razin and Bulavin.

Razin's revolt, however, was more than a response to government recovery operations. It was the culmination of a great wave of violence which swept the Russian empire in the middle decades of the century. This was indeed a time when social upheaval engulfed the whole European continent, from France, Portugal, and Ireland to Hungary, Russia, and the Ukraine, a phenomenon which some historians interpret as a general crisis with deep-seated spiritual as well as political and economic causes.[7] In several countries, including Russia, outlying regions rebelled against the center to resist crushing tax burdens and infringements of local liberties. Everywhere there was discontent with the growing state edifice, which existed primarily for making war. Everywhere outbursts were directed more against unpopular governors, ministers, and bureaucrats than against the monarchs they served. Everywhere there was a drift of people from village to town, a sharp rise in the cost of living, and a widening gulf between the rich and the poor. Peasants and craftsmen were further squeezed by the exploitation of landlords and merchants and by rising taxation to feed the expanding state machine. The result was widespread poverty, dislocation, and popular resentment, which found expression in mass revolts and millenarian religious movements. An apocalyptic wave swept much of the continent from the Atlantic to the Urals. "These days are days of shaking," declared an English preacher during the Puritan Revolution, "and the shaking is universal." In nearly identical language, after the Moscow "salt rebellion" of 1648, an angry commoner from the *posad* warned the boyars that more violence was yet to come "because the whole world is shaking." "The times are bad," he said, "there is great shaking, and the people are troubled." [8]

In Russia, where the church was torn by a great schism both social and spiritual in character, apocalyptic feelings were intense and widespread. Religious dissenters regarded Patriarch Nikon as Antichrist and Tsar Alexis as the Beast of the Apocalypse prophesied in the Book of Revelation and believed that the end of the world was at hand.[9] And if the bulk of the people continued to distinguish between the well-meaning sovereign and the "wicked boyars" who kept him under their spell, a growing number began to criticize Alexis himself for bowing to the wishes of his advisors. "The sovereign," it was said, "is a young fool and looks on everything through the eyes of the boyars Morozov and Miloslavsky. They dominate everything, and the tsar, though he knows what is going on, keeps quiet, for the Devil has taken away his understanding." [10]

During Alexis' reign popular outbursts occurred more frequently and on a larger scale than ever before. The chief causes have already been indicated. By the middle of the seventeenth century the Russian empire had become a vast armed camp, overburdened with taxation and military recruitment and living under the harsh regimentation imposed by an increasingly centralized and bureaucratic regime. The government was not only engaged in continuous warfare on its western frontiers but was simultaneously extending its commitments in the south and east, where a line of fortified outposts was steadily being pushed farther and farther into the steppe and beyond the Volga into the Ural mountains and Siberian forests. As a result, the human and material resources of the country were being strained to the limit; indeed, such protracted warfare and intensive colonization would have drained the wealth of nations far more prosperous than Muscovy, which had yet to recover fully from the Time of Troubles.

When violence erupted, it began in the towns rather than in the rural districts. As in Bolotnikov's day, the peasants, for all their hardships, remained passive until stirred to rebellion by neighboring urban disorders. In the towns of Russia the *posads* were overflowing with potential insurgents. Mingled with the tradesmen and artisans, who themselves eked out a precarious existence, was an assortment of unstable elements—beggars, thieves, casual laborers, drifters—who lived in a state of unrest and were forever on the edge of violence, ready to fall on the privileged inhabitants of the citadel, outside of which they camped, in sight of the golden domes. Lacking even the meager security of the soil and the village community, the residents of the *posad* were dependent on a fluctuating market for their daily bread and were directly exposed to the arbitrary and contemptuous treatment of urban officialdom. They formed a kind of preindustrial *Lumpenproletariat*, impoverished, rootless, overburdened with taxes, and resentful of government monopolies on alcohol, salt, and other basic items of consumption. Their plight was aggravated by competition from markets and workshops maintained by monasteries and private estates, and by the tax privileges granted to foreigners and to the affluent Russian merchants (*gosti*) who handled the tsar's own commercial dealings. Moreover, the *streltsy* and other minor servitors were also allowed to carry on trade without paying taxes, placing ordinary civilians at a considerable disadvantage. All these factors conspired to keep the inhabitants of the *posad* on the margin of subsistence. Only a slight deterioration in their economic situation might menace their very survival. Thus it is hardly surprising that they should possess a more volatile temperament than their rural counterparts and should be the first to rebel in times of abnormal tension. Any sudden misfortune, such as famine or war, might provoke them into a frenzy of violence against their real or imaginary tormentors. For the most part their political attitudes were conservative; ardent defenders of the tsar, they were always ready to take up arms against his alleged enemies, the "traitorous boyars." But in moments of extreme stress the urban poor could become a vicious, uncontrollable mob, beating at the palace gates to demand relief from their sovereign.

But their outcry was seldom heard. The government, in constant need of funds, continued to levy inordinate taxes on the towns, the "fifth money," a special assessment imposed on artisans and traders, being a notorious example. On top of this the merciless exactions of corrupt administrators made life difficult to bear. Thus in 1648, when the already onerous salt tax was quadrupled, revolt broke out in Moscow, the mob venting its worst fury upon foreigners and state officials. According to a Dutch eyewitness, the commoners petitioned Alexis

> concerning the intolerable great taxes and contributions, whereby they were overburdened for some years . . . so they with their wives and children are thereby ruined; besides which the great oppressions which the boyars did lay daily upon them, and that they were not able to hold out any longer. Yea, they desired rather with their wives and children to undergo a present death than to suffer any longer in such a transcendent oppression.

When their appeals went unheeded, the *posad* folk proceeded to sack the foreign quarter and the houses of boyars and merchants, and "all the stately and precious things they found they hewed in pieces with axes." [11] Fires broke out throughout the city, and soon half of Moscow lay in ashes. The *streltsy*, called into action, turned a blind eye to the rampaging crowd. For even though they enjoyed tax advantages over the civilians, their wages had fallen into arrears, and to a certain extent they shared the rebellious outlook of the lower classes from which they originated.

From Moscow the rioting spread swiftly. Town after town broke out in revolt. Even such conservative northern communities as Ustiug, Solvychegodsk, and Yaroslavl rose in protest against the government's fiscal and administrative abuses; and insurgents in the remote Siberian town of Tomsk declared their intention to "start a Don [that is, a Cossack republic] on the upper Ob."

In 1650 violence against the "boyar traitors" and their "German friends" flared up in Pskov and Novgorod, where ancient memories of independence and popular rule had been kept alive through nearly two centuries of Muscovite domination.[12] After days of savage fighting each of these risings was put down, and on the surface at least, quiet prevailed in the towns for the next dozen years. In 1662, however, the protracted war with Poland and Sweden brought on a fiscal crisis of greater dimensions than any in the past. To satisfy the mounting demand for funds, the treasury minted low-grade copper coins in identical size and shape to the silver pieces in use at the time, and a wild spate of money speculation ensued during which unscrupulous men hoarded the available supplies of silver and flooded the market with counterfeit copper coins. The result was a ruinous inflation which threatened the whole monetary system with collapse. As prices skyrocketed, the desperate residents of Moscow renewed their violence. Seditious leaflets appeared on the walls of churches and public buildings demanding the severest punishment for boyars, merchants, and officials who had seized the opportunity to enrich themselves at the expense of the poor. As in 1648, fiscal agents were savagely beaten and homes of the wealthy pillaged. The rising reached a climax when an angry mob marched on the tsar's suburban palace at Kolomenskoe, the village from which Bolotnikov had directed his siege of the capital sixty years before. When the sovereign emerged, one of the protestors clutched at his robes, and the others clamored for the heads of the profiteers. Troops were rushed in, and a wholesale massacre took place. According to a contemporary estimate, 7000 lost their lives in the disorder and twice as many suffered the knout or branding or amputation of arms and legs.[13] Thousands more were deprived of their property and banished to the garrison towns of the middle and lower Volga, where a few years later they would furnish eager recruits for Razin's campaign against Moscow.

In 1667 the prolonged war with Poland was finally brought to an end. Nearly a fifth of the Russian population had fallen in combat or died from the ravages of famine and plague. Widespread disorders, particularly in the towns, had compounded the government's difficulties. But the greatest rebellion was yet to come. For the war had increased the regimentation of Russian

life and sharpened the edge of discontent. All the ingredients for
a mass upheaval—bondage, bureaucratic despotism, spiritual crisis
—had steadily accumulated. All, that is to say, save one: the appearance of a charismatic leader to rally the people to his banner.

2. Razin

It is not hard to explain why each of the four great revolts of
the seventeenth and eighteenth centuries should have been led
by a Don Cossack or, in Bolotnikov's case, by a slave who ran
off to the Cossacks and spent his formative years among them.
The Cossacks were distinguished by an aggressive nature and a
fighting capacity all but unknown among the mass of ordinary
villagers and townsfolk to the north. Descended of fugitives from
Muscovite oppression, they cherished their freedom and independence and felt a strong sympathy for the inhabitants of the
heartland, where the last vestiges of personal liberty were being
torn up by the roots. It was this sympathy, combined with an un-
quenchable thirst for excitement and adventure, which thrust
them into the vanguard of every major upheaval in Russia over
a 200-year period. Until the nineteenth century the Cossacks were
the very symbol of popular freedom, audacious rebels who rejected domination from every source. "Warrior muzhiks," Alexander Herzen christened them, "knights-errant of the Russian
common people." [14]
More than anything else the Don Cossacks prided themselves
on their autonomy and self-rule. True to their libertarian spirit,
they recognized no authority but that of their own general assembly, or *krug*, which gathered periodically in the Cossack capital
of Cherkassk, situated on a large fortified island in the lower
Don. Presiding over the *krug* was the elected chieftain of the
Host, the *voiskovoi ataman*, assisted by a body of elected elders,
under whose guidance the assembly meted out justice and decided
on matters affecting the community as a whole, such as the ad-
mission of new members and the organization of military campaigns or expeditions of plunder. Questions of local concern were
dealt with by the individual Cossack villages—there were some

fifty in Razin's time, strung out along the Don and its tributaries
—which had their own assemblies, *atamans*, and elders on the
model of Cherkassk. Cossack government thus took the form of
a rough-and-ready folk democracy which, though tempered by
the oligarchic propensities of the elected officials, who tended to
dominate the proceedings of their respective assemblies, stood in
marked contrast to the increasingly centralized and bureaucratic
despotism of Muscovy. By setting an example of autonomy and
self-determination, imperfect though it might be, the Cossack
"republic" on the Don presented a challenge the Romanovs could
not long afford to ignore.

Independent and headstrong plainsmen, the Don Cossacks resented government interference in their affairs and resisted all
attempts to control them. They refused to pay taxes to Moscow
—indeed, they expected to be rewarded for patrolling the frontier,
acting as guides, and other services. Nor would they humble
themselves before Russian landlords and officials. Symbolic of
their autonomy was the fact that their relations with the tsar
were conducted through his foreign office, the Posolski Prikaz,
which sought to preserve amity with the raucous horsemen, on
whom the crown relied for border defense against the Crimean
Tatars and other warlike tribes. In return for this service the
Cossacks received an annual subsidy (*zhalovanie*), partly in money
and partly in food and military supplies, especially powder and
lead. Periodic delegations were sent from Cherkassk to Moscow
to negotiate the amount of the *zhalovanie;* and on special occasions, such as after a victorious campaign, extra subsidies of
cloth, grain, and wine were dispatched to the Host to be distributed among its members.[15] The whole question of *zhalovanie*
—how much would be paid, how often, and to whom—was a
thorny one which figured largely in the frequent Cossack mutinies against the state. The payments fluctuated widely according
to the condition of the treasury, falling off sharply in times of
war when available funds were earmarked for the regular army.
And with warfare being almost continuous in the mid-seven-
teenth century, the cry for *zhalovanie* went up frequently among
the Cossacks, becoming a major source of friction between Cherkassk and the central government.

To demand higher subsidies, however, was to risk government
intervention in Cossack affairs, which the Host tried desperately

to avoid. One of the chief preoccupations of the Cherkassk leadership was to keep the Muscovite system, which was drawing nearer and nearer with the advance of colonization and the fortified frontier, from penetrating their domain. As a precautionary measure, extensive agriculture was forbidden within the territory of the Host, for agriculture was inevitably linked with serfdom and government controls. They would guard the borders of Muscovy, the Cossacks declared, in return for "the waters and grasses but not for estates." [16] Farming, in their eyes, was a menial occupation unworthy of a warror and plainsman. The settled life of the peasant they held in great disdain. Restless adventurers, they refused to be fettered to the plough like beasts of burden, but rather preferred to roam the prairie without trammels of any sort:

Not with the plough is our dear, glorious earth furrowed,
Our earth is furrowed with the hoofs of horses;
And our dear, glorious earth is sown with the heads of Cossacks.

They feared, and feared rightly, that the introduction of agriculture on a significant scale would lead to the disruption of their ancient "liberties" and of their traditional way of life.

Shunning the plough, the Cossacks won their livelihood by netting fish in the Don and its tributaries, hunting the abundant game of the steppes, and herding cattle, horses, and sheep. In some districts salt extraction and beekeeping were important occupations, while Cossacks of a more predatory stamp pillaged merchant convoys on the Volga and outfitted small fleets of shallow-draft longboats (*strugi*) for hit-and-run raids against Tatar settlements and Turkish and Persian towns on the coasts of the Black and Caspian seas. In exchange for their fish, animals, and booty, the Cossacks imported grain from the black-earth provinces of south-central Muscovy, especially from the regions of Tambov and Voronezh on the upper Don, to which the traders from Cherkassk carried, along with their goods, a message of liberty and self-rule.

Yet, for all their efforts to ward off agriculture, the Cossacks were fighting a losing battle. Apart from being menaced by the relentless advance of Muscovite colonization, they were inundated by runaway peasants who brought their rustic occupations with them. The untamed prairie, as we have seen, was a traditional sanctuary from the thrall of serfdom and autocracy; and the territory of the Don Cossacks was particularly tempting because anyone who reached its borders was considered a free man. "From the Don no one is handed over," was a basic Cossack axiom. Nor would the search parties from Muscovy dare venture into the southern no-man's-land in defiance of this injunction. Small wonder that after the Code of 1649 and the outbreak of war with Poland the influx of runaways into the Don area assumed the proportions of a flood. By 1670, the year in which Razin launched his rebellion against Moscow, the population of the Don region had jumped to 25,000, three times what it had been when Alexis mounted the throne a generation before. Thus, ironically, the wedge that enabled the Muscovite system to penetrate the Don was formed by the runaway peasants themselves, for it was only a matter of time before landlord and tax collector would follow in pursuit.

The influx of refugees had a profound effect on the character of the Don community. As the century wore on there developed a growing cleavage between the old-time Cossacks, who lived mainly downstream in the vicinity of Cherkassk, and the new peasant fugitives, who settled along the upper reaches of the river and along its northern tributaries, nearer the areas from which they had fled. The downstream Cossacks, whose ancestors had arrived on the Don generations before, were known as the "house-owning" (*domovitye*) element. It was they who enjoyed the best fisheries and hunting preserves, who owned extensive herds of livestock, and who carried on a lively trade both locally and with the market towns to the north. It was they who dominated the local and central *krugs* and furnished the *atamans* and elders who managed the affairs of the community. And, finally, it was they who received the much-coveted *zhalovanie* from Moscow and, in contrast to the disgruntled upstream fugitives, enjoyed reasonably good relations with the central government. Over the years they had lost their taste for plunder and adventure. Abandoning their seminomadic ways, they built flourishing towns on the lower Don and began to adopt a more settled existence, making more and more compromises with their Muscovite neighbors, on whom they relied for grain and subsidies.

The newcomers, by contrast, known as the "naked" ones, the *golytba* or *golutvennye*, without land or property of their own, were the lawless and discontented, the rootless and desperate men whose mentality differed sharply from that of their prosperous and settled downstream neighbors, for whom circumstances often compelled them to work as hired hands. They, of course, received no subsidies from the government from which they had fled and which they hated with an abiding passion. Memories of the knout, of forced recruitment, of unbearable taxes were still fresh. And now, arriving on the Don, they found that their troubles were not over. For their membership in the community had to be passed upon, after a long waiting period, by the general assembly in Cherkassk, which was controlled by the Cossack establishment. Even worse, they were prohibited from earning their traditional livelihood by cultivating the soil. Little wonder their resentment was bitter. They were forever in a condition of ferment and unrest. And as their numbers increased, so too did the antagonism between the new and the old, the poor and the rich.

In effect, then, a miniature sectional conflict was developing on the Don between its upstream and downstream inhabitants. So long as the newcomers remained disorganized, the elders were able to control them and to retain their monopoly of power. It fell to Razin to alter the situation. It is not surprising that the elders, in the words of a government report of 1669, should have "strongly lamented his return to the Don," [17] fresh from a triumphant campaign of plunder on the Caspian. For under Razin's dynamic leadership the disorganized rabble became a serious threat to the Cherkassk establishment; and as a result, the "house-owners" threw in their lot with Moscow to help crush his insurrection, just as the service gentry had turned against their social inferiors in Bolotnikov's day. Thus the government was once again to benefit from internal divisions among its opponents—this time, indeed, to the extent of bringing the Don Host under its control. Hereafter the downstream Cossacks, like the minor nobility, were to remain loyal·servants of the sovereign and were to betray Bulavin as well as Razin into his hands.

In the meantime, the plight of the upstream newcomers had become acute. Denied both their traditional agricultural pursuits and a share of government subsidies, they cast about for a means of survival. At length, finding no alternative, they resorted to expeditions of piracy. These were sponsored by the downstream Cossacks, who though themselves no longer active participants in the quest for booty, were ready to supply boats, weapons, and supplies in return for a share of the proceeds. For more than a century Cossacks had been launching raids down the Don and into the Black Sea, penetrating as far as the shores of Anatolia. In these maritime adventures they showed extraordinary courage and ingenuity, striking with lightning speed at the coastal settlements of the Turks and Crimean Tatars, then escaping in their light and maneuverable *strugi* before any effective force could be collected against them. Their predatory activities, however, were sharply curtailed when the Turks built fortifications at the mouth of the Don to block their passage. In 1642 the Turkish bastion of Azov was reinforced after an army of Don Cossacks seized it by storm and held it for five years, until Tsar Michael asked them to withdraw. Cossack excursions into the Black Sea became still more hazardous in 1660, when the Turks bolstered their defenses at the mouth of the Don with a garrison of 5000 troops and as an added precaution stretched thick iron chains across the river between the watchtowers on either bank.[18]

Thereafter Cossack raids on the Black Sea were few and far between. Deprived of their traditional areas of plunder, the marauders shifted the direction of their attacks to the east, sailing down the Volga into the Caspian. Not that Cossack raids in these waters were anything new. In fact they had been occurring since the late sixteenth century, after Moscow's conquest of the Volga basin. In 1636, when Adam Olearius, secretary of an embassy to Muscovy from the Duke of Holstein, began a trip down the Volga, the *voevoda* of Nizhni Novgorod warned him to stay on the alert for Cossack pirates, "a barbarous and inhumane people, and more cruel than lions." [19] On his way down the Volga Olearius saw gallows on a hill near Tsaritsyn which were used to hang Cossack buccaneers who crossed over from the Don at a point above the town where the two rivers bend sharply toward each other, forming an easy portage. A few years later, during the 1650s and 1660s, Don Cossacks took to plundering merchant vessels on the Volga from a fortress near Panshin, at the bend of the Don between its Tishina and Ilovlia tributaries. Often these raiding parties would winter on the Yaik River, east of the Volga, and when spring arrived would sail into the Caspian in search of further loot, a pattern which Razin was to follow on the eve of his great rebellion. Before long, however, even these easterly waterways became more difficult of access, for the tsar, while encouraging raids against the Turks and Tatars on the Black Sea, frowned on this shift of operations to the Caspian, a Persian lake. Moscow wished to protect its flourishing commerce with the Middle East and valued its good relations with the shah, a potential ally against their common Turkish adversary. Moreover, the appearance of predatory Cossacks on the Volga posed a threat to local Russian trade between Nizhni Novgorod and Astrakhan. For these reasons the government branded the new expeditions "piracy" and took urgent steps to prevent them.

With their marauding operations hampered on both the Black Sea and the Caspian, the upstream Cossacks found themselves in a desperate economic situation. Compounding their plight was a severe food shortage throughout the Don territory. "In many Don settlements," reads a government report, "runaway peasants have come from neighboring areas with their wives and children, and as a result there is now great hunger on the Don." [20] Owing to the war with Poland, food shipments from Tambov and Voronezh were being diverted for military use; this, coupled with an increased demand on the Don created by the influx of refugees, caused the price of grain to skyrocket. Upriver, the "naked" population was faced with starvation.

During the summer of 1666, in the twelfth year of the Polish war, hunger and privation called into being a movement of protest among the upstream Cossacks led by an obscure freebooter named Vaska Us. As the forerunner of Razin, Us played a role akin to that of Khlopko, whose ill-starred campaign against Moscow in 1603 anticipated the more formidable revolt of Bolotnikov three years later. Unlike Khlopko, however, Us was destined to survive defeat and become one of Razin's principal lieutenants. The plan he conceived was to ride with his followers to the capital and ask the tsar to admit them into government service, in return for the *zhalovanie* which had hitherto been denied them.

Collecting a band of 500 men, Us rode north to Voronezh, where he was joined by 200 additional volunteers who arrived on foot or in small boats. From Voronezh they proceeded toward Tula, the town in central Muscovy where Bolotnikov had made his last stand sixty years before. "Oh Us, Us, came into Rus," begins a folksong which tells of his invasion of the Russian heartland. By the time Tula was sighted more than 2000 peasants had flocked to his company, attacking and plundering the neighboring estates and sending the landowners and their families scurrying to the safety of the town. The Tula *voevoda* hastily mobilized his gentry militia and sent an urgent call for help to Moscow. In response the tsar dispatched a large force led by Prince Yuri Bariatinsky, an able commander who was later to oppose Razin as well. But now his task was simpler. Hearing that troops were on the way, Us's following disintegrated, the peasants scattering to their villages and the Cossacks to their sanctuary on the Don.[21]

Us's brief adventure was only a foretaste of what was to come. Less than a year was to pass before the same *golytba* who had followed him to Tula rallied to a far abler leader in a fresh quest for booty and excitement. Their new *ataman* was Stepan Timofeevich Razin, born of an established Cossack family in Zimoveiskaya Stanitsa, an old settlement on the lower-middle Don within the immediate orbit of Cherkassk. Razin, then, was not himself a destitute fugitive from Muscovite oppression. Indeed, his godfather was none other than the *voiskovoi ataman*, Kornilo Yakovlev, who would later turn against him when he challenged the house-owning oligarchy from which he himself had sprung. It is worth noting that Frolka Razin, Stenka's younger brother and fellow rebel, was one of the signatories of a letter from Yakovlev to the tsar promising to punish Vaska Us for his unsanctioned escapade into the heartland,[22] which suggests that, at this point at least, Frolka was a loyal member of the establishment.

The same was true of Stenka. We first hear of him in 1652, when, as a young man of twenty-one or twenty-two, he made the long pilgrimage to the Solovetsky Monastery on the White Sea, traveling by way of Moscow, which he saw for the first time. It was a tradition among the Don Cossacks to visit the famous shrine and pray to its founders, Saints Savva and Zosima, whose remains were widely credited with miraculous powers. Six years later, in 1658, young Razin made his second visit to Moscow as a member of a Cossack delegation sent to negotiate the annual *zhalovanie*. In 1661 the *krug* in Cherkassk entrusted him with another important mission: to negotiate an alliance with the Kalmyks against the Nogai Tatars, fierce vassals of the Turks who launched frequent raids of plunder from their base on the lower Volga. Later the same year we find Razin again in Moscow, reporting to the Posolski Prikaz on the success of his mission to the Kalmyks and receiving permission to make a second pilgrimage to the Solovetsky Monastery.[23] Beyond his diplomatic assignments, Stenka, as an able-bodied Cossack, performed his share of military duty. In 1663, for instance, he took part in an expedition against the Crimean Tatars launched jointly by the Don and Zaporozhian Cossacks, in which they liberated some 350 prisoners seized by the Tatars during their periodic forays into the steppe.[24]

Clearly, then, Razin was no "naked" newcomer athirst for revenge against Moscow. He had served the Host with distinction and had won its trust and respect. Why then should he come forward as the *ataman* of the poor and raise a revolt in their name? The reasons remain obscure. Yet often throughout history rebel leaders have come from comfortable backgrounds; indeed, this would seem more the rule than the exception. Seldom have the oppressed themselves led the way, but rather those who have been aroused by their suffering and degradation. It is significant, in this connection, that Stenka was not the only member of his family to take up the insurrectionary torch. During his rising both his uncle and brother headed large rebel detachments, and even his mother, Matryona, was to be captured and executed by government troops after participating in a bloody battle on the Northern Donets River at the height of the revolt.

But their motives are shrouded in mystery. Some sources relate that Razin, after his own capture, cited the execution of his elder brother as the reason for his rebellion.[25] In 1665, so the story goes, Stenka's brother, who commanded a detachment of Don Cossacks on the Polish front, asked for leave to go home during a lull in the fighting. When his superior, Prince Yuri Dolgoruky, denied the request, Razin left anyway, only to be overtaken and brought back to his camp, where a furious Dolgoruky ordered him hanged as a deserter. It was this act which supposedly kindled within the Razin family a desire for revenge against the Muscovite aristocracy. The story, however, cannot be supported by any documentary evidence. Indeed, the very existence of an older brother is in doubt. Contemporary records mention several Don Cossacks named Razin,[26] but none who fits the circumstances in question.

For a more convincing explanation of Stenka's rebellious career one must turn to the nature of the man himself. By all accounts he was a born leader, a Cossack of striking personality and appearance, endowed with charismatic powers to influence the behavior of others. Jan Struys, a Dutch seaman who saw Razin in Astrakhan in 1669, describes him as "a brave man as to his person, and well-proportioned in his limbs, tall and straight of body, pock-pitted, but only so as did rather become than disfigure him, of good conduct, but withal severe and cruel." [27] Stenka was then about forty years old, a seasoned warrior whose determination, resourcefulness, and restless energy are traits on which all contemporary sources agree. He was also a man of strong, at times ungovernable, passions. According to an anonymous English mariner from the *Queen Esther*, docked in Archangel at the time of Razin's rebellion, "nothing but his malicious and rebellious temper hath impelled him to this infamous undertaking," the execution of his brother being merely a pretext to escape the same fate.[28]

That Razin was capable of sudden changes of mood, particularly when under the influence of alcohol, is attested to by his contemporaries. At times his bouts of drinking brought on paroxysms of violence which claimed innocent lives. Yet among the rootless inhabitants of the frontier he acquired an aura of benevolence and magical prowess that survived long after his death. He had an instinctive understanding of simple men, and his ability to incarnate the popular ideal of the deliverer was unsurpassed by any other rebel leader. At some point in his life he evidently conceived a hatred for men of privilege and authority and turned his truculence and pent-up energies against them. At the same time, he accurately gauged the mood of the lower classes, the castaways of the Don and the Volga, and knew that they were ripe for revolt. Nikolai Kostomarov, in what remains

while, the Tsaritsyn *voevoda*, Andrei Unkovsky, sent an emissary
across to Razin's headquarters to propose negotiations, to which
Stenka replied with a threat: should Unkovsky attempt to stop
him, he would attack Tsaritsyn and burn it to the ground. Amid
growing alarm, Moscow turned to the Cossack establishment
and directed Ataman Yakovlev to prevent Razin from leaving the
Don. But again no action was forthcoming, for Yakovlev had
no quarrel with his godson, who had yet to challenge his authority.
Indeed, by diverting the restless *golytba* to the Volga and Caspian, Yakovlev might have hoped to prevent an attack on the
downstream communities over which he presided. Nor was the
ataman, as protector of the Host's independence, prepared to
truckle to the commands of the Muscovite authorities. It was
only later, when Razin became a threat to the Cossack oligarchy,
that he would take active measures to curb him.

   In the meantime, Razin and his party, which numbered nearly
a thousand, had left their camp for the Volga. The Cossacks were
in luck, for they arrived just in time to intercept a large convoy of trading vessels owned by the tsar, the patriarch, and a
merchant named Vasili Shorin, one of the opulent *gosti* whose
homes had been ransacked in the Moscow riots of 1662. Aside
from a rich cargo of merchandise, the convoy was carrying a
group of political prisoners to exile in Astrakhan and Terki, and
so was guarded by a contingent of *streltsy* who, but for the element of surprise, might have offered serious resistance. Attacking
from ambush, the Cossacks quickly overwhelmed all opposition.
Those who resisted were thrown into the Volga, while the rest
were invited to join Razin's company. "Go wherever you please,"
he told them. "I shall not force you to join me, but whoever
chooses to come with me will be a free Cossack. I have come to
fight only the boyars and the wealthy lords. As for the poor and
plain folk, I shall treat them as brothers." [31] These words, if
indeed spoken, reveal that even at this early stage Razin's movement displayed that peculiar mixture of brigandage and revolt
which characterized all the mass uprisings of the period. At first,
to be sure, piracy was the dominant element; but the latent forces
of insurrection were not slow to emerge, so that what began
chiefly as an expedition of plunder was soon to be transformed
into a full-scale social rebellion with immense and far-reaching
consequences.

The convoy once subdued, Razin's flotilla, laden with booty and prisoners, sailed down the Volga unopposed. Surprisingly, as it passed Tsaritsyn, the guns of the fortress remained silent. Perhaps Unkovsky, mindful of Razin's warnings, feared for the safety of his city if he should open fire. Or possibly, as a recent authority suggests, his gunners sympathized with the Cossacks and refrained from loading their weapons.[32] At any rate, Stenka's boats were able to pass safely downriver. And with this episode was launched the myth of his invulnerability. Thereafter he was to enjoy the reputation of an invincible warrior endowed with supernatural powers and immune to bullets and cannonballs, a reputation that won him many supporters and survived in song and legend even after his execution.

From Tsaritsyn Razin proceeded down the Volga toward the Caspian. Just below Cherny Yar, the next government strong-point, he encountered and routed an armed flotilla sent against him, then, passing Astrakhan, sailed through the mouth of the river and into the open sea, heading eastward toward the Yaik. A series of *streltsy* detachments was sent in pursuit, but there was disaffection among them because of irregular pay, besides which many of the troops, coming from the same lower-class background as Razin's men, had no desire to oppose them. The first detachment to overtake Razin, on the northern coast of the Caspian, defected in a body. The second, which caught up with him at the mouth of the Yaik, mounted an attack but was easily overcome and its officers put to death. Thus in July 1667 Razin's band arrived outside the town of Yaitsk in full force. But the city, surrounded by a thick stone wall and defended by a garrison of 500 *streltsy*, was not an easy target. Stenka, rather than squander the lives of his men, resorted to a simple ruse, the first of many he employed with great success during his campaign. In the guise of pilgrims, he and 40 of his men approached the main gate and asked for permission to pray in the town cathedral. Once inside, they overpowered the warders, opened the gates to their comrades, and occupied the town without a struggle. The garrison commander and 170 of his troops who refused to join the intruders' ranks were slaughtered on the spot.[33]

In keeping with his plan, Razin spent the fall and winter in Yaitsk, preparing for the campaign ahead and rebuffing further government expeditions sent to stop him. The largest of these, some 3000 strong, arrived in February 1668, but the men as usual proved reluctant to fight and failed even to breach the Cossack defenses. In the meantime, a messenger came with a pardon from the tsar if Razin would give up his adventure and return to the Don, but Stenka stalled by demanding a second document to confirm the original. Soon afterward a team of negotiators arrived from Saratov, only to be arrested and to have the officer in charge drowned in the Yaik.

With the arrival of spring Razin was ready to embark for the Caspian. In March 1668 some 30 *strugi*, each mounted with light cannon and holding 40 to 50 men, set sail down the Yaik, leaving behind a small force of *streltsy* defectors to guard the town. These, however, were quickly overwhelmed by a new government expedition, put in irons, and banished to Kholmogory on the White Sea. Razin was thus cut off from his base of supply. But by now he had already begun what a contemporary called his "furious inroad into Persia." [34] In their fast and maneuverable longboats the brigands ravaged the coast of Dagestan from Derbent to Baku, "plundering and sinking all the small shipping, wasting and depopulating the cities and villages, and using the people very inhumanely." [35] At Baku alone the raiders made off with 150 prisoners and 7000 sheep. Not until Resht did they encounter serious resistance; but there, after celebrating their triumph in the usual drunken orgy, some 400 Cossacks were slaughtered by Persian troops in a surprise attack. With the Persians in hot pursuit and his men badly in need of a respite, Razin sent a delegation to the mountain capital of Isfahan with a request for permanent sanctuary, promising to enter the "eternal bondage" of the shah in return for a grant of land.[36] While the talks were still in progress, Razin and his band, having recouped their strength, mounted a new series of raids along the southern coast of the Caspian. Disguised as merchants, they landed at Farahabad and for several days innocently traded in the market place until, at a prearranged signal from their leader, they fell upon the townsmen and plundered their houses and shops. The next day the Cossacks returned for a repeat performance. At length, laden with booty and captives, they took to their ships and continued their raids eastward along the Caspian shoreline.

When cold weather set in, the Cossacks made camp in the

swampy forests of the Mian Kaleh Peninsula between Farahabad and Astrabad. There they spent a hard winter, withstanding repeated attacks by Persian forces. Lacking food and fresh water, their numbers were gradually reduced by starvation and disease. When spring came, however, the Cossacks felt strong enough to establish a new base on an island in the Caspian, from which they attacked Turkmen settlements on the eastern shore. But their days in the Caspian were numbered. The Turkmen put up a fierce resistance, killing hundreds of Cossacks, among them Razin's ablest lieutenant, Serezhka Krivoi. A greater threat presented itself when the Persians collected a large fleet with 3700 troops under the command of Menedi Khan and sent it to destroy the intruders. In June 1669 a great battle took place in the Caspian, but the heavy Persian galleys proved no match for Razin's *strugi*, and the Cossacks won a stunning victory. When the fighting was over, only three Persian vessels remained afloat. Razin had seized thirty-three cannon and numerous prisoners, including Menedi Khan's son. His reputation now acquired new glory, and songs were sung comparing him to the legendary hero Ilya Muromets. But his victory was achieved at great cost. Five hundred Cossacks had been killed, many more were wounded, and hundreds were deathly ill, "all sick and swelled" from drinking the salty water of the Caspian when their supply of fresh water ran out.[37] The Cossacks had had their fill of adventure. They were weary and longed to return to the Don and divide up their rich booty. So, the following month, Razin left his island camp and, covered with fame and riches, headed toward the Volga and home.

4. Astrakhan

In August 1669 Razin and his followers were approaching the mouth of the Volga when they carried out their final act of piracy in the Caspian. They encountered two Persian merchantmen, boarded them and seized a rich cargo, including a gift of thoroughbred horses from the shah to Tsar Alexis. Thus Razin was not surprised when some hours later his lookouts sighted a fleet of Russian warships approaching at top speed. The ships had been dispatched by Prince Ivan Prozorovsky, the new Astrakhan *voevoda*, who, informed of Razin's approach, ordered his able assistant, Prince Semyon Lvov, to intercept him. But Razin chose not to fight. Instead he directed his vessels to turn about and make for the open sea. Badly outnumbered, short of provisions, his men ridden with disease and weary from their long campaign, he did not want to risk defeat and the loss of his hard-won loot. Prince Lvov, for his own part, had no desire for an armed contest with the hardened marauders and sent a courier in a fast boat to overtake Razin with an offer of peace. The Cossacks were told that they could return to the Don unmolested and under full pardon from the tsar if they would surrender their heavy guns and larger vessels and restore the Persian goods and thoroughbreds seized at the Volga estuary; in addition, they were also to return their Persian prisoners from the battle in the Caspian as well as the *streltsy* who had defected or fallen captive on the Volga and the Yaik two years before.[38]

Razin agreed to these terms, though it is doubtful that he intended to abide by them. His flotilla rode into Astrakhan harbor to the salute of cannon and church bells, and the brigands, "in very costly attire and with great pomp," made a triumphal entry into the city.[39] Sharing out their booty in equal portions, they carried on a lively trade in Astrakhan's bazaars, while Razin, it is said, scattered Persian coins to the friendly populace who thronged the streets. Already surrounded by legend, he was greeted not as a pirate but as an invincible warrior fresh from a victorious campaign. The townsfolk called him *batko*, their dear father, the title earlier bestowed on him by his Cossack followers. Prince Lvov entertained Razin as his own house guest, and a lasting affection grew up between the two men, for which Lvov, it will be seen, would have reason to be thankful at a less cordial moment.

Stenka, aware of his immense popularity, thought it necessary to carry out only a small part of the bargain he had made with the *voevoda*. Contrary to the agreement, he kept all his ships and most of his cannon, insisting that they were needed to get safely past the Tatars on the way back to the Don. He also kept the Persian horses and refused to give up the *streltsy*, who, he maintained, had joined him voluntarily, so that to surrender them would be to violate the Cossack rules of sanctuary. He did, however, surrender his Persian captives, including the son of Menedi Khan, whose fleet he had annihilated in their Caspian encounter. According to Jan Struys, there was also a daughter whom Razin kept as his concubine and later threw in the Volga when her presence upset the camaraderie of his men (it was forbidden by Cossack custom to have women along on expeditions). "The lady was of an angelic countenance and amiable," wrote Struys, "of a stately carriage of body, and withal excellently well qualified as to her parts, being of singular wit and always pleasing in her demeanor towards him when he was in the heat of fury, and yet at last became the instance of his cruelty." [40] The beautiful princess, however, was probably a figment of Struys's imagination. Other witnesses, while confirming the existence of a son (of which we know from official documents), are silent about a daughter.[41] Nevertheless, Struys's account gave rise to a legend, celebrated in one of the most popular of Russian folksongs, in which the Persian princess sows discord among Razin's followers, whereupon her lover consigns her to a watery grave in the Volga.

When Razin reneged on their agreement, the *voevoda* made no move to enforce it, for which he was later castigated by the tsar. Prozorovsky knew that, quite apart from the civilian population, even his *streltsy* were in sympathy with the Cossacks and could not be trusted in any armed engagement. Moreover, there are indications that he had been placated by a handsome gift of Cossack booty. Thus when Razin left Astrakhan in September 1669, he carried away his treasure largely intact, as well as a reputation for defiance which warmed the hearts of the destitute, who saw him as their avenger. On his way to the Don he stopped briefly in Tsaritsyn for a last round of excitement before returning home. Entering the city unopposed, his men broke open the jail and let out the prisoners. Andrei Unkovsky, the same *voevoda* who had failed to block Razin's passage two years before, fled through a window of his house but was promptly caught, dragged through the streets by his beard, cursed and humiliated, but at length allowed to purchase his freedom.

Razin then departed and crossed over to the Don. With some

1500 followers he made camp on an island near the village of Kagalnik and fortified it with earthen ramparts to which he transferred the cannon from his ships. From Cherkassk, a two days' journey downstream, he sent for his wife and children and brother Frolka, who spent the winter with him in relative tranquillity. Meanwhile, his reputation had swelled to godlike proportions. Stories of his exploits echoed up and down the Don, and the landless and destitute flocked to his camp, hungry for loot and drawn by the hope of new adventure. Throughout the Don valley, according to a contemporary report, there was hunger and "great poverty." [42] Even some of the house-owning Cossacks joined Stenka's ranks, their *zhalovanie* having dwindled to a mere trickle; and by the spring of 1670 his following had swelled to some 4000 men nursing strong grudges against Moscow and Cherkassk. The Cherkassk elders felt themselves threatened, for Kagalnik had become a rival fortress populated by desperate men over whom they had no control. The existence on the Don of two island strongholds symbolized the growing cleavage between the "naked" and propertied elements. What was emerging, as we have seen, was a miniature sectional conflict similar to that which divided the country as a whole. Now the upstream poor could boast of their own army, their own *krug*, their own *ataman*; and the authority of Cherkassk hung in the balance. For Moscow, too, the swelling host of disgruntled Cossacks had become a force to be reckoned with. The government, having looked askance at Razin's escapades in the remote Caspian, would hardly tolerate his unruly band on the upper Don, within striking distance of Muscovy itself.

Moreover, Razin's movement had undergone a change. His following, as one historian put it, had been transformed from a *shaika* into a *voisko*, that is, from a gang of pirates into a rebel army.[43] From 1667 to 1669, during his campaign on the Volga, the Yaik, and the Caspian, plunder had been the overriding object. Yet even then social rebellion was never far beneath the surface, for it was poverty and dislocation that had made the upriver Cossacks hungry for loot and adventure. The social implications of Razin's actions had already manifested themselves in his murder of officers and bureaucrats and in his declared intention to fight "only the boyars and wealthy lords" but not the poor, whom he welcomed as brothers. He showed little respect for governmental authority. Even before his return to the Don, a foreigner in Astrakhan noted that Razin was "a discontented person and one of great power . . . bearing a sovereign awe among [his followers]." [44] His dramatic success on the Caspian surely strengthened his self-confidence and sense of power, as did the aura of invincibility which now surrounded him. Impressed, moreover, by the weakness of the Russian administration in Tsaritsyn and Astrakhan, he began to conceive a plan against the government itself, a plan to master the Volga, along which, so he hoped, a mass of discontented townsmen and peasants would rally to his banner as he moved upriver toward the capital.

Stenka's first move, we learn from the English narrative, was to attack the official church within the Don territory, "driving away many priests and hindering divine service, and intruding himself in church affairs." His object, according to reports reaching Moscow, was to banish regular priests from the Don and live "without marriage, thereby forcing true Christians to violate and defile God's teaching." [45] But still more dangerous, from the point of view of the government, were his efforts to forge an alliance with the Dnieper and west Ukrainian Cossacks and create a "great Host, stalwart and menacing, of the Don, the Yaik, and Zaporozhie," [46] an echo of Bogdan Khmelnitsky's appeal for a united Cossack republic throughout the south. Owing to deep-seated rivalries, however, nothing came of these overtures, except that a number of Zaporozhian Cossacks went over to Razin of their own accord in defiance of their *ataman*'s orders.

The tsar was of course greatly alarmed by these developments. In December 1669 he sent an envoy to Cherkassk, Gerasim Evdokimov, to demand that Ataman Yakovlev restrain the would-be rebels. Two years before, it will be recalled, Yakovlev had refused to act against Razin. This, however, did not imply any disloyalty to Moscow. Yakovlev, indeed, was a veteran of several campaigns on behalf of the tsar. An intelligent and capable leader, deeply respected by his fellow Cossacks, he was torn between his duties to Moscow and his determination to preserve the autonomy of the Host. But if he had earlier turned a blind eye to his godson's transgressions, now that Stenka, at the head of an organized *golytba*, posed a threat to the Cherkassk oligarchy, he was ready to act.

Thus when Evdokimov arrived, Yakovlev gave him a cordial reception. A *krug* was at once summoned, and Evdokimov, in the name of the tsar, promised a full resumption of the annual *zhalovanie* as soon as Razin had been dealt with. In the midst of the proceedings, however, Stenka himself burst in and turned the meeting into a bedlam. He angrily accused Evdokimov of being a spy for the aristocracy rather than a true representative of Alexis. "Who sent you," he demanded, "the Great Sovereign or the boyars?" [47] Seizing the unfortunate envoy, his men beat him savagely and threw him in the Don to drown. When some of the elders protested, they were killed on the spot, and Yakovlev was threatened with the same punishment if he dared to interfere. When news of Evdokimov's murder reached Moscow, the enraged tsar immediately cut off the remaining *zhalovanie* and ordered the *voevodas* of neighboring districts to sever all supply routes to the Don. Razin had meanwhile left Cherkassk and returned to his camp. By killing Evdokimov he had taken his first step of open rebellion. He now declared his intention to march on Moscow and deal with the boyar traitors. Yakovlev, for his part, fished Evdokimov's body from the Don and gave it an honorable burial, a token of his collaboration with the government against the rebels.

In March 1670, with the arrival of good weather, Razin mobilized his army for the new campaign. Nearly 7000 Don Cossacks, augmented by a few hundred Zaporozhian volunteers, gathered at Panshin near the crosspoint to the Volga, from which Razin's first expedition had been launched three years before. Stenka summoned a *krug* and in a dramatic speech proclaimed his ambition "to go from the Don to the Volga and from the Volga into Rus against the Sovereign's enemies and betrayers, and to remove from the Muscovite state the traitor boyars and Duma men and the *voevodas* and officials in the towns . . . and to give freedom to the common people." Characteristically, he did not attack the tsar himself, but only his underlings. It was because of their treachery, he said, that the people were hungry and oppressed and that the Cossacks were receiving no *zhalovanie*. "I will not raise my sword against the Great Sovereign," he declared, unsheathing it from his scabbard. "I would rather cut off my own head with it or be drowned in the river." The Cossacks shouted their agreement: "We are ready to serve and die for the House of the Blessed Virgin and for the Great Sovereign. But the boyars have barred our way to the sea and the Volga, and we have thus become naked and hungry. And now we shall go to the Volga against the boyars and *voevodas*, so that the boyars and *voevodas* do not starve us to death." [48]

The rebels left Panshin in mid-April and soon reached the Volga above Tsaritsyn. Among Razin's lieutenants was Vaska Us, who in 1666 had been the first to lead the *golytba* into Muscovy. Now Stenka, barred from the Black Sea by the Turks and from the Caspian by the Persians, was following Us's example. At Tsaritsyn the old *voevoda*, Andrei Unkovsky, had meanwhile been replaced by Timofei Turgenev, who was nervously awaiting a detachment of Muscovite *streltsy* sent to reinforce his garrison after the murder of Evdokimov. Razin, for obscure reasons, left Us in charge of the siege while he himself galloped off with a party of Cossacks to raid a Tatar settlement to the south. When he returned three days later (with a herd of Tatar horses and other booty), he was delighted to find the city already in Us's hands. It had been taken in typical Cossack fashion, "by perfidy and deceit," in the words of a contemporary.[49] Us, having learned that reinforcements were on the way from Moscow, sent agents to spread the rumor in the town that the troops were coming not to drive away the Cossacks but to punish the inhabitants for supporting them. The townspeople—whether because of this deception or from fear of reprisals if they resisted—opened their gates to the rebels. The *voevoda* with the gentry and a small group of loyal soldiers barricaded themselves in one of the watchtowers of the citadel and put up a fierce resistance, but the tower was taken by storm, and the defenders, with the exception of Turgenev, were butchered on the spot. Turgenev was led about the town in cruel mockery, pricked with lances, and finally speared like a fish and thrown into the Volga.

The rebels had been in Tsaritsyn for several weeks, celebrating their victory by plundering the houses of the merchants and nobility, when their scouts reported the approach of the government flotilla containing the regiment of *streltsy* sent to defend the city against the Cossacks. Its commander, Ivan Lopatin, had no inkling that Tsaritsyn already lay in rebel hands, and a few miles above the town the flotilla was ambushed from both banks of the river. The *streltsy* put up a stiff fight and cut their way through a swarm of Cossacks, expecting to find shelter in the town. But to their horror, when they reached its walls they were greeted with a murderous cannonade and, after a brief battle with heavy losses, were forced to surrender. All the officers, including Lopatin, were immediately drowned in the Volga. Of the 400 surviving troops only a handful voluntarily joined the insurgents —the Moscow *streltsy* being more reliable than their provincial counterparts—while the rest Razin "took with him against their will" as oarsmen for his Volga campaign.[50]

In Tsaritsyn, self-government was inaugurated in the Cossack manner, complete with a town assembly, an elected *ataman* (for which post Razin nominated a trusted companion), and several elected elders to assist him. Razin detailed a few hundred Cossacks to defend the city against further government interference and sent another detachment upstream to capture Kamyshin, for which another ruse was employed: the Cossacks disguised themselves as a Muscovite relief force, entered the town unopposed, and overwhelmed its small garrison. Razin then held a *krug* in Tsaritsyn to determine the next move. Opinion was sharply divided. Some wanted to sail down the Volga and seize Astrakhan, while others favored making straight for Moscow "to annihilate the traitor boyars."[51] After a heated discussion the former prevailed. Some historians consider this a fatal mistake. Soloviev, for one, contends that Razin, had he immediately marched north instead of giving the government time to gather its forces against him, would have had Moscow at his mercy. Bulavin and Pugachev were to face a similar choice, and they too would decide to consolidate their hold in the peripheries before heading for the capital. Nor is this surprising. For it was in the border areas that government control was weakest and that the insurgents enjoyed their strongest support. Whenever the risings approached the heartland, they tended to lose momentum as the sectional balance tipped against them.

Yet, fatal or not, their decision afforded the crown a badly needed respite; and Alexis made the most of it. His first move was to mobilize the service gentry of the central districts and middle Volga and to strengthen the garrisons at Tambov, Voronezh, and other key strongpoints along the defense perimeter between Moscow and the steppe. The *voevodas* of these towns were ordered to stop fugitives and vagrants from joining the rebels. Hundreds were intercepted and slaughtered between the Don and the Volga by loyal Kalmyk tribesmen, who at the same time seized the opportunity to raid Cossack settlements in the upper Don valley and make off with livestock and property. Nevertheless, during the summer of 1670 an increasing number continued to get through on foot or in small boats, including several hundred Cossacks from the Dnieper, whose military talents were a particularly welcome asset to Razin's motley army. The tsar, forced to redouble his efforts, enlisted the aid of the church in winning the allegiance of the population, and ecclesiastical charters were sent to every town and village denouncing "the bandit Stenka Razin who has lost his fear of God and forsaken the holy Orthodox and apostolic church and utters abusive words against our Lord Jesus Christ." [52]

In the end, however, it was military might that proved decisive. As the century advanced, Russia had been moving in the direction of a standing army, conscripted for life and drilled on western European lines. The Time of Troubles had demonstrated the need for a drastic modernization of the armed forces; and though it would take a Peter the Great to whip a genuine standing army into shape, much of the groundwork was laid by his father Alexis, during whose reign Russia's fighting force, spurred by incessant foreign wars and domestic upheavals, doubled in size from 50,000 to 100,000 men.

Yet at the time of Razin's outbreak on the Volga it was still in a rather primitive state. One disaffected nobleman, Grigori Kotoshikhin, called the cavalry a "shameful thing to behold" and likened the infantry to a "herd of cattle." [53] The backbone of the infantry, the *streltsy* musketeers, formed by Ivan the Terrible in the sixteenth century, was stationed in the capital and in the garrison towns strung out along the Muscovite defense perimeter in the south and east. In most cases they lived with their families in a special quarter on the outskirts of town, just beyond the

posad, from whose population they originated and whose grievances and instability they tended to share. Their weapons—the
sabers and halberds, muskets and battle-axes in use for nearly a
century—were outmoded, and the reliability of the men was poor.
During a campaign their one desire was to return home; and it
was by no means uncommon for them to abandon the field in
the midst of battle, only to be hunted down, beaten with the
knout, and returned to duty. In peacetime their way of life was
barely distinguishable from that of their *posad* neighbors. Given
a house with a small plot of land, they grew their own vegetables
and often kept domestic animals. To supplement the *zhalovanie*
which they, like the Cossacks, gatekeepers, and other petty "men
of service," received from the tsar, they were permitted to engage
in handicrafts and small trade without paying taxes. They could
also make alcoholic beverages for their own consumption, a privilege of which they availed themselves often, much to the detriment of military discipline. Men of volatile temper, they often
clashed with their officers—noblemen whose status they envied
or, in a rising number of cases, foreigners who aroused their powerful xenophobic feelings. Their principal grievance, however,
was the irregular receipt of their *zhalovanie*. Low pay and mounting arrears were a constant source of friction, precipitating frequent outbursts of mutinous violence. As we have seen, during
the riots and insurrections which plagued Alexis' reign, the
streltsy would often stand idly by or even join the urban poor in
their looting and destruction. And they were especially untrustworthy in the garrison towns of the lower Volga—Tsaritsyn,
Cherny Yar, Astrakhan—to which many had been reassigned after
the Moscow riots of 1662.

Such was the opposition Razin faced when, in June 1670, he left
Tsaritsyn and headed down the Volga. His army now numbered
more than 7000 men, some traveling in *strugi* and some on foot
or horseback along the flat meadow side of the river. Their immediate objective, Cherny Yar, was the only important government stronghold between Tsaritsyn and Astrakhan; and it did not
prove hard to take, for on Razin's approach the local *streltsy*
rose in mutiny, slaughtered their officers, and opened their gates
to the rebels, to whom they defected in a body. A new challenge
presented itself when the Astrakhan *voevoda*, Ivan Prozorovsky,

sent Prince Lvov with 2600 *streltsy* to intercept the insurgents. The two armies met below Cherny Yar, but Lvov's men refused to fight. Instead they arrested their commander and sent a delegation to Razin with an offer to help him "kill the masters, *voevodas*, officials, and other ranks of noblemen." Their proposal was promptly accepted, and a special *krug* was held at which Stenka welcomed them into his army. Hitherto, he said, they had been "fighting for the traitors," but now they would be "fighting with his Host for the Sovereign." [54] When he finished speaking, according to Ludwig Fabritius, a young Hollander serving as one of Lvov's officers, the Cossacks and *streltsy* "began embracing one another and swore with life and limb to stand together and to exterminate the treacherous boyars, to throw off the yoke of slavery, and to become free men." The *krug* then considered the fate of the officers, many of whom, like Fabritius and his stepfather, were foreigners. Their strange talk, newfangled methods, and efforts to impose discipline were bitterly resented by their charges, who wanted to kill them outright. Though Razin objected that "there must be a few good men among them who should be pardoned," the troops were adamant; and in the end all the officers were put to death except Fabritius, whom a sympathetic soldier helped to escape, and Prince Lvov, whom Razin personally spared over the objections of the men, who cried for his blood along with the rest.[55] Razin's leniency was not out of character: except when inflamed by drink he was never as bloodthirsty as his followers. In this case, though, he had a special motive for intervening, for he had developed a strong liking for his former Astrakhan host and thought he might prove useful in the coming assault on the city.

Astrakhan, Moscow's "window on the East," was a place of great wealth and strategic importance. Situated at the gateway to Persia, it was Russia's chief entrepôt of trade with the Orient. In its crowded bazaars gathered merchants from many lands, attracted primarily by the flourishing commerce in silk. The city was famous too for its excellent fish and caviar; the mouth of the Volga abounded with sturgeon, herring, and carp, while perch and pike were also plentiful. Salt was extracted in great quantity from the surrounding marshes, and if grain, the staple of the Russian inhabitants, was in scarce supply, the area was rich in wildfowl and fruit. The town itself, "with its many towers and lofty piles of buildings," presented a noble sight, as Razin had observed after his Caspian adventure the year before. Small wonder, then, that he and his followers, now 10,000 strong, should choose "to go to Astrakhan and rob all the merchants and traders." [56]

But the town was no easy target for plunder. Like Cherkassk and Zaporozhie, it stood on a strongly fortified island, at the center of which was the citadel, encircled by a high stone wall with six gates and ten watchtowers and surmounted by four or five hundred brass cannon. Stationed in the fortress was a garrison of 6000 *streltsy*, whose chief mission was to keep the neighboring Kalmyks and Nogai Tatars at bay. Thus, barring treachery from within, Astrakhan was well situated to withstand a siege by even the most powerful enemy.

Treachery, however, was an ever-present danger. The town had a history of internal upheaval dating from the Time of Troubles, when its lower-class inhabitants launched "Tsarevich Peter" on his violent career, a history that was to continue into the next century, the last important eruption occurring on the eve of Bulavin's revolt in the reign of Peter the Great. It will be recalled, moreover, that when Razin returned from Persia the previous summer, the townsfolk had greeted him as a savior and called him their "dear father," an epithet normally reserved for the tsar. The bulk of the population came from a background similar to that of the Cossacks and nursed similar grievances against the gentry and officials. Indeed, the whole atmosphere of the place was restless and predatory. More than a few political dissidents had been exiled there by the tsar. Worse still, the *streltsy* were unreliable. Though reinforced when Prozorovsky took up his duties as *voevoda*, the garrison had lost several detachments to Razin on the Yaik two years before, and the defection of Lvov's contingent at Cherny Yar had had a devastating effect on morale. Pay, as usual, was badly in arrears, and at a time when grain prices in the city were abnormally high owing to Razin's seizure of a supply convoy on the Volga. The *streltsy* in any case displayed a strong tendency toward brigandage, that curious blend of piracy and rebellion of which the Cossacks were the outstanding practitioners. They too longed for a share of plunder and adventure. In contrast to their Moscow counterparts, they were separated from their kin and lacked the stabilizing influence of family life and peaceful occupation. And their poverty, like that of the lower classes in general, contrasted sharply with the wealth of the local merchants, with their flourishing shops and sumptuous houses.

Prince Prozorovsky had no illusions as to the reliability of his garrison, and to defend his city he relied mainly on the foreign officers of the sailing ship *Orel*, which lay at anchor in Astrakhan harbor. The *Orel*, the first ocean-going vessel in Russian service, had been constructed on the Oka River the previous year and sailed down the Volga to Astrakhan, arriving there in August 1669, on the eve of Razin's return from Persia. Its Irish commander, David Butler, had collected a European crew in Amsterdam, among whom was Jan Struys, whose description of Razin was quoted earlier. By Butler's account, Prozorovsky now invited him to dinner, showered him with gifts, and commissioned him a lieutenant colonel in his service.[57] Thirteen guns were removed from the *Orel* and installed atop the walls of the citadel. With an English colonel named Thomas Baily, Butler made the rounds of the city, inspecting the artillery and fortifications, with particular attention to the Voznesensky Gate, the main entry to the town, through which the Cossacks were expected to attack. Apart from the officers of the *Orel*, Prozorovsky pressed into service a Persian envoy in Astrakhan, who obtained the rank of colonel as well as an opportunity to settle accounts for Razin's humiliating attacks on the Caspian.

To boost the morale of the residents, Metropolitan Iosif organized processions with crosses and the icon of Our Lady of Kazan, one of Russia's most venerated religious treasures, and at each of the town gates, which had been buttressed with heavy blocks of stone, the Metropolitan intoned a prayer for victory. Prozorovsky, to placate the *streltsy*, paid them part of their arrears from a fund raised by the Metropolitan and the Trinity Monastery. But this only whetted their appetite for more and further undermined the *voevoda*'s waning authority. Razin, whose success depended on the extent to which he could fan popular discontent, meanwhile smuggled agents into the town "to stir up the soldiers against the governor."[58] Equally effective was his ability to implant terror in the hearts of the citizenry. The fear of reprisals gripped the entire population, and especially the *streltsy*, who trembled lest they should share the fate of their obdurate comrades whom Razin had massacred in Yaitsk three years before after capturing that city. Stenka's fifth column had done its part to create this atmosphere of terror mingled with excitement at the prospect of his arrival. In both the garrison and the *posad*, as Butler noted, there was "whispering and murmuring against the governor." [59] An apocalyptic frenzy had seized the city, whose inhabitants looked for signs which, according to the prophetic tradition, would herald the approach of the millennium. Men reported a strange shaking of the earth beneath their feet, and it was said that the night before Razin's coming an eerie ringing of bells sounded from the Cathedral of the Blessed Virgin. To a superstitious people these omens betokened imminent redemption. According to Struys, a crowd gathered in front of the town hall and shouted to the officials inside: "Now, now the times begin to alter. It will be our turn next to lord it. You villains come out and show yourselves to the world." [60]

The following day the rebel flotilla sailed into Astrakhan harbor. Razin sent two of his men, a dissident priest and a household servant of Prince Lvov, to the *voevoda* to demand his surrender. Prozorovsky responded by throwing the priest in the dungeon of the Trinity Monastery and beheading his companion outside the town walls, in full view of the rebels, whom the grisly act aroused to a dancing fury. Razin decided to attack that very night, while the lust for revenge remained acute. When darkness fell he sent a small detachment to feint an assault on the Voznesensky Gate, while the rest of his army attacked in strength on the opposite side of town. The plan was a total success. Attacked from the rear, the defenders were seized by panic and began to massacre their officers. Meanwhile the insurgents, aided by sympathetic townsmen, clambered over the walls on ropes and scaling ladders and alighted inside the citadel. Prozorovsky and his brother, who had been awaiting the rebels at the Voznesensky Gate, rushed to the other side and headlong into a swarm of attackers. The *voevoda*, though gravely wounded, managed briefly to escape, but his brother was seized and shot on the spot, and he himself was soon captured. Resistance in the fortress was quickly overcome, except for a small group of Circassian tribes-

men who barricaded themselves in a watchtower and began to
fire on the rebels. "When they ran out of ball," recalled Ludwig
Fabritius, "they used copecks, so that afterwards many copecks
were cut out of the villains by the surgeons." [61] But their supply
of coins was soon exhausted, and the defenders were cut down
as they tried to flee.

Razin, in the words of a government report, fell on Astrakhan
"like a wolf falling on the Christian flock." [62] Once in his hands
the town was given over to plunder. The rebels confiscated the
government treasury and pillaged the cathedral, the bazaars, and
the houses of the wealthy. Then, in accordance with Cossack
tradition, they divided up the loot in equal shares. Official documents were burned, and the insurgents toasted their victory in
the usual debauch, followed by a long orgy of bloodletting. The
voevoda, still bleeding from his wounds, was tortured at great
length, then cast down from the high tower in the middle of the
fortress. After this, says an eyewitness report, "they slew the
clerks and officials, the colonels and *streltsy* captains, the Moscow
gentry and Astrakhan gentry—all of them they slaughtered." [63]
Persian and Armenian merchants were butchered together with
their Russian counterparts. According to witnesses, a river of
blood flowed past the cathedral toward the town hall. Prozorovsky's two sons, aged eight and sixteen, were dangled by their
heels all night. In the morning the older was cut down, tortured,
then thrown from the ramparts, "which was the death his father
suffered." [64] Atrocities of this sort were commonplace. The
voevoda's secretary was hung by the rib on fleshhooks and tortured to death. The Persian envoy whom Prozorovsky had commissioned met a similar fate, and Razin also hanged the son of
Menedi Khan, whom he had released the previous year as part of
his bargain with the *voevoda*, but who for unknown reasons had
not yet returned to his homeland. The dead were collected—there
were 441 in all—and buried in a common grave at the Trinity
Monastery. Fortune, however, smiled again on Prince Lvov, who,
still in Razin's good graces, was merely placed under house arrest. Prozorovsky's younger son was returned to his mother
"beaten half dead," and both were put under guard in Lvov's
palace. David Butler, after a long ordeal in rebel hands, succeeded
in escaping to Persia, where he set to paper the horrible scenes

he had witnessed. His ship, the *Orel*, was destroyed during the assault.[65]

Though over 400 dead seems a grim enough figure, the toll might have been heavier but for Razin's intervention. Most of the victims fell during the storming of the city, and only 66, it appears, in the massacre that followed. Stenka himself, it has already been noted, was not a bloodthirsty individual, and during his month-long reign in Astrakhan he succeeded in imposing an impressive degree of discipline within his army. "Although this brigand tyrannized in such an unheard of manner," observed Fabritius, "he nonetheless insisted upon strict order among his men." [66] Under his supervision a Cossack-style regime was established on the model of the Don Host. The Astrakhan population was divided into thousands, hundreds, and tens, with a town *krug* and elected officers, though Stenka himself picked the *ataman* (Vaska Us) and his chief lieutenants. At the first session of the *krug* the townsmen swore an oath "to stand for the Great Sovereign . . . and to serve him, Stenka, and his Host, and eliminate the traitors." [67] But after Razin's departure discipline quickly fell apart. The upper classes suffered appallingly at the hands of the Cossacks and the mob. Murder became rampant, the victims including the Metropolitan and Prince Lvov, while the widows and daughters of slain merchants and officials were taken by the rebels as their "wives." Razin in due course would learn of these atrocities. For the moment, however, his thoughts were turned in another direction, up the Volga toward Moscow.

5. The Volga

It was on July 20, 1670, that Razin began his ascent of the Volga. His army numbered some 6000 stalwarts, the others having remained in Astrakhan or absconded with their loot. Half his men sailed in a fleet of 200 *strugi*, barges, and smaller craft, while the rest went on foot and horseback on the flat bank of the river. In Cherny Yar and Tsaritsyn they were greeted as heroes and attracted a swarm of new adherents. By mid-August thousands more had flocked to the horsetail standard of the rebel movement.

The town of Saratov, having risen on Stenka's approach, was occupied without a struggle. Next came Samara. Here too the gates were opened by the inhabitants, who had risen as the Cossacks approached and massacred the loyalists, including the *voevoda* and all his officials. The way had been prepared by an advance guard of agitators who preceded Razin into the garrison towns and aroused the lower classes against the authorities.

Once again, as with Bolotnikov, the main base of popular support, at least in the early stages, was not the countryside but the town. Nor, we have seen, is this hard to understand. Herded together in appalling conditions, the residents of the *posad*—traders and artisans, *streltsy* and watchmen, porters and servants, vagrants and barge haulers—were far more susceptible to revolutionary propaganda than their rural cousins scattered over wide areas and cushioned by traditional ties to the land and the village commune. The urban poor suffered not only from economic hardship but also from the psychological effects of disorientation, the result of their displacement from the village, to which, for all its poverty and frustrations, they longed to return. So it was that town after town rose in revolt at Razin's approach. The pattern was everywhere the same. Emissaries arrived with leaflets proclaiming that Stenka was "going to Rus to establish the Cossack way there, so that all men will be equal." [68] Roused by this message, the townsfolk would rebel, overthrow the authorities, and welcome the Cossacks with bread and salt. Officials were executed, property confiscated, prisons thrown open, taxes abolished, records destroyed. Then, amid general rejoicing, the old administration was replaced by Cossack self-rule, complete with *krug* and *ataman* (usually hand-picked by Razin) and elected elders.

As he moved upstream, Razin bent every effort to win the support of the peasantry. His messengers roved the countryside disseminating their inflammatory proclamations—"seditious letters," the authorities called them—with remarkable effect. "Stepan Timofeevich is writing to all you common folk," reads one of these leaflets. "Whoever wants to serve God and the Sovereign and the great Host, as well as Stepan Timofeevich" come join us and help "eliminate the traitors and the bloodsuckers of the peasant communes." [69] In the words of a contemporary chronicle: "The bandits and insurgents with their satanic enticements stirred up the God-fearing against the boyars. Alas and alack, father went against son, brother against brother, and friend against friend, slaughtering each other with their weapons . . . and the bandits told the people: We are going to kill the boyars and let you have a privileged life for many years." [70]

Vast stretches of the Volga valley were lit by the fires of insurrection as thousands of peasants heeded Razin's call. Manor houses went up in smoke; title deeds were destroyed; landlords fled to nearby towns, only to be slaughtered there by bands of invading Cossacks. On some estates the peasants seized their masters and brought them to the rebels to be killed. Elsewhere they sent delegations to the Cossacks to ask their help in meting out justice, or taking up their pitchforks and axes, carried out the grisly deed themselves. "The peasantry," wrote Struys, "who indeed are very tyrannically dealt with throughout all the Emperor's dominions, here found an occasion to be revenged of their liege-lords, and to show their manhood brought the heads of their lords and threw them at the feet of a provost or executioner thereto ordained, who gave them a reward for their pains." [71] Yet for all the bloodshed this was a mere foretaste of what the nobility were to experience a century later, during the rebellion of Pugachev. In Razin's time the peasants, though they burned and looted with little restraint, generally shrank from murder. Most of the killing was done by the urban mobs and by Stenka's own Cossacks, some of whom, having fled to the Don from these very same districts, were paying off old grudges against the local officials or landlords.

Additional recruits were drawn in large numbers from the non-Russian peoples of the Volga, who yearned for relief from increasing Muscovite intrusions into their territory. These tribesmen—notably the Mordva, Mari, and Chuvash—were mostly peasants whose lands had been confiscated by Russian gentry and ecclesiastics and by Tatar princes (*murzy*) who had submitted to baptism and, like other nobles, were granted estates in return for service. In some areas, moreover, the tribes were subjected to a campaign of Christianization. During the 1650s, for example, the Archbishop of Riazan had baptized thousands of Mordva by force, for which he now paid with his life. [72] For these reasons Razin's emissaries had little difficulty in stirring the natives to revolt, and they streamed to his banner by the thousands. The rebellion, as in Bolotnikov's time, spread through the tribal districts of Alatyr, Arzamas, Kurmysh, and Kozmodemiansk, but on a vaster scale than before. Mordva and Mari delegations came to the towns to ask for Razin's manifestoes and to invite the Cossacks to their villages to visit destruction upon the nobility. Besides these settled Finnish peoples, a sprinkling of seminomadic Bashkirs, Kalmyks, and Tatars could also be found within the rebel ranks. But the Bashkirs, who had rebelled against Moscow in 1662 and were to play a major role in the *Pugachevshchina* a century later, lived mostly in the Urals, remote from the area of Razin's movement, and so did not participate in any real strength. The Kalmyks and Tatars, moreover, were traditional rivals of the Cossacks and for the most part remained loyal to the tsar. This was especially true of the Edisansky Tatars, whose settlements below Tsaritsyn Razin had raided in the spring, and still more of the Tatar *murzy*, who often held estates in Mordva districts and whose interests conformed in most respects to those of their Russian counterparts. The Russian gentry, incidentally, did not, as in Bolotnikov's revolt, make common cause with the rebels. The feuds which divided the landed classes during the Time of Troubles had long since evaporated; more than that, the Code of 1649 had removed the gentry's principal grievances, and their ties with the throne were more firmly cemented than ever. But Razin, determined to win as many adherents as he could, and particularly adherents with military ability, instructed the peasants to leave unmolested any landlords who might be willing to join him.[73] Such efforts, needless to say, had little practical result, and in the end only a handful of noblemen were to acclaim the rebel cause.

It was the urban and rural poor, as we have noted, from whom Razin won his largest following, that vast floating population of the Don and Volga valleys—Cossacks and *streltsy*, peasants and tribesmen, convicts and vagrants—who lived on the edge of starvation and responded eagerly to revolutionary agitation. Among the first to join were the Volga boatmen who pulled the barges from Astrakhan to Nizhni Novgorod and whose life, says their proverb, was one of "toil and drudgery till they dig your grave."[74] Women, too, took an important part, not only as camp followers and nurses but as disseminators of propaganda and even, in a few cases, as commanders of rebel detachments. Razin's own mother is a case in point; but the most remarkable of these Amazons was a widow from Arzamas—described by some as an apostate nun—who dressed in men's clothing, led a force of 7000 partisans, and fought "bravely in this war" until captured and burned as a rebel and witch.[75]

An essential place in the rising was occupied by the lower clergy, an astonishing number of whom sided with the insurgents, some doubtless out of fear but the majority from genuine sympathy with Razin's cause. At one point defections became so numerous that Patriarch Ioasaf issued a circular to every parish, urban and rural, cautioning the priests "not to be allured by the enticements of the bandit and traitor Stenka Razin and his comrades." [76] But his warning went largely unheeded. For the priests, coming of peasant stock, shared the poverty of their parishioners ˌand their grievances against landlords and bureaucrats. They were able, merely by greeting the rebels with the traditional bread and salt, to draw whole villages and towns into the rebellion. There were many, however, who assumed a more active role. Some conducted prayers and religious processions for a rebel victory, while a few took command of guerrilla bands and plunged into the thick of the fighting. But the most critical function of the clergy was to write "seditious letters" for the predominantly illiterate Cossacks. The authorities, alive to the effects of this propaganda, took strong measures to stop it. There are many cases on record of priests, monks, and sextons being tortured, banished, and even executed for putting the inarticulate yearnings of the lower classes into a simple but vivid language that all could understand.[77] What is more, the presence of so many clergymen lent an element of religious fanaticism to the rebellion, in the same way, as will be seen, that the Old Believers were to inject a millenarian strain into the rising of Pugachev.

Even more than in Bolotnikov's day, rebel propaganda played a crucial role in winning popular support. Razin's seditious letters circulated in nearly every corner of the land, penetrating beyond the Urals into Siberia and even into the northern forests of Karelia. In the Volga area they were so numerous that a government commander was able to send a whole sackful to Moscow for the tsar's personal examination.[78] A few had already reached the capital through Razin's agents and sympathizers, with the result that "men began to speak openly in his praise, as if he were a person that sought the public good and the liberty of the people." The tsar, adds the English narrative, from which the preceding words are quoted, "was necessitated to make a public example of some to deter the rest." For instance, one old Muscovite, "being asked what should be done in case that Stenko should approach the city, answered that the people should go and meet him with bread and salt, which among the Russians is a token of love and friendship. For which this man was taken and hanged." [79]

What message did the propaganda contain that made it so effective? Most important was Razin's general promise of deliverance from the landowners and bureaucrats. "Everywhere he promised liberty," says the English narrative, "and a redemption from the yoke (so he called it) of the boyars or nobles, which he said were the oppressors of the country." [80] Beyond this, a few variations were included to meet the special grievances of different groups. Thus while one leaflet, addressed to the Russian peasants of the Kozlov district, declared that the rebels stood "for the House of the Blessed Virgin, for the Great Sovereign, for the good father (*batiushka*) Stepan Razin, and for the whole Orthodox Christian faith," a similar proclamation to the Kazan Tatars substituted Mohammed for the Blessed Virgin: "This is our watchword: For God and the Prophet, for the Sovereign and the Host." [81] A constant feature was Razin's claim to be defending the tsar against the machinations of his advisors, in keeping with the widespread belief that the misery of the people was the work of treacherous bureaucrats who kept the sovereign in ignorance while exploiting his subjects for their own gain. The chief villains remained the "boyars," a catchall embracing the whole nobility from small gentry to landed magnates and state officials. Alexis, it was said, even if he knew of their deception, might not be willing or able to act; for "God is high in the heavens," went the proverb, "and the tsar is far away." To compensate for this, there emerged in the popular mind the image of a substitute tsar, an ideal ruler, just and merciful, who lived close to his subjects, listened to their complaints, and acted to relieve their suffering. It was Razin, of course, who now filled this role, even though he himself never masqueraded as the sovereign. He merely claimed, like Bolotnikov before him, to be fighting on the tsar's behalf in order to rid the country of treason. To his followers, however, he was a *batko* or *batiushka*, a father figure who would deliver his children from their oppressors. They saw in Stenka a man of more than human qualities, a messiah sent by Providence to lead them to the Promised Land, and the government launched a vigorous campaign to shatter this image. Razin was denounced as a brigand and an apostate, luring the ignorant into heresy and damnation. A striking example of this counterpropaganda was the following charter issued by the patriarch in September 1670:

> From time immemorial the Devil, who hates everything good, has filled his vessel with flattery and cunning and poured out his bile and poisoned the hearts of the faithful. He has stung the flesh of the innocent like a viper emitting its venom. And now from the cave of vipers comes the bandit and traitor and desecrator of the cross, the Don Cossack Stenka Razin. With his cursed accomplices he has caught true Christians in his embrace like a serpent and pulled them down with him into the ditch of ruination. Like a carnivorous lion on the prowl, he has been gnawing at them, not at their flesh and possessions but at their very souls, despoiling them of their oath of allegiance to the Great Sovereign Tsar and Grand Prince, Alexis Mikhailovich. Having lost the fear of Almighty God and forsaken the Holy Orthodox and Apostolic Church, and having forgotten his oath to the Great Sovereign, the brigand has betrayed him, the Great Sovereign, and the whole Muscovite state.[82]

But efforts to discredit Razin were of little avail. The popular desire for a redeemer was too strong to be easily dissipated, and a host of pretenders appeared during Alexis' reign to challenge the existing regime. In the district of Tver, for instance, peasants wearing red shawls and armed with muskets carried around in a sedan chair a man whom they called the real sovereign.[83]

Razin was quick to exploit the situation. Following Bolotnikov's example, he brought forward a new "tsarevich," falsely reported dead, who was marching with him to Moscow to recover the throne. What was the basis for this story? In March 1669 the tsar's wife, Maria Miloslavskaya, had died, followed ten months later by the death of their elder son, Alexis Alekseevich, at the

age of sixteen. In June` 1670, by an odd coincidence, the Tsare-
vich Semyon, aged four, also died. That this succession of princely
deaths at a time of acute tension should have stimulated rumors
of foul play is not surprising. Razin encouraged the rumors. More
than that, he spread the word that Tsarevich Alexis had escaped
"the violent hands of the boyars and great lords, and taken his
refuge to him, adding that he, Stenko, was come by order of the
Great Czar to put to death all the boyars, nobles, senators, and
other great ones (that were too near his Majesty) as enemies
and traitors of their country." [84] And "to color the lie the better,"
as the English narrative puts it, he employed a simple ruse. On one
of his barges, covered with red velvet, he kept a young Circassian
prisoner, about the same age as the tsarevich, whom he claimed
to be the rightful heir to the throne, riding with him to eliminate
the traitors. The government countered that the tsarevich was indeed in the grave and that Razin was an ordinary cutthroat trying
to conceal his crimes behind a bogus pretender. But the story
caught on, with the result that "the ignorant people were inflamed
to fight furiously, and those of them that were taken prisoners
underwent death with a wonderful resolution as being possessed
with the persuasion of dying for a good cause." The authorities
responded with increasing brutality, so that in Smolensk a citizen
was hanged merely for stating that he had seen the tsarevich in
Razin's company.[85]

In a second barge—decked out in black velvet—Razin displayed
yet another imposter. This one posed as the disgraced Patriarch
Nikon, whom the tsar had banished to a monastery in the remote
north. Razin had actually sent emissaries to Nikon with a promise
to restore him to office in return for his cooperation, but Nikon,
who like Luther in Germany would have no truck with peasant
rebellion, refused to see them. So Stenka resorted to an impostor,
and moving upriver, urged the people to kiss the cross to the
tsarevich and to recognize Nikon as patriarch. Again the government reacted sharply, and a village priest was hanged after con-
fessing that he had "uttered words in praise of the former Patriarch Nikon and prayed to God for him and for the rebel
Cossacks." [86]

It may seem odd that Razin should wish to collaborate with a
patriarch whose reforming zeal had alienated a broad segment of

the lower classes. There are some, indeed, who regard this as Stenka's worst blunder, costing him the support of the Old Believers, which might have altered the outcome of the rebellion. The error is usually attributed to Razin's political naiveté and indifference to spiritual matters, and up to a point this may be true. But on closer inspection his maneuver does not appear quite so ill-conceived. For Nikon too was a sworn enemy of the boyars and of the existing political order. He was born on the Volga of Russian and Mordva peasants, and his background differed little from that of the typical insurgent. To the aristocracy, moreover, he was an unwelcome upstart whose position in the church and influence on the tsar they deeply resented and were determined to counteract. Nikon, of course, resisted such designs. He resisted the growing domination of the state in church affairs and yearned for the old theocratic monarchy of the early Muscovite princes. After his disgrace he severely condemned the Code of 1649, in which the emerging order of secular absolutism had received legal sanction. In all this he and the rebels saw eye to eye. It was easy for Razin to cast him as the victim of a boyar conspiracy. Was it not through their treachery that he had been deposed? To all who opposed the established order Nikon could thus become a martyr and could, despite his hated reforms, be annexed to the rebel cause.

It is true that the Old Believers played only a small role in the insurrection. Razin was denounced in government charters as a heretic and devil's disciple but never as a schismatic, and known links between the schism, or *raskol,* and his movement were limited to sporadic participation of Old Believers in the Nizhni Novgorod area and to the Old Believer rising in the Solovetsky Monastery on the White Sea, in which a number of Stenka's veterans took an active part.[87] But if few schismatics joined Razin's revolt, this had little to do with his espousal of Nikon. It was merely because the *raskol* had not yet become a major force of social protest in the borderlands. Along the Don and the Volga there was, to be sure, a strong atmosphere of religious dissent which doubtless helped the rebels attract a following, but till the late 1670s the number of Old Believers in the south was still small. On the other hand, it was more than mere coincidence that the territory of future militant Old Belief should overlap so extensively with the territory of Razin's movement or that Razin should appear in future Old Believer legend as an ardent schismatic who had received Avvakum's blessing. Indeed, in the immediate aftermath of his defeat social rebellion and religious dissent were to merge in a single current which would erupt with unprecedented violence in the century to come.

6. Simbirsk

By late summer of 1670 Razin was at the height of his success. His revolt had spread up the Volga almost to its bend—a stretch of some 800 miles—and threatened to move toward Moscow. Astrakhan had been captured, and Cherney Yar, Tsaritsyn, Saratov, and Samara had opened their gates without resistance. Razin's popularity was immense. He was looked on as a sort of Robin Hood, come to avenge the poor on the property and lives of the wealthy. His program, for all its vagueness, had widespread appeal. He promised to "remove" the boyars and root out treason, to eliminate state officials and restore the ancient bond between tsar and people. Townsmen and peasants, tribesmen and vagabonds greeted him as their liberator. By mid-September his legendary prowess and seditious letters had attracted nearly 20,000 adherents, a motley army driven by anger and a craving for vengeance. His coming let loose the fury of the lower classes, and it swept toward the capital, spreading chaos in its wake. Arson and looting flared out of control. The Volga trade was thoroughly disrupted. Razin, in the words of a contemporary, "wrought great devastation . . . and ordered many to be killed." [88]

The government, however, did not remain idle. After the debacle at Astrakhan, troops were collected from all over the country to put down the rising. To lead them the tsar's choice fell on Prince Yuri Dolgoruky, a seasoned officer about sixty years old, who had proven his ability in the recent war with Poland. It was the same Dolgoruky who, as legend had it, had executed Stenka's brother, thus arousing his thirst for revenge. Dolgoruky's army consisted largely of gentry cavalry; and though the lack of infantry was a drawback of which he was to complain more than once in the coming campaign, the foot soldiers on hand were of good quality. Many were veterans of the Polish War, and some had been trained by foreign officers, though their field commanders were nearly all Russian noblemen. The troops, moreover, were equipped with up-to-date muskets and artillery and were inspected by the tsar himself before being sent against the rebels.

Razin's prolonged stay in Astrakhan had given the authorities a welcome reprieve. But his ascent of the Volga had been so rapid that by September 1, when Dolgoruky left Moscow, he was already approaching Simbirsk, the last major stronghold before Kazan, where the river turns westward toward the capital. It was at Simbirsk that the fate of the rebellion was decided. Founded by Alexis in 1648, Simbirsk (now Ulyanovsk, the birthplace of Lenin) boasted of strong natural defenses, with a citadel perched on a terraced hill high above the rest of the town. Its *voevoda*, Prince Ivan Miloslavsky, was an able officer and administrator who, in contrast to his downstream colleagues, had won the unswerving loyalty of his garrison. Four regiments of *streltsy* were at his disposal, as well as a few hundred noblemen who had fled to Simbirsk from the surrounding countryside on news of Razin's approach. In addition, the *voevoda* of nearby Alatyr had come to join him with a small party of landowners. But his strongest asset was a cavalry detachment of Russian gentry and Tatar *murzy* under Prince Yuri Bariatinsky, the officer who had dispersed Vaska Us's band four years earlier. Bariatinsky, traveling at breakneck speed, had arrived in Simbirsk on August 31, only four days in advance of the rebels.

Razin's army outnumbered the defenders by about four to one. But apart from a seasoned core of Cossacks and *streltsy*, it was a heterogeneous and poorly equipped collection, totally destitute of training and discipline. Though most had joined voluntarily, some had been forced into battle on pain of death. Their arms were an odd assortment of cudgels, spears, sickles, axes, pitchforks, staves, and stones. Prone to drinking and looting, they were extremely untrustworthy and liable to panic when opposed by regular military formations. Yet their numbers compensated to some extent for these deficiencies; and more important, they enjoyed the support of the local population and, except in siege operations, were able to put their guerrilla methods to effective use.

On September 4 the rebels sailed past Simbirsk, singing a hymn of war:

> We have come to claim our freedom,
> With our *ataman* Stenka Razin,
> From wicked judges and officials.[89]

They camped above the town for the night, and Razin planned his attack. The following morning he marched on Simbirsk and tried to take it by storm. Bariatinsky rode out with his cavalry to meet him. The ensuing battle raged till sundown, but Bariatinsky, short of infantry, could not mount a counterattack and was finally forced to withdraw across the Sura River and make for Kazan to obtain reinforcements. Miloslavsky, fearing that the residents of the outer city would now open their gates to the insurgents, retired to the citadel, in which the barracks, cathedral, government buildings, and houses of the wealthier citizens were located. The citadel was well defended with artillery and encircled by a wooden wall and a moat. The *voevoda*, determined to hold out at all costs, buttressed the wall with sacks of earth, flour, and salt. It was essential to delay the rebels long enough for Dolgoruky, in Kazan, to deploy his army against them. "Though death may come, I will not surrender to the brigand," vowed Miloslavsky.[90] Razin meanwhile entered the outer city unopposed. Following the established pattern, the inhabitants were proclaimed free men and a Cossack-style regime was introduced amid general jubilation.

As usual, the news of Stenka's victory drew an influx of fresh recruits to the rebel camp. Peasants, tribesmen, and barge haulers flocked to Simbirsk, anxious to take part in the assault on the fortress. Razin, opposed by some 4000 well-entrenched defenders, made careful preparations for the attack. Carts filled with wood, hay, and straw were brought up and emptied into the moat beside the wall. On September 15 this material was set alight and the fortress encircled by fire. While the defenders struggled to put it out, the rebels attacked through a thick screen of smoke. Scaling ladders were thrown upon the wall, and waves of insurgents tried to clamber up, only to be mowed down by the men within. Miloslavsky's troops, like their commander, fought "with extraordinary courage," [91] raining cannonballs down on the enemy and working feverishly to repair their damaged defenses. The women of the fortress hurried to the wall with ammunition and with water to put out the flames and to refresh the defenders. By nightfall the assault had been rebuffed.

The second assault came three days later, under cover of darkness. The Cossacks threw incendiary missiles filled with oil and kindling into the citadel, while Mari and Mordva hunters shot burning arrows into the air which fell on the roofs inside. Much of the fortress was soon in flames. "Here and there," an eyewitness noted, "the flames were high, and from the town they brought canvas and poured out water." [92] The defenders were sent scurrying to put out the fires, and a number of rebels mounted the wall but were beaten off after ferocious hand-to-hand fighting. Losses were very heavy on both sides. But the rebels did not give up. A third assault was made a few days later, again at night to escape the deadly fire from within. It was preceded by a prolonged barrage from cannon mounted on earthen ramparts erected alongside the citadel wall. As before, flaming missiles were hurled over the wall, and tinder was thrown into the moat and set alight, but again the attack was rebuffed. The defenders, who knew that they were fighting for their lives, were sustained by the hope that Bariatinsky might return at any moment with reinforcements. Yet the strain was beginning to tell on their nerves, and there was growing anxiety over the dwindling supply of food and munitions. Bariatinsky would have to come soon if Simbirsk was to be saved.

The month-long siege of Simbirsk saw the climax of Razin's revolt. While the siege was in progress, large rebel detachments, each led by a Cossack *ataman*, fanned out over the surrounding districts, inciting the inhabitants to attack the towns, monasteries, and estates. During this period the rebellion even spread across the Volga into western Siberia, where, in the words of the Tobolsk *voevoda*, Cossack bands distributed "alluring rebel leaflets to seduce the ignorant and propertyless." [93] It has been argued that by dispersing his forces in this manner Razin committed a serious, perhaps even fatal, error. If he had used all his men to storm the Simbirsk citadel, he might have been able to capture it, thereby opening the way to Kazan and Nizhni Novgorod, and perhaps to the capital itself. On the other hand, hav-

ing taken every other Volga town without a struggle, Razin may
not have anticipated the determined resistance he met at Simbirsk.
Moreover, he was anxious to broaden his base of support, convinced that only in this way could he win a lasting victory. It
was for this reason that he had sent his envoys to the Ukrainian
Cossacks and the Kazan Tatars and sent leaflets into every corner.
Thus, rather than concentrate all his forces at one point, perhaps
he believed that by sending out detachments in every direction
he was ensuring his mastery over the country at large. It is ques-
tionable, in any case, whether he was able to control the movements of his restless lieutenants, always on the lookout for loot
and adventure.

Three of the rebel detachments were of particular importance
and merit our special attention. The first, led by Mishka Kharitonov, struck out to the southwest, captured Penza and Saransk,
and put their *voevodas* to the sword. At Penza, Kharitonov was
joined by another Don Cossack, Vaska Fedorov, who came with
his band from Saratov. Together they made for Verkhni and
Nizhni Lomov, killed the *voevodas*, and wreaked havoc on the
merchants and officials. A second detachment, under Prokopi
Ivanov, traveled up the Volga and, skirting Kazan, seized the town
of Kozmodemiansk, whose inhabitants, led by a priest, had risen
on their approach. The largest detachment was led by Maksim
Osipov and numbered several thousand, predominantly peasants
and tribesmen with a small nucleus of Cossacks. Heading northwest toward Nizhni Novgorod, Osipov sacked the town of
Alatyr, then set it ablaze. The *voevoda* and his family, together
with the local nobility, were all burned alive in the cathedral,
where they had taken refuge. Osipov entered Kurmysh and
Yadrin without firing a shot but was forced to bypass Arzamas,
as Dolgoruky had just arrived there from Kazan with a large
troop of cavalry augmented by gentry from the surrounding
countryside. The Cossack leaders, as a rule, tried to avoid direct
clashes with government regulars, for though their peasant and
native followers knew the country and had the advantage of
numbers, they were virtually useless against disciplined formations. They were at their best in guerrilla warfare, erecting roadblocks, obstructing rivers, and ambushing parties of landowners
on their way to join the government forces; and it was by such

maneuvers that they succeeded in delaying Bariatinsky, who was hurrying with reinforcements to lift the siege of Simbirsk.[94]

During September, as Razin strove to reduce the fortress, a full-scale jacquerie raged out of control throughout the middle Volga. In such districts as Alatyr and Arzamas, Saransk and Kurmysh, manor houses were invaded by mobs of peasants and tribesmen on whose merest whim hung the lives of the owners and their families. Unpopular landlords were butchered on the spot, together with their wives and children.[95] Others were spared if they surrendered their money and belongings. Many took to the woods, whose shelter was closest to hand, or fled to the nearest town, where if they were in luck, government troops had arrived to protect them. In most of the towns, however, it was the rebels who held sway, having massacred the governors and officials. A few *voevodas*—those of Kadom and Kerensk are examples—managed to flee to safety or, in exceptional cases, were spared by the residents as enlightened administrators.[96]

Meanwhile, as Razin prepared his fourth assault on the Simbirsk citadel, Bariatinsky arrived from Kazan with a fresh and well-equipped army on October 1, 1670. For a month Miloslavsky had defied every rebel effort to capture the fortress. The delay was crucial, for it not only allowed Dolgoruky to marshal his forces but also enabled Bariatinsky to return in time to save the city. Stenka was informed of Bariatinsky's approach and rode out to meet him with a detachment of 6000 men, leaving the rest of his army to continue the siege. His troops, however, were not the same as those which had swept up the Volga with such terrifying speed. What was once a powerful force of Cossacks and musketeers had been fatally diluted by an ill-assorted mob of peasants, tribesmen, boatmen, convicts, and flotsam from the neighboring towns. Unreliable soldiers, good perhaps at the first onrush, they were easily discouraged if not at once successful and were hardly a match for Bariatinsky's picked troops, which, besides the usual horsemen and *streltsy*, included some of the tsar's best regiments, the cream of the Russian army, trained in the European manner and equipped with the latest handguns and artillery.

As Bariatinsky deployed his troops, the rebels forded the Sviiaga River and rushed in to attack, screaming their battle cries and urged on by drums seized during earlier encounters with the government. These sounds, however, were quickly drowned out by the roar of Bariatinsky's artillery, which launched a terrific bombardment that tore gaping holes in the ranks of the attackers. Peasants and tribesmen dropped their primitive weapons and scattered toward the river for safety. Only the Cossacks offered serious resistance, but they too were soon forced to give ground before Bariatinsky's cannonade. As the rebels fled, Bariatinsky ordered his dragoons into action, and the dead began to pile up. Razin himself, wounded in the head and leg, owed his life to a brave Cossack who used his own body to protect his fallen leader. Carried off the field by his men, Stenka was taken to the main army besieging the citadel. Meanwhile thousands of terror-stricken peasants streamed across the Sviiaga in full flight, heading for the safety of the forests beyond. More than a hundred, however, were taken prisoner and executed on the spot. Four cannon, fourteen standards, and a number of drums were also lost to the enemy.

Thus Razin had suffered his first defeat. It was shattering, even decisive, and worse was still to come. On October 3 Bariatinsky hastily threw two bridges across the Sviiaga, over which he led his army to liberate Miloslavsky and his weary soldiers in the beleaguered fortress. The fourth assault was still in progress when he mounted his attack, driving the insurgents into full retreat. He overtook them on the banks of the Sviiaga, and on October 4 a bloody battle was fought that lasted all day. Once again Bariatinsky used his artillery and cavalry with deadly efficiency against the frightened and demoralized rebels, who broke in panic and scattered in all directions. When all was lost the Cossacks fled with their wounded *ataman* to their boats, pursued by Bariatinsky's horsemen. There was a great crush at the moorings; many of the craft capsized and hundreds of rebels were drowned. Yet most of the Cossacks, Razin among them, managed to escape, leaving the peasants and tribesmen behind to certain death. Bariatinsky showed no mercy for the conquered mob. Reprisals began at once on the banks of the river, where hundreds of rebels— many already wounded—were hanged, quartered, or shot. Others were hooked onto posts on wooden rafts and floated down the river as a lesson to their sympathizers.

About the same time, a similar disaster overtook Razin's followers on the Don. Toward the end of September, while the rebels were preparing their last assault on Simbirsk, Frolka Razin collected an army and sailed up the Don into the grain-producing districts of south-central Muscovy. His objective was twofold: to reopen the supply routes blocked by the government and to enlarge the scope of the rebellion. Frolka's thrust formed the second prong of the Cossack campaign into the heartland, each following a major waterway along which a mass of discontented humanity was concentrated; and it had probably been ordered by his brother in yet another effort to broaden the base of his movement. Toward the same end fresh overtures were made to the Ukrainian Cossacks to mount a concerted drive against Moscow, but again they fell on deaf ears—indeed, the Ukrainian hetman, far from collaborating with the insurgents, sent a thousand men to assist the government in crushing them.[97]

As Frolka approached Voronezh, at the headwaters of the Don, there occurred nearby one of the few episodes of the rising in which a nobleman joined forces with the insurgents. In the town of Ostrogozhsk the commander of the garrison, Colonel Ivan Dzinkovsky, incited his troops to mutiny and executed the *voevoda* and his deputy. Dzinkovsky's motives are unclear, but as he had once been a confederate of Bogdan Khmelnitsky, the famous hetman of the Ukraine, Razin's revolt perhaps reawakened in him old dreams of a united Cossack republic throughout the steppe. At any rate, he summoned a *krug* and urged the townsmen to "go with [Stenka] to Moscow and eliminate the traitors and boyars."[98] The mutiny soon spread to Olshansk, whose *voevoda* was put to death. But it got no further, for Dzinkovsky was arrested by one of his own officers, who had won control of the garrison. Soon after, Prince Grigori Romodanovsky, the tsar's most capable commander in the area, arrived with a large detachment and crushed all remaining resistance. Dzinkovsky, as a traitor to the tsar and to his class, was quartered alive, then hanged; and in their fury Romodanovsky's officers executed his wife as well. Apart from Dzinkovsky, only a handful of gentry cast their lot with the rebels, and all met a similar fate.[99]

Frolka, meanwhile, was having troubles of his own. On Septem-

ber 27 he placed the town of Korotoyak under siege with every
hope of success, but Prince Romodanovsky, fresh from his triumph at Ostrogozhsk, hurried to the scene and drove the Cossacks
to flight. Like his brother on the Volga, Frolka took to his boats
and sailed down the Don toward home.

7. Suppression

The defeats at Simbirsk and Korotoyak were grave setbacks to
the rebel cause, for the two prongs of Razin's assault were simultaneously blunted and the Cossacks forced to withdraw to the
peripheries from which they had come. Stenka himself, severely
wounded and vanquished in combat, lost the aura of invincibility
which had clung to him for more than three years. Yet his rebellion was far from over, for popular excitement once aroused was
not easily subdued. In Kadom and Kurmysh, Saransk and Lomov,
Kerensk and Tambov, the jacquerie continued for months to
come. A number of Volga towns remained in rebel hands throughout the autumn and winter. Roving bands of Cossacks, peasants,
and tribesmen went on burning, looting, and massacring, and
dozens of pitched battles had to be fought before order was
restored. In the meantime, the rebellion spread all the way to the
Oka, sending shivers of fear through the citizens of the capital.

After Simbirsk, however, the tide turned unmistakably in favor
of the government. Dolgoruky on the Volga and Romodanovsky
on the Don pursued the bands of rebels and dispersed them one
by one. To facilitate the task of repression, fresh regiments were
collected from all over the country and sent to Kazan and
Voronezh, headquarters of the punitive armies. Some were first
inspected by Alexis himself on a field outside the capital; in the
largest review, which took eight days to complete, some 60,000
men paraded before the tsar.[100] Fortunately for the government,
the Polish War had ended before the revolt began, and a supply
of experienced soldiers was available to crush it. In the next century major wars were to coincide with the risings of Bulavin
and Pugachev, making the task of suppression much more difficult

for lack of troops and equipment. Alexis, by contrast, was able to dispatch some of his best units with up-to-date weapons against the insurgents. Tambov, for example, received an extra company of dragoons trained in the German manner and equipped with "thirty pairs of pistols with holsters and thirty carbines with slings and hooks," all of the latest European design.[101]

In the Volga theater of operations Dolgoruky had the benefit of two remarkable officers, Fyodor Leontiev and Prince Konstantin Shcherbatov. Acting as a team, they won a series of victories in which large numbers of rebels "were killed and captured, cannon, supplies, handguns, banners, and drums taken, and the captured bandits executed." [102] One a prince and the other a service landowner, their collaboration was symbolic of the fusion, in progress since the Time of Troubles, of boyars and gentry into a single class of noblemen. Their primary mission was to intercept the detachment of Maksim Osipov, some ten or twelve thousand strong, which having swept through Alatyr, Kurmysh, and Yadrin, was heading toward Nizhni Novgorod. In early October Osipov, still ignorant of Razin's defeat at Simbirsk, laid siege to the Makariev Zheltovodsky Monastery near the confluence of the Volga and the Oka. Monasteries were frequent victims of rebel attacks, not because of their religious function (though this may have provoked some of the insurgent tribesmen) but because of their combined roles as landlords, trading centers, and outposts of Muscovite colonization. The Makariev Monastery, an affluent market and producer, attracted the insurgents mainly by its promise of booty. For ten days its monks and peasants put up a desperate resistance, but the rebels finally breached the walls and carried away rich plunder in money, livestock, and grain.

Osipov planned to move next on Nizhni Novgorod, but a messenger arrived with news of Razin's defeat, and he swung around and headed south, in the direction from which he had come. Approaching Arzamas, the field headquarters of Dolgoruky, he "began to think that the weather was unfavorable," [103] so he skirted the town and made for Lyskovo and Murashkino, from which many of his peasant adherents originated. Until recently the two villages had belonged to Boris Morozov, tutor, brother-in-law, and favorite of Alexis, who had granted him vast estates in the area. Gifts of crown lands in the Volga districts were becoming increasingly common, much to the chagrin of the peasants, whose condition after conversion to serfdom took a sharp turn for the worse. Morozov, for one, had tripled the quitrent (*obrok*) of his villagers and forced them to supply potash without payment. Earlier, his notorious profiteering had made him the chief target of the Moscow mob in the "salt rebellion" of 1648. When he died in 1664, Lyskovo and Murashkino reverted to the crown, but no improvement followed. The peasants continued to pay heavy taxes and to supply potash to the state for export and domestic sale. An indication of their poverty is that three out of four households owned no horses.[104] Small wonder, then, that Lyskovo and Murashkino saw some of the worst rioting of the rebellion. When Osipov passed through on his way to Nizhni Novgorod, he was met by a procession with icons, crosses, and bell-ringing, and hundreds of villagers joined him for the raid on the Makariev Monastery, having long coveted its rich possessions. Accomplishing their purpose, the rebels returned home to divide up the spoils.

But Shcherbatov and Leontiev were not far behind. On October 22 they reached Murashkino and defeated the rebels in a two-day battle in which 21 cannon, 880 cannonballs, and numerous muskets and banners were taken. Hundreds of captured rebels, mostly local peasants, were hanged or beheaded. Lyskovo experienced a similar ordeal, after which Leontiev and Shcherbatov informed Dolgoruky that the area had been "cleared of the brigands" and that the peasants had taken the oath to the tsar.[105] But the rising was not yet over. Still another battle occurred a few days later at Bolshaya Kondorat in which a well-armed government force inflicted a crushing defeat on the rebels. A witness reported that "on the fields and roads horses and wagons could not pass because of the corpses; so much blood was spilled that it ran in rivulets, as after a heavy rain." Government parties continued to sweep the countryside, mopping up isolated pockets of insurgents. By the end of November Dolgoruky could advise the tsar that the whole territory "from Simbirsk to Kazan and from Kazan to Moscow" had been pacified.[106] Osipov himself fled down the Volga but was captured in Tsaritsyn and hanged.

Meanwhile, Romodanovsky was carrying out a similar mission

in the south. Rebel activity reached a climax here during October and November. Several towns, including Mayak and Tsarevo-Borisov, were taken by bands of insurgents who called on "all the common folk" to join their cause "lest we all perish because of them, the traitor boyars." [107] At the same time, Frolka Razin launched a new campaign up the Don. His target was Tambov, where he hoped to link up with the large detachment of Mishka Kharitonov, who was riding westward from the Volga toward Shatsk. In the past few decades the crown had granted many estates in this region to Russian and Tatar gentry, against whom the peasants harbored both national and social grievances. Thus if Frolka and Kharitonov could join forces, they might start an immense jacquerie throughout the area. Aware of the danger, Romodanovsky made every effort to stop them. Though hampered by wholesale desertions among the *streltsy* and other petty servicemen of the garrison towns, and by incompetent *voevodas* who abandoned their posts or otherwise failed to rally their forces against the rebels, he was fortunate that the governors of two key strongpoints—Yakov Khitrovo of Tambov and Stepan Khrushchev of Kozlov—were capable men who, like Miloslavsky in Simbirsk, commanded the devotion of their troops. As a result, he was able to concentrate his own efforts against Kharitonov and disperse his band before it could reach Shatsk. Frolka meanwhile placed Tambov under siege, but his repeated attempts to storm the citadel were as fruitless as his brother's at Simbirsk. On December 3, after a five-week siege, the Cossacks finally penetrated the fortress, only to be repulsed by the timely arrival of two of Romodanovsky's detachments. After a bloody battle they fled through the adjacent forests, their adversaries in close pursuit. The next day the rebels were overtaken at the village of Boikino, and the two armies joined in a ferocious struggle. The government, outnumbered by three to one, suffered heavy losses. But rebel losses were even heavier, thanks to the superior artillery at Romodanovsky's disposal, and the Cossacks were forced to withdraw to their home territory on the Don. The rebellion had been halted before it could endanger the heartland. To the end, the central districts remained little affected, apart from sporadic and isolated rioting, which Romodanovsky had no difficulty in bringing under control.

Little by little the rebel army was reduced to a handful of
exhausted bands, fleeing in terror from their pursuers. Hundreds
of Cossacks were caught while trying to escape eastward to Siberia
or westward to their Zaporozhian cousins on the Dnieper. Others
hid out in the forests until the repressions were over. A few
made the long journey to the White Sea to join the beleaguered
monks in defending the Solovetsky Monastery against a government invasion. The majority, however, were hunted down and
executed or banished to Siberia or the frozen north. A contemporary observer estimated that 100,000 insurgents lost their lives
in combat and a similar number in the repressions that followed.
Though this is surely an exaggeration, the number of dead
nevertheless rose into the tens of thousands.[108]

The brutality of the repressions by far exceeded the atrocities
committed by the insurgents. Where rebel violence was largely
spontaneous, occurring amid the breakdown of local authority,
the violence of the government was a calculated policy ordered
and approved by the tsar to terrorize the populace into submission and to discourage future outbursts. Captured rebels were
impaled on stakes, nailed to boards, torn to shreds by fleshhooks,
and flogged or strangled to death. Throughout the main theaters
of the rising, public hanging, quartering, disemboweling, beheading, and breaking on the wheel went on for many months.
Rebel leaders were decapitated in market squares or strung up at
town gates for display. Arms and legs were amputated and nostrils
torn out with iron pincers. Countless bodies were hung by a rib
on metal hooks and set floating down the rivers as a grisly
warning to the population. The paths of Dolgoruky and Romodanovsky were marked by gibbets, corpses, and burning villages. In some districts where reprisals were especially brutal, the
population was decimated. Thus in Lyskovo and Murashkino 35
percent of the inhabitants died in battle, 30 percent fled, 7 percent were impressed into the army, and 4 percent were executed.[109] The cruelest scenes, however, were reported in the
town of Arzamas, where Dolgoruky maintained his field headquarters. "The place was terrible to behold," wrote the anonymous Englishman from the *Queen Esther*,

> and had the resemblance of the suburbs of Hell. Round about it
> were gallows, each of which was loaded with forty or fifty men.

In another place lay many beheaded and covered with blood. Here
and there stood some impaled, whereof not a few lived unto the
third day, and were heard to speak. Within the space of three
months, there were by the hands of the executioners put to death
eleven thousand men, in a legal way, upon the hearing of
witnesses.[110]

Some of the most tragic episodes occurred in the tribal districts near the bend of the Volga between Kazan and Nizhni
Novgorod. Thousands of Chuvash, Mordva, and Mari, as well
as Russian peasants of the neighborhood, were executed or
flogged and their villages razed. Prince Bariatinsky reported
that in the town of Kozmodemiansk, whose inhabitants had
risen and slain their *voevoda*, some 400 were put to death and
another 100 deprived of their limbs or beaten with the knout.
"I have marched against the bandits," the new *voevoda* reported
to Moscow, "and with the aid of Almighty God, the Blessed
Virgin, and the Great Sovereign have defeated them and beheaded or hanged five hundred in different villages." [111] When
their work was done, a party of officers appeared before the
tribal assembly of one Mari village and called on the natives to
remain loyal to God and the tsar, "even though the Cheremis
[Mari] were not baptized in the name of the Father, the Son,
and the Holy Spirit." The villagers admitted they had been
aroused by the "many alluring rebel leaflets" brought to their
settlement by Razin's emissaries. They added, however, that
they had sought only to regain the ancestral lands of which the
state had deprived them. "There is no more stateless land any
place," the officer replied, and advised the Mari to rest content
with their present lot, "to live [peacefully] in their homes, and
wander freely in the forests." [112]

Meanwhile, a grateful tsar began to lavish rewards upon the
victors. Wholesale promotions and large bounties went to officers
and men wounded in battle, while nobles who had deserted
or refused to serve were deprived of their estates. In January
1671 Alexis received Dolgoruky and Bariatinsky in the Kremlin
and granted them large sums of money in token of his gratitude.
Dolgoruky, as commander-in-chief of the punitive army, also received a silver goblet and a sable coat lined with velvet.

It remains to inquire into Razin's fate after his defeat at Simbirsk. In early October he fled down the Volga toward the southern frontier. Samara and Saratov, which only a few weeks earlier had thrown open their gates to the triumphant *ataman*, now refused him shelter, fearing the reprisals of a vengeful government. Stenka continued downriver to the portage above Tsaritsyn, and from there to his native Don. Back in his island fortress, he nursed his wounds, which, thanks to his robust constitution, quickly healed. As his strength returned, so too did his chronic restlessness, and before winter had passed he was already planning a new venture, this time against the downstream elders. In February 1671, collecting a band of "naked" Cossacks, a mere remnant of his once enormous army, he sailed to Cherkassk with the object of unseating the established authorities. For a whole week he tried to rouse the rank and file there to "kill the elders and create disturbances in the Host," then join him in a new campaign against Moscow.[113] But the powerful loyalist party—headed by Kornilo Yakovlev and Mikhail Samarenin (who lately had been alternating with Yakovlev as *voiskovoi ataman*)—prevented him from entering the city. Finally admitting defeat, Razin returned to his longboats and sailed back to Kagalnik to map out a new strategy.

The immediate effect of Razin's bid for power was to strengthen the hitherto tenuous links between Cherkassk and Moscow. For four years Yakovlev had shrunk from interfering with his troublesome godson. He had cherished the traditional independence of the Don Host and refused to take orders from any higher authority. But Razin had renewed his threat to the privileged position of the house-owning oligarchy; moreover, failure to act now, after Razin's revolt against the government, would surely invite the tsar to send his own forces to crush the insurgents. Thus Yakovlev chose to collaborate. Ironically, it was Stenka himself who precipitated precisely what he had all along been struggling to prevent, a Muscovite presence on the Don. Alexis, resuming his *zhalovanie*, dispatched to Cherkassk a large consignment of grain and several pieces of artillery, but also 2000 Muscovite dragoons, the first such force ever to enter the Don territory, arriving there in March 1671. That same

month, on instructions from the tsar, Patriarch Ioasaf anathematized Razin and his cohorts in a solemn ceremony at the
Kremlin.[114]

Meanwhile, the Cossack elders decided that the time had come
to wipe out the rebel nest at Kagalnik. Yakovlev mustered his
followers and sailed to the island. On April 14, under cover of
darkness, he silently surrounded the bastion, stacked firewood
and dry reeds against its walls, and set them alight. He then led
his men through the smoke and swiftly crushed all resistance.
Razin and his brother were clapped in irons and removed under
heavy guard to Cherkassk. The fortress was burned to the
ground. From now on only one Host remained on the Don,
though among the "naked" Cossacks there survived a legacy
of opposition that never completely abated.

Soon afterward, Yakovlev and Samarenin, heading a convoy
of seventy-six Cossacks, set out with their prisoners for Moscow. They had strict orders from the government to guard
the rebel leaders "with great caution" during the long trip north.
At the town of Serpukhov, some twenty miles below Moscow,
they were met by a company of *streltsy* who provided an escort
for the final leg of the journey. It was thus, as a prisoner rather
than a conquerer, that Razin was to enter the capital. Yet even
now he retained his faith in the mercy and justice of the
sovereign. He requested an audience with Alexis, "always imagin-
ing that he had many things to say, very important for the
Czar to know." [115] A mile before Moscow a wagon awaited the
convoy to carry Razin into the city. A remarkable drawing made
by the visitor from the *Queen Esther* shows Stenka with his
neck chained to a scaffold mounted on the rear of the wagon,
and Frolka, going on foot alongside, fastened to the wagon
by an iron chain (see illustration No. 6). In this position the great
Cossack was trundled into Moscow, "and so," wrote the Englishman wryly, "fulfilling his prophecy of the honor he should have
in entering the town." [116]

Razin's desire to see the tsar was soon realized. Alexis interrogated his prisoner, then put him through a series of hideous
tortures: he was beaten with the knout, his limbs were pulled
out of joint, a hot iron was passed over his body, and the crown
of his head was shaved and cold water poured on it drop by

drop, "which they say causeth very great pain." [117] Razin, it is said, endured all his torments without a sound. On June 6, 1671, he was taken to the execution block on Red Square where his crimes were read aloud, followed by his sentence: "For evil and loathsome acts against God, for betraying the Great Sovereign Tsar and Grand Prince Alexis Mikhailovich, and for bringing ruin and devastation upon the whole Muscovite state [Stepan Razin] by order of the Great Sovereign and the boyars is condemned to the execution of the wicked, quartering." According to a German witness, Razin replied with "angry and hate-ridden gestures that Russia preferred to be ruined by alien action rather than to gain freedom." He then crossed himself and was quartered, during which he "gave not the least sigh." Finally, his head and limbs were mounted on stakes and his torso thrown to the dogs. [118]

About the same time, Razin's mother and uncle were executed in Tsarevo-Borisov for their part in the rebellion. Frolka's death sentence, however, was not immediately carried out. He is believed to have prolonged his life by claiming to know the whereabouts of hidden booty or of hidden leaflets that the authorities were eager to examine. Kept in prison for five years, he was finally decapitated in May 1676, shortly after the death of Alexis. [119]

After Stenka's execution, Yakovlev and Samarenin returned to Cherkassk laden with rewards from the tsar. Apart from the full restoration of their subsidy, they received a special allotment of munitions, grain, and wine, which led the upstream Cossacks to accuse them of selling out for mere *zhalovanie*. Yet, given the relentless expansion of the state, Muscovite domination was probably inevitable; the irony is that it might have been delayed if not for Razin's rebellion. At any rate, in August 1671 envoys arrived from Moscow to administer the oath of allegiance, and the Cossacks, who had refused to do so in the past, swore fealty to the sovereign in a ceremony that marked the beginning of the end of their traditional independence. [120] No longer could they boast, as they had for nearly two centuries, that "the tsar rules in Moscow but the Cossacks rule on the Don." Though they retained internal autonomy, they had now become Muscovite subjects and in future years were to take an oath of allegiance with the accession of each new ruler. As time wore on, moreover, their remaining autonomy was to wane with the waning power of the steppe and the growing power of the central government.

By the spring of 1671 only Astrakhan, the principal rebel stronghold on the Volga, remained unsubdued. It will be recalled that Razin had left Vaska Us in charge of the city when he embarked on his campaign against Moscow. But Us, "that former destroyer of Orthodox Christians," as a contemporary chronicle describes him, had meanwhile "come to a wicked end," succumbing to an attack of intestinal worms.[121] In May 1671 his successor, Fyodor Sheludyak, announced his intention to renew Stenka's campaign and "go up river to Moscow and defeat and eliminate the traitor boyars." [122] Leading some 5000 Cossacks up the Volga, he got as far as Simbirsk only to be routed there, like Stenka before him, by a well-equipped army and forced to return to Astrakhan. Embittered by their failure, the Cossacks threw all restraint to the winds, and in July a terrible bloodbath took place in the city. Metropolitan Iosif was flung down from the ramparts of the citadel, while Prince Lvov, without his protector to save him, was beheaded and his house given over to plunder. "And the gentry and officials of all ranks serving the tsar in Astrakhan," reads a contemporary report, "all of them were killed, some being thrown from the parapet." [123]

To Prince Ivan Miloslavsky, the heroic defender of Simbirsk, fell the task of reducing the last rebel bastion. In August 1671 he led an army of 30,000 down the Volga and camped above Astrakhan. His strategy was to starve the Cossacks into capitulation, so he blocked the river and prevented any supplies from entering the city. As winter set in, hunger overtook the defenders. Yet for three months Sheludyak, "a servant of the Devil, in the company of Judas," managed to hold out.[124] In an effort to break the blockade he launched repeated sorties against the government camp, but without success. As supplies dwindled, dissension arose among the insurgents, recalling Bolotnikov's experience at Tula in 1607. One group was ready to surrender, but another, headed by Sheludyak, vowed "to sit in siege and together suffer privations and even death, regarding every privation as a blessing." [125] To fan the discord Miloslavsky, like Shuisky at Tula, promised the rebels clemency if they would surrender. For the moment, however, the diehards prevailed. It was left to the Circassian prince Kaspulat Mutsalovich to break the impasse. The year before, it was his courageous tribesmen who had fired coins at the Cossacks and fought them to the last man. Kaspulat now avenged their death by a trick not unworthy of the Cossacks themselves. Offering to negotiate, he lured Sheludyak to his headquarters and clapped him in irons, whereupon Sheludyak's followers lost the will to fight and, yielding to the moderates, accepted the government's offer of amnesty. On November 26 Miloslavsky entered the city, and after a year and a half of mutiny, restored government control. Miloslavsky, in the words of a witness, "deployed his troops, then stopped at the cathedral to recite his prayers. Next he went to the town hall to get the tsar's seal, which he affixed to the stores of powder and lead. And these were placed beside the warders at the gates and on the watchtowers, where they had been before the bandits came with their destruction." [126]

Faithful to his promise, Miloslavsky left Sheludyak and his men at liberty to wander about the city. For six months the authorities, seeking to avoid a fresh outbreak, took no action against them. In the end, however, "eternal torment awaited them for their sins." [127] During the summer of 1672 the tsar appointed Prince Yakov Odoevsky as the new Astrakhan *voevoda*, a post he had held from 1663 to 1666, earning a reputation for arbitrariness and brutality. Fierce retribution followed immediately after his arrival. Sheludyak and his main confederates were rounded up, tortured, then sent to Moscow to be hanged. Many other rebels were quartered or burned at the stake. The more fortunate had their tongues cut out and were banished to Archangel and Kholmogory in the far north.

By the end of 1671, however, the last embers of revolt had been stamped out. In January 1672 services were held in the capital to celebrate the victory and to honor the troops who had fallen in the struggle. The shah of Persia, whose own subjects were among the first to suffer at the hands of the Cossacks, sent congratulations to Alexis for suppressing the rebellion. So too did Charles II of England, whose memories of the Puritan Revolution and of his father's beheading inspired in him a loathing of all who opposed their legitimate ruler.[128]

8. Conclusion

Razin in many ways carried on the tradition launched by Bolotnikov at the beginning of the century. In the first place, both movements were what one historian has described as struggles "between the depths and heights of society," [129] elemental outbursts of the lower orders against the landowners and officials who held them in subjection. In both rebellions, moreover, there was a wide overlap between banditry and social protest. Razin's movement, in fact, originated as a campaign of plunder; but by igniting the underdog elements of the frontier, it was quickly transformed into an outright revolt against the state. Furthermore, like its predecessor, it was as much a sectional as a social conflict, pitting the expanding center against the retreating frontier. The Don and the Volga became conduits of rebellion alive with an assortment of disaffected groups—tribesmen and peasants, convicts and vagabonds, Cossacks and boatmen— following their redeemer along the path of destruction. Razin's strength lay chiefly in those districts which had only recently been colonized by Moscow and in which government control was still weak. In the central provinces, where the authorities were firmly entrenched, the revolt never penetrated to any significant extent. The same was true of the northern stretches from the upper Volga to the White Sea, where, as before, the commercial towns, dependent on the Volga for their livelihood, rallied behind the government against the challenge from the steppe. In the north, moreover, serfdom and service estates were extremely rare, so that the rebels would have found few supporters among the peasantry even if they had penetrated into the area. Thus, for all the turmoil to the south, the northern region remained quiet except for the Old Believer rising at the Solovetsky Monastery, which raged on for eight years before the government could suppress it.

Razin's rebellion, far from being an isolated event, stands as a dramatic episode in that great struggle between the centralizing aspirations of monarchs and the traditional rights and liberties of their subjects which was raging all over Europe in the seventeenth century. As far as Russia was concerned, it was another chapter, as Kostomarov put it, in the age-old struggle

116

between "the appanage-*veche* and the autocratic" traditions,[130] a struggle in which regional autonomy ultimately collapsed beneath the weight of the rising autocracy. Throughout the realm townsmen and peasants were losing their freedom. Along the Volga, tribal autonomy was rapidly succumbing to Muscovite colonization. And on the Don the Cossacks, the very symbol of the vanishing seminomadic life, were forced to surrender their traditional independence and proclaim their loyalty to the tsar.

Like Bolotnikov, however, Razin lacked a coherent vision with which to combat the emerging order. His program was essentially destructive: to eliminate the landlords and officials so that the people could run their own affairs as they saw fit, on traditional lines of local self-government. Yet his aim was not to destroy the state as such. What he wanted was a popular government with a popular tsar. He wanted to replace the new bureaucratic autocracy with a decentralized, Cossack-style regime of local assemblies and elected officials, such as he inaugurated in the towns of the lower and middle Volga. Nor was it his aim to destroy the official church, as his opponents maintained. He himself, despite his early pilgrimage to the White Sea, was admittedly not attached to any organized church. He appealed to religion only as a means of attracting new followers; and he was just as ready to invoke Nikon, if this should suit his purpose, as he was to appeal to the Moslem tribesmen in the name of Mohammed. In religious as in political matters he was content to allow each region to determine its own practices. Thus when he dispensed with Orthodox wedding ceremonies in his own camp, it was less from any hostility to the church than because this was a longstanding custom on the Don, where clergy were in short supply and where priests who did live in the area were generally elected by the inhabitants,[131] a practice of which Stenka doubtless approved.

But Razin—again like Bolotnikov—failed to realize his objectives. Indeed, his revolt hastened the very developments he had hoped to forestall. Cossack independence was fatally impaired and the way opened to further Muscovite encroachments on the Don. The ties between the tsar and the nobility were strengthened owing to their mutual fear of similar outbreaks in the future. And in the ensuing years the government became increasingly authoritarian, serfdom was clamped down more firmly than ever, and the last vestiges of popular freedom and local autonomy were trampled underfoot.

In resisting all this, Razin, however vaguely and inarticulately, was resisting the modernization and secularization of Russian life. It is no accident that his rising should have occurred at a time when Russia was being drawn ever more closely into contact with western Europe. And it is symbolic that European-trained forces should have played a key part in crushing the rebellion. For it was the state, with its increasingly Western orientation, which played the "progressive" role in Russian history; and while the state was working to discard outmoded customs and habits, the bulk of the population looked backward to a simpler and purer age which perhaps had never existed outside their own imagination. The gulf between the Western-oriented ruling stratum and the mass of ordinary citizens who clung to their native traditions, a gulf that was to characterize Russian society for centuries to come, was already in the making.

Although the stratum upholding the government was extremely thin, the rebels were unable to undermine it. And they failed for much the same reasons that Bolotnikov had failed before them. For one thing, as it has been seen, they lacked a constructive program. But even more serious were their deficiencies in arms and military experience, which, whatever their program, were bound to spell defeat. Stenka's followers, for all their numerical strength and cyclonic fury, had little discipline or organizational unity. In the end they proved a poor match for the tsar's picked regiments with their up-to-date weapons and European training. "For if this power of the rebels," wrote the Englishman from the *Queen Esther*, "consisting of two hundred thousand men, had been united and unanimous, it would have been difficult for the forces of the Czar to have resisted and mastered the same." [132] Corrupt and unwieldly as the government was, it always proved stronger in sustained combat than the movements of destruction from the steppes. If Bolotnikov, during the Time of Troubles, had been able to reach the gates of Moscow, it was only because of the political vacuum created by the absence of a "born tsar." In Razin's case, as the rebels approached the capital, their quality became diluted by an influx of peasants, tribesmen, and derelicts, while the government's forces, though weak in the peripheries, were both more numerous and more trustworthy in the center. Hence the Oka line encircling the heartland was never breached.

Yet, for all the parallels between the revolts of Bolotnikov and Razin, there were a number of important differences. Bolotnikov, we have said, unlike Razin, succeeded in crossing the Oka and in laying siege to the capital. Furthermore, although the same segments of the population sided with the rebels in each case, they did so in strikingly different proportions. In comparison with its predecessor, there were few slaves in Razin's movement, for slaves in Russia were a vanishing class whose members were being converted into taxpaying serfs. The proportion of peasants, by the same token, was much greater. While only the peasants of the Komaritskaya district joined Bolotnikov in any strength, in Razin's time a vast jacquerie, the largest in Europe during the seventeenth century, engulfed the whole region of the middle Volga, where serfdom had taken firm root. Serfdom was by now a well-advanced institution, sanctified in the nation's code of laws. And the peasants, for their part, were beginning to show signs of a rudimentary class consciousness almost entirely lacking a generation or two earlier. Class lines were in general more sharply defined, particularly after the Law Code of 1649, and only a handful of noblemen, mainly for personal and discreditable reasons, cast their lot with the rebels, in constrast to Bolotnikov's time. Yet again the jacquerie was confined largely to the peripheries, scarcely touching the rural districts within the Oka perimeter. This, as we have seen, was chiefly because Razin's bands, owing to the government's strength in the center, were unable to penetrate the area and rouse the villagers to revolt. The peasants of the Volga, moreover, like those of Komaritskaya in Bolotnikov's day, were still sufficiently independent to resist the encroachments of Moscow. Since they were only recently enserfed, their backs were not so bent nor · their spirit so crushed that they would not rise in protest when a charismatic leader appeared to lead them.

Aside from the larger peasant element in Razin's movement,

the Cossacks also took a more prominent part, serving as its spearhead and most effective fighting force. An interesting feature was that the social conflict dividing the country as a whole was reproduced in miniature along the Don, where the "naked" Cossacks locked horns with the more prosperous downstream elements. Razin, as his followers sang, refused to "walk with the elders" or to "think as they thought," [133] but preferred to harness his chariot to the propertyless *golytba* and to challenge the privileged stratum from which he himself had sprung. The tribes of the Volga were another group which rose in greater strength than before, Muscovite colonization having made enormous strides since the Time of Troubles. Crushed by taxation and robbed of their lands, the tribesmen shared the grievances of the Russian peasantry, but national differences were too pronounced for any effective collaboration against the authorities. The clergy, too, participated in unprecedented numbers, some hundreds of village priests flocking with their parishioners to the rebel cause. The Old Believers, however, had not yet emerged in strength, and so played only a marginal role. Finally, the towns once more occupied a central place, though again there was little coordination with the outbreaks in the rural districts. In the garrison towns of the frontier, *streltsy* mutinies were more serious than any in the past, whether in Bolotnikov's rising or in the urban insurrections of more recent years, and foreshadowed the great *streltsy* revolts of the end of the century which led Peter the Great to disband this volatile group once and for all.

Razin's revolt was crushed in blood. Like Bolotnikov's, it failed to alter the immediate course of Russian history. But it nevertheless had far-reaching consequences. It awakened, however dimly, the social consciousness of the poor, gave them a new sense of power, and made the upper classes tremble for their lives and possessions. Moreover, it left a myth of rebellion which would inspire future generations with dreams of liberation. Above all, it created a martyr whose memory was preserved in ballad, lore, and epic. Of the four great rebels of the seventeenth and eighteenth centuries, Razin, whom Pushkin called "the one poetic figure in Russian history," was the one most revered by the people. According to one authority, he is the subject of more songs and legends than any other popular hero.[134] Long after his death he was regarded as a sorcerer endowed with superhuman powers: bullets could not harm him, he could cast a spell over snakes, open locks by magic, and escape from prison merely by drawing a boat on the wall with charcoal or chalk and sailing away. These legends gave rise in turn to the legend of his immortality. He had not really died, it was said, but was hiding out in the forests or hills or on a remote island, and at a critical moment for the people would return "with his golden banner" and deliver them from their oppressors. Along the middle and lower Volga, rocks, ravines, and burial mounds were named after him and were said to be the sites of his hidden treasure. Below Saratov, we are told, stands a hill bearing Razin's name, and, according to legend, whoever climbs it at night will learn his secret—the secret of class war.[135]

Razin was the bravest and most colorful of the four rebel leaders. People admired his adventurous spirit, his daring in battle, and his sense of honor and justice. He was admired too for his unflinching courage under torture and on the execution block. In the eyes of some he was a Christ-like martyr sacrificing his life to save the poor and bring about a golden age that would last forever. Within a short time after his death a whole legend grew up about his second coming. During the 1680s Old Believer agitators on the Don, convinced that he would rise again and lead them to the Promised Land, preached a doctrine of self-immolation to escape their tormentors "until the new coming of Razin." [136] In many poems and ballads Stenka is referred to as the "resplendent sun" (*krasnoe solnyshko*), an epithet suggesting renewal and resurrection and associated with that earlier messianic redeemer, the False Dmitri, and before him with Prince Vladimir of Kiev, the tenth-century saint who brought Christianity to the Russians:

> Rise, oh rise, resplendent sun,
> Warm us hardy, stalwart lads,
> Us poor folk, poor orphans.
> No thieves, no brigands we,
> But Stenka Razin's comrades.[137]

Afterward, songs about a "son of Razin" were to evolve into songs about Pugachev, a kind of apostolic succession in which the myth of the rebel savior martyred for the people was kept alive. As late as the 1840s Nikolai Kostomarov met an old peasant on the Volga who was convinced that Pugachev had been the "second coming of Razin after a hundred years." [138]

The persistence of such myths is far from accidental. That a futile adventure by an obscure and illiterate Cossack should survive in popular memory bears witness to the mood of rebellion which continued unabated in Russia down to the twentieth century. Periodically, new messiahs would appear in various guises to resurrect Razin's promise of liberation. On May 1, 1919, Lenin himself, in a speech at the notorious execution block on Red Square, claimed Razin as his forebear in the struggle against slavery and exploitation. [139]

But Razin left more immediate heirs. After his death a number of partisan bands sprang up in the Don territory and, though never strong enough to mount a new campaign against Moscow, aroused considerable alarm within the government. In 1673 one Don Cossack, a veteran of Razin's revolt who called himself "Tsarevich Semyon Alekseevich," collected a band of followers against the tsar but was crushed before his movement could spread. [140] Further disturbances occurred as religious dissent took root along the Don. In 1682 a group of schismatic Cossacks who planned an expedition to the Caspian under Razin's horsetail banner were subdued by the *voiskovoi ataman*, and fifteen ringleaders were taken to Cherkassk and hanged. In 1688 and 1689 Old Believers again rose on the upper Don and had to be crushed by force of arms. A former *ataman* and an unfrocked priest were arrested and executed for "plots against the Great Sovereign and the Russian state and for wicked rebellious acts, aiming to gather like-minded bandits and launch a campaign up the Volga to Moscow, just as Stenka Razin had done." [141] In spite of the most savage repressions, however, the southern frontier remained a powder barrel for many years to come. In 1707, during the reign of Peter the Great, another major revolt erupted on the Don under the leadership of an upstream *ataman* named Kondrati Bulavin, among whose lieutenants was an old Cossack who had been "with Stenka Razin for seven years." [142] The torch of rebellion had passed to a new generation.

1. The Siege of Moscow, December 2, 1606

2. Prince Mikhail Skopin-Shuisky

3. Samara and Tsaritsyn in the Seventeenth Century

STENKO RADZIN
Haupt Rebellen in der
Mostau / ist grausam
hingerichtet am 27
May 1671.

4. Stenka Razin,
   a Contemporary Engraving

5. Razin's Capture of Astrakhan, June 24, 1670

6. Razin and His Brother Being Taken to Moscow

7. Beard-Clipping During
the Reign of Peter
the Great, a
Contemporary Cartoon

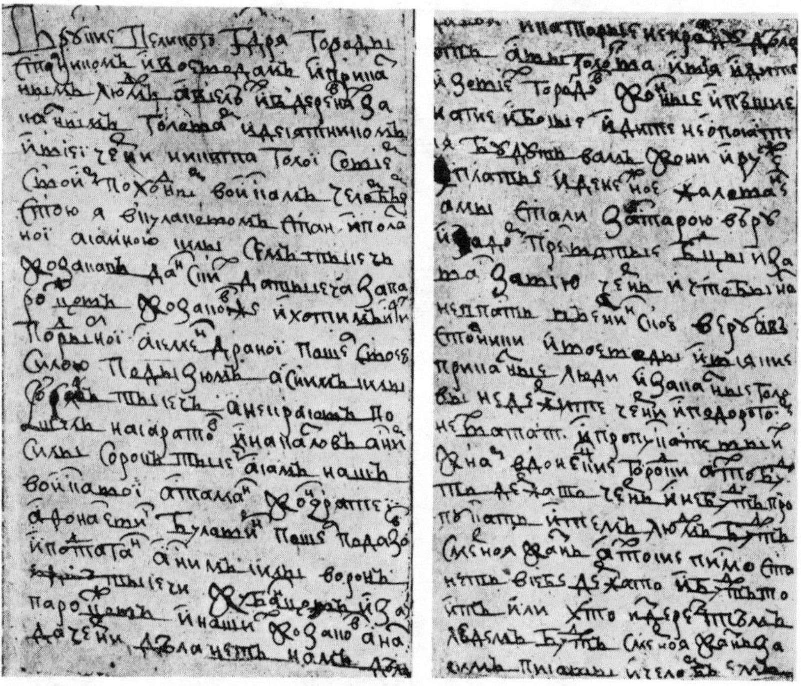

8. "Seditious Letter" of Nikita Goly, July 1708

9. Portrait of Pugachev Painted from Life, September 21, 1773, over a Portrait of Catherine II

10. Colonel Ivan Mikhelson

11. Pugachev in His Cage,
   a Contemporary
   Engraving

III Bulavin

1707–1708

1. The Streltsy

With the accession of Peter the Great in 1682, the dominant trends of Russian historical development received a powerful new impetus. Peter's expansionist foreign policy, his sweeping reorganization of the government and the army, his financial and industrial reforms, his extension of serfdom and of compulsory state service, his importation of foreign advisors and techniques— all these had their origins in the past; but he carried them out with such unprecedented energy and on so grand a scale that, by the end of his reign in 1725, Russia was transformed into a power of the first magnitude whose destiny was firmly tied to the destiny of Europe as a whole.

In this sense Peter's reign marked a watershed in Russian history. Owing to his all-embracing reforms, the emergence of centralized absolutism proceeded apace. Completing the work of the Legal Code issued by his father in 1649, he sharpened the division of the population into separate classes, each with its specific duties to the state. And it was during his reign that Russia saw the final merger of boyars and gentry into a single service nobility, and of peasants and slaves into a single class of serfs. All this, however, was achieved at the cost of appalling sacrifices. Regimentation reached a climax. Peter's edicts, as Pushkin put it, were "written as though with the knout." And if the peasantry, as we shall see, bore the heaviest burden of his policies, the entire population was harnessed to the state and driven forward by a dynamic ruler whose energy was as boundless as his appetite for power was insatiable.

There was little of the traditional tsar in Peter's makeup. He was an iconoclast who, for the sake of efficiency and modernization, overturned time-honored values and beliefs. His whole bent was pragmatic and utilitarian. He rejected every appeal to religious or regional custom. His loathing for the backward and primitive elements in Russian life was as keen as his admiration for foreign achievements in warfare and technique. His overriding ambition was, in his own words, "to sever the people from their former Asiatic customs and instruct them how all Christian peoples in Europe comport themselves." [1] After his return from the West in 1698, he spared no effort to impose new habits and values on an unreceptive population. He personally shaved off the beards of his courtiers and ordered them to discard their flowing robes for knee-length German or Hungarian coats. These measures, when extended to other segments of the population, aroused bitter resentment. Ordinary Russians, in the words of a foreign visitor, "had a kind of religious respect and veneration for their beards," [2] and to shave was to desecrate the image of God in which man had been created. Faced with mounting opposition, the tsar partially relented. Peasants and priests were left unmolested and townsmen could wear beards on payment of a special tax. But in the years ahead, unshaven chins and native dress became badges of opposition to the innovating state, and along the Don and the Volga the mere rumor of beard-cutting was enough to trigger violent outbreaks against the authorities which had to be crushed by force of arms.

Peter's campaign of Westernization struck a blow at the obstinate conservatism of the old Muscovite order. In an effort to propel backward Russia into the eighteenth century, he recruited foreign technicians, modernized the calendar, simplified the alphabet, translated Western books, launched the first Russian newspaper, and founded technical schools to prepare sons of the gentry for state service. The introduction of European culture drove a wedge between rulers and ruled, between new and old, which profoundly affected the subsequent course of Russian history. While the government and its supporters looked ahead to a future of technical modernization and economic development on Western lines, the mass of ordinary citizens were determined to remain loyal to their sacred customs and traditions. Peasants and Cossacks, *streltsy* and Old Believers, and even the aristocratic boyars insofar as they had not been assimilated to the service gentry, resisted Peter's innovations and clung to an idealized past undefiled by the emergence of a disciplined secular state. The tsar, in their eyes, had diverted the nation from its natural path and set it on a new and alien course that, sooner or later, would surely spell disaster for the people. Yet they too, for all their tenacious conservatism, had revolutionary ambitions, yearning as they did for a vanished age of personal freedom, local autonomy, authentic religion, and harmony between the tsar and his subjects—in short for Holy Russia as against the new secular order in the making. Thereafter two distinct cultures faced each other across a widening gulf of dress, habit, language, and religion. A small body of landowners and bureaucrats, clothed in Western styles and educated in Western ideas, enforced their will on a mass of rural and urban poor—illiterate, superstitious, and resentful of each new change imposed from above. With the expansion of the state, moreover, a growing number of gentry were of "alien" blood as well as habits, while the lower classes retained in large measure their ethnic and cultural homogeneity. All this goes a long way to explain the fury with which the peasants were to attack their masters during Pugachev's revolt in the 1770s, as compared with their milder behavior in the past, when Russians of all classes were still more or less united in a single Muscovite culture.

Apart from Westernization, war and territorial expansion—the root causes of popular misery—were the dominant themes of Peter's reign. His initial thrust was southward against the Turkish fortress of Azov at the mouth of the Don. Sixty years earlier, in 1637, the Don Cossacks had seized Azov and held it for five years so their ships might pass freely into the Black Sea on expeditions of plunder. When they withdrew on Tsar Michael's orders, the Turks rebuilt the fortress as a bulwark against further depredations. Now Peter, thanks to a new Russian fleet and a modern assault force, succeeded in capturing it on his second try in 1696. Four years later, when the outbreak of war deflected Peter's attention to the Baltic, popular disturbances flared up in the south at Azov, Astrakhan, and along the Don. The most serious of these outbreaks was that of Bulavin, one of whose aims, it will be seen, was to wrest Azov from Muscovite control and reopen the Black Sea to Cossack entry.

Russia was at war almost continuously throughout the forty years of Peter's reign, during which the tsar bent every effort to modernize his armed forces. What this entailed was a more efficient chain of command, a greater reliance on foreign specialists, and, above all, a determined push toward regular and permanent service. Before his accession a standing army had already begun to take shape, trained and officered largely by Westerners. The old tradition of a landowner appearing when called, with a specified number of men, was rapidly yielding to a system of direct conscription for life. By the 1680s regular troops constituted more than half of Russia's fighting force, some 90,000 out of 165,000 men. But their ranks were being depleted at a rapid rate by combat, disease, and mass desertion. Moreover, Peter's wars on two fronts called for reinforcements on a larger scale than ever. Peasants were conscripted by periodic levies, so many recruits from so many households, the normal ratio being one to twenty. To meet the rising demand, recruitment was extended to categories of the population hitherto exempt from military service. Neither townsmen nor vagrants nor even clergy escaped the recruiting sergeant's net. Between 1705 and 1709 levies were repeated on an annual basis, until the Swedish war had passed its climax and Bulavin's rising had been subdued.

All told, during the first decade of the eighteenth century, some 300,000 men from a total population of 14 million had been put into uniform and compelled to serve for life rather than for the duration of a campaign.[3] At the same time, modern equipment was introduced on a wide scale. The pike was abandoned for the bayonet, the flintlock musket replaced the outmoded firelock, and new types of light artillery were brought into service. These weapons, of course, could be deployed against internal as well as foreign enemies. The bayonet and flintlock made possible the development of new tactics which, when combined with mobile artillery, enabled infantry to stop Cossack cavalry charges. It will be recalled that Prince Bariatinsky had used similar innovations to smash Razin's army at Simbirsk. Thus the new weapons threatened the independence—perhaps the very survival—of Cossack horsemen in the same way that gunpowder had contributed to the extinction of the medieval knight. Up-to-date artillery, moreover, made the defense of towns against invading rebels more effective. Peter, at the same time, redoubled his efforts to attract military specialists from abroad and constructed factories in the Urals and near St. Petersburg to keep his troops supplied with the latest munitions. As a result, the government in the eighteenth century was able to cope with domestic uprisings even while simultaneously embroiled in major external wars.

Peter's modernization of the army was bitterly opposed by the turbulent *streltsy*, who stood to lose more from it than any other military group except perhaps the Cossacks. At the beginning of Peter's reign there were some 50,000 *streltsy* throughout Muscovy, half of whom were stationed in the capital and organized in 22 regiments of 1000 men each. A deeply conservative lot, they were exceedingly hostile to newfangled methods which might threaten their customary way of life or, indeed, their very existence as a privileged armed force. Unlike the new peasant conscripts, who served continuously with no privileges and little pay and lived in barracks often remote from family and village, the majority of *streltsy* had their own homes with garden plots and carried on trade and crafts on a tax-free basis. Their chief preoccupation was to protect their special status against the emergent standing army and to prevent themselves from falling to the level of bondsmen. But under the pressures of modernization their position was rapidly deteriorating, and they were being reduced to a disgruntled element opposed to innovation and to the whole emerging order. The decline in their status paralleled that of the Cossacks, peasants, and tribesmen, who clung with nostalgic fervor to their former customs and religion. The *streltsy* yearned for the traditional military organization just as the Cossacks yearned for their former "liberties," the Old Believers for their ancient ritual, and the serfs for "land and liberty." Like the Cossacks, moreover, they chafed over arrears in their *zhalovanie* and were prone to run amok when inflamed by rumor or drink. They had showed how troublesome they might be during Razin's revolt and during the urban riots of 1648 and 1662, in which they played a destructive role, joining rather than restraining the Muscovite mob in its outbursts of arson and plunder. Faced now with outright extinction, they were in a state of profound unrest, aggravated by the abuses of their gentry commanders. Their morale was low, their discipline lax, their deep-seated xenophobia excited by the large-scale introduction of foreign officers, weapons, uniforms, and drill. The early years of Peter's reign saw them erupt in periodic riots and mutinies which, far from improving their lot, were to precipitate their ultimate downfall.

Little wonder, then, that Peter should resolve to replace the *streltsy* with a modern standing army. His vast military program demanded a more reliable and efficient infantry; and since the *streltsy* also served as civic police and palace guard, their chronic unrest was all the more intolerable. Beyond this, Peter had first-hand recollections of their violent outbursts dating from the beginning of his reign in 1682. As a boy of ten, he had witnessed a savage mutiny in which the Moscow *streltsy* invaded the Kremlin, butchered a number of his relatives, and installed his ambitious half-sister Sophia as regent. Drink, rumor, irregular pay, and the fear of losing traditional privileges had combined to touch off the explosion. The rumor in this case was that the boyar "traitors" had murdered Peter's half-brother and co-ruler Ivan. The rioters, having avenged his fictitious death in blood, proceeded to loot the houses of the nobility and to tear up the title deeds of their serfs, scattering the pieces over Red Square. Peter himself was left unharmed in the Kremlin, while the mutiny was put down and the ringleaders summarily executed. Twelve *streltsy* regiments were transferred to the borderlands, where, as in the past, they formed hotbeds of social and religious discontent for years to come.[4]

This, however, was but the first of a series of *streltsy* revolts during Peter's reign. It is important to dwell on them because they were at once links to the risings of the past and harbingers of what was to come. In a number of ways, we shall see, they anticipated Bulavin's rebellion in the south. In 1689, seven years after the first outbreak, a rumor that the *streltsy* were on their way to murder Peter sent him galloping to safety in the Trinity Monastery of St. Sergei. It proved, however, to be a false alarm. The next real trouble occurred in 1698, while Peter was away on his celebrated journey to the West. What sparked the disturbances was an announcement that four *streltsy* regiments would be transferred from Moscow to reinforce the recently won fortress of Azov. For the *streltsy* this amounted to virtual banishment, and they rose in protest, determined to remain in the capital where their roots were deep and they led a relatively comfortable existence with their own homes and economic privileges. An investigation by the secret police revealed that bogus rumors of Peter's death had convinced the rebels that the time was ripe to act. Their object, they announced, was to kill the boyars and foreigners who, in the tsar's absence, had taken the reins of government in their own hands. For Peter, however, the *streltsy* were "nothing but begetters of evil, and not soldiers," [5] and he hurried back to Moscow to deal with them once and for all. The coup of 1682 was now revenged in mass torture and execution. Hundreds of rebels were done to death and their bodies left hanging for months as a grisly warning to their sympathizers. The remaining regiments were disbanded and scattered with their families to the peripheries. Of these a large number were banished to Azov "to dig trenches." [6] They were to cause further trouble in the years ahead. But their backbone had been broken. Never again, as B. H. Sumner observed, was the capital to be threatened by these unruly musketeers, so closely tied to the past and so hostile to Peter's innovations. By liquidating them Peter removed at a single stroke the chief obstacle to his military reforms and the one armed force that resisted his efforts to alter the course of Russian history.[7]

Along the southern frontier, however, the *streltsy* remained a nuisance for several more years. In 1697 a group of them in Taganrog, Peter's new naval harbor on the Sea of Azov, had already sought to attract the Don Cossacks into a joint campaign against the authorities. "I shall go to Moscow and do what Stenka Razin had done," declared their leader.[8] Their appeal struck a sympathetic chord among the poorer Cossacks, who longed to repeat Razin's exploits, but the movement was nipped in the bud and its instigators taken to Moscow for execution. After the 1698 revolt, pockets of exiles persisted in their seditious behavior. In 1699, for instance, a band of disgruntled *streltsy* made common cause with the Cossacks for the first time since Razin, proclaiming their ambition to "go to Moscow to stir up the common folk and kill him, the Sovereign." "When Razin revolted," boasted one of the insurgents, "I went with him." They cursed Peter for transferring them to godforsaken Azov and forcing them to labor day and night with little compensation. But their worst venom was reserved for the boyars and "Germans" (i.e., foreigners), whom they regarded as the true source of their oppression. One of their leaders expressed this feeling in graphic terms: "In the earth there are worms, in the water demons; in Moscow there are boyars, in Azov Germans." [9] On the eve of Bulavin's revolt the *streltsy* in the south were finally disbanded. But long afterward dissident petty servitors—soldiers, Cossacks, deserters—remained the chief agitators and rumor-mongers who stirred the poor to rebellion and who, in Pugachev's time, even posed as the messiahs who sought to lead them to a better world.

2. Christ or Antichrist?

The *streltsy*, for all their turbulence, were by no means the only group with strong grievances against the state. The weight of Peter's policies fell just as heavily on the taxpaying peasants, traders, and artisans of the villages and towns. To meet the voracious needs of the treasury, levies were imposed on them in ever-increasing amounts. "Gather ye money where ye may," Peter instructed the Senate, "for money is the artery of war." Existing taxes were raised, and new taxes invented by a special corps of "profit-makers" who caused, in the words of a contemporary, "wailing amongst all the populace." The profit-makers were resourceful men who, as Kliuchevsky noted, "attained virtuosity and almost insane ingenuity." The Hanoverian resident in Russia compared them to birds of prey who regarded their duties merely as opportunities to suck the marrow from the peasants' bones and build their personal fortunes on the ruin of others.[10] From 1704, when the profit-makers were organized, some thirty new taxes were introduced—on land, beards, hats, boots, horse collars, beehives, baths, chimneys, coffins, firewood, foodstuffs, and other items—arousing widespread discontent. In 1707–1708, the period of Bulavin's rising, the average peasant household paid five times the annual taxes it had paid in 1700.[11] Although the number of taxpayers had, according to the census of 1710, declined by more than a fifth during the last thirty years, owing partly to military recruitment, partly to the merger of households, and partly to the continuing flight of peasants to the frontier, the burden was merely shifted to those who stayed behind. As the demand for money increased, so did the murmurs of opposition among the people. A mass explosion seemed inevitable.

Another source of unrest was the large-scale conscription of peasant labor for government construction projects. Tens of thousands from all parts of Russia were forced to work building Peter's "paradise" on the marshes of the Neva. An appalling number succumbed to dysentery, disease, and sheer exhaustion, reminding some observers of how the Pharaohs erected their pyramids. St. Petersburg, it was said, was a city built on bones, a mass grave.[12] In the south, additional conscripts were sent to build ships at Voronezh, fortifications at Azov, and a naval station at Taganrog. The demand for labor was insatiable. At Azov alone

more than 5000 were put to work strengthening the fortress,
which Peter was only to relinquish to the Turks in 1711. Thousands more, herded like cattle, labored at digging a new canal
that was to link the Don and the Volga, thereby creating an uninterrupted waterway from Moscow to Azov. The project, however, was abandoned after the loss of Azov and not completed
till after the Second World War, nearly 250 years later. On the
upper Don near Voronezh, where the first Russian fleet was being
constructed under the direction of Western artisans and engi-
neers, whole villages were conscripted to labor in the shipyards
and to cut wood in the surrounding forests. Wages were irregular, sickness rankled, desertion mounted. "The years have become
hungry years and taxes are heavy upon us," complained a
peasant from the area. "We have no food and God alone knows
how we exist, how we pay. And now we are dragged to Voronezh
to work forever as carpenters, which leaves our own villages without wood." [13] According to the figures of the Azov governor,
from 1704 through 1709 an annual call went out for some
30,000 laborers in the south; and though fewer than half actually
reported, the effect on the villages was severe.[14] The number
appearing for work dropped sharply in 1706, on the eve of Bulavin's revolt, a sign of the disaffection among the Don inhabitants.
Sporadic disturbances broke out among the forced laborers at
Taganrog harbor and among the woodcutters and carpenters at
the Voronezh shipyards. There was trouble too among the raftsmen recruited to float timber from the forests to the sites of
construction.

The fact that foreigners were everywhere in charge of the
work contributed in no small way to the growing ferment. Another interesting development was that the tsar himself came
in for as much criticism as his hirelings and subordinates. A
noticeable shift was taking place in the popular attitude toward
the ruler. The files of the secret police contain hundreds of complaints about Peter's oppressive activities. Peasants denounced
him as a drinker of their blood, a tormentor of their flesh, a de-
vourer of their village (*miroed*). "What kind of tsar is he?" asked
one distraught villager of her interrogators. "He has driven the
peasants from their homes and taken our husbands as soldiers.
He has made orphans of us and of our children and left us to

weep forever." [15] Opponents of the government cursed Peter and all his works—his centralized bureaucracy, his new army and navy, his wars and taxes, his conscription of labor, his destruction of old values and beliefs. Their most earnest wish was to rid themselves of this tyrant and restore a more traditional and less onerous social order. All sorts of rumors were circulated about him by vagrants and deserters, by runaway peasants and dissident priests, rumors which a superstitious people accepted as the only explanation of their suffering. Some said he was a changeling substituted for the real tsar during his travels abroad. Others insisted he had been murdered in Stockholm and a German installed in his place. Dozens of such stories were heard throughout the country. Peter, in the popular mind, became an evil impostor, a false tsar, a creature possessed of the Devil, born of an impure virgin, the very antithesis of an Orthodox sovereign. This, indeed, was why he massacred the *streltsy*, hobnobbed with foreigners, burdened his subjects with recruitment and taxes, cut off beards, donned strange coats, smoked tobacco, and—a reference to his calendar reform—stole eight years from God. Antichrist, they said, sat on the throne of Holy Russia with smoke issuing from his mouth. The same thing had been said of his father, but now it was clear that Peter was the true Antichrist.[16]

But it was Peter himself who was attacked and not the institution of tsardom. The idea of Russia without a sovereign remained beyond the popular imagination. As Sumner put it, the tsar in some form was accepted as something given, like the sun and the moon.[17] Indeed, the belief in a popular ruler hiding from the treacherous nobility was stronger and more widespread than ever. A hermit on the Don spread the rumor that Ivan Alekseevich, Peter's feebleminded half-brother whom the conservatives had always favored, "is alive in Jerusalem and that is why the boyars are stealing; for Peter loves the boyars while Tsar Ivan loves the common folk." [18] A group of Cossacks were so excited by this tale that they resolved to kidnap Peter on his next trip to the Don and hand him over to the Turkish sultan, a plan, however, that they never had a chance to put into effect. In a similar way Peter's son Alexis was later to become the hope of conservative elements of society, outraged by the tsar's alien and heretical innovations. In the light of these widespread yearnings for a "just" ruler, a "people's tsar," it is odd that Bulavin did not exploit them. Not once during the course of his revolt did he attempt to put forward a pretender to the throne. By failing to do so he forfeited a good deal of potential support, and this, it will be seen, was one of the chief reasons for his downfall.

The belief that Peter was the Antichrist was, as one might expect, especially strong among the Old Believers, who were largely responsible for spreading it among the people as a whole. The Old Believers were shocked by the tsar's flagrant impiety and disrespect for traditional modes of worship. He melted down churchbells for cannon, pressed clerics into military service, and organized a mock church council that indulged in drunken parodies of venerated religious rites. More than that, Peter's reign saw the final subjugation of the church to the state begun by his predecessors. The office of patriarch was allowed to lapse and a holy synod subsequently founded in its place on the Protestant model of Sweden or Germany. For the schismatics this was nothing but a betrayal of the tradition that Moscow was the true and uncontaminated vessel of Christianity. They drew a sharper line than ever between the state-dominated official church and the native Orthodoxy of their "fathers and forefathers." In their eyes, the former was a heretical institution shorn of sacramental grace, the latter the third and last surviving Rome. They longed to return to the original faith of Holy Russia, when, in the words of their seventeenth-century progenitor Avvakum, "under our pious princes and tsars the Orthodox faith was pure and undefiled, and in the church was no sedition." [19] They clung to the strict observation of established ritual as a necessary preliminary to salvation. They resisted conscription, taxation, and even the census, recalling the biblical account of David's sin of "numbering" the people.[20] To yield to the dictates of state power or of the church hierarchy, they felt, would lead to certain damnation. The issue was clear. It was, as an English preacher phrased it during the Puritan Revolution, "whether Christ or Antichrist shall be lord or king." [21]

But the Old Believers were more than mere religious fanatics struggling against the modification of church ritual. Religious issues, though important in themselves, provided an outlet for social and political discontent. The dissenters were as much opposed to the expanding state and to the whole new pattern of life which it imposed as they were to changes in the spelling of "Jesus" or in the number of fingers used in making the sign of the cross. They saw the deeds of Antichrist not only in Peter's irreverent mockery of religious worship but also in his ruthless accumulation of power at the expense of the people. For them the centralized state was an artificial body forcibly grafted upon Russian society, an alien growth weighing heavily on the poor and responsible for their suffering. Their tenacious loyalty to traditional habits found wide support among small tradesmen, independent peasants, and other elements within the conservative core of the taxpaying population, and also among the mass of underprivileged and dispossessed who clung to everything old because everything new fell on their shoulders with a heavy weight. They were particularly numerous among the Cossacks and *streltsy*, semiautonomous groups which, threatened with the loss of traditional privileges and status, expressed their social grievances in religious dissent. Old Belief, paradoxically, was a deeply conservative movement that simultaneously became a restless and even a revolutionary factor in Russian life. It formed a nucleus around which all dissident social elements, all elements opposed to the secularized, bureaucratic, and Westernized power-state in the making, might rally. It is not surprising, therefore, that the *streltsy* rising of 1682 should have taken as its manifesto an Old Believer tract drawn up by a schismatic priest (Nikita Dobrynin, known as Pustosviat) and appealing, among other things, for the right to make the sign of the cross with two fingers, as in the past. From that time on, all popular rebellions in which *streltsy* and Cossacks took the lead were to be fought under the banner of Old Belief, the risings of Bulavin and Pugachev being the most notable cases in point. Thereafter the restoration of traditional rituals and texts would be inseparably linked with the abolition of serfdom and centralized absolutism.

Old Belief and popular rebellion had still another important feature in common. As products of the seventeenth and eighteenth centuries, an era of emergent national feeling in Russia, both were inspired by nativist tendencies and ideas. They were movements of national as well as plebeian opposition to the Europeanized gentry-dominated state and to the state-dominated official

church.²² They aimed to root out alien elements in both society
and religion. With the rapid absorption of new territory, Russia
was becoming a multinational empire and, as such, was losing
whatever ethnic, religious, and cultural homogeneity it had formerly possessed. This process, accelerated by the influx of Western merchants, technicians, and military specialists, brought about
a profound nativist reaction. In the popular mind, Europeans and
the Europeanized gentry were identified with the forces of
modernization and change that were working to the detriment of
the lower classes. The governing strata, it was thought, did not
belong to the Russian folk, but formed a class apart, an alien
breed of parasites sucking the blood of the poor. Beliefs of this
sort sharpened the hostility of serf against master and, as was
noted earlier, help to explain the widespread massacre of landowners during Pugachev's revolt in the late eighteenth century.
It was in this combined social and cultural schism, moreover, that
the gulf between the "dark" masses and the educated minority
had its origins, as did much else of what was to divide Russian
society in future years, down to the Revolution of 1917 and even
beyond.

The Old Believers, finally, were in part responsible for the
religious overtones and quasi-religious vocabulary exhibited by
movements of social protest in the seventeenth and eighteenth centuries. These were manifested most dramatically in the millenarian
quest of Bulavin and Pugachev for a golden past when men were
free from the shackles of serf-owner and bureaucrat. Since the
time of Avvakum, indeed, rebels and schismatics looked back to
a holier Russia uncontaminated by the rise of serfdom and of the
barracks state. They were convinced that the end of the world
was at hand, that the sun would be eclipsed, the stars fall from
the sky, the earth burn up, and that on Judgment Day the Archangel's trumpet would summon the righteous to God's kingdom.
During the 1670s and 1680s peasants on the Volga, in anticipation
of these events, abandoned their fields and, dressed in white
shrouds, lay down in coffins hollowed from tree trunks to await
the trumpet call. The brutal persecutions by the government only
heightened their fanaticism. "Let us go into the flames," declared
their leader Avvakum, "for in the other world our shirts will be
of gold, our boots of red leather, and there will be plenty of

honey, nuts, and apples. It is better to burn alive than to serve Antichrist." [23] In response to his appeal no less than 20,000 schismatics sacrificed their lives in paroxysms of self-immolation. Among them, as we have seen, were Old Believers on the Don who sought purification by fire "until the new coming of Razin."

The tide of religious and social opposition was to reach a new climax with Bulavin's rebellion of 1707–1708. But two years earlier a violent outbreak in Astrakhan, that perennial hotbed of revolt, provided a foretaste of what lay ahead. The apocalyptic mood there, so strong in Razin's time, had, if anything, deepened during the reign of Peter the Great. The town's inhabitants, many of whom were Old Believers, continued to look for signs heralding the end of the world. These appeared in abundance with the launching of Peter's reforms. Following orders from Moscow, the *voevoda*, Timofei Rzhevsky, began in 1704 to levy taxes on baths and laundries, cellars and taverns. Citizens complained of beard-cutting, innovations of dress, and curtailment of traditional fishing rights. It was even rumored that all Russian girls would be forced to wed foreigners, which led to the hasty performance of a hundred marriages in a single day.[24] Rzhevsky, moreover, was an extremely unpopular governor, loathed for his cruelty and extortion. The *streltsy*, for whom Astrakhan was the last remaining stronghold, accused him of embezzling their *zhalovanie* while overloading them with new labor duties beyond their already heavy obligations.

In July 1705 the lower-class inhabitants, headed by *streltsy*, schismatics, and other malcontents, rose in revolt and slaughtered the *voevoda* and some 300 noblemen, officials, and foreigners. Then the insurgents, harking back to Razin and Sheludyak, held a *krug* in the Cossack manner, elected an *ataman*, and resolved to avenge the massacre of their fellow *streltsy* in Moscow by killing the tsar. "He calls himself tsar," they said of Peter, "but he has forsaken the Christian faith." [25] The time had come to act, they thought, for the army was embroiled with the Swedes, leaving the capital virtually defenseless. Some of the rebels, on the other hand, later told their police inquisitors that they had merely wished to see if the tsar were alive, because rumors had circulated that he had died in Stockholm and that an impostor had taken the throne. "We decided to go to Moscow," they said, "to question the boyars about the sovereign, then raise a rebellion and kill them all." This apparent contradiction stems, perhaps, from their implicit belief in a "true" sovereign who sided with the people against their oppressors. At any rate, their aim was "to go to Moscow and kill the government administrators, military officers, and above all the foreigners . . . and to swear allegiance to the sovereign so he should restore the old faith and not require the wearing of German clothes or the shaving of beards." [26]

As the preceding quotation indicates, the nativist element in the rising was very strong. Since the arrival of the *Orel* in 1669, an increasing number of European ships and technicians had been coming to Astrakhan, and among the *streltsy* and Old Believers xenophobic feelings were running high. According to John Perry, an English engineer hired for the dredging of the Volga–Don canal, "all the strangers that were in the city were cut to pieces in a revengeful manner, without sparing either man, woman, or child." [27] The victims included the entire crew of a Dutch-built vessel outfitted to sail on the Caspian.

From Astrakhan the revolt spread quickly to the nearby garrison towns of Cherny Yar, Krasny Yar, Guriev, and Terki. At one point the rebels, following an established tradition, sent emissaries to Cherkassk to solicit the aid of the Don Cossacks, to whom they complained that their beards were being shaved and Western clothes introduced by force, a charge that Bulavin was to repeat when seeking support for his own rebellion. But the *ataman*, Lukian Maksimov, and the Cossack elders refused to collaborate. Some, in fact, lent their services to the government in suppressing the revolt. The following year a grateful tsar rewarded them with a special *zhalovanie* and issued a charter praising the Host for its loyalty at such a critical moment.[28]

The Astrakhan revolt continued for eight months, until a government expedition was sent to crush it. To carry out the task Peter summoned from the Swedish front one of his ablest officers, Field Marshal Boris Sheremetiev, to whom he allotted several Muscovite regiments and a detachment of Kalmyk tribesmen supplied by Khan Ayuka Taisha. The Kalmyks, like the Cossack loyalists, were receiving a handsome subsidy from the crown, to which they had earlier demonstrated their loyalty in the suppression of Razin. Sheremetiev's army arrived in March 1706 and, after a fierce struggle, put down the rebellion. The ring-leaders were sent to Moscow to be interrogated and then were hanged. A few, however, eluded capture and fled to the Don to await a new opportunity to challenge the government.

3. Bulavin

Despite the loyalty of the Don Cossacks during the Astrakhan rising, their relations with Moscow were very strained. Nor are the reasons far to seek. With the expansion of the state to the south and the simultaneous growth of the Cossack Host to the north, the competition for land became keen. Little by little Muscovite landlords were advancing into the northern Don terri-tory, carrying in their train what the Cossacks had always feared: agriculture, serfdom, and government control. "Where the Mos-kals go, tears and blood flow," went a Cossack proverb.[29] With less and less land available in the center, the tsar took to distrib-uting new estates in the south and east, the recipients being both newer service gentry and powerful older families such as the Romanovs, Repnins, and Naryshkins. Monasteries, too, cramped by Peter's restrictions in the heartland, were extending their hold-ings in the peripheries, particularly along the upper Don and its tributaries. At the same time, Cossack influence in these areas was on the rise. This was especially apparent in the valleys of the Aidar and Northern Donets rivers, where every month new villages sprang up, settled by runaway peasants who looked to Cherkassk rather than Moscow for protection.

Inevitably the ill-defined, shifting border between Moscow and the Don became a source of bitter contention. In February 1702, for instance, the foreign office in Moscow, which continued to handle relations with the Cossacks, warned the Host not to fish, poach, or trap, nor even to graze cattle or keep bees on the bishop of Tambov's new estate on the Khoper River, a tributary of the Don. The Cossacks in a defiant reply told the "trespassers" to get off *their* land or be "thrown into the water."[30] But the gov-ernment, for which the Don was the base of its new fleet and the highway to mastery over the Turks, was determined to make its authority felt. In 1702 a decree was issued prohibiting the Cossacks to fish near recently conquered Azov. Over the next few years fishing rights along the rest of the Don and its tributaries were progressively curtailed. Woodcutting was also limited in order to conserve timber for the shipyards at Voronezh. Restrictions on the use of forests in turn impeded hunting, trapping, and beekeeping, the traditional means by which the Cossacks gained their livelihood. Finally, a government edict of February 28, 1706, forbade the Cossacks to occupy empty land throughout the whole territory of the upper Don. The two sides had reached a deadlock. The Cossacks were bent on stopping further encroachments. on what they claimed to be part of their own territory, while the government insisted that the land belonged to the tsar and "that the Don Cossacks not extend their settlements any further." [31]

An additional source of friction was the extraction of salt in areas claimed by both the Cossacks and the government. Salt, a highly valued commodity, gave rise to repeated clashes between the competing parties. In 1704, for example, Colonel F. V. Shidlovsky of the Izium regiment, which consisted of military Cossacks in regular government service, seized the salt works at Bakhmut on the Northern Donets. The local Cossacks who had opened the works in 1701 were evicted as mere squatters with no legal claim to the salt. The following year a Cossack band led by the Bakhmut *ataman*, Kondrati Bulavin, retaliated by destroying the works in a surprise attack. Word of the dispute reached Moscow, and the tsar ordered an inquiry. Nothing was settled, however, for though Shidlovsky won control of the salt deposits, the conflict simmered till the fall of 1707, when it merged with Bulavin's mass rebellion.

For the elders in Cherkassk an old dilemma was revived. Since the middle of the seventeenth century they had been engaged in two simultaneous struggles, one against the expanding autocracy, the other against the impoverished fugitives from the central districts. Once again they had to decide whether to support the government and risk further encroachments on their "liberties" or to side with the upstream newcomers who posed a threat to their wealth and security. Neither was an attractive alternative. On the one hand, the danger of government domination was greater than ever. Since the 1660s new stockades had been going up along the northern fringes of the Don territory. On the Northern Donets, for instance, fortified blockhouses had been erected at Tor in 1668 and Izium in 1680, intended chiefly as buffers against the Crimean Tatars, who, though no longer able to penetrate the heartland, continued to menace the outlying southern districts. If necessary, however, they could also be used against the Cossacks, as during the dispute over the salt works at Bakhmut. With the capture of Azov in 1696, the Cossacks found themselves caught in a government vise. Well-equipped garrisons stood on the north and south. The Cossack *strugi*, moreover, were no match for Peter's modern fleet at Voronezh and Taganrog. In Cherkassk the influence of Moscow was perceptibly increasing. A council of elders friendly to the tsar was beginning to supplant the authority of the general assembly. The independence of the *ataman*, moreover, was on the wane. And since the Old Believer revolts of the 1680s, the government had been attempting to interfere with the Cossack tradition of electing their own priests. The clergy, however, were still, for the most part, chosen by their parishioners; and within the Cossack oligarchy discord persisted between those who favored closer ties with Moscow and those who sought to protect their shrinking autonomy.

On the other hand, the old-timers were being swamped by the rising tide of immigration from the center. In Razin's heyday there had been some 50 Cossack settlements on the Don with a population of 20,000 to 25,000. Now, a single generation later, there were more than 120 settlements with as many as 50,000 or 60,000 inhabitants. The new arrivals settled mainly along the upper Don, the Northern Donets, and their tributaries. On the Khoper River, for example, where only 8 villages had existed in Razin's time, there were 26 when Bulavin took up the torch of revolt. The settlers included former *streltsy*, urban poor, and a large number of military deserters. Many were Old Believers who complained that "in Moscow there are many churches but neither God nor justice." [32] But the vast majority were runaway peasants whose situation had become worse since Peter's coronation. The fetters of bondage were everywhere tightened. Slaves were subjected to taxation and recruitment, while serfs were reduced to

virtual slavery, so that the distinction between them was obliterated. Monastery peasants were, if anything, even worse off
than the hard-pressed serfs on private estates. And if conditions
were somewhat better for peasants on state lands, they too suffered from the mounting burden of taxes, conscription, and
forced labor. For peasants of all categories flight remained the
chief means of protest. The urge to wander, to escape from
tyranny and oppression, was a permanent trait of the rural inhabitants, and the broad, underpopulated expanses of the south
and east offered full scope to their quest for a freer life. The
flight of whole villages was not unknown, the fugitives often
plundering the manor and, on rarer occasions, even killing their
master before departing for the frontier.

The influx of runaways brought the dilemma of the downstream Cossacks to a head. The sharp increase in the number of
newcomers threatened to shift the balance of strength against
the entrenched oligarchy. The older Cossacks, as we have seen,
enjoyed a virtual monopoly on trade, *zhalovanie*, and political
authority. They willingly employed the *golytba* to fell their
timber and tend their herds and as hired laborers in their fisheries,
apiaries, and salt works. But they drew the line at admitting them
into the Host. Newcomers were accepted as Cossacks only
after a seven-year residence period and on the vote of the *krug*
in Cherkassk. Lately they were being rejected with greater
frequency than in the past because the older residents were
reluctant to spread the government subsidies any thinner and
also because of the tendency of the runaways to bring agriculture
into their new settlements. The downstream Cossacks regarded
the peasant refugees with more contempt than sympathy, boasting that they themselves "neither sow nor reap nor spin but
live well just the same." [33] Their worst fear was that the Don
would fall under the plough, and on its upper reaches at least
this fear was becoming a reality.

Thus the elders and the government had something in common: both wanted to stem the tide of fugitives into the steppe.
For Peter the Great, bent on marshaling the population to serve
the state, the drain of manpower to the frontier was intolerable.
In 1703 he sent two officers to the Don to take a census of old
and new residents, setting 1695 as the cutoff date. Settlers who

had arrived after that year were to be rounded up and sent back to the towns and villages from which they had fled. The Cossacks, however, refused to cooperate, and the officers returned to Moscow with their mission unfulfilled. New emissaries were sent, but without result. For if the established Cossacks looked askance at the newcomers, they were not prepared to surrender them at the government's demand. They kept faith with their motto, "From the Don runaways are not handed over." Some, their livelihood already menaced by government restrictions on fishing, woodcutting, and salt extraction, regarded this new interference as intolerable. For Bulavin, at any rate, it was the immediate cause for rebellion.

Peter, however, refused to countenance the right of sanctuary any longer. With the expansion of the northern war his demands for the return of runaways became more and more insistent. In May 1705 he sent a charter to the Don ordering the immediate transfer of new settlements beyond the Northern Donets boundary and the return of all fugitives to their place of origin. During the Astrakhan revolt he relaxed his demands lest the Cossacks be driven into an alliance with the insurgents. He was relieved and gratified when they remained loyal, and in February 1706, as we have seen, sent them a special subsidy as a reward. Some of the elders, notably Efrem Petrov and Yakim Filipiev, actually took part in quashing the uprising. Others sympathized with the rebels but shrank from joining them for fear of government reprisals and a further reduction of Cossack independence. The majority, however, including the *ataman*, Lukian Maksimov, favored a show of obedience and even a certain measure of collaboration in order to preserve their dwindling autonomy, and until the outbreak of Bulavin it was their position that prevailed.

In July 1707 the tsar took a decisive step, sending Colonel Prince Yuri Dolgoruky with a detachment of 300 men to enforce the charter of May 1705. Dolgoruky's was but one of a long series of search parties sent to the frontier since the middle of the seventeenth century. The difference, however, was that for the first time recovery operations were extended into the Don territory on a significant scale. Peter instructed Dolgoruky —a relative of the officer of the same name who subdued Razin's rising—to track down the "*posad* folk and peasants of various landlords who, not wanting to pay their regular taxes, abandon their work . . . and conceal themselves on the Don with their wives and children." The Cossacks, Peter complained, "do not drive these fugitives from their settlements but harbor them in their homes." [34] Dolgoruky, in addition, was ordered to look into the simmering quarrel between the Don and Izium Cossacks over the Bakhmut salt works.

Arriving in Cherkassk on September 2, 1707, Dolgoruky was received with little enthusiasm by Ataman Maksimov, who rightly saw his mission as part of a broader Muscovite effort to colonize the steppe and to mobilize the wealth and manpower of the Cossacks for the service of the state. What then was to be done? Maksimov settled on a compromise. He refused to allow any interference in the Cherkassk area, yet, rather than antagonize the government, agreed to cooperate in a search of the upper Don and the Northern Donets, where the bulk of the newcomers was concentrated. He assigned to Dolgoruky seven experienced men, among them the loyalist elder Efrem Petrov, to act as guides. Dolgoruky divided his force into four separate posses and sent them along the rivers of the upper Don territory to root out fugitives. The populace was roughly handled and the knout freely applied. Each day hundreds of settlers were rounded up—ecclesiastical peasants, peasants from crown and private estates, townsmen, barge haulers, and runaway soldiers and laborers from the new bases at Azov and Taganrog, whom Peter was especially anxious to retrieve. In a month's time Dolgoruky recovered some 3000 runaways, though more than a few insisted that they had come to the Don long before the cutoff date and had participated in the Azov campaigns of 1695 and 1696.[35]

Dolgoruky's mission was not only a direct violation of traditional Cossack immunities; it was a challenge to the principle of autonomy to which the Cossacks owed their very existence. The Cherkassk elders recognized this but felt powerless to resist. Instead, they were content to deflect the government's efforts away from their own immediate bailiwick and against the newer settlements to the north, about which they themselves had cause for apprehension. It was left to the local upstream *atamans*, headed by Kondrati Afanasievich Bulavin, to offer opposition.

Of Bulavin's early life very little is known. The son of a village *ataman*, he was born about 1660 in Trekhizbianskaya Stanitsa on the Northern Donets, and so was old enough to remember Stenka Razin, with whom he had much in common. Like Razin, he was from an established Cossack family, though from an upstream settlement where government intrusions were directly felt and deeply resented. He appears, like Stenka, to have been illiterate. And as a young Cossack—once again like his predecessor—he won his spurs in campaigns against the Kuban and Crimean Tatars, undertaken jointly with the Zaporozhian Cossacks as in the past. During these campaigns Bulavin apparently became acquainted with Mazepa, the celebrated hetman of the Ukraine. From 1704 to 1706 Bulavin served as *ataman* of Bakhmut, a settlement not far from his birthplace. It was at this time that he first showed his rebellious spirit, leading an attack on the salt works seized by government troops, a harbinger of things to come.

When Dolgoruky arrived on the upper Don and began to carry out his recovery mission, Bulavin resolved to stop him. For this purpose he collected a band of some 200 Cossacks and runaways, among whom was at least one veteran of Razin's rebellion, a Cossack named Ivan Loskut. Their anger had been aroused not only by reports of atrocities committed by the searchers, but also, as in Astrakhan, by the rumor that the authorities intended to cut off their beards, for which they had "a high veneration," as a foreigner noted, "in as much as they think they make them resemble God Almighty, whom their painters represent with a beard." [36] On October 8 Bulavin ambushed Dolgoruky at night in the village of Shulgin on the Aidar River (a branch of the Northern Donets) and slaughtered him and most of his men, then flung their corpses into wolf pits. The survivors fled in terror to Voronezh, while Efrem Petrov hurried to alert his comrades in Cherkassk.

Bulavin later tried to justify his action in a letter to the tsar. The Cossacks, he wrote, had asked nothing more of Dolgoruky's party than "to recognize the Don and other rivers, as of old, as Cossack territory of our grandfathers, our fathers, and ourselves," yet "without the advice or consent of the whole Don Host, they went through many settlements, wreaking destruction and subjecting many men to torture and the knout; they took our wives and daughters to bed by force, hung our children by the legs from trees, and without cause slit the nostrils of many Cossacks." Others, continued Bulavin, were cursed and humiliated, their possessions confiscated, their villages burned, and old residents of at least twenty years' standing sent "against their will into Russia." Bulavin further charged, in a letter to the Kuban Cossacks, that the intruders "began to shave beards and mustaches . . . and wanted to introduce the Hellenic faith." [37]

Following the attack, Bulavin rode through the surrounding villages and appealed to the inhabitants to join him. At Stary Borovsky Gorodok, the local *ataman* greeted him with bread, wine, and honey, and summoned a village assembly in his honor. In a speech worthy of Razin, Bulavin promised arms and horses to all who would go with him against Azov and Taganrog to liberate the exiles and conscripts. Once freed from their tormentors, he said, they would become "our faithful comrades" and march with us on Voronezh and Moscow.[38] Bulavin's exhortations, accompanied by threats of reprisal against those who refused to cooperate, won an immediate response. During the next few days several hundred Cossacks rallied to his standard. Ataman Maksimov, alarmed by his success, offered a 200-ruble reward for his capture and gathered a force against him.

On October 18, just as the rebellion was gaining momentum, it suffered a major setback when Maksimov overtook Bulavin on the Aidar and, in a long and savage struggle, soundly defeated him. Bulavin escaped with a small group of followers into a neighboring forest. The captives were harshly dealt with; more than a hundred had their nostrils slit, and ten of the ringleaders were taken to Moscow for interrogation and hanging. According to the British ambassador, Charles Whitworth, they were "willing to own no more than that it was a sudden uproar caused by the imprudent severity of Mr. Dolgoruky and his party, who, under pretense of searching for deserters, plundered the inhabitants and abused the heads of some of their villages." [39]

Maksimov's collaboration with the government thus exceeded his original intentions. Though at first he merely supplied a few guides for the searchers, when confronted with the prospect of a general rising by the upstream Cossacks, a rising that might endanger his own position and bring the government down on his head, he acted, as Yakovlev had done against Razin, to suppress it. After the battle of October 18 an uneasy calm settled on the upper Don territory. Maksimov reported to Moscow that the "banditry of Kondrat Bulavin has been eradicated and all is quiet in the Cossack villages." But Whitworth, a shrewd observer, sounded a note of caution. "So they said," he wrote to the foreign secretary in London, "when the rebellion at Astrakhan first broke out and, I believe, there is more danger than they are willing to own." [40]

4. The Rebels

After hiding out for a week or two in the Khoper forests, Bulavin and a dozen close confederates, including his brother Ivan, Semyon Drany, who was a local *ataman* from the Northern Donets, and an Old Believer monk named Pitirim, made their way across the steppe to the Dnieper. In November they arrived in the town of Kodak on the main route from Zaporozhie to Moscow, at the point where the Dnieper bends toward the Northern Donets. Joined by forty more Don Cossacks, they spent the rest of the winter there, planning their next move. In December, however, Bulavin went down the Dnieper to the headquarters of the Zaporozhian Cossacks and tried to drum up support for a new insurrection. Addressing the Cossack assembly, he revived Razin's proposal for a joint campaign "into Russia." [41] The dream of a united Ukraine, momentarily realized by Khmelnitsky half a century before, remained alive, and the Cossacks listened with sympathy to Bulavin's appeal, though in the end only a fraction were to join him.

In the meantime, the tsar had learned of Bulavin's whereabouts and sent an envoy to Hetman Mazepa demanding that he arrest the rebel and hand him over to the government. Mazepa's feelings about his former comrade-in-arms were ambivalent. To arrest him might give the appearance of bowing to Moscow's orders and thereby weaken his autonomy. More important, the hetman had already begun secret negotiations with King Charles XII of

Sweden for an alliance against Peter, so he might well have regarded Bulavin as a welcome thorn in the tsar's side. But he was
not prepared at this stage to show his hand and fight openly
against Moscow. Cooperation with Bulavin might bring government reprisals before his deal with the Swedes could be imple-
mented. Beyond this, he may have resented Bulavin as an upstart
against the Cossack oligarchy, whose seditious example was not
to be encouraged. In the end, while he forbade his men to join
Bulavin, he allowed him to return unmolested to Kodak. At the
same time, however, he ordered him to be detained if he should
go again to Zaporozhie for support.

With the passing of winter the traditional time approached
for launching a Cossack adventure. In Kodak, Bulavin prepared
to return to the Don with a small band of Zaporozhian volunteers
who, as in Razin's time, had joined him in defiance of their
ataman's orders. In March 1708 they began their eastward trek,
sending agitators in the van with seditious letters to stir up the
populace. One proclamation, "For the True Faith," was directed
at the Old Believers, who made up a large proportion of the
steppe's inhabitants. In another, which was addressed to the
"Brave Atamans" of the Don territory and was among the most
eloquent to be issued during the rebellion, Bulavin appealed to
all who wanted "to roam the open fields with him, to go in style,
to drink sweetly, eat well, and ride fine horses." He called on
them to spread his message and to throw open the prisons but
warned against wanton killing and plunder. Our aim, he declared, is

> to stand with all our fervor for the house of the Blessed Virgin,
> for the true Christian faith, for the pious tsar, and for our own
> souls and heads. Son with father, brother with brother, comrade
> with comrade, we shall die as one [rather than] remain silent and
> submissive before the wicked deeds of evil men—princes and
> boyars, profiteers and Germans—who are leading us into the
> Hellenic faith and away from the true Christian faith.[42]

Given the widespread conviction—particularly among the Old
Believers, on whom Bulavin relied for support—that Peter was
the Antichrist, it is odd that he did not attack the tsar directly,
rather than perpetuate the traditional legend of a "pious tsar"
surrounded by alien and wicked men who deceived him and op-

pressed the people. It is possible, of course, that the "pious tsar" of Bulavin's manifesto refers not to Peter but to the "true" sovereign of popular imagination, the long-awaited savior who would liberate the poor and restore their cherished traditions. Yet this is not borne out by the evidence, for there is no further reference in rebel propaganda to a "substitute" tsar, nor did Bulavin ever put forward a claimant to the throne. A more likely explanation lies in the political naiveté of these primitive rebels, exhibited earlier in Razin's endorsement of Nikon, who, like Peter, was widely regarded as an agent of the Devil.

At all events, Bulavin reached the upper Don toward the end of March and chose Pristansky Gorodok, a settlement on the Khoper near the town of Borisoglebsk, as his base for collecting an army. From Pristansky Gorodok he issued a torrent of leaflets appealing for support. The response was remarkable. By the end of April no less than 33 settlements along the upper Don and its three major tributaries—the Khoper, the Buzuluk, and the Medveditsa—with nearly 7000 inhabitants had joined him. At the same time, a dozen settlements on the Northern Donets with 1700 residents went over to Bulavin's lieutenant, Semyon Drany. Thus, as in Razin's movement, it was the Don Cossacks, the disgruntled upstream *golytba* for the most part, who provided the leadership as well as much of the rank and file of the rebel army. Such figures as Semyon Drany ("ragged") and Nikita Goly ("naked") were poor Cossacks in fact as well as in name. Drany, according to some accounts, was a former serf from the Voronezh area who had fled to the Northern Donets only a few years before the rebellion. As the rising gained momentum, moreover, an increasing number of Zaporozhian volunteers—perhaps 2000 or 3000 in all—crossed the steppe to join it, particularly after a letter arrived from Drany calling for "Cossack brotherly love and assistance, so that our Cossack rivers should be as before." "We are ready to die with you as one," said Drany, "so that Russia might not rule over us and that our common Cossack glory might prevail." [43] The overriding aim of the Cossack insurgents was, of course, to stop Muscovite expansion, and especially recovery operations, in what they regarded as their territory. As a rebel leaflet put it, "Our first task is to keep our old land and hold it firmly." [44]

The composition of the rest of the rebel following—peasants and townsmen, deserters and clerics—was largely the same as in Razin's day. "Many are swine—runaways, service men of various ranks from the towns escaping from service and taxes, monastery and landlords' peasants fleeing dues and payments to their masters," declared G. I. Volkonsky, the unpopular *voevoda* of Kozlov.[45] Of the peasant adherents most were from Volkonsky's own district or from neighboring Tambov, where fugitives from the north abounded. In March and April a rebel party under Lukian Khokhlach, a Cossack from Bulavin's native village who played a leading role in the uprising, rode through the area with incendiary leaflets urging the peasants to "annihilate the boyars, Germans, and profiteers" and hereafter to "plow for yourselves." [46] By the end of April more than 700 Russian and Mordva villagers were added to the rebel ranks, though some, it appears, had to be recruited by force. In May and June the jacquerie spread northeast toward Verkhni and Nizhni Lomov, where Razin had won a large following. In many villages Cossack self-rule was introduced, with local *krugs* and elected *atamans* and elders. Estates were pillaged, towns sacked, and officials murdered or taken to the Cossacks for execution. In a report to Prince Menshikov, one of the largest landlords in Tambov, thanks to lavish gifts from the tsar, Volkonsky wrote that "there was much destruction, plunder, and killing." [47] Actually only one Tambov landowner lost his life, though many were injured and there was widespread arson, woodcutting, and theft of grain, cattle, and horses. During the year 1708, peasants rioted in forty-three districts throughout the country. Though only a fraction of incidents were directly related to Bulavin's revolt, the number indicates the wide extent of rural unrest and the danger it presented to the government. In eighteen districts manors were attacked, and in seven landowners or stewards put to death,[48] a warning of what was to occur later in the century. An occasional nobleman—an official in Korotoyak, for example—joined hands with the insurgents, but instances of class defection were even rarer than in Razin's time.

In the towns, by contrast, the rebellion failed to take root. The situation was very different from what it had been in the seventeenth century, when towns constituted the principal rebel strongholds. By Peter's time even the most volatile of the garrison towns were being transformed into market and trading centers with a more settled population that was less responsive to seditious propaganda. In addition, government control was more firmly entrenched and the troops more efficient and reliable. Few merchants and traders were convinced by Bulavin's assurances that they had nothing to fear since his quarrel was only with "the boyars and Germans." [49] In most cases they wasted little time mobilizing against the insurgents. The most notable rebel victory in a town occurred at the end of April, when Khokhlach swept through Borisoglebsk, just north of Bulavin's headquarters, slaughtered the officials, burned public records, and inaugurated a Cossack-style regime. Khokhlach next laid siege to Tambov but was forced to withdraw when Colonel Stepan Bakhmetiev arrived with a fresh regiment of dragoons. On the Volga, as we shall soon see, a number of towns (including Tsaritsyn) were briefly occupied, only to be evacuated on the arrival of reinforcements.

An important place in the rising was occupied by the lower clergy—monks, priests, sextons—especially those adhering to the old ritual. One of Bulavin's original confederates was an Old Believer monk who fled with him to the Dnieper. Bulavin's Cossack lieutenants Nikita Goly and Ignati Nekrasov were Old Believers, and possibly Khokhlach and Bulavin himself; [50] but since most of the Cossacks were illiterate, it was left to the monks and priests to draft the rebel manifestoes, many of which called for the restoration of traditional religious practices. "We stand for the old faith," proclaimed one of Goly's leaflets, "and for the house of the Blessed Virgin, and for you, the common folk, that we should not fall into the Hellenic faith." [51] Beyond this, renegade clergymen conducted religious ceremonies for the rebels, and a few even commanded detachments that took an active part in the fighting.

A new element in the revolt was the labor force conscripted largely from the rural districts. Included in this group were—apart from barge haulers, who had already supported Razin in considerable numbers—carpenters and stevedores, woodcutters and raftsmen, uprooted, overworked, underpaid men "without horses, without weapons, without money," [52] and eager to settle accounts with their oppressors. The situation was complicated, however, when Cossack raiders attacked and destroyed the timber-collecting station on the Khoper, killing its director and alienating many of the workers by their indiscriminate violence, an error Pugachev was later to repeat, though on a much larger scale, in the factories and mines of the Urals.

Finally, a word must be said about the Volga tribesmen, who had figured so predominantly in Razin's uprising. Now, apart from a small number of Mordva peasants in the Tambov area, their participation was negligible. The main reason was that, in comparison with Razin, the territory mastered by Bulavin was rather small. Owing to the government's growing strength, he was unable to establish even a tentative foothold in the territory where the tribesmen were concentrated, but remained confined to the Don region and a few adjoining districts. At most he could issue vain appeals to the Kalmyks and the Kuban Tatars for support, but since they were traditional rivals of the Cossacks, their response was predictably negative. The Kalmyks, moreover, under Ayuka Taisha, were receiving a substantial *zhalovanie* from the tsar and were not likely to risk it for an adventure that may have seemed doomed from the outset.

What is puzzling, however, is Bulavin's failure to approach the Bashkirs, who were themselves in rebellion against Moscow and who were later to furnish Pugachev with some of his best warriors. The Bashkir rising had erupted in 1705, sparked by forced baptisms, searches for Russian deserters, and mounting levies of horses and tribute for the war. The tribesmen feared, moreover, that Peter's new foundries in the Urals would crowd them off their land. Their grievances, then, were akin to those of the Cossacks, and, like the Cossacks, they opposed the disruption of their customary way of life. Thus Bulavin's failure to try to draw them into an alliance seems all the more mystifying. Reports that he did in fact do so [53] are without foundation. He did, however, write to the Turkish sultan, calling on him to attack Azov, his former possession. The Russians had long been worried lest the Turks unite with their Volga coreligionists (to say nothing of the Cossacks) and menace their southern frontier. But beyond some exchanges of messages no joint action was forthcoming.[54] Apart from the Bashkirs, the tribes remained quiet. However, the prospect of the Cossacks and Bashkirs making common cause doubtless alarmed the government, which, aided by the Kalmyks, redoubled its efforts to crush them; and within a few years the task was accomplished, though the dreaded combination was indeed to materialize later in the century with devastating results.

5. Cherkassk

Meanwhile, at Pristansky Gorodok, each week brought hundreds of volunteers to the rebel camp. In early April Bulavin summoned a general assembly and announced his intention "to march on Cherkassk, destroy Azov, and remove from all the towns the boyars, profiteers, and Germans." He vowed, moreover, "to kill the *ataman* because he collaborates with the Azov boyars." [55] Lukashka Khokhlach, for his part, proposed to attack Voronezh and burn Peter's new fleet. To forestall these plans Maksimov decided to take the offensive. Mobilizing his followers, he sailed up the Don and, on April 8, encountered a rebel force of 3000, with Bulavin himself at the head, on the banks of the Liskovatka River above Panshin. Maksimov, with a detachment of Kalmyks and government troops from Azov to complement his Cossacks, outnumbered the insurgents by more than two to one. Nevertheless, he accepted a proposal to negotiate and sent Efrem Petrov to represent him. The parleys, however, were nothing more than a ruse. For no sooner had Petrov returned to make his report than the rebels launched a fierce surprise attack. Part of Maksimov's army immediately defected, while the rest, taken unawares, were thrown into disorder. For Bulavin the victory was complete: four cannon were seized, together with a large quantity of powder and lead, and—a particularly coveted prize—8000 rubles of government *zhalovanie*. Maksimov's battered troops meanwhile beat a swift retreat to Cherkassk to nurse their wounds and prepare for the rebel assault.

As usual, as the news of victory spread, a swarm of new recruits swelled the rebel ranks, so that by the latter part of April Bulavin had an army of 7000 men. The situation, from the government standpoint, was grave. The Cherkassk loyalists had been soundly beaten. Azov was alarmed. The tsar himself was wor-

ried, for at a time when the Swedes were marching toward the
Russian frontier, badly needed soldiers had to be diverted for use
against the rebels. Colonel Stepan Bakhmetiev was dispatched with
a regiment to Tambov and Kozlov, where a peasant jacquerie was
in full blaze, but was unable to quell the disorders. Thus Peter,
on April 12, four days after Maksimov's defeat on the Liskovatka,
summoned from the Swedish front one of his best officers, Guards
Major Prince Vladimir Dolgoruky, brother of the slain colonel
whose expedition had precipitated the rebellion. The tsar allotted
Dolgoruky two Muscovite regiments (one dragoon, one infantry)
and ordered him to spare no effort "to extinguish the flames of
revolt." [56] Peter also sent a contingent from his crack Preobrazhensky regiment and 400 dragoons from Voronezh, replacing
the latter with a fresh infantry regiment under Lieutenant Colonel William Rykman, whose chief mission was to guard the shipyards against a rebel assault. The Voronezh dragoons, drawn
largely from the local population, proved unreliable; some, indeed, deserted with their weapons to the rebel camp. At the same
time, the governor of Azov, Ivan Tolstoy, warned that seditious
propaganda was threatening to subvert his entire garrison. Peter
found it necessary to mobilize additional gentry against Bulavin,
"a cousin to that rogue, traitor, and accursed criminal, Stepan
Razin." [57] In addition, Hetman Mazepa, on the eve of his own
betrayal of Moscow, sent at the tsar's behest 1000 Ukrainian Cossacks, so that, all told, Dolgoruky had an army of 32,000 with
which to deal with the insurgents.

Khokhlach, marching on Voronezh, was the first to encounter
the government forces. On the night of April 16 he forded the
Bitiug River and attacked Rykman's dragoons, who, though
caught off guard, managed to drive off their assailants. On April
28 a second encounter took place on the banks of the Kurlak.
By now, however, Rykman had been joined by Bakhmetiev and
by Colonel Ivan Teviashev, commander of the Ostrogozhsk regiment, and what occurred was a slaughter rather than a battle.
The rebels, despite their preponderance of more than two to one,
were no match for the picked government troops. Of some 1500
insurgents, many of them peasants with only staves and cudgels
for weapons, nearly 1000 were killed and another 143 captured
(along with three of their horsetail banners), the rest fleeing

into the adjacent woods and swamps. On the government side, although Rykman was wounded, losses were very few.

That same day, April 28, Bulavin sailed down the Don against Cherkassk. Cherkassk, like Astrakhan and the Zaporozhian Sech, was built on a narrow island with a thick wall surmounted by mortars and artillery. The surrounding area, moreover, was studded with fortified Cossack settlements defended with some forty or fifty cannon. Cherkassk, then, was virtually impregnable—were it not for the human element. For Bulavin's propaganda had aroused dissension among the defenders, and five villages guarding the approaches to the Cossack capital allowed him to pass unopposed. Within the city itself the Cossacks were torn by factional conflict. On May 1, rebel sympathizers rose in revolt, drowned a number of elders, and admitted Bulavin's army. Though some of the loyalists escaped to Azov, Maksimov, Petrov, and several of their supporters were handed over and, at a specially summoned *krug*, condemned to death. Before the assembly Bulavin himself beat them with a whip to find out where their treasury was hidden. At length some 20,000 rubles were unearthed and divided up among the insurgents. On May 6 the loyalists were beheaded. "Though I die by your hands," declared Petrov on the execution block, "the Sovereign will cleanse this great river and exterminate you bandits." [58] On May 9 another *krug* assembled and Bulavin was elected *ataman* of the Host, thus succeeding—at least for the moment—where Razin before him had failed.

Once ensconced in Cherkassk, Bulavin, like Razin at Simbirsk, strove desperately to secure his position and to broaden his base of support. One of his first acts was to write to Peter and ask him to recall Dolgoruky and his troops. He insisted that, as the British ambassador put it, "he aimed at nothing but to live quietly under their old privileges, and therefore he wondered the Czar was sending an army against him, who was a good subject." What he had done, he said, was merely to depose the "unjust" elders so that the Cossacks might live peacefully "as before." He had no quarrel with the throne, he added, but if Peter's troops should advance he would resist with all his might and, if necessary, flee to the Kuban and put his Cossacks under the protection of the Turks.[59] Bulavin wrote in a similar vein to the foreign office and to government headquarters at Voronezh, requesting that *zhalovanie* be sent to Cherkassk as in the past. At the same time, however, he sought military aid from a number of sources—the Kalmyks, the Kuban Tatars, the Kuban and Zaporozhian Cossacks, the Turkish sultan—against a Muscovite invasion. He wrote finally to the governor of Kiev, Prince D. M. Golitsyn, threatening to send an army unless his wife and son, imprisoned in Belgorod, were released at once.[60] But all his efforts were in vain. Apart from some Zaporozhian volunteers, no assistance was obtained from any quarter. Moreover, the government, far from softening its stand, was more determined than ever to bring the insurgents to heel. As for Bulavin's wife and child, they remained behind bars till after the rebellion, when a worse fate overtook them.

Thus Bulavin was compelled to fall back on his own resources. During May and June he sent his Cossack bands in all directions, just as Razin had done, in an effort to enlarge the scope of the rising. His aim was to advance "into Russia, from town to town, as far as Moscow"—or to flee to the Kuban if the tide should turn against him.[61] While Goly hurried north to block the government forces descending from Voronezh, Drany, joined by 1500 Zaporozhians, extended his operations along the Northern Donets, and Khokhlach, Nekrasov, and Ivan Pavlov headed eastward in an attempt to ignite the Volga valley.

On May 13 Khokhlach, with 1000 men, occupied the Volga town of Dmitrievsk na Kamyshinke (formerly Kamyshin), which Razin had taken by ruse in 1670. This time, it seems, the inhabitants themselves—at any rate the lower classes of the *posad*—invited the rebels to come and admitted them without opposition. The rebels, "children of the arch-cunning Devil" in the description of a government official,[62] seized and drowned the director of the local salt works and, assisted by the townspeople, played havoc with the commercial traffic on the Volga. Then Khokhlach, joined by 1500 Dmitrievsk poor armed with picks, hoes, and spades, linked up with Nekrasov near Saratov. On May 26, with a combined force of 4000, they placed the town under siege. At night they tried to storm the gates but were beaten off with heavy losses. A second attempt, on May 29, was cut short by the appearance of Ayuka Taisha's Kalmyks, some 10,000 strong, fresh from a victorious engagement with the rebellious Bashkirs. In the ensuing struggle the insurgents lost 200 dead and several hundred wounded or captured, as well as a large number of horses and weapons. The survivors fled to safety down the Volga. Khokhlach crossed over to the Don and made his way to Cherkassk, while Nekrasov and his men joined forces with Pavlov, who had meanwhile laid siege to Tsaritsyn, a favorite target of Cossack marauders since well before Razin's day. The Tsaritsyn *voevoda*, Afanasi Turchaninov, with only 500 defenders against some 3000 rebels, withdrew to the citadel to await reinforcements. Seven weeks were to pass before his fate, as we shall see, was decided.

The Cherkassk period (May–June 1708), during which Bulavin was *ataman* of the Don Host, marked the high point of his rebellion. It was also one of the most precarious moments of Peter's reign. On the Volga the Bashkir rising continued to rage out of control (not till 1711 was it finally quelled). Bulavin's movement by now had nearly 30,000 adherents and threatened to grow still larger. Some 2000 Zaporozhians had cast their lot with the insurgents, and Mazepa, the Ukrainian hetman, was on the point of joining forces with Sweden. The Swedes themselves, with their formidable King Charles XII at the lead, were nearing the Russian frontier in strength, and Count Loewenhaupt was distributing leaflets calling on the population to depose Peter and choose "a legal and just tsar under whose authority the lives and property of the Russian people can be safe and secure." [63] The Swedish general, by invoking the myth of a "just tsar," showed greater political sense than Bulavin, who never once made use of this powerful weapon, much less bring forth a pretender to the throne, even though he had lost his faith in Peter and forbidden his men on pain of death to utter his name. Nor did Bulavin, like Mazepa, seek an alliance with Charles XII. His captured followers, questioned under torture, were steadfast in their denial of any contacts with the Swedes.[64]

The tsar, however, was extremely anxious over the possibility of collaboration between his internal and external enemies. He worried, moreover, lest his new bases at Azov and Taganrog succumb to rebel propaganda or to a direct rebel assault. After Bulavin's capture of Cherkassk, he instructed Dolgoruky to "spread the rumor that I shall be there," and at one point, it seems, he seriously considered hastening to the Don to direct military operations in person.[65] Though this did not prove necessary, he did feel constrained, at the end of June, to send Dolgoruky an additional regiment of dragoons and one of infantry, to be followed soon after by an infantry battalion from Poland and two infantry regiments from Narva. For "the rebels are very dangerous," noted the British ambassador, "most of the cozaks on the Don being up in arms; and what is worse, the new raised forces sent from hence desert to them in whole companies." [66]

Peter's fears for his southern outposts were well founded, for at the beginning of July Bulavin made ready to march on Azov. His decision, however, aroused considerable opposition, especially among the "house-owning" Cossacks, who were far from being reconciled to Bulavin's "election" as *ataman*. Ever since his coup in May, they had considered him a usurper and awaited the moment to depose him. They feared that if Azov were attacked, relations with Moscow would be irreparably impaired, the flow of *zhalovanie* would cease, and total government control would be the final result. They felt threatened, moreover, by the "bareback" element which initiated the revolt, and saw their only hope in a reconciliation with the tsar. What occurred, in short, was a repetition of the split which had earlier sealed the fate of Razin's rebellion and of Bolotnikov's before it.

A plot to oust Bulavin, in which some 500 Cossacks were to be involved, had begun to take shape from the moment he occupied Cherkassk. The leader, Ilya Zershchikov, was a former opponent of Moscow who had come to recognize the dangers of Bulavin's movement—or simply wanted power for himself. Zershchikov and his accomplices began to spy on the rebels and to feed information to the Azov governor, Ivan Tolstoy, "about their roguish and wicked schemes." [67] On the night of July 1 the conspirators, hoping to forestall the drive on Azov, dispersed the rebel horses grazing outside Cherkassk. But Bulavin was not so easily deterred. The horses were rounded up, and on July 6 an army of 5000 under Lukian Khokhlach began their march. When they neared the fortress, a regiment of cavalry rode out to meet them but failed to stem their advance. Four companies of infantry moved up to bolster the horsemen, and the rebels were driven back to the Kalancha River, where they fell under cross-fire from the fortress and from government warships anchored nearby. Hundreds were killed outright or drowned while swimming for safety. The rest broke in panic and fled into the surrounding woods. A tattered remnant made its way back to Cherkassk to report the news of the disaster.

A few days earlier the rebellion had sustained another major setback on the Northern Donets, where Semyon Drany held sway with a force of 7000 Cossacks, including 1500 Zaporozhians. Drany, having sacked the town of Tor on June 30, withdrew to the east at the approach of a large government detachment under Brigadier (formerly Colonel) F. V. Shidlovsky, Bulavin's erstwhile adversary in the Bakhmut salt controversy. Drany was overtaken, however, the following afternoon at the village of Krivaya Luka and driven back against his supply wagons by a sudden onslaught in which hundreds of his men were shot or speared with lances. Fierce fighting continued long after dark and rebel casualties mounted. Many drowned in the Northern Donets and adjoining swamps while trying to escape. All told, more than 1000 insurgents, Drany among them, lost their lives in the debacle. Part of the Zaporozhian contingent got away but were overtaken at Bakhmut and all but annihilated. On Shidlovsky's orders Bakhmut was reduced to ashes.

The double blow at Azov and Krivaya Luka led, as one might expect, to defection and betrayal. In Cherkassk, Bulavin's position and the morale of his followers were irreparably undermined. Khokhlach was treacherously murdered by one of his own lieutenants. Discontented veterans of the Azov campaign flocked to Zershchikov's conspiracy. Overnight even the staunchest insurgents became turncoats. For the plotters the time had come to act. Marshaling their forces, they seized control of the city. In most cases the rebels were disarmed without incident, but Bulavin and his closest confederates barricaded themselves in a Cossack house and offered stiff resistance. The plotters surrounded the house and set it afire, then, taking up their axes, smashed their way through the door and windows. Inside they found Bulavin dead, a bullet in his brain. With his pistol he had killed two attackers and then, if Zershchikov is to be believed, saved the last round for himself. A Soviet specialist maintains,

however, that he was killed by his assailants and that Zershchikov, fearing responsibility for the act, put it down as suicide.
The truth must remain uncertain. "About Bulavin," wrote the
governor of Kazan, P. I. Khovansky, to the tsar, "many say that
certainly the Cossacks in Cherkassk killed him and Lunka Khokhlach, but others say that they killed themselves." [68] At any rate,
twenty-six of Bulavin's associates, including his brother and
Drany's son, were taken alive and held in irons under heavy
guard till government troops could arrive and escort them to
Moscow.

The following day, July 8, Bulavin's body was sent to Azov
and suspended by the feet on the banks of the Kalancha, where
his army had suffered defeat two days before. His head, however,
was cut off and preserved in alcohol. In Moscow word of his
fate was acclaimed with jubilation. Writing to Tolstoy in Azov,
Peter said: "We have received with great joy news of the death
of the scurrilous villain Bulavin." [69] One of Peter's ministers proposed a public celebration, but this was not done for fear of
touching off riots, in view of the widespread hostility to the tsar
and sympathy for the rebel who had opposed him. Instead, a
thanksgiving service was held at Peter's field headquarters at
Mogilev, and nearby, it was said, the Swedes could hear the noise
of Russian cannon saluting the victory over the rebels. With the
pacification of the steppe a good part of Dolgoruky's army could
be transferred to the Swedish front. As Charles Whitworth noted:
"Thus the tranquillity of [the Don] is resettled, and near fifteen
thousand men of regular troops are left at liberty to be employed
by his Czarish Majesty on other occasions." [70]

But Whitworth's remarks were a trifle premature. Along the
Volga, the Don, and the Northern Donets the rebellion simmered
and in places broke out with renewed violence. On July 17 Nekrasov and Pavlov, after a seven-week siege, finally captured the
Tsaritsyn citadel, massacred the *voevoda* and officials, and inaugurated Cossack self-rule. Their triumph, however, was short-
lived. Only three days later a well-equipped government regiment
under Colonel Lewiston arrived from Astrakhan and, after a brief
struggle, forced the Cossacks to abandon the city. Embittered
by defeat, the leaders fell to quarreling over their next destination.
Nekrasov wanted to return to the Don, while Pavlov argued for

sailing down the Volga to the Caspian, as Razin had done forty
years before. When Nekrasov departed, Pavlov and his men
drowned their anger in drink, and many were slaughtered when
Lewiston chose the moment to launch a surprise attack against
them. The survivors fled in panic to their boats with the government troops close behind. On the point of being overtaken, they
were forced to scuttle their vessels and make it back to Panshin
on foot.

Once in Panshin, Nekrasov and Pavlov patched up their differences and threatened to sail against Cherkassk to seek revenge
for Bulavin's death. On July 27, however, the Cossack capital
was occupied by Dolgoruky, and they had to abandon their plans.
Dolgoruky's entry into Cherkassk was a momentous occasion.
With banners flying, Zershchikov, in his new role as *ataman*,
went out on horseback to meet him, knelt, and swore an oath
of fealty to the tsar. The Preobrazhensky guards, in their short
green tunics and three-cornered hats and armed with new muskets
and bayonets, must have been a hateful sight to the Cossacks. The
latter, nevertheless, sang hymns of welcome and "kissed the
cross" to Peter, swearing that "in the future they would not rise
up or be enticed into rebellion, they would kill and destroy no
more, hold no more mutinous gatherings, join no more with
bandits and mutineers, distribute no more seditious letters either
openly or surreptitiously, and stand no more behind brigands
and insurgents." [71] Despite this show of submission, there was no
mercy for the conquered. At Dolgoruky's command some 200
rebels were hanged in the main square of Cherkassk, and on
August 4 Bulavin's headless corpse, having been retrieved from
Azov, was quartered and the limbs mounted on stakes for all to
see. The twenty-six captured ringleaders, however, were temporarily spared for questioning, and a large number of dissidents
escaped to Panshin to join Pavlov and Nekrasov.

Panshin and nearby Esaulov, to which Nekrasov shifted his
headquarters in early August, were rallying points for the scattered remnants of Bulavin's movement. Determined to wipe them
out, Dolgoruky mustered his troops (bolstered by Cossack loyalists) and marched up the Don valley, reaching Esaulov on August
22. In the struggle that followed, the rebels were dealt a crushing
blow. Of some 5000 defenders nearly 1000 perished in the fight-

ing, while at least 200 were selected from the survivors to be
hanged on gibbets or mounted on rafts and floated down the Don
as a warning to their supporters. The local *ataman* was quartered
alive, as were two schismatic monks—one for leading a guerrilla
detachment, the other merely for conducting prayers for a rebel
victory—and their heads and limbs were paraded about the
village.

But Nekrasov managed to escape. He and his followers, some
2000 in all, fled to the Kuban and placed themselves under the
protection of the Crimean khan. Peter's demands for his return
fell on deaf ears, and for the next two decades he appeared on
the steppes raiding with the Tatars and stirring up trouble for
the tsar.[72] Seventy years later, in 1778, the Nekrasovites, augmented by fugitives from Pugachev's revolt, moved to Anatolia,
settling near Constantinople, where they have remained for nearly
200 years, clinging to their old religion and traditional Cossack
ways. Some of their descendants, lured by a promise of autonomy,
returned to the Soviet Union in the 1920s, only to fall victim to
Stalin's collectivization drive, while in 1963 others, still looking for the Promised Land, emigrated to the United States.

No sooner had Dolgoruky routed the insurgents at Esaulov than
another government expedition, led by the able governor of
Kazan, P. I. Khovansky, attacked their second stronghold at
Panshin with equally devastating results. In a fierce battle on
August 23, half of the 4000 defenders were killed, some being
speared in the Don like fish by Kalmyk horsemen fighting on
the government side. Six rebel banners, eight cannon, and all
the rebel supply wagons were taken, and Panshin, the base of
Cossack pirates for over a century, was razed.

By now the only sizable rebel force still intact was that of
Nikita Goly on the upper Don. Goly had established headquarters
in the village of Donetsky Gorodok, where he enjoyed the full
cooperation of the local *ataman*, Nikolai Kolychev. In a last-ditch
effort to rally support for the waning rebel movement, he issued,
in August 1708, what was probably the most eloquent leaflet to
appear during the course of the uprising. It declared:

> We have no quarrel with the common people. Our quarrel is
> only with the boyars and those who do injustice. You bare-
> backs and poor folk, come all of you, come out of your towns,

on horse or on foot, naked and barefoot. Come, have no fear.
There will be horses and guns, clothing and money for you.
We have stood for the old faith and the house of the Blessed
Virgin, and for you, for all the common people, that we should
not fall into the Hellenic faith. . . . And whoever would seize the
common people and not let them pass, he shall be hanged to
death.[73]

On October 3 Goly and Kolychev won a stunning victory over
the government below Donetsky Gorodok when they captured
a fleet of barges from Azov laden with money and provisions
and defended by more than 1000 troops. The commander, Colonel Ilya Bils, was ignominiously taken in by the simplest of Cossack tricks. Pretending to be friendly, Goly hailed him to shore
by shouting that he had a message from the tsar. When the barges
pulled over they were overwhelmed by the rebels, who drowned
Bils and his officers in the Don. On hearing the news Peter
was furious. "That fool Bils," he wrote to Dolgoruky. "Such a
fine regiment lost through his stupidity!" [74]
But this was the last rebel triumph of any consequence. Moreover, the government's revenge was swift. That same month Dolgoruky himself led a large force up the Don to deal with Goly
and his followers. In a brief fight on October 26 Dolgoruky
wiped out the rebel nest at Donetsky Gorodok, hanged 150
survivors, and burned the village to the ground. Goly, however,
had fled with the bulk of his detachment to Reshetevskaya Stanitsa, where Dolgoruky overtook them on November 4. They
joined in an uneven battle which left nearly 3000 rebels strewn
on the banks of the Don while hundreds more were drowned
or shot as they tried to swim to safety. Two cannon and sixteen
Cossack standards were taken. Beyond this, 300 captives from
Bils's regiment were liberated, with four of their flags. Reshetevskaya Stanitsa was relieved of its grain, then gutted, as were two
neighboring villages that supported the rebels. In the two engagements the government lost only 17 dead and 57 wounded.
Though Goly again escaped, his following of 5000 men had been
virtually annihilated, and except for the mopping up of isolated
rebel pockets, his defeat marked the end of the rebellion. During
the next few months the remaining insurgents were hunted down
and exterminated. Kolychev was captured in November and

taken to Moscow for questioning by the secret police. Goly himself was caught and executed in February 1709. His wife and mother had already been drowned in the Don by Cossack loyalists. A similar fate most likely befell Bulavin's wife and son in Belgorod, where they had been held prisoner since the beginning of the revolt. His twenty-six comrades seized in Cherkassk on the day of his death were sent to Moscow for interrogation, torture, and hanging. The suppression was carried out with ruthless cruelty, "and no quarter given to man, woman or child." [75] Dolgoruky in his memoirs reckons the total number of rebel dead at 28,500, and though half this figure would be a more accurate estimate, it was still a large number considering the comparatively small scope of the movement. In September Peter ordered all new settlements on the upper Don and Northern Donets to be razed. The villagers were rounded up, "their homes destroyed and burned without mercy, and they themselves returned to the places from which they had fled." [76] Crops were destroyed and scores of villages leveled, though a few were spared after declaring their loyalty to the tsar.

Thus, in the critical months before Poltava, the last embers of the revolt were extinguished. Yet, in the opinion of some observers, had Peter been defeated by the Swedes, he would have faced a new and even greater upheaval. "It is certain," wrote John Perry, an English engineer whom the tsar had hired during his historic journey to the West,

> that not only the Cossacks, but the Russes too, who were everywhere ripe for rebellion, and who had before taken up arms in several places, and had been defeated, would, if the Czar had lost the battle of Poltava, have made a general revolt, in hopes of relief to their grievances complained of in the Czar's administration, and to be restored to their old superstition and ignorance, to be rid of the foreigners whom they were always dissatisfied with, and to be eased of the burden of their taxes, and drain of their people, occasioned not only by the long war, but by the other public undertakings of the Czar. Such particularly as the erecting and fortifying of new places on the frontiers (whither they with their families, gentlemen as well as soldiers and peasants, were obliged, upon the Czar's commands, to remove and inhabit), as also the building of fleets, with works for making rivers navigable, which they reckoned they had no occasion for, and which they nor their fathers had never known.[77]

On April 19, 1709, after the victory of Poltava was assured, Peter went to Cherkassk to celebrate on the spot the crushing of the rebellion. Bulavin's head, preserved for the occasion, was exhibited on a pike, as was the head of Ilya Zershchikov, who had been executed after Goly denounced him as a former opponent of Muscovite policy. Thereafter Peter tightened his grip on the Cossacks. Some of their best lands he claimed for his own. He ordered the dismantling of their fleet as a danger to Azov and Taganrog, and forbade the construction of new *strugi* on the Don. Although the Cossacks retained their local administration, military organization, and unique way of life, the presence of the government was increasingly felt as the years passed. In 1721 dealings with the Host passed from the College of Foreign Affairs to the War College, and the Don territory became in effect an integral part of the empire. The following year, 1722, the War College established a department of Cossack affairs to carry on relations with Cherkassk. Soon after, the Cossacks lost the right to elect their own *ataman*, who was henceforth appointed in Moscow. Stripped of its independence, the Don lost its attraction as a sanctuary for the oppressed, and the size of the Host, which had expanded very rapidly since the sixteenth century, was to remain fairly stable for more than 150 years to come.

6. Conclusion

Perhaps the most striking feature of Bulavin's revolt was its close resemblance to Razin's revolt a generation before. The parallels are so numerous, in fact, as to warrant calling the former a virtual replica of the latter, though on a smaller scale in area and in the number of participants. Both rebellions attracted much the same social elements into their ranks. Both were partly Cossack insurrections against the increasing encroachments of the state, partly peasant risings against the institution of serfdom, the bonds of which in Bulavin's time were greatly strengthened by a ruler for whom work and service were the chief reasons for existence. Both at bottom were sectional struggles of the frontier against the center, of the untamed Cossack prairie against the disciplined Muscovite autocracy, and in an age, moreover, when Western habits and ideas were progressively challenging the traditional patterns of Russian life. As Europeanization increased the capacity of the government to deal with its opponents, the contest became more and more one-sided. Nevertheless, it was to persist down to the twentieth century, when Don Cossacks under Ataman Kaledin, pitted in civil war against the Bolsheviks, could still see themselves as heirs of Razin and Bulavin, defending their traditional liberties against the tyranny of the central government.[78]

To a certain extent, indeed, Bulavin's revolt seems to have been consciously patterned after its predecessor. One of Bulavin's "colonels," Ivan Loskut,[79] provided a living link between the two movements, which were fought under the same horsetail banner, with the same slogans and tactics, and for essentially the same objectives. Nor was the government blind to these similarities. For Peter, indeed, Bulavin was "a cousin to that rogue, traitor, and accursed criminal, Stepan Razin." And a member of the privy chancellery, on the occasion of Bulavin's death, described his rising as a typical display of Cossack banditry, "just as Razin's had been." [80]

But Bulavin's rebellion differed from Razin's in a number of important respects. For one thing, it was more exclusively a Cossack affair, with the peasants assuming a decidedly secondary role. The jacquerie encompassed only those districts contiguous to the territory of the Don, districts in which serfdom was just beginning to take hold and in which the population was unstable and government control as yet insecure. Moreover, for reasons already indicated, the towns were little affected in comparison with the revolts of the seventeenth century. Nor did the tribesmen play a significant role, apart from scattered rioting among the Mordva peasants of Tambov and the serious but independent Bashkir rising further east. Unlike Razin, Bulavin had little success along the Volga. His Cossack bands succeeded in occupying only Dmitrievsk and Tsaritsyn, and then only briefly. On the other hand, his was the first mass uprising to involve the Old Believers on a large scale. The schismatics, like the Cossacks and peasants from whom they drew so much of their following, longed to return to a vanished past in which their ancient faith and customs were as yet unimpaired by the rising secular state. The same longing for a golden past gripped yet another new element in the revolt, the conscripted workers, whose participation, like that of the religious dissenters, provided a warning of what was to come with Pugachev's outbreak later in the century.

Bulavin, moreover, succeeded in one respect where Razin had failed. He occupied Cherkassk and installed himself as *voiskovoi ataman*. But his tenure was brief. He never gained a secure foothold on the lower Don, and in the end, like his predecessor, was doomed to be defeated by the Muscovites with the aid of the Cossack oligarchy. The main reason for his downfall was the overwhelming strength of the government, which was able, although embroiled in a major war with Sweden, to keep the rebellion from spreading beyond the confines of the Don. Owing to Peter's reforms, a centralized bureaucracy was replacing the old rough-and-ready rule of the *voevodas* in the outlying provinces. Furthermore, the bulk of the Russian army was now equipped and trained on Western lines, and the number of foreign officers employed against the rebels—Rykman, Lewiston, Bils, to name only the most prominent—was far greater than in the past, as, indeed, was the nativist reaction against them.

But in part the failure stems from Bulavin's own inadequacies as a leader. He lacked, so far as one can tell, Razin's immense charismatic powers. No legend grew up around him after his death. One of the few songs devoted to his exploits (specifically to his ambush of Yuri Dolgoruky) does not even mention his name:

> Thereupon they rose in commotion,
> Flung themselves upon the boyar,
> Cut off his proud head,
> And threw his white body into the quiet Don.[81]

Nor was he a particularly effective military commander. He never became undisputed chieftain of the rebellion but remained throughout merely first among equals, with only a tenuous control over the actions of his lieutenants. For two whole months he lingered in Cherkassk, while Peter gathered his forces against him. His legions were dispersed over a wide area rather than marshaled in a single concerted attack against Azov or Voronezh.

By such a strategy, it is true, he might avoid pitched battles with superior government troops and conduct his struggle by means of small, mobile guerrilla bands, scattering the sparks of sedition far and wide in hopes of igniting a general conflagration. Such hopes, however, were in vain. He failed to conquer Azov, to master the Volga, or to penetrate the Muscovite heartland. Beyond the Don territory his rebellion did not take hold. He won no outside support, either from the Tatars or the Turks or from the other Cossack hosts—save for a number of volunteers from the Dnieper. He secured no assistance from Mazepa, his erstwhile comrade-in-arms against the Crimean Tatars; on the contrary, Mazepa furnished a Cossack detachment to help suppress the rebellion. He made no effort to combine his revolt with that of the Bashkirs. Nor did he collaborate with the Swedes, though contemporary observers conjectured that a synchronized campaign might have altered the outcome of his rising. As it was, Peter was able to tackle his enemies one by one and curb the Cossacks before the Swedish threat had reached its climax. Finally, and perhaps most important, Bulavin failed to put forward a pretender. His was the only one of the four mass revolts not to employ this effective device. Had he done so he would undoubtedly have won much broader support. For Peter lacked the popular devotion enjoyed by earlier rulers—indeed he was widely hated and feared, as inquests by his secret police revealed. Moreover, given the widespread belief that he was not the true tsar but a German changeling or even Antichrist himself, it is all the more surprising that Bulavin did not bring forward a claimant to the throne, in the convenient guise, say, of Ivan Alekseevich, whom dissident elements had always preferred to his innovating half-brother.

For all these reasons Bulavin's movement was fated to dissolve into sporadic, localized outbursts which the government had little difficulty in stamping out. After 1709 the intensity of warfare, both external and internal, gradually abated. Bulavin was defeated in 1708, Mazepa and Charles XII in 1709, the Bashkirs in 1711. But Peter's troubles were far from over. On the foreign front much fighting was still to be done against the Swedes, the Turks, and the Persians. And at home isolated bands of Cossacks and peasants continued to haunt the steppes, and again and again troops had to be called in to quell them. From 1722 to 1724, near the close of Peter's reign, new rioting flared up in many districts owing to poor harvests and to the introduction of the poll tax. Among the Cossacks, however, the disturbances centered no longer on the Don but on the Yaik in the remote Urals, where the government administration had yet to strike firm roots. Once again it was mainly the refusal of the Cossacks to return runaways that sparked the violence, though another cause was their unwillingness to serve in Peter's ill-conceived war against Persia, for which the tsar had ordered a thousand Cossacks to muster for duty.[82] Some of the instigators, it seems, were veterans of Bulavin's rebellion, but carrying their grievances to the Urals, they shifted the scene to a new location from which, half a century later, the last and greatest of the mass revolts was to be launched.

IV Pugachev
1773–1774

God, what a sad country our Russia is!
—ALEXANDER PUSHKIN
on reading Gogol's *Dead Souls*

1. The Yaik

In the first three risings, as we have seen, Cossacks of the Don and Volga played a critical role. After Bulavin, however, the seedbeds of revolt shifted farther east, following the retreat of the frontier. Thus, while Pugachev was himself a Don Cossack, it was the Yaik Host which formed the spearhead of his insurrection. Unyielding frontiersmen, the Yaik Cossacks were descended largely from Don and Volga Cossacks who had fled into the Urals to escape Muscovite expansion. Some, however, traced their ancestry to the first Cossacks who appeared in the region after Ivan the Terrible's conquest of the Volga in the mid-sixteenth century. They insisted that Tsar Michael, in return for guarding the frontier, had promised their forebears full "possession of the Yaik River with its tributaries and all its adjacent land from its source to its mouth [so they might] gather there to live as free men." [1] Whatever the validity of this claim, the Yaik Cossacks did in fact receive a small subsidy from the government as a reward for border service against the Tatars, Kalmyks, and Kirghiz. Their main livelihood, however, was fishing, supplemented by cattle herding and salt production, which had replaced the marauding operations of an earlier age. The Yaik, they said, referring to its plentiful supply of fish, was "the golden Don with a silver lining." [2]

By the early part of the eighteenth century, however, not even the remote Yaik was safe from government intervention. Little by little the Urals were being settled by Russian colonists, industry was expanding under government tutelage, and the new frontier, like the old, was vanishing. The revolt of Pugachev represented a last-ditch stand against this Muscovite expansionism, a final battle between frontier and heartland, after which there was no more steppeland to conquer save in the distant stretches of Siberia and central Asia.

Peter the Great, near the end of his reign, took the first steps to incorporate the Yaik Cossacks into the expanding state system. In 1721 the Yaik Host, together with its parent body on the Don, was placed under the jurisdiction of the War College in St. Petersburg. The Cossacks were so outraged that they burned down their capital, Yaitski Gorodok (Yaitsk for short), and prepared to flee to the Kuban or to the Kirghiz steppes in central Asia. But Peter sent an army to stop them, and adding insult to injury, appointed his own *ataman* to rule over the Host, a practice continued by his successors. Peter, ever hungry for new recruits, sought ultimately to absorb the Cossacks into the regular military service; and though he himself died in 1725, his object was partly fulfilled, toward the middle of the century, when a chain of forts and outposts was built along the Yaik and the governor of Orenburg (founded in 1735) was given full authority over the Cossacks in the area.

The Cossacks themselves were torn by dissension. As on the Don, two parties took shape: the more prosperous loyalists, headed by the elders and the government-appointed *ataman*, and the dissident rank and file, numbering between 3000 and 4000 and filled with the spirit of rebellion. As in Bulavin's revolt, disputes broke out over salt extraction and over attempts by the authorities to recover runaway serfs. But the main source of friction was the right to fish in the Yaik, over which the government had established a monopoly, compelling the Cossacks to lease concessions for a large annual payment. During the 1760s, shortly after the accession of Catherine the Great, a scandal erupted when a group of dissidents accused the *ataman*, in league with the elders, of pocketing part of the payment. He denied the charges and ordered his accusers beaten with whips. A government commission sent to investigate the affair found that the *ataman* had indeed embezzled some 2000 rubles intended for the treasury in St. Petersburg. Yet no punishment was forthcoming. This infuriated the dissident party, who took matters into their own hands. Disturbances broke out, and troops had to be sent from Orenburg to restore order. But tensions continued to mount, reaching a climax on the eve of Pugachev's appearance.

Meanwhile, a new crisis arose over the question of military service. Hitherto the Yaik Cossacks, though under the general jurisdiction of St. Petersburg and Orenburg, enjoyed considerable autonomy, serving on a voluntary basis in their own detachments with their own elected officers. In 1765, however, new regulations came down from the War College, headed by Zakhar Chernyshev, who more than anyone else was responsible for the explosion that followed. From now on service was made mandatory for all able-bodied Cossacks, and the practice of electing officers was abolished. The rank and file indignantly refused to submit to this new violation of their traditional liberties, but Chernyshev was adamant and troops sent from Orenburg began taking conscripts by force.

With the outbreak of war with Turkey in 1768, matters became still worse. The authorities began to recruit Yaik Cossacks into a regular unit of the Russian army, which from the standpoint of the Cossacks meant being reduced to ordinary serfs. As regular recruits, they would be outfitted in Western-style uniforms, shorn of their beards, and subjected to rigid discipline by Muscovite and foreign-born officers. "From the very beginning of our existence there have never been such regulations as are now being introduced," the Cossacks protested. They particularly objected to the loss of their beards, which as Old Believers they prized "almost equal to their lives." [3] A series of delegations made the long journey to St. Petersburg with petitions for redress, only to be evicted without ceremony on Chernyshev's orders. In the end, however, Catherine relented. The war with the Turks was not going well, and she needed loyal soldiers, not potential mutineers, for her army. Anxious to placate the Cossacks, she disbanded the regular detachment and allowed them to return to their old system of service. Moreover, in December 1770 she ordered a new commission to look into their grievances on the Yaik.

The commission, headed by Major General von Traubenberg of the Orenburg garrison, did not arrive until the end of the following year and, when it finally came, showed little sympathy for the complaints of the rank and file. Indeed, it began its work by arresting seven of the dissidents and having them shaved and whipped in the public square as a lesson to their sympathizers. A more provocative act would be hard to imagine, and the enraged Cossacks declared they would retaliate by "shaking up Moscow." [4] As a first step they ambushed a government convoy and liberated their shorn and beaten comrades, who were being taken as recruits to Orenburg. Then, on January 13, 1772, a band of Yaik dissidents fell upon Traubenberg's commission, slaughtered the general and most of his subordinates, and sacked the houses of their own elders. When word of the outbreak reached St. Petersburg, Catherine ordered a regiment of infantry from Moscow under Major General Fyodor Freiman to suppress it and punish the ringleaders. Freiman reached Orenburg in May 1772 and, reinforced by a detachment of service Cossacks, proceeded toward Yaitsk. On June 3 he was intercepted by a force of Yaik rebels who set fire to the grassy steppe in an effort to stop him, but smashing his way through the flames, Freiman pressed on by forced march to Yaitsk, which he seized with few casualties. Severe repressions followed. Dozens of Cossacks had their nostrils slit, scores were beaten with the knout, and more than a hundred were exiled with their families to Siberia. Moreover, the commander of the Yaitsk garrison, Lieutenant Colonel Ivan Smirnov, replaced the regular *ataman* of the Host, which was saddled with a heavy fine. The mutiny was crushed. But discontent smoldered, and barring a cessation of government encroachments, a new rebellion seemed inevitable.[5]

2. The "Third Emperor"

When Russians are unhappy, as Kliuchevsky observed, the way is opened for a pretender. At about this time, rumors arose among the Cossacks of the reappearance of Peter III, who had been murdered in 1762 by a group of Catherine's favorites. Peter's violent death at the hands of the aristocracy conjured up the traditional myth of the good tsar martyred for the people, and murmurs of his resurrection and imminent return gained widespread acceptance.

In many respects, Peter was an unlikely candidate for the role of a "people's tsar." A German by birth and culture, he harbored an ill-concealed aversion for the Orthodox church and Russian traditions. His idol was Frederick the Great, and for Prussian institutions, especially the Prussian army, his admiration was boundless. Yet there was ample reason why, at least in retrospect, he should have emerged as a popular ruler. During his brief reign he had reduced the onerous salt tax, abolished the secret police, and converted ecclesiastical serfs into state peasants. He had also forbidden merchants to buy serfs for factory labor, a sop to the nobility which nevertheless endeared him to the peasantry. More than that, he had permitted Old Believers who had fled abroad to return to Russia and settle in the southeast, particularly along the Irgiz River in Saratov province, a statute, we shall see, of which Pugachev was to make use. The schismatics, in addition, were given freedom to worship as they pleased, which together with the other reforms convinced many citizens that Peter had "a heart inclined to goodness." [6]

His most celebrated act, however, was to emancipate the gentry from compulsory service. By the manifesto of February 18, 1762, noblemen were permitted to retire to their estates, to travel freely abroad, and even to enter the service of a foreign government. It was a revolutionary step which aroused immediate hopes among the peasants that their own emancipation was in the offing. The conversion a few weeks later of monastic serfs into state peasants seemed a prelude to this general emancipation. But it failed to materialize. Instead, Peter was dethroned and assassinated by a court conspiracy, and the peasants concluded that the nobility had murdered him in order to keep them in chains.

So it was that Peter III, whatever his defects as a ruler, came to be regarded as a martyr in the people's cause. His short-lived reign, his decrees favoring peasants and schismatics, his sudden and mysterious disappearance all contributed to his reputation as a "just tsar" betrayed by the wicked aristocracy. Next to his wife, Catherine, he seemed, despite his own German birth and upbringing, the very model of an Orthodox sovereign. Catherine was an uncompromising Westerner, a self-proclaimed daughter of the Enlightenment, whose foreign ways, like those of Peter the Great, aroused widespread resentment. As a woman and a usurper, with neither Russian blood nor legal claim to the throne, she could hardly inspire the customary reverence among the people for their anointed father and protector. On the contrary, she incurred their profound hostility and suspicion. One of her first measures was to return the ecclesiastical serfs to their former masters, an act which set off such violent disturbances, with tens of thousands of participants, that she was forced to reverse herself and restore them to the state peasantry. In 1767, when she summoned the Legislative Commission to prepare a new code of laws, rumors of a general emancipation quickly revived, only to be denounced in a notorious decree which not only upheld the existing system but also prohibited serfs from petitioning the crown against their masters on punishment of the knout and forced labor for life in Siberia. The following year the Legislative Commission was dissolved, and hopes of reform turned to disappointment. Far from being liberated, the peasants were subjected to tighter restrictions, heavier exactions, and closer supervision by their lords. At the same time, the most hateful policies of Peter the Great—war, expansion, and bureaucratic repression—were revived, with their attendant burdens of increased taxation and recruitment.

Small wonder that ordinary Russians, as their grievances accumulated, looked back to Peter III with increasing nostalgic affection. Small wonder, too, that during Catherine's reign more than twenty pretenders appeared to haunt the empress and her supporters. In the decade preceding the Pugachev rebellion no less than ten impostors came forward. In fact, rumors that Peter III was still alive began to circulate almost immediately after his death. He had liberated the serfs, it was said, but the gentry had suppressed the decree and tried to murder him; like the Tsarevich Dmitri, however, he had escaped his assassins and a soldier who resembled him had been buried in his place.

Rumors of this sort found especially rich soil along the southern frontier where dissident elements were heavily concentrated— where peasants, Cossacks, and schismatics, yearning for their old way of life, had long hoped that a good tsar would someday appear and by the stroke of his pen grant them freedom, happiness, and prosperity. Old Believers, with their apocalyptic cast of mind, were particularly prone to believe in the coming of a messiah who would deliver them from their oppressors, and they did much to encourage the rumor that Peter III, who had shown them leniency, was about to reclaim the throne. As early as 1762, the year of Peter's death, word spread among the Yaik Cossacks that the tsar was hiding among them, and in the village of Chesnokovka, near Ufa, a focal point of Pugachev's revolt a decade later, the local priest and sexton recited prayers for his miraculous resurrection. Before long, rumors swept through the Ukraine that the "third emperor [i.e., Peter III] did not die" but was "traveling to Kiev to inspect Little Russia." [7]

The first pretenders on record, a Ukrainian peasant and an Armenian trader, made their appearance in 1764 but only very briefly, the former being arrested and the latter fleeing to an Old Believer colony across the Polish border where Pugachev himself was to take refuge. Like their numerous successors, both men were uprooted wanderers who tramped from village to village in the outlying areas of the empire, armed with a sackful of bogus manifestoes. The typical impostor was a runaway serf, deserter, Cossack, or free homesteader from the so-called *odnodvortsy*, who like the Cossacks, were fighting a losing battle to retain their former privileges. In 1765 a runaway soldier from this homesteader class (about which more will be said later) appeared in Voronezh province and, claiming to be an emissary of Peter III, distributed a decree which suspended taxes and recruitment for a dozen years. The response was electric and peasants from the surrounding area flocked to greet him. Emboldened by his success, he began to claim that he himself was the emperor, but he was seized by the authorities, publicly knouted in each village where he had spread his false tidings, branded with the words "Deserter and Impostor," and banished for life to the Nerchinsk mines of Siberia. Four years later another runaway soldier of homesteader origin posed as the slain tsar, but he too was quickly arrested and deported to Nerchinsk, where he continued to call himself Peter III, attracting a considerable following among the exiles.[8]

During the late 1760s and early 1770s the borderlands spawned a whole series of impostors—Cossacks, homesteaders, soldiers, peasants—who suspended taxes and recruitment, converted serfs into state peasants, promised to restore the old ritual, and sparked off disturbances among the poor. Between 1762 and 1772, according to one estimate, there were forty serious outbreaks in the rural districts of the south, many of them triggered by pretenders or false manifestoes.[9] As in Razin's day, village priests played an important part by reading the manifestoes to their parishioners or by recognizing the pretenders and performing the traditional rites in their honor. One by one, however, the impostors were hunted down, arrested, and banished to forced labor in Siberia. A bizarre case occurred in far-off Montenegro, where a wandering stranger was rumored to be the Russian emperor seeking refuge from his would-be murderers. It was said that he wept on hearing the name of the Grand Duke Paul and on seeing a portrait of Peter III; and though he seemed to know no Russian, many accepted him as the deposed tsar who was honoring Montenegro with his presence, a thought which thrilled the popular imagination and fed hopes of liberation from the Turkish yoke. In 1773, however, the stranger was murdered and his movement collapsed.[10]

Inside Russia itself, the pretender who attracted the widest attention before Pugachev was a runaway serf named Fedot Bogomolov, a typical drifter who (like "Tsarevich Petrushka" in Bolotnikov's time) had worked as a Volga boatman, lived among the Kalmyk tribesmen, and finally joined the Volga Cossacks, who in 1772 recognized him as Peter III when he showed them the "tsar's signs" (scars in the shape of a cross) on his body. Actually he bore not the slightest resemblance to the late emperor, but "the passing of many years had changed him," his followers explained.[11] Supported by Cossacks, boatmen, parish clergy, and urban poor, Bogomolov started a rebellion in Tsaritsyn which spread through sections of the lower Volga valley, but when the tide turned against him he was betrayed by his fellow Cossacks and handed over to the authorities. Branded, whipped, his nostrils slit, Bogomolov died en route to Siberia, where he was to have served a life sentence at hard labor.

In November 1772, while the memory of Bogomolov was still fresh, Emelian Ivanovich Pugachev arrived on the Yaik and identified himself as Peter III. The last of the great Cossack rebels, he was the first to style himself tsar. Thirty years old, he was of medium height, broad-shouldered and narrow-waisted, his face slightly pockmarked and with a short dark beard already flecked with gray. A disgruntled Cossack with Old Believer sympathies, a deserter from military service, a fugitive from justice, a wanderer on the outskirts of society, he fit the pattern set by earlier pretenders of Catherine's reign. By an odd coincidence he came from the same Don settlement (Zimoveiskaya Stanitsa) as Stenka Razin. At the age of seventeen, already married to a Cossack girl from Esaulov, he was called to the army and received his baptism of fire in the Seven Years' War against Prussia. He became the orderly of Colonel Ilya Denisov (who was to help crush his rising fifteen years later) but was "mercilessly whipped" for allowing the colonel's horse to get away during an enemy raid.[12]

Trivial though it may seem, this is just the sort of incident which rankles and, with the accumulation of similiar grudges, may set a man on the path of rebellion.

In January 1762, with the accession of Peter III, Russia withdrew from the war, and Pugachev was able to return home. In 1764, however, he was called up again and sent to recover fugitive Old Believers across the Polish border, where he himself was to seek refuge when hunted by the authorities. In 1768 he was mobilized a third time with the outbreak of war against Turkey. Now a noncommissioned officer, he took part in the siege of Bender under General P. I. Panin, another future opponent in his revolt. After Bender, he fell ill with pains in his chest and legs and was sent home to recuperate. Though his illness persisted, his application for early retirement was refused, and he tried in vain to flee to the Terek. After two arrests and two escapes, he made his way across the Polish border to the Old Believer colony at Vetka, which his unit had raided in 1764.

Founded in the late seventeenth century, Vetka had since been conducting a lively trade with the Ukraine and White Russia and supplying numerous communities on the Don and the Volga with Old Believer icons and crosses. From the time of Peter the Great, however, it had been raided repeatedly by Russian troops, who crossed the border in violation of Polish sovereignty. During the attack of 1764 the colony was largely destroyed, but many refugees were allowed to return to Russia under an amnesty of Peter III, of which Pugachev himself now took advantage. From Vetka he made his way to a border post in White Russia where returning schismatics were processed and, claiming to be an Old Believer, applied for resettlement in the Irgiz valley. By now the idea of posing as Peter III had already been planted in his brain. Characteristically, it was a runaway soldier at the internment center who remarked—probably with mischievous intent—that Pugachev resembled the late emperor; and a merchant suggested that he go to the Yaik and deliver the Cossacks from their tormentors. Actually, Pugachev looked no more like Peter III than did his predecessor Bogomolov. Neither eyewitness descriptions nor contemporary portraits of the dark and solidly built Cossack bear any similarity to the tall, fair, and round-shouldered emperor, who had in any case been born fourteen years earlier than

Pugachev. Nevertheless, by the time he received his passport, the idea of styling himself tsar had taken firm root. And no one, least of all Pugachev himself, could have foreseen the consequences.

3. The Urals

When he reached the Irgiz, Pugachev stopped at an Old Believer monastery that served as a way station for dissidents fleeing to the Yaik. Its abbot, a former Moscow merchant named Filaret, maintained close contact with a network of fellow schismatics around the country, who formed a sort of underground railway for fugitive religious nonconformists. To Filaret, Pugachev revealed his plan to pose as Peter III and lead the Yaik Cossacks to some happier land—perhaps Turkey, perhaps the Kuban—farther south. This, of course, was the route which Nekrasov had taken in 1708 and which the Yaik Cossacks had themselves been considering since the 1720s, after their subordination to the War College by Peter the Great. For the Cossack rank and file, as for other discontented elements of Russian society, relocation was a powerful urge, nourished by their messianic expectations and by their belief in a Promised Land to the south, nearer the Holy Land where Christ was born, a New Jerusalem where no authority would tamper with their ritual or inhibit their freedom. Both these myths—of a deliverer and of a Promised Land in the south—were embodied in Pugachev's plan, and Filaret proved a sympathetic listener. He told Pugachev about Bogomolov's rising and about the recent disturbances on the Yaik. Though he did not think Pugachev resembled the tsar, the Yaik Cossacks were profoundly unhappy and ready for a deliverer to guide them to the "land of the Golden Mosque." [13] For Pugachev himself the urge to resettle in a happier place was very strong, a fact to which his long odyssey bears testimony. Encouraged by Filaret, he assumed the guise of a fish merchant and began to put his plan into practice.

He arrived on the Yaik in November 1772. An experienced soldier, a man of physical strength, restless energy, and compelling character, he was well endowed with the qualities of a leader. And he came at a favorable moment, barely a month after the sentences against the murderers of Traubenberg had been announced: sixty-two condemned to death and hundreds to be beaten with whips, shorn of their beards, and sent into the army. If ever a deliverer was needed it was now, and Pugachev began to announce himself as the tsar. But before his movement could get off the ground one of his confidants betrayed him and he was taken to prison in Kazan. His confinement was brief. Claiming to be an Old Believer persecuted for "cross and beard," he won over a guard who helped him to escape. He returned at once to the Yaik, where he found the Cossacks more agitated than ever. The sentences against the mutineers, though much reduced by the government, had been carried out, arousing a strong desire for revenge.

Somehow Pugachev established contact with a group of dissidents who were hiding out to avoid punishment. Appearing before them, he assumed the role of Peter III, who had come to redress their grievances. Nor was it hard to win their support; imitating Bogomolov, he exhibited marks on his body which he said were the tsar's. He then delivered an extraordinary speech into which all the rumors and legends about the late emperor were woven—that the gentry had tried to remove him because of his sympathy for the people, that he had escaped his assassins and gone into hiding, that he had wandered a dozen years but had now returned to claim the throne, liberate the poor, and punish their oppressors.

I was in Kiev, in Poland, in Egypt, in Jerusalem, and on the Terek River. From there I went to the Don and then came to you. And I hear that you have been wronged and that all the common folk have been wronged. There is great reason why I am not loved by the gentry: many of them, young men and others of middling years . . . though fit to serve and given posts, went off into retirement and lived at their will off the peasants in their villages and quite ruined them, poor folk, and they alone almost ruled for themselves the whole empire. So I began to compel them to service and wanted to take away from them their villages, so that they serve only for wages. And the officials who judge suits unjustly and oppress the people I punished and wished to hand over to the block. And so, for this they began to dig a ditch for me. And when I went to take a row on the Neva River they arrested me there and they made up a false tale about me and they forced me to wander over the face of the earth.

He had returned, however, for he "wanted to see how the common people were faring and what oppressions they have suffered from the officials." Now he would join his son Paul (reputed to be on bad terms with Catherine) and go to St. Petersburg and send Catherine to a nunnery or back to her own country. But "if she meets me with bad words, I know already what to do then." [14]

The speech was precisely what the Cossacks wanted to hear. It played upon their nativist hostility toward the German empress, their hatred of Muscovite landlords and bureaucrats, their yearning for justice and retribution, and their sympathy for the peasants, who, in contrast to the gentry with their arrogance and foreign ways, were of their own kind and faith. Moreover, it appealed directly to their own vanity and self-interest. "If God helps me to gain the throne," said Pugachev, "then Yaitsk will be the capital instead of Moscow or Petersburg, and the Yaik Cossacks will enjoy superiority over everyone else." In addition, to quote a contemporary, Pugachev "was artful enough to take advantage of their religious prejudices, which he openly professed to espouse and protect." [15] That he was in fact an Old Believer seems doubtful. Indeed he himself later denied it, although the British ambassador calls him a "schismatic Cossack" and Pushkin says the same in his history of the rising.[16] He had, it is true, professed the old ritual in Vetka and on the Irgiz and in Kazan prison, but this was doubtless for reasons of expediency. And if now, before the Yaik Cossacks, he promised to uphold the "cross and beard" and to replace the four-pointed cross of the Nikonians with the eight-pointed cross of the dissenters, he would later promise the Moslems to respect their faith and, when passing through predominantly Orthodox territory, would refrain from promoting schismatic demands.

For the moment, however, he firmly defended the old ritual, and the Cossacks gave him an enthusiastic reception. Whether they truly believed he was the "third emperor," however, is open to dispute. That he bore no resemblance to Peter has already been indicated, but the Cossacks, already on the verge of open insurrection, needed little convincing to win them over. His closest supporters, men like Ivan Zarubin, Maksim Shigaev, and Timofei Miasnikov, appear to have been knowing accomplices rather than dupes. General Bibikov, Pugachev's most formidable opponent, went so far as to call him their "puppet," while Pugachev himself later testified—possibly to minimize his own guilt—that his confederates "did as they pleased." [17] Veterans of the mutiny against Traubenberg, they were anxious to resume their rebellion and saw the advantages of a pretender to attract a larger following. As Miasnikov testified, "we accepted him as the deceased sovereign, Peter Fyodorovich, so that he would restore our customs and destroy all the boyars, who think they are so clever in everything. We hoped that our undertaking would be supported and our power multiplied by the common folk, who also are oppressed and headed for ruin." The government, he added, was trying "to introduce a new kind of military state that we have never agreed to accept. . . . It does not matter to us whether he is the sovereign or not. Out of mud we can make a prince. Even if he does not seize the Muscovite throne, we shall make the Yaik our own kingdom." [18]

The mutineers began spreading the news that Peter III had come to restore their former independence, and hundreds of Cossacks flocked to his banner. On September 17, 1773, to attract further adherents, Pugachev issued his first manifesto to the Yaik Host. Since he himself was illiterate, it was drafted by an accomplice, Ivan Pochitalin, and appealed to immediate Cossack interests: "I the sovereign, Peter Fyodorovich, pardon you of all your sins and grant you the river from its source to its mouth, the earth and the grass, and a subsidy of money, lead, powder, and grain. All this grant I, the great sovereign and emperor Peter Fyodorovich." [19] The same day Pugachev marched on the Cossack capital of Yaitsk. The rebellion had begun. Yaitsk, however, with its large garrison and strong fortifications, proved too difficult a target, so he bypassed the town and, advancing along the Yaik River in the direction of Orenburg, seized a series of isolated outposts with their artillery and munitions. At each stockade his messengers preceded him, waving their hats and shouting to the defenders that "all should rejoice because [the tsar] has risen and is now coming here." To those who were ready to join him Pugachev promised immediate deliverance. "I shall grant you eternal freedom, the rivers and seas, and all sorts of benefits and subsidies, food, powder, and lead, rank and honor, and liberty for centuries to come," reads one of his early proclamations.[20] Those who would resist, on the other hand, were threatened with torture and execution, which was usually enough to dispel any doubts about his true identity. On September 21 the town of Iletsk, with a garrison of 300 service Cossacks, surrendered without a fight. With church bells clanging, the residents came out to greet the "emperor," while parish priests with icons and crosses kissed his hand and offered the traditional welcome of bread and salt.

One by one forts and settlements took the oath to the impostor, and by early October he could boast more than 2000 followers and a large arsenal of cannon and rifles. Resistance was sporadic. At Fort Ilyinsk, when the rebels demanded entry in the name of the tsar, the gatekeeper replied: "We have in Russia the Sovereign Empress Catherine Alekseevna and her heir the Grand Prince Paul Petrovich. Aside from them we have no other sovereign." Taking the fort by storm, Pugachev rounded up the officers and asked why they had opposed their sovereign. "You are not our sovereign," they replied, "and we do not recognize you as such. You are a bandit and an impostor"—whereupon they were hanged on the spot.[21]

The rebels met with stiffer opposition at Fort Tatishchev, which guarded the crossroads to Orenburg and Yaitsk. Perched on a hill high above the Yaik, it was the main strongpoint on the southeastern defense perimeter, with large stores of supplies and equipment and a well-armed garrison of a thousand soldiers under the command of Colonel Fyodor Elagin. A few days before Pugachev's arrival the garrison was reinforced by 400 soldiers under Brigadier Christian von Bülow. Sent from Orenburg to intercept the impostor, Bülow learned that Pugachev had already collected some 3000 followers and a sizable quantity of guns, so he retired to Tatishchev to join forces with Elagin. As usual, Pugachev's messengers preceded their leader with warnings not to resist him. But while some of the defenders defected, the fort had to be taken by storm. Using a familiar tactic, the rebels set stacks of hay

ablaze and breached the walls while their opponents were occupied with extinguishing the flames. The garrison surrendered,
Elagin and Bülow were put to death, and the jubilant Cossacks
celebrated their triumph in a three-day debauch.

The fall of Tatishchev made a great impression on the surrounding population. It was the first major victory for the insurgents and, as in past uprisings, drew a swarm of fresh adherents
to their camp. In addition, it opened the way to Orenburg, the
main administrative center of the region. But why bother about
Orenburg? Why not make directly for the heartland, arouse the
peasantry, and catch the government off balance? A similar choice
had confronted both Razin and Bulavin in the early stages of
their ·risings, and both had chosen the peripheries, where the
government was weakly entrenched and where they, by contrast,
enjoyed the support of the people and an intimate knowledge of
the terrain. To Pugachev not only did the same considerations
apply with equal weight, but the driving force of his rebellion
was the Yaik Host, for whom Orenburg, with its decrees and tax
collectors, its recruiting parties and punitive expeditions, was the
direct source of their misery and the chief object of their hatred.
Now they would settle accounts.

Orenburg girded itself for the attack. Fortifications were
strengthened, bridges were destroyed, and the people were mobilized and armed. Yet the governor, General Ivan Reinsdorp, remained apprehensive, for his garrison had fewer than 3000 men,
only a fraction of whom were regulars, the rest being an assortment of Cossacks, Tatars, Kalmyks, and new recruits, many of
them overage and poorly equipped. As for his officers, remarked a
contemporary, "it is best to remain silent." [22] Pugachev's agents
had already penetrated the town, sowing dissension with the
news of "Peter Fyodorovich's" approach. To scotch the rumors
Reinsdorp denounced Pugachev as an "impostor, scoundrel, and
monster," which merely added to the fear and confusion.

The siege began on October 5. At first the populace was
plunged in despair. "All the inhabitants thought about death,"
noted a local priest in his diary, "and there was great wailing
and disconsolate sobbing." [23] But the panic faded as quickly as it
came, and the residents settled down to endure the siege, which
lasted nearly six months. Meanwhile, as winter set in, a particu-

larly severe one even by Russian standards, the rebels blockaded
the city in an effort to starve the population into submission. Cannon deployed around the walls subjected the defenders to a continuous bombardment, which was answered in kind from within.
While the siege dragged on, Pugachev established headquarters in
the village of Berda, about three or four miles north of Orenburg. There he reigned as Peter III, at the head of a rebel "government," while keeping Reinsdorp beleaguered all winter. At
the same time, like Razin at Simbirsk and Bulavin at Cherkassk,
he sent out riders in every direction to scatter the sparks of sedition. Hundreds of leaflets were issued, in Arabic, Tatar, and
Turkic as well as Russian, promising freedom to those who cooperated and death to those who resisted. For the rural and urban
poor it was not a difficult choice, and each week hundreds of new
recruits flocked to Berda to serve the "third emperor."

Throughout the southern Urals the air was filled with messianic expectations. Each day the conviction grew that "Peter
Fyodorovich is alive," risen like Christ from the dead to save the
humble and punish their oppessors. "Our time has come," said
the common folk. "Now we shall get to the top, and we have
nothing to fear." [24] Cossack bands roved the countryside raiding
gentry estates and announcing that the tsar had sent them "to
give the peasants freedom." Villagers were ordered to cease toil-
ing for their masters or be impaled. "Why do you work for the
landlords when the sovereign, Peter Fyodorovich, has given you
liberty?" demanded the Cossacks.[25] A reward of 100 rubles was
offered for the death of a landowner and the destruction of his
home; and for ten gentry victims—1000 rubles and the rank of
general. Village priests were upbraided by the Cossacks for conducting services with the three-fingered sign of the cross, and
were threatened with execution if they did not follow the old
rites.

"I know that the common people will greet me with joy once
they hear of my coming," said Pugachev.[26] And his prophecy
was correct. In a few weeks he had raised a large if motley army:
Cossacks and serfs, schismatics and priests, miners and foundry
workers, and a variety of tribesmen—Bashkirs, Tatars, Kalmyks,
Kazakhs—streamed to his standard. To these must be added a
host of vagrants of every description—army deserters, escaped

convicts, unfrocked monks, highwaymen, political exiles, and even a few ruined or disgruntled noblemen, as well as officers of the Polish Confederation who joined in November and December when the revolt spilled over into their place of banishment in western Siberia. "Great and small, poor and rich—all will be esteemed as one class by the sovereign and merciful tsar," proclaimed one of Pugachev's early manifestoes.[27] No wonder, given such disparate origins, the rebels were from the outset plagued by dissension. But they were united in their opposition to the existing order, with its infringement of traditional liberties, and their lives being wretched or their ambitions keen, they were eager to follow a leader who promised salvation.

During the early stages of the rising, Pugachev's most numerous and effective supporters, apart from the Yaik Cossacks, were the Bashkirs and the factory peasants of the Urals region. The semi-nomadic Bashkirs, who differed markedly from the settled agricultural peoples of the Volga valley, gained their livelihood chiefly by hunting, herding, trapping, and beekeeping. Of Magyar stock, Turkic language, and Moslem religion, they fell increasingly under Russian domination after the fall of Kazan and Astrakhan to Ivan the Terrible in the 1550s. The founding of Ufa in 1586 heralded a wave of Russian colonization in Bashkiria, and over the next two centuries the pace of expansion quickened as settlers streamed in from the west, noblemen carved out estates, garrisons sprouted up, and officials imposed tribute, monopolized the salt trade, recruited native horsemen, and demanded provisions for their new stockades and forts.

At the same time, every device of persuasion or force was used to convert the tribesmen to Christianity. Missionaries were dispatched, tax concessions granted, mosques destroyed, and whole villages baptized at gunpoint. As if these outrages were not enough, from the time of Peter the Great, Russian industry began moving into the area on a large scale, and the tribesmen, beyond their normal tribute of furs and honey, were compelled to supply wood for factory furnaces and hay for factory horses. Step by step, with the seizure of grazing lands and game preserves, with the leveling of forests used for trapping and beekeeping, the Bashkirs were deprived of their traditional means of subsistence, and no relief was in sight. Colonization and industrialization con-

tinued on their relentless course. Indeed, with the founding of
Orenburg in 1735, new enterprises sprang up at an unprecedented
rate, causing a rapid change in the social and economic structure
of the region.[28]

The impact of these developments on a nomadic people is not
hard to imagine. Nor, indeed, is the ferocity with which the intruders were resisted. From the 1640s to the 1770s accumulating
social, religious, and national grievances touched off half a dozen
major risings, each more furious than its predecessor, till in
Pugachev's time the whole of Bashkiria raged out of control in
a last-ditch struggle for independence. The first serious outbreak
of the eighteenth century coincided, as we have seen, with the
revolt of Bulavin under Peter the Great and continued for the
better part of a decade. For the Bashkirs, however, there was no
relief. In fact their situation continued to deteriorate at such a
rate that the founder of Orenburg, Ivan Kirillov, warned of a
new explosion if a "clever rogue like Stenka Razin" should appear to lead them.[29]

No new Razin was destined to appear for another generation,
but the Bashkirs were unable to wait. In 1735 they rose against
Kirillov himself to prevent the construction of Orenburg as a
new center of Russian colonization. The Russians, said the insurgents, "want to own all the land," and if Orenburg is built "there
will be no more freedom." [30] After a savage six-year struggle a
tsarist army subdued the Bashkirs, with orders "to crush them
to death and raze their dwellings." Nearly 30,000 tribesmen were
tortured and executed or died in prison or were given into bondage. Thousands were forced to convert, and the tribal aristocracy
was decimated. Some 400 settlements were burned and countless animals, along with goods and money, were seized as booty.
But the Bashkirs refused to capitulate. In 1755 they rose again
under the mullah Batyrsha Ali in a renewed effort to expel the
intruders. Orenburg was sacked, mines and foundries were destroyed, and hundreds of settlers were massacred. In the end,
however, arrows and spears were no match for the cannon and
rifles of the enemy. The rising was crushed in blood, followed
by burning and looting in which thousands of natives were killed
and hundreds of villages destroyed.

Faced with vastly superior arms, the Bashkirs were doomed to defeat so long as they fought unaided. Their only hope lay in an alliance with other discontented groups, Russians of course included. Thus when rumors began to reach them that Peter III was alive and was summoning all the oppressed into one united army, many of the tribesmen, however skeptical of his real identity, were eager to respond. For with the return of the "male sex" to the throne, they believed, their troubles would come to an end. "Whether or not Pugachev is the tsar does not interest us," they said. "Pugachev is against the officials, the generals, and the boyars—that for us is enough." [31] Pugachev, for his own part, was anxious to have their support. In October 1773 manifestoes reached the Bashkirs from the "sweet-tongued, merciful, soft-hearted tsar," promising to restore their former way of life: "I grant you hereafter the lands, the waters, the forests, the fisheries, the dwellings, the meadows and seas, the grain, your own faith and law, the crops, bodily nourishment, garments, subsidies of lead, powder, and provisions—in a word, everything that you have desired all your lives. Be again like the untamed animals of the steppe." [32] Yet his appeal, for all its magnanimity and eloquence, had a mixed reception. Among the Bashkirs, as among the Cossacks, there were deep-seated divisions which the government had long been exploiting in order to impose its control. Rather than join a rebellion which might threaten their privileged position, many of the tribal elders remained aloof or even, during a later stage of the fighting, cooperated with the government against the insurgents. The divisions, moreover, cut across class lines. For most Bashkirs, whether needy or prosperous, cooperation with the Russians was no easy matter. And they disliked not only the landlords and officials but also the simple peasants who settled on their lands, the ordinary workmen who labored in the foundries, the Yaik Cossacks who helped put down their rebellions—in short the very groups who constituted Pugachev's main supporters. On the other hand, they shared with these groups common grievances against the state, a common hatred of the gentry, a common desire to recapture a golden past; and for some this was enough to set aside, at least temporarily, their religious and national differences.

The most prominent of Pugachev's early Bashkir adherents was an elder named Kinzia Arslanov, who joined him in October with a few hundred men. It was a modest beginning, but Kinzia, determined to win further adherents, sent to the villages agitators armed with Pugachev's manifestoes and with bogus news that the Tsarevich Paul was about to join his father with a large force of Don Cossacks. Kinzia's efforts were so successful that Pugachev made him a "colonel" in charge of a Bashkir regiment that took part in the siege of Orenburg. By the end of November, Bashkirs made up nearly half of Pugachev's entire army and had laid siege to Ufa, the capital of Bashkiria, assisted by Tatars, Mari, and Russian peasants, so that the three principal towns of the southern Urals—Yaitsk, Orenburg, and Ufa—were now in danger of capture.

The discontents of the Bashkirs were equaled, or perhaps exceeded, by those of the factory peasants, whose participation in the *Pugachevshchina* added a distinctive new element, a sort of incipient proletariat, to these primitive mass upheavals. The industrialization of the Urals, already begun on a small scale in the late seventeenth century, assumed major proportions under Peter the Great and his successors. Rich beds of copper and iron as well as an abundance of woodlands for fuel and of rivers for transportation favored a rapid development of the area. Mines, furnaces, and smelting works, founded by the state or by resourceful merchants and gentry, such as the Demidovs, the Stroganovs, the Tverdyshevs, and the Miasnikovs, sprang up in every corner, reaching a high-water mark during the 1740s and 1750s, when the number of enterprises more than doubled, so that a hundred factories dotted the Urals by the time of Catherine's accession in 1762.[33]

It is here that one must look for the prototype of the Russian working class—not in the towns of European Russia, apart from the state arsenals of Petersburg and Tula, but in the mines and foundries of the Urals, where a factory life akin to that of the next century was already beginning to emerge. This labor force, as in agriculture, was founded on the institution of bondage. In 1721 Peter the Great permitted merchants with industrial establishments to purchase villages of serfs, who were bound to the enterprises rather than to the owners. In addition, whole villages of state peasants, largely from the middle Volga, were "ascribed" to Urals factories as seasonal laborers. And as the need for labor increased, paupers, vagabonds, convicts, dissenters, tribesmen, and other combustible elements were recruited for the metal works and mines. Finally, by a decree of 1736 all free workingmen, together with their families, were converted into bondsmen and tied forever to the factories, completing the legalization of forced labor.

The period of rapid industrialization in the mid-eighteenth century saw a sharp rise in the number of ascribed workers, who made up the bulk of the Urals labor force. From 100,000 in the 1740s the figure more than doubled by the time of Pugachev's outbreak. As unskilled peasants, the ascribed workers were saddled with the heavy tasks of mining ore, felling trees, and hauling wood and charcoal, at which they toiled under appalling conditions and for little reward. The climate was severe, the hours were long, the wages were meager and often in arrears, the factories were shoddily built with damp, earthen floors, leaky roofs, and poor lighting and ventilation. Crowded into squalid huts or dormitories, the workmen were ill-clothed, even worse fed, compelled to pay exorbitant prices at factory stores, and subjected to extortions, fines, and beatings by callous foremen and administrators. Worse still, they were sometimes ascribed to enterprises 300 or 400 miles from their native villages, requiring weeks of travel with no pay.[34]

By Catherine's reign the ascribed peasants had been reduced to "utter squalor and ruin," to quote from one of their numerous petitions to the authorities. "Just look at the factory workers," wrote an army officer to the empress, "especially the ascribed peasants, who have been sacrificed completely to the factory owners, and those predators think about nothing but their own gain and greedily devour all the property of the peasants."[35] Government inspectors concurred and recommended drastic reforms, but none was forthcoming. Yet, for all their grievances, there was little solidarity or class feeling among the Urals workers. Like their Cossack and Bashkir allies, they formed two distinct groups whose interests seldom coincided. There was a nucleus of more or less skilled workmen who lived permanently at the factories (in which they were employed the whole year round) and were considerably better off than the ordinary seasonal laborers. As artisans or foremen, not only did they receive higher wages and have less tedious duties, but they also received an allotment of free grain (akin to the *zhalovanie* of the Cossack hierarchy) and were allowed to engage in trade outside working hours. Although their lives were far from easy, they acquired a certain stake in their enterprises and, while eager for improvements, were not opposed to factory life as such. For the uprooted peasants, by contrast, the routine and discipline of factory work was hard to accept after the seasonal cycle, the rhythm of hard and slack labor, and the freedom of the outdoors to which they were accustomed. It was a dismal existence, tantamount in their eyes to penal servitude, and they found adjusting to it difficult. Rather than better conditions, they wanted to rid themselves of the factories and return to their rural life, which, for all its hardships, seemed a lost paradise by comparison. They yearned to be restored to the state peasantry, which they considered their rightful status, but their petitions to the government were unavailing.

Small wonder that, in contrast to the skilled workers, they should have resorted to violence as an outlet for their grievances. During the 1750s and 1760s a wave of riots and disturbances swept the Urals region. At one Demidov factory in 1760, troops were called in and ordered the peasants to return to work. "We do not want to work at Demidov's," was the reply, "and we will not listen to any decrees. You can send ten decrees and as many soldiers as you like, but we will not go back to work as long as there is no decree from the senate with the personal signature of the empress." [36] When such decrees were not forthcoming, the peasants began to manufacture their own, or to circulate bogus edicts brought in from outside. In 1762, following Peter III's emancipation of the gentry, counterfeit manifestoes appeared liberating the ascribed workers from the factories and restoring them to the state peasantry. When Peter prohibited the further acquisition of serfs by factory owners, these manifestoes gained wide credence and workers began returning to their villages. "If we are hunted down and forcibly sent back to the factories," they warned, "there will be killing on both sides." [37]

A special trouble spot in those years was the Avziano-Petrovsk iron works, one of the largest enterprises in the Urals and a center of worker discontent since its construction in the early

1750s. For the next two decades it was the scene of repeated violent outbursts, one of which coincided with the Bashkir revolt of 1755 and brought severe government reprisals. Not surprisingly, then, it was to the Avziano-Petrovsk works that Pugachev sent an emissary, Khlopusha by name, in search of weapons and volunteers. Himself a former metal worker, Khlopusha had turned to brigandage, had been four times beaten with the knout, had twice escaped from Siberia, and was languishing in an Orenburg prison, with torn nostrils and branded forehead, when Governor Reinsdorp offered him freedom if he would go to Berda and denounce Pugachev as an impostor. Eager to escape his chains, Khlopusha accepted, but on arriving in Pugachev's camp promptly defected to the rebels. Pugachev sent him on a new mission, to drum up support among the Urals workers, and this time he faithfully carried out his assignment. With a Cossack escort he arrived at Avziano-Petrovsk in October 1773 and, in the name of Peter III, granted the workers "personal liberty and freedom from all taxes." [38] The announcement was greeted with jubilation, and hundreds of workers joined him, bringing cannon, horses, and supplies. From Avziano-Petrovsk they rode through the surrounding area promising "to shut down all the factories." At each enterprise the pattern was the same. Swearing an oath to the emperor, the ascribed peasants (but only a fraction of the skilled workmen) attacked the factory office, plundered the strongbox, burned official documents, and pillaged the homes of the administrators. News of the tsar's return was received with wild excitement. Nor did the workers trouble themselves about Pugachev's real identity so long as he told them what they wanted to hear. As one of them put it: "They are all tsars to us, whoever they are!" [39] Pugachev, indeed, was more than a tsar. He was a Christ-like messiah heralding the dawn of a new age. With a millennial fervor the workers rejoiced that "our resplendent sun, hidden beneath the earth, now rises in the east, shedding rays of mercy over the whole universe and warming us lowly orphans and slaves." [40]

Khlopusha's mission was a great success. In November 1773 he returned to Berda laden with cannon, rifles, powder, and money, and with 1000 recruits for the rebel army. For the duration of the winter Pugachev pressed his siege of Yaitsk, Ufa, and Orenburg, laid siege to half a dozen lesser administrative centers, and sought additional forces to guarantee the success of these operations. When volunteers did not suffice, he sent detachments into the countryside to gather recruits by force. By the end of the year his army numbered between 10,000 and 15,000, of whom there were some 1500 Cossacks, 5000 Bashkirs, and 1000 workers, the rest including serfs, Tatars, and Kalmyks, with a sprinkling of other tribesmen, religious dissenters, convicts, priests, and an occasional merchant or nobleman. It was a motley body, loosely organized, poorly armed, short of horses and supplies, fluctuating in numbers and quality, and except at the outset when the government was unprepared, not particularly effective. The Cossacks, it is true, formed a seasoned and comparatively well-armed nucleus that could deploy more than eighty cannon obtained from captured factories and forts. But the infantry was inexperienced and badly equipped. Rifles and pistols were in short supply, so that the ragtag troops had to rely on knives, cudgels, and sharpened stakes, and occasionally fought with nothing but rocks and bare fists. Discipline, moreover, was a constant problem, which Pugachev answered with severe measures. One rebel was hanged merely for boasting that he knew where "the emperor" really came from. To increase their efficiency Pugachev formed his men into regiments according, so far as possible, to national or social origins, placing each under the command of a trusted associate. The Yaik Cossacks, for example, comprised a regiment under Andrei Ovchinnikov, Pugachev's ablest commander. Similarly the factory peasants were organized under Khlopusha, the Bashkirs under Kinzia Arslanov, and so on. Each regiment was in turn divided into companies which elected their own officers in the Cossack manner. But the regimental commanders, or "colonels," were appointed by Pugachev himself, each having his own banner of red or gold silk embroidered with Old Believer crosses and with images of Christ or of St. Nicholas the Miracle Worker. Near every major target—Orenburg, Yaitsk, Ufa, or the newly beleaguered towns of Ekaterinburg, Cheliabinsk, and Kungur—local headquarters were established by one of the colonels, who enjoyed considerable autonomy in his own bailiwick. To impose a measure of control, however, a "War College," modeled after the one in St. Petersburg, was set up at Berda in November 1773, and strove with limited success to coordinate operations. Beyond this, it functioned as a logistical center, maintaining supply lines with the Urals factories, from which it ordered cannon, mortars, and ammunition.

Pugachev was by all accounts an able commander-in-chief. In the most difficult engagements, his confederates later testified, he was to be seen at the head of his troops issuing orders and urging them forward. Foreign observers compared him—both as a rebel and as a military leader—to Oliver Cromwell. From his Cossack upbringing and long army experience he was acquainted with tactics and organization, but his particular strength was artillery. At the height of the rebellion he had 100 cannon (captured from government forts or forged in the Urals foundries), which gave him a military might of which Bolotnikov, Razin, and Bulavin could scarcely have dreamed. His gun emplacements at Berda were of such outstanding quality that, according to Governor Reinsdorp, "Vauban himself could not have constructed better." [41] To give the impression of even greater strength, he ordered decoy cannon to be fashioned from wood and painted to look like the real thing. In the field, moreover, his guns were mounted on sledges for easy mobility, and by a series of lightning marches, such as only Cossacks were able to perform, government outposts were overwhelmed and, except for the more strongly defended administrative centers, the vast territory from the Urals to the Volga fell under effective rebel control.

At the same time, Pugachev inaugurated a rebel government over which he ruled as Peter III. Choosing for his palace the finest house in Berda, he assumed the role that people would expect from a true emperor and played it with evident relish. He surrounded himself with a personal guard of twenty-five Cossacks who called him "your excellency" and "dear father" (*batiushka*) as they would the real tsar. On special occasions he wore a white embroidered shirt, a robe of red velvet, and a black lambskin hat with a crimson lining. As the Duke of Holstein (a title of Peter III) he displayed an old Holstein banner that one of his men had captured during the Seven Years' War. And on a wall of his headquarters hung a portrait of the Tsarevich Paul, of whom he spoke with feigned paternal affection.

Berda, in short, became a grotesque parody of the Russian capital, though Pugachev called it his Moscow instead of St. Petersburg, perhaps because the old capital, the traditional center of serfdom, remained the foremost symbol of aristocratic oppression. But he had his Petersburg too, in the town of Kargala, and a Kiev as well, in Sakmarsk. Moreover, aping the imperial court, he dubbed his closest confederates with the names of Catherine's favorites, so that Ovchinnikov became Count Panin, Zarubin Count Chernyshev, Shigaev Count Vorontsov, and Chumakov Count Orlov. In Pugachev's mock court the rebels amused themselves with heavy drinking, peasant dances, and bawdy Cossack songs. Pugachev himself seemed a curious mixture of Petersburg emperor and people's tsar, a Cossack warlord in velvet robes at the head of a popular government. With his colonels and counts and other Western paraphernalia, he distinguished himself sharply from earlier rebel leaders, who had rejected European customs. Yet his up-to-date image was superficial. Unlike his predecessors, he was playing the role of an emperor, and for this his imperial trappings were necessary props. But beneath the thin exterior was a traditional popular rebel whose goal was a popular tsardom with extensive local autonomy. "If God sees fit that I should conquer the throne," Pugachev declared, "then I shall allow everyone to pursue the old faith and to wear Russian clothing. But none shall be allowed to shave his beard, and I shall command everyone to cut his hair in the Cossack style." To make this dream a reality, he would "go to Moscow and then to Petersburg and conquer the whole state" and eliminate the boyars.[42] With such a program it was not hard to convince the people that he was their true ruler. They wanted desperately to believe it, and he in turn, because of their response, tried to live up to his role, becoming the servant of his own myth. To some extent, perhaps, he may actually have come to believe it. At any rate, it was with a measure of genuine conviction that he spoke of liberation and proclaimed a new era of popular justice.

4. Bibikov

It was several weeks before news of the uprising reached St. Petersburg, and the government's response was desultory. Pugachev's claim to be Peter III, and his declared intention to join with the tsarevich and depose Catherine, may have irritated the empress, but she was not unduly alarmed. For Pugachev was merely one of a long line of false Peter IIIs, and his outbreak seemed merely another local Cossack disturbance on the fringes of the empire, which the Orenburg governor could handle without difficulty. In any case, with her troops engaged against the Turks, Catherine was unable to spare more than a small force to suppress the revolt, and it was not until November that these reinforcements made their appearance. Nor did the delay pass unnoticed. In fact it added to the rumors that the true tsar had returned. For if Pugachev was an impostor, asked the workers of one Urals factory, why were no troops sent to put him down?[43]

Some troops were actually on the way, though an insufficient number to contain the rebellion. To prevent speculation by foreign observers, the government maintained a strict curtain of silence, so that Sir Robert Gunning, the British ambassador, could not even learn the correct name of the officer sent from Moscow to deal with the insurgents. It was not "Bauer,"[44] but Vasili Kar, who was ordered in mid-October to raise the siege of Orenburg. Of Scottish lineage, though born and educated in Russia, Kar was a veteran of the Seven Years' War who had risen to major general; yet despite his rank and experience he was a mediocre officer, and he had only 500 men and 6 guns at his disposal. Fortunately, a larger force was dispatched about the same time from western Siberia under General Ivan Dekolong (de Colongues), an officer of French extraction and a veteran of numerous campaigns. Two additional detachments were summoned from the Volga, one from Simbirsk under Colonel Chernyshev (no relation to the minister of war) and the other from Kazan led by Brigadier Korf.

With four government parties converging on him, Pugachev would appear to have been in grave danger. But this was not at all the case. Kar and his colleagues had vast distances to cover; communications between them were virtually nonexistent; none knew the plans or precise whereabouts of the others; and so they were unable to mount a concerted attack. Moreover, they had little reliable information about the activities of the rebels, while the rebels received a good deal about theirs from sympathetic tribesmen and peasants, and were of course better acquainted with the terrain. Thus Pugachev had the advantage of surprise; and he was able to deal with his opponents singly rather than as one formidable army.

Orenburg was heartened by the news of Kar's approach. But his progress was slowed by heavy snowfall and severe frost. At last he reached the area, only to discover that the rebel army was much larger and better armed than he had expected; and "owing to faintheartedness and poor behavior," as a contemporary put it, he "allowed himself to be beaten." [45] On November 8 a large rebel force under two of Pugachev's ablest commanders, Andrei Ovchinnikov and Ivan Zarubin, encircled Kar at the village of Yuzeevka. With the Cossacks shouting at them not to oppose "the emperor," Kar's troops were thrown into confusion, and nearly a hundred defected when the rebels promised them "the lands, seas, and forests, the cross and beard, and full freedom." [46] Worse still, according to a French officer exiled in Kazan, Kar had gone into battle without reconnoitering his opposition. As Kar himself testified: "The rogues swept in like the wind from the steppe, and their artillery did much damage." Nor, he said, did they "shoot the way one might expect of peasants." [47]

Kar beat a swift retreat to Kazan, where news of his defeat threw the gentry into a panic. Many decided to flee, and though the governor, Yakov von Brandt, tried to calm their fears, his efforts failed when it became known that he had sent his own family to safety and emptied his house of its furniture. From Kazan, Kar proceeded to Moscow "with as much haste as he had left it," and Catherine, furious at his "weakness of spirit," cashiered him and instructed the Moscow governor to tell him "not to dare show himself before my eyes." [48] Meanwhile Pugachev was not idle. Following up his victory over Kar, he led the defeat of Chernyshev near Orenburg and had him executed with 32 other officers and one of their wives. But Korf managed to slip past him and into the besieged city with his badly needed contingent of 2500 men and 22 guns.

By now Catherine realized the gravity of the situation. At the end of November she offered a 1000-ruble reward for Pugachev's capture, a figure which would increase sharply as the revolt expanded. But a more important step was her appointment of General Alexander Bibikov to take charge of the pacification.

Bibikov was an excellent choice. Born of a military family, he had twice been cited for bravery in the Seven Years' War and had later distinguished himself against the Poles. Moreover, he had proved his ability to tame domestic unrest by crushing factory riots in the Urals. A statesman as well as an officer, he had served in both the Senate and the War College and as Speaker of Catherine's short-lived Legislative Commission. "His known probity," noted the British ambassador, "his unaffected patriotism and his great military knowledge gave him the justest title to favour and confidence of his mistress." [49] Bibikov, in short, was a model imperial servant. He and Pugachev represented two distinct worlds, as Catherine understood when she advised him to use the "superiority which courage, education, and culture always afford against an ignorant mob driven only by the stormy fanaticism of religious and political superstition and obscurantism." [50] To Catherine the Bibikovs stood for enlightenment, civilization, progress, the Pugachevs for superstition, barbarism, reaction. Pugachev, in her eyes, was not merely a brigand and a traitor; he was a "monster of the human race," an offender against the public order and against those divine and secular laws without which no empire could stand.

Such, at any rate, were the terms in which she denounced the pretender in a manifesto of December 1773, on the eve of Bibikov's departure for Kazan. That Pugachev should take the name of her late husband was a source of particular irritation, owing perhaps to an uneasy conscience over his death. "It would be superfluous here," she wrote in the manifesto, "to prove the absurdity of such an imposture, which cannot even put on a shadowy probability in the eyes of sensible persons." But the empress was plainly troubled—so much so that she conjured up the memory of the Time of Troubles, when, "because of an impostor, towns and villages were ravaged by fire and sword, when the blood of Russians was spilled by Russians, and when the unity of the state was in the end destroyed by the hands of Russians themselves." It was an unwise analogy, as her advisors pointed out, since it could "only recall unpleasant events and encourage the insurgents." [51] The parallels between Peter III and Tsarevich Dmitri— their sudden and mysterious death followed by their miraculous reappearance under the banner of insurrection—were better left unstated.

In December 1773 Bibikov hurried to Kazan with a regiment of cavalry and two of infantry and wide powers to deal with the rebels. Meanwhile the contagion continued to spread. Toward the end of the month, following a three-month siege, Yaitsk fell to the insurgents, except for the stockade, to which a force of Cossack loyalists and the garrison commander had retired. Repeated attempts to breach the walls were rebuffed at considerable cost, and as time wore on the loyalists were reduced to eating their horses, and "cold and hunger," one of them recalled, "brought us to a state of despair which increased with each day." [52] At one point there was a momentary respite when the attackers paused to celebrate Pugachev's marriage to a local Cossack girl who had caught his fancy. It was a lavish wedding, as befitted a royal couple, the ceremony performed to the accompaniment of cannon and church bells. Yet its effect was to damage the pretender's image and to sow doubts among his followers. How can an emperor marry an ordinary Cossack? it was asked. And what about the empress Catherine (to say nothing of his real wife and children on the Don)?

For the moment, however, such doubts were put aside, and by January 1774 the revolt, according to a foreign witness, had 30,000 adherents and was growing "more serious every day." [53] At Ufa and Orenburg the situation became desperate, as provisions dwindled and morale sagged. Further east a force of Bashkirs and ascribed workers placed Cheliabinsk under siege and a mutiny broke out within the town in which an angry mob dragged the governor through the streets by his hair before his troops could restore order. The rebel commander, Ivan Griaznov, an Old Believer with a talent for millenarian propaganda, bombarded the inhabitants with leaflets which cast Pugachev in the combined role of Christ rescuing the poor and Moses leading the Israelites to the Promised Land:

> Our Lord Jesus Christ wishes through his holy providence to free Russia from the yoke of servile labor. We all know who has brought Russia to this state of hunger and exhaustion. The gentry own the peasants, and though in God's law it is written that the

peasants too are God's children, yet they treat them not merely as servants but as lower than the very dogs with which they hunt rabbits. The company men have got hold of most of the factories and have so burdened the peasants with work that there is nothing at all like it, not even in exile at hard labor. How many are the tears shed to the Lord by the workers and their wives and small children! But soon, like the Israelites, you shall be delivered out of bondage.[54]

To this was added another popular myth: that Peter Fyodorovich, having liberated the gentry, had drawn up a manifesto freeing the serfs as well, but that the landlords had suppressed it and deposed the tsar, who, wandering like Christ in the wilderness for eleven years, had now returned to carry out his intentions. Pugachev, said Griaznov, was no impostor. He was the true Russian tsar, come at last to emancipate the poor.

Throughout the winter factory peasants and Bashkirs continued to provide the Cossacks with their most zealous supporters. While Khlopusha and Kinzia remained indispensable leaders, new men of equal ability now made their appearance. A notable example was Ivan Beloborodov, about the same age as Pugachev and born near Kungur in the heart of the Urals mining region. When the Seven Years' War broke out, Beloborodov was conscripted to work in a munitions factory near St. Petersburg. After seven years of hard labor, with no prospect of release, he feigned illness and was allowed to return to Kungur, where he married and set up shop as a trader in beeswax and honey. But in January 1774, when a Pugachev courier read a manifesto in the market square, Beloborodov was won over. Organizing a force of workers from a Demidov foundry near Ekaterinburg, he moved from factory to factory emptying the strongboxes, burning official records, and seizing a large quantity of supplies and ammunition. At each enterprise Beloborodov told the workmen that the "great sovereign" was coming to free them from compulsory labor and to cancel their dues and taxes. Calling his adherents Cossacks, and himself their *ataman*, he divided them into hundreds and distributed loot in equal portions. He put his own factory experience to good use by supervising the production of weapons and teaching his men how to use them. One by one the large enterprises of the Ekaterinburg area were taken, and the city itself was gradu-

ally encircled, for which the government commander, Colonel
Vasili Bibikov, must be held partly responsible. For unlike his
namesake, the colonel was a listless officer whose preparations for
the assault were grossly inadequate—indeed at one point he even
considered fleeing to save his own neck. Yet despite his incom-
petence Ekaterinburg managed to hold out until reinforcements
arrived.

Among the Bashkirs the outstanding new leader was Salavat
Yulaev, the son of a prominent elder, Yulai Aznalin, who had
fought against the Prussians in the Seven Years' War and had
been decorated for bravery against the Polish Confederation.
Yulai was thus a Bashkir loyalist, a common phenomenon within
the tribal hierarchy. In fact he and his son had been sent by
Governor Reinsdorp to fight the insurrectionists but were taken
prisoner by Ovchinnikov and promptly defected. Salavat, though
only twenty-one, already had three wives and two sons; and with
his dark hair and eyes and tall green cap, as a Bashkir song describes
him, he cut a handsome figure. What was more, he was a popular
folk poet who read and wrote Tatar and knew the Koran by
heart. Highly esteemed by his fellow tribesmen, he had little
trouble recruiting an army "to serve the sovereign," [55] and, occupying Krasnoufimsk without a struggle, he marched on Kungur,
whose *voevoda* fled in panic, leaving the defense of the city to
the local merchants and gentry and a small contingent of troops.

With Ufa and Orenburg under siege, Kungur and Ekaterinburg
threatened, and Yaitsk all but taken, General Bibikov had his
work cut out for him. Arriving at Kazan toward the end of December, he reprimanded Governor von Brandt for his lack of
initiative and set about organizing the local gentry into an effective fighting force. In addition, he posted a 10,000-ruble reward
for Pugachev's capture, while Pugachev, for his own part, ordered
a gibbet constructed with a sign in gold letters "For Bibikov." [56]
Bibikov was quick to size up his adversary. He saw that Pugachev's rising, like those of the past, was a broad social struggle
of the have-nots against the haves, a clash of two cultures, of the
two social and spiritual worlds into which the nation was divided.
Pugachev "may be even more dangerous to the nobility and the
rich than he is to the empress," he told the Kazan aristocracy.
"This is a revolt of the poor against the rich, of the slaves against

their masters." The pretender, Bibikov recognized, could have made little headway but for the widespread unrest, the ground swell of discontent, which underlay his movement. "Pugachev himself is not important. What is important is the general indignation." [57] A similar observation was made about the same time by the future poet Gavriil Derzhavin, then a young lieutenant under Bibikov's command:

> One must determine whether, in the event we kill him, there will not appear a new and even more dastardly swine calling himself the tsar. Is he the only one who calls himself by that name, or are there many who do so? Do the people look on him as the real deceased sovereign, or do they know that he is in fact just Pugachev, though their coarse instincts for insurrection and robbery do not allow them to reject him? [58]

Nor was Catherine herself blind to what the *Pugachevshchina* represented: a rising of peasant Russia against its ruling aristocracy. In a letter to Bibikov she pointedly numbered herself among the landowners of Kazan and pledged that the security and well-being of the gentry "are inseparable from our own and our empire's security and well-being." [59] She increased the reward on Pugachev's head, and ordered his house on the Don burned, the ashes scattered to the winds, and his family sent to Kazan, where Bibikov tried to use them to discredit the pretender by telling the people his true identity.[60]

All this was to no avail. But Bibikov had other weapons that were far more effective. Between January and April a number of capable officers with well-armed troops came under his command, and one by one they relieved the Urals towns. Toward the end of January the siege of Kungur was lifted by Major Dmitri Gagrin with two rifle companies from Dekolong's Siberian army. For several days Salavat had tried to capture the city, but he had not reckoned on Major Alexander Popov, whom Bibikov ranked among his best garrison commanders. Popov ordered drums beaten to drown out rebel demands for surrender. Then, launching a sudden attack, he caught Salavat off guard and forced him to withdraw to Krasnoufimsk, where Gagrin overtook him and dealt a decisive blow. Gagrin next headed his troops toward Ekaterinburg to deal with Beloborodov. In a series of savage engagements factory after factory was cleared of insurgents, Beloborodov fled to Berda, and Ekaterinburg was out of danger. Gagrin then moved against Griaznov, who had occupied Cheliabinsk on Dekolong's premature withdrawal, and again the rebels were defeated, although what became of Griaznov, a remarkable figure about whom little is known, remains a mystery.

Meanwhile, Ufa had also found its liberator in Lieutenant Colonel Ivan Mikhelson, second only to Bibikov himself as the outstanding hero of the government forces during the rebellion. A brilliant young officer from the Baltic nobility, Mikhelson enjoyed a well-earned reputation for courage in battle. He had served under Bibikov in the Seven Years' War, had been wounded at both Zorndorf and Kunersdorf, and had fought with equal distinction against Turkey and Poland, receiving the Order of St. George for bravery in combat. Little wonder that Bibikov, his former commander, should choose him now to lift the siege of Ufa. Since the previous November Ufa had been under continuous attack by Zarubin's predominantly Bashkir army. Cold and hunger gripped the inhabitants, whose stores were seriously depleted. Yet Zarubin (like Bolotnikov at Moscow) was unable to impose a total blockade, so that a trickle of supplies continued to flow into the city. The defenders, fearing a massacre by the tribesmen, were determined to hold out at all costs, and repeated rebel attacks were thrown back with heavy losses. Quarreling broke out between the Bashkirs and the Russians in Zarubin's camp, and energies were further squandered in raids on factories and estates, so that by mid-March, when Mikhelson's crack carbine regiment arrived in the area, the insurgents were tired and discouraged. Still, they outnumbered their opponents by more than ten to one; and the tribesmen were fighting on native territory which they were loath to surrender to the invaders. On March 24, under cover of darkness, Mikhelson mounted a swift attack, with his troops on skis to increase their mobility. Once again training and equipment told heavily against the rebels, who offered fierce resistance before being dispersed. Many of the Bashkirs refused to be taken alive, and hundreds were left dead in the snow, while Mikhelson, if government figures are to be credited, had only twenty-three killed and thirty-two wounded.

While Mikhelson was liberating Ufa, a large army under Generals Golitsyn, Mansurov, and Freiman converged on Orenburg to lift the six-month siege, of which Pugachev himself was in charge. Here again the rebels, though superior in numbers, were vastly outdistanced in arms and discipline. Of their 9000 adherents fewer than a third were Cossacks, the rest being a disparate assortment of Bashkirs, Tatars, Kalmyks, serfs, factory peasants, and vagrants, with an arsenal ranging from axes, stones, and clubs to the latest cannon and carbines. Apprised of the government's strength, Pugachev moved his motley forces to Fort Tatishchev, the scene of his first major victory a half year before. It was here that he made his stand. Using an old technique, the defenders piled snow around the fort, over which they poured water to form a solid barrier of ice. The device, however, was outdated. On March 22 the generals brought up their heavy artillery and, in a three-hour bombardment, reduced the defenses to rubble. When the barrage ended, infantry rushed in from three sides and overwhelmed all resistance. More than 2000 rebels were killed—their corpses littered the fort and the surrounding roads and woods—and all their cannon were taken. By comparison the government's losses (150 dead and 500 wounded) were trivial. The site of Pugachev's initial triumph became the site of his first shattering defeat, after which, as always, support quickly evaporated.

But the pretender was still at large. Retreating to Berda, he tried desperately to regroup his forces. But his camp was buzzing with intrigue, and, fearing betrayal, he collected what followers he could and raced through Kargala (his "St. Petersburg"), then on to Sakmarsk (his "Kiev"), where disaster overtook him. On the night of April 1 General Golitsyn quickly encircled the town, and of the rebel leaders only Pugachev and Ovchinnikov managed to escape, leaving most of their confederates—Khlopusha, Shigaev, Pochitalin, Gorshkov, Padurov, Miasnikov—in Golitsyn's hands. (Zarubin had already been captured at Ufa.) All told, nearly 3000 were taken prisoner. Pugachev, fleeing northward into Bashkiria with a remnant of his once-powerful army, became the object of a determined manhunt that kept him in hiding for several weeks.

Ovchinnikov, with a small party of Cossacks, rode west to Yaitsk, the sole remaining rebel stronghold. The Cossack capital, where the revolt had originated, was the last town to be relieved.

On April 15, when General Mansurov arrived, Ovchinnikov was already there, but his tired followers, outnumbered and out-gunned, were quickly dispersed. The next morning Mansurov entered the town in triumph, amid cries of joy from the ex-hausted and half-starved garrison, whose commander, Colonel Simonov, received an estate with 600 serfs from a grateful empress.

In the end, none of the major administrative centers of the Urals was taken, with the sole exception of Cheliabinsk, and then only briefly. Orenburg, Ufa, Kungur, Ekaterinburg, and the Yaitsk citadel all held out until government relief arrived. Similarly, during the coming summer, rebel forces entering the towns of the Volga would be quickly put to flight. Why did Pugachev fail where his predecessors had succeeded? Why did his revolt fail to take root in the towns, where Bolotnikov and Razin (though not Bulavin) had found so much of their support? Lack of organiza-tion and discipline—internal discord, national antagonisms be-tween Russians and Bashkirs, the dispersal of forces over a wide territory, the waste of energy in raiding and plunder—undoubt-edly played a part. But more important than the weaknesses of the rebels were the strengths of their opponents. Both economi-cally and politically the towns were more developed and less given to popular disturbances than in the past century. The im-proved quality of troops and equipment was another critical factor. Thus the government, for all its inefficiency, proved more than a match for the destructive whirlwind from the southeastern frontier.

In Moscow and Petersburg it was widely believed that the re-bellion was over. The pretender's army was smashed, his support vanishing, his confederates captured, his movement in disarray. In March 1774 Bibikov could report that the rebels had "been defeated, and hour by hour we are approaching peace and tran-quillity." [61] But Bibikov did not live to see his victory consum-mated. Toward the end of March, while his troops were dispers-ing the remaining rebel concentrations, he suddenly fell ill at his field headquarters, between Kazan and Orenburg. Doctors sent from Moscow arrived too late, and on April 9, at the brink of success, he died. Bibikov "came to get the sovereign, but seeing him face to face took fright, and from a button of his coat drank a powerful poison and died." Such was the interpretation of a

Urals workman, to whom no boyar malefactor could be a match for the true emperor. Bibikov, at any rate, died before his work was finished; and his death, the British ambassador feared, could "give new courage to the insurgents." [62] The rebel movement, though damaged, was not completely broken, while the government's drive was interrupted, allowing Pugachev a much-needed respite during which, deep in the hills of Bashkiria, he could begin to raise a new army. The first act of the rebellion was over. But a second and more formidable act was soon to begin.

5. Kazan

On May 1, 1774, Bibikov's second in command, General Fyodor Shcherbatov, was appointed to succeed him. Shcherbatov, though an experienced officer and a veteran of Zorndorf and Bender, was a disappointment compared with his predecessor. He had little of Bibikov's imagination or ability to command devotion. His gravest defect was a quarrelsome nature which embroiled him in continual disputes with his subordinates, who on the whole were a capable lot with whom Bibikov had maintained smooth relations. During the spring and summer, owing partly to Shcherbatov's limitations, the rebellion again flared out of control, and more than six months were to elapse before it was finally extinguished.

Pugachev, meanwhile, his army dispersed and his "War College" in prison, had taken refuge in the hills of Bashkiria where, after lying low for most of April, he began to collect a new following. After their defeat at Yaitsk, Ovchinnikov and Beloborodov came to join him, and by the middle of May they had gathered nearly 8000 recruits. The rebels, in the words of a Swiss journal, had been "reborn from their own ashes." [63] Husbanding his strength, Pugachev shook off pursuing detachments and avoided pitched battles. He fought only when forced to fight. He was constantly on the move, sweeping through villages, factories, and stockades, carrying out hit-and-run raids and gathering men and equipment. Shcherbatov and his officers seldom knew his exact whereabouts. Mobility was his chief strength, enabling him to appear quite suddenly where least expected, attack his target by surprise, and withdraw as quickly as he had come. His adherents, largely Bashkirs from the surrounding area, could make their way through mountains and valleys impenetrable to regular government formations, with their cumbersome weapons and supply trains.

Yet, for all Pugachev's evasiveness, his pursuers were never far behind. On May 21 Dekolong and Gagrin surprised the rebels in their camp, groggy with drink like Razin's Cossacks at Resht, and cut them to pieces. Pugachev managed to escape, only to run headlong into Mikhelson, who inflicted heavy casualties and seized the bulk of his munitions. But the impostor again got away and soon drew a fresh batch of recruits. Word of his reappearance had meanwhile swept through the Urals and western Siberia. "'Under Pugachev,'" declared a convict in Omsk prison, "salt is sold for twenty copecks and wine for a ruble a bucket. Maybe this will happen in Omsk if we live to see the day when Pugachev comes here to the fortress." [64] Whereupon he was hanged on Dekolong's orders for spreading malicious rumors.

Even more than before, Pugachev relied on the Bashkirs and the factory peasants as his chief source of volunteers. The government made every effort to stem the flow from these groups into the rebel ranks. Shcherbatov, for instance, sent emissaries to the Bashkir elders with a promise of subsidies if they shunned the revolt; and more than a few, fearing class war within their tribe, now broke with Pugachev just as the service gentry had broken with Bolotnikov and the Cossack oligarchy with Razin. When persuasion failed, the tribesmen were threatened with violence. "I will execute you, hang you by the legs and ribs, burn your homes, your property, your grain and hay, and destroy your cattle," declared one of Shcherbatov's officers. "Do you hear me? If you do, then take care, for I am not in the habit of lying or joking." Such language, however, merely strengthened their will to resist. Nor was the Holy Synod's denunciation of Pugachev as "the disciple of Antichrist Mahomet" calculated to win their allegiance.[65]

During the spring of 1774 the Bashkirs attacked Russian villages and factories with unprecedented fury. On May 26, according to a government report, the huge Avziano-Petrovsk metal works was "reduced to ashes" by raiding tribesmen. At another large enterprise, the foundries, the office, the church, the dwellings—"everything was burned down," noted an eyewitness.[66] The extent of the damage was enormous. Of some 120 Urals factories, at least 90 were forced to stop production at some point during the rebellion, 74 were attacked and plundered, and 56 were occupied by rebel detachments. All told, more than half were destroyed or seriously damaged. For several months production was at a near standstill, and it took the rest of the decade for output to reach former levels. The raids, moreover, unleashed a mass exodus of ascribed peasants, most of whom returned to their villages, so that by the end of the rising only half the workers were still on the job.[67]

At the same time resistance to the raiders was often quite fierce, particularly in the larger factories equipped with garrisons, watchtowers, and artillery. Nor was it only the soldiers and administrators who fought against the rebels. Skilled artisans and year-round workmen, for whom the factory was the sole means of existence, often aligned themselves with the defenders. As the number of raids increased, more and more workers complained that the Bashkirs were threatening them with ruin. And as national antagonisms sharpened, a growing number of ascribed peasants began to side with their fellow Russians against the "heathens." But in most cases they either fled to their villages or joined in the plunder and destruction, and at one factory they warned a supervisor against resisting "while your belly is still in one piece." [68]

The previous fall and winter there had been comparatively little destruction, for Pugachev's lieutenants had been able to restrain their tribal adherents. But the situation had changed. Zarubin had been captured and Pugachev severely trounced. For the Bashkirs it was now or never. They were determined once and for all to remove the monuments of colonialism from their midst: "'Go home! Your time is done! Our fathers who gave you land are dead, and we will suffer you no longer." [69] By now, moreover, Pugachev's own position had changed. He no longer wished to restrain them. On the contrary, he himself ordered the factories destroyed and personally led raiding parties against them. There were several reasons for this shift. In the first place he wanted to placate the Bashkirs, his mainstay of support, whom he in any case could no longer control. A second motive, as Roger Portal has suggested, was sheer military necessity: the factories, having been reoccupied by the government, were no longer sources of munitions, but were enemy strongpoints which had to be destroyed by lightning raids.[70] Finally, Pugachev no longer needed them, for he had decided to abandon the Urals and strike at the heart of the empire.

In June 1774 the rebellion took an ominous turn. Where before it had been confined to the peripheries beyond the Volga and Kama, now came the alarming news that Pugachev was marching westward toward the central core of Muscovy. "Instead of being crushed, he is become more formidable than ever," reported Sir Robert Gunning to the foreign secretary. "This rebel spreads terror and devastation wherever he turns; and according to the last accounts seems inclined to correct his first error, and march towards Casan and Moscow, that is to say, into the heart of the empire; where it is much feared that he will find a great number of discontented persons." [71] This was indeed his intention. He would march on Kazan, he told his confederates, "and after taking it go to Moscow and then to Petersburg and conquer the whole state." Before him rode his couriers with their leaflets and manifestoes, and ascribed peasants, returning to their native districts, spread the news of his coming. The peasants of the Volga and Kama, astir with promises of freedom, suspension of taxes, and relief from compulsory military service, awaited their savior with eager anticipation. Some, unable to wait, sent deputies to the insurgents with a plea to come at once and deliver them from their masters. Disturbed by these reports, Catherine ordered her governors not to exact unusual work from their peasants or provoke them in any way, but rather to remove the causes of unrest and restore "peace and quiet" to their provinces.[72] But her celebrated favorite, Grigori Potemkin, sounded a less conciliatory note. Incensed by Pugachev's promise to abolish taxation and recruitment, he firmly defended the existing system: "Who will guard the borders of our state when there are no soldiers? And there will be no soldiers without recruiting. How will the soldiers be maintained without the soul tax? Where would the Turks have got to by now if Russia had no troops?" In the same vein he denounced Pugachev's egalitarian pretensions and his war on landlords and bureaucrats: "Try to imagine who would administer the towns and villages if we had no officials. Who would judge in court, restrain wickedness and injustice, and ward off the oppressor if there were no legal authorities? And who would command the armed forces if there were no distinctions of rank? How patently absurd are the malicious delusions of Emelka Pugachev!" [73]

Yet precisely such "delusions" had inspired a mass movement which pointed directly at Moscow. On June 21 the rebels occupied Osa, a small town on the Kama River southwest of Kungur. Behind them forts, factories, and estates lay in ruins, the countryside was ravaged, and Russian settlements were in embers from Bashkir assaults. Osa put up a determined struggle, pouring a hail of missiles and boiling oil upon the attackers, but when Pugachev prepared to set the walls alight, the townsmen decided to surrender. The pretender entered in triumph. In a scene repeated elsewhere, an old soldier who claimed he had once seen Peter III came forward and confirmed that Pugachev was the emperor. But though the town had capitulated, Pugachev ordered it burned anyway, a sign of things to come.

It was early July when the rebels, some 7000 strong, forded the Kama and advanced on Kazan. Kazan was the chief administrative and commercial center of the middle Volga region and the gateway to central Muscovy. Yet it was ill-prepared for an attack. The inhabitants, wrote General Pavel Potemkin (a cousin of Catherine's favorite), who was in charge of defending the city, were in "great desperation and terror," and many had fled to points west.[74] Pugachev's sudden move against Osa had taken Shcherbatov unawares. Most of his troops were still hunting the rebels in the remote Bashkiria highlands, and frantic calls were issued for reinforcements, but they arrived too late. Meanwhile, to bolster the garrison at Kazan, which contained only 700 regulars, ordinary civilians, including students of the local gymnasium, were mobilized and armed. But they were of little use against Pugachev's savage followers, and on July 12, when the attack began, they hastily retired to the citadel.

The outer city was quickly overrun and given up to pillage and destruction. The streets swarmed with insurgents who moved from house to house laden with stolen goods. The prison was thrown open, reuniting Pugachev with his wife and three children, though at first he refused to recognize them, insisting they were the family of an ordinary Don Cossack of his acquaintance. Also liberated was the Old Believer Abbot Filaret, who had set the impostor on his rebellious path and had afterward been arrested. Buildings, once ransacked, were burned. The wooden structures went up like tinder. Fires blazed out of control in every part of the city. On the main street, according to a local merchant, "not a post was left standing." [75] Of 2873 houses in the city, only 810 survived the holocaust. Twenty-five churches and three monasteries were stripped of their valuables (largely by Bashkirs and other tribesmen) and gutted. Townsmen without beards or in "German" clothing were set upon and beaten or killed. In a single day of violence Kazan lost 162 dead, 129 wounded, and 468 missing without a trace. Survivors recalled the scene with horror for many years to come.

Pugachev meanwhile trained his guns on the citadel and launched a continuous bombardment, which took a heavy toll. As casualties mounted, more and more defenders wanted to surrender, and Potemkin hanged two of his men as an example to the rest. "The greatest misfortune," he wrote on the day of the attack, "is that the people are not trustworthy." [76] The whole province, he said, was ready to revolt. But help was on the way. Mikhelson, after a forced march from the Urals, arrived the next day, July 13, and though his men were tired and woefully outnumbered, he immediately formed them in columns and charged the rebel positions. "The scoundrels greeted me with a great shout and with such a hail of fire as I, who have fought against many different opponents, seldom have seen and from such barbarians did not expect," he wrote.[77] By nightfall, however, the rebels were compelled to withdraw, leaving 800 dead and an equal number of prisoners.

Three times Pugachev regrouped his forces and returned to the fight, but each assault was driven back with heavy losses of men and equipment. The final encounter lasted several hours, and the pretender, sacrificing 3000 followers and all his artillery, barely managed to escape, fleeing across the Volga with Mikhelson in pursuit. Kazan was liberated. The rebels were again dispersed; and though Pugachev had slipped away, Beloborodov, having found refuge in a nearby forest, rashly returned to the city, where he was recognized and arrested.

With the sacking of Kazan panic seized the residents of Moscow. The upper classes feared that Pugachev, having reduced Kazan to a heap of blazing ruins, would now make directly for the heartland. St. Petersburg too was alarmed, so much so that the court even considered retreating to Riga. According to a contemporary, "a panic seized half the country; and the same spirit of sedition which animated Pugatcheff had infected the rest." [78] For the moment, however, it was Moscow, where lower-class discontent had been dramatically revealed during an outbreak of cholera in 1771, that experienced the greatest terror. The geographical heart of the empire and the bastion of serfdom, the old capital remained the chief target of mass revolts long after Petersburg had replaced it as the official seat of government. A sprawling congeries of gentry residences, markets, shops, and hovels of the poor, it was densely populated with household serfs and peasant laborers whose sympathies were overwhelmingly with the pretender. Each week saw hundreds arrested, some merely for drinking to Pugachev's health, so that the prisons were crammed with "seditious people." [79] Records of the secret police reveal that throughout the surrounding countryside the peasants were ready to rise for the "third emperor." "Praise God, we shall not have to live for our masters much longer," a villager declared, "for now Peter Fyodorovich is coming to us and he will ascribe all the peasants as his own and hang the nobles. He is the true tsar." [80]

Given such expectations, it is small wonder that Moscow was gripped by panic. It was a moment of immense danger and terrifying suspense. If Pugachev could arouse the central provinces, the classical region of serfdom, the whole existing order might collapse. Would he try to make for Moscow? Would he touch off a general rising of the serfs against their masters? Such questions, arising at the climax of the Turkish War, provoked great interest all over Europe, where the revolt was widely reported in the press. In fact word of the *Pugachevshchina* spread as far afield as the New World, where it was carried in the *Virginia Gazette* in the summer of 1774. The interest displayed abroad encouraged a tendency among Russian officials to see the revolt as a plot hatched by hostile foreign powers: some thought Pugachev an agent of the Polish Confederation, others of the Turks or the French or the Swedes. But no evidence has come to light of any foreign complicity, though the Swedish king wryly remarked that Catherine had cause to be grateful that he did not conclude an alliance with the pretender. The Secret Commission in Kazan, charged with examining the causes of the revolt, made a thorough investigation and concluded that Pugachev had received "neither outside guidance nor assistance" but had been backed only by the "ignorance of the people of this land, their simplicity and gullibility." [81]

One question was on everyone's lips: Would Pugachev, having crossed the Volga, now head his movement toward Moscow? Nervous officials in the former capital could already scent the smoke of burning manor houses. Yet had they recalled the history of past rebellions they might have been less pessimistic. For Razin and Bulavin had faced a similar decision and both had opted to remain in the peripheries lest, like Antaeus, they should lose their strength if cut off from their native soil. The government might have taken comfort from this fact. Indeed, for Pugachev there was even greater reason to avoid the central districts. For the second time in less than six months his army had been defeated, whereas Moscow was strongly defended and expecting reinforcements at any moment. Furthermore, Mikhelson had swept around his flank to cut off any attempted drive into the heartland. Thus Pugachev chose to follow the example of his predecessors. For a few days he clung to the west bank of the Volga, heading upstream in the direction of Moscow; but at the town of Kurmysh he turned abruptly southward in hopes of igniting the Volga valley as Razin had done before him. Should he suffer defeat, however, he would hold to his course and, as he had planned the previous autumn, lead his followers to safety in the south.

6. The Volga

During the summer of 1774 an immense jacquerie broke out along the western bank of the Volga, marking the climax of the rebellion. Though defeated at Kazan, the movement had not been broken. In fact, as the pretender moved down the Volga, he touched off new outbreaks on a greater scale than ever. "Pugachev was fleeing," noted Pushkin, "but his flight seemed an invasion." [82] For as he fled he scattered the sparks of sedition in all directions, and for two months insurrection engulfed the Volga valley from Nizhni to Tsaritsyn, from Simbirsk to Tambov, the same peasant and tribal districts which had rallied to Razin a century before. "The damned owl frightened Kazan on July 12," wrote the archimandrite of Our Savior of Kazan Cathedral, "and though his wings are damaged, it is evident that his bats are flying all over the outskirts, barring all the roads, so that during this month there have been neither couriers nor post from or to Kazan." [83]

The months of July and August were the high-water mark of the rebellion. A vast stretch of territory—Kazan, Nizhni Novgorod. Arzamas, Alatyr, Sviiazhsk, Simbirsk, Penza, Shatsk, Saransk, Tambov, Voronezh—became the scene of savage violence encompassing more than three million people, or nearly an eighth of the population of the empire. It was the third time in nine months that revolt had flared up over a broad area. But now its social composition was somewhat altered. As the scene shifted from the Urals to the Volga, so too did the base of rebel support, with a sharp increase in numbers but a decline in military efficiency and in the degree of control imposed from above. In place of Cossack and Bashkir horsemen and Urals gunsmiths it was peasants and agricultural tribesmen who filled the rebel battalions. The largest group were serfs from private estates, who rose on a scale and with a fury unmatched in rebellions of the past.

Why were they so ripe for revolt? The answer is not far to seek. The reign of Catherine marked the golden age of the Russian nobility and the zenith of Russian serfdom. With their emancipation from compulsory service, many landowners returned to their estates, where they exercised virtually absolute power over their peasants. By Pugachev's time the government had all but ceased to interfere in the nobleman's treatment of his serfs. He could reduce their land allotment, raise their dues and quitrents, increase their labor obligation, and compel them to work in his factories. And his control over their private lives was more complete than ever. He might seize their property, interfere with their marriages, convert them into domestic servants, or sell them apart from the land and even from their wives and children. The trade in peasants reached a peak during Catherine's reign, breaking up families and immeasurably increasing frustration and despair. The empress herself, by giving away hundreds of thousands of crown peasants—many of them in provinces to be affected by Pugachev's revolt—transformed them overnight into private serfs at their master's beck and call. The lord, moreover, exercised manorial justice. He could have a peasant beaten or put in chains. He could send him to prison or into the army or to Siberia—and at government expense. Finally, he might emancipate—that is, cast off—old or infirm serfs who were no longer useful as servants or field hands. By the 1770s, in short, the serf had become a mere chattel at his owner's disposal. As a leading authority on the Russian peasant has noted, "the landlord ruled a little monarchy within the great one." [84]

Against the arbitrary powers of his owner, the serf had no legal redress, which goes a long way to account for the frequency of flight and rebellion in the seventeenth and eighteenth centuries. He was forever at the mercy of his master's moods and appetites. Nor did the state intervene to protect him. During Catherine's long reign only twenty cases are on record where landlords were punished for mistreating their serfs. In August 1767, as we have seen, Catherine went so far as to forbid complaints against masters on penalty of the knout and of banishment to hard labor in Siberia. Some lords, no doubt, dealt humanely with their peasants, looking after them in times of hardship and famine, but unbridled power is not conducive to humanitarian behavior; rather, it tends to bring out the worst in men, corrupting even the most enlightened, so that brutality and exploitation remained constant features of the master–serf relationship.

During Catherine's reign, moreover, the economic position of most serfs deteriorated. In some provinces the average quitrent (*obrok*) more than tripled, while on estates where servile labor (*barshchina*) was performed the accepted standard of two or three

days a week was increasingly ignored, and some landowners required their serfs to work continuously until the harvest had been
gathered and prepared for market. As the demand for grain
increased both at home and abroad, driving prices steadily higher,
more and more proprietors switched from *obrok* to *barshchina*
in order to raise their output. For the peasant this represented
another serious setback, entailing as it did closer supervision by
his owner and less freedom in managing his own affairs. Like the
conversion of state peasants to serfs, it meant a sudden reverse
in terms of autonomy and status as well as economic position,
and it is significant that some of the worst rioting of Pugachev's
revolt occurred in districts where *barshchina* was emerging as the
dominant form of obligation.[85]

At bottom, then, the grievances of the peasantry were as much
a matter of status as of economic oppression. Their aspirations
were essentially the same as those of other disaffected groups who
flocked to Pugachev's banner. Like the Cossacks and schismatics,
the Bashkirs and ascribed workers, they yearned to recover the
traditional "liberties" of which the gentry and the state had
deprived them. As they saw it, the emancipation of the nobility
by Peter III had overturned the only legitimate foundation on
which serfdom had rested, as part of the overall system in which
service was required of all segments of the population. With
Peter's manifesto of 1762 the peasants felt that their masters,
being freed from their obligation to the state, had no further
claim to their services; and, as has been seen, rumors became rife
of a second manifesto liberating the serfs from their proprietors.

What the 1762 manifesto inspired, however, was not so
much the desire for absolute freedom as for the relative freedom
of the crown peasantry, a status which some of Pugachev's followers had enjoyed until Catherine transferred them to her favorites. For the private serf the dream of emancipation assumed the
concrete shape of conversion to a state peasant, by which he
would become the property of the sovereign rather than of the
noble. Nor was Pugachev blind to this aspiration. As he moved
down the Volga he issued a flood of proclamations releasing the
serfs from their masters and converting them into crown peasants. More than that, he promised them free use of the land and
unrestricted personal liberty, as well as free distribution of salt

and exemption from taxes and recruitment. Catherine dismissed this propaganda as "essentially that of simple Cossacks." [86] But this was precisely what made it so effective. For it told the people what they wanted to hear, and in terms they could understand. The manifestoes, wrote Pushkin in *The Captain's Daughter*, a novel based on the Pugachev revolt, were written "in crude but forceful language, and must have produced a strong impression upon the minds of the simple people." Catherine, steeped in Western culture, could not appreciate that other world of folk eloquence embodied in Pugachev's appeals.

The most striking of these manifestoes, issued in July 1774, deserves to be quoted at length:

> By this decree, with sovereign and paternal mercy, we grant to all hitherto in serfdom and subjection to the landowners the right to be faithful subjects of our crown, and we award them the villages, the old cross and prayers, heads and beards, liberty and freedom, always to be Cossacks, without recruiting levies, soul tax or other money taxes, with possession of the land, the woods, the hay meadows, the fishing grounds, the salt lakes, without payment or rent, and we free all those peasants and other folk hitherto oppressed by the malefactor gentry and the bribe-takers and judges in the towns from the dues and burdens placed upon them. We wish you the salvation of your souls and a peaceful life here on earth, for we too have tasted and suffered from the malefactor gentry much wandering and hardship. . . . Those who hitherto were gentry in their lands and estates, those opponents of our rule and disturbers of the empire and ruiners of the peasants—seize them, punish them, hang them, treat them in the same way as they, having no Christian feeling, oppressed you, the peasants. With the extermination of these enemies, the malefactor gentry, everyone will be able to enjoy a quiet and peaceful life, which will continue evermore.[87]

This was by far the most extraordinary document to emerge from the rebellion. It expressed in vivid language the essence of Pugachev's program. By canceling taxes and military service, converting private serfs into state peasants, restoring the old faith, and declaring war on bureaucratic despotism, it fulfilled all the popular expectations associated with the late emperor. With strong millenarian overtones it cast the pretender in the role of a messiah who had come to eliminate the oppressors and to restore the ancient bond between the people and their anointed father. Biblical myth was mingled with a pagan demonology in which the nobility formed an alien breed of parasites sucking the blood of the people. Pugachev's was a Manichaean vision which pitted the forces of good, embodied in the common folk, against the forces of evil, embodied in the landlords and officials. And though the tsarist framework was retained, Pugachev himself emerged as the sovereign ruling in the people's interests.

The manifesto had an enormous impact. Up and down the Volga, wrote Derzhavin to Shcherbatov, the peasants "eagerly awaited Peter Fyodorovich on whom they have set all their hopes." According to Frederick the Great, who followed the revolt with keen interest, "the rural population went in crowds to meet Pugachev and greeted him as their savior." The excitement began in advance of his arrival. It was enough to hear that the "third emperor" was on the way to set off a violent reaction. "In their blind ignorance," wrote General Golitsyn, "the common people everywhere greet this infernal monster with exclamations of joy." It was said that he was Stenka Razin come to life again to punish the wicked and liberate the peasants. In Penza province villagers and priests met him with icons and hailed him as their true sovereign: "We never believed he was dead, and here he is alive, and henceforth all will be state, not landlord's, peasants." [88]

Nor was it mere ignorance or superstition that led the peasants to believe in the pretender. They were always inclined to believe what favored their interests and to reject what did not. For them Pugachev was the true tsar whoever he was, as they sometimes put it. And his strength owed much to their conviction that they were rising not only for themselves but for their sovereign, whose manifestoes set the royal stamp of approval on their actions. Captured serfs often claimed innocence of wrongdoing on grounds that "Peter Fyodorovich" had removed them from the jurisdiction of their masters. When they attacked their owners and put them to flight, orders from the tsar had given them legal sanction.

In this connection, the role of the parish priest was of critical importance. As in the risings of Razin and Bulavin, the lower clergy—priests, sextons, monks—participated in large numbers. They greeted the pretender with icons and crosses, conducted services on his behalf, and prayed for his safety and success. All this, of course, strengthened the peasants' conviction that they were fighting for the legitimate sovereign. Indeed, one village priest assured his congregation that "there is no empress, but there is an emperor, Peter III." [89] Nor was he alone in doing so. Whether from sympathy or fear of reprisals, the vast majority of parish priests sided with the pretender, identifying their cause with that of the peasants to whom they ministered. Such was the attitude of two priests in a village near Penza who drank a toast "to the health and success of the former emperor, Peter III." For us common folk, they said, Pugachev is "not a rogue but our friend and protector." [90] Some clergy, however, remained steadfast in their loyalty to the empress. A village priest near Kazan, for example, urged his parishioners "to defend the faith and the fatherland against the insurgents." But the peasants refused to listen. Pugachev, they insisted, was the "real emperor" who had come to free them from their masters and who, so they heard, would pay five rubles to whoever served him—whereupon they drove the priest from the village.[91] Recalcitrant clergymen were sometimes the victims of rebel violence. During the course of the rising more than 200 priests and their wives were killed, and 63 churches and 14 monasteries were sacked, mostly, however, by marauding Cossacks and vengeful tribesmen rather than local peasants.

The non-Russian peoples of the Volga responded to Pugachev with the same enthusiasm with which they had greeted Stenka Razin a century before. By Catherine's time most of the tribesmen had been baptized and classed as state peasants, and economically they were better off than their Russian counterparts. Yet they continued to harbor strong resentment against the Muscovite intruders, so that when Pugachev arrived with promises of land and liberty and freedom of worship they hailed him as their "own father." [92] A group of Chuvash villagers near Kazan cast their lot with the rebels because their Russian landlord had taken their livestock and compelled them to till his fields as virtual slaves. "Nor are we the only ones to suffer such insults," they said, "but there are many villages that weep because of him." Similarly, Votiak tribesmen testified that they joined because forced baptisms, heavy tribute, and the confiscation of their lands had reduced them to "unbearable exhaustion and privation." [93]

Another group that played an important part in the rebellion were the so-called *odnodvortsy*, or homesteaders, who were especially numerous in the black-soil districts of Tambov and Voronezh, where they constituted a majority of the taxpaying population. As we have seen, several of the pretenders who preceded Pugachev came from the homesteader class, and whenever a would-be messiah appeared in their midst they were eager to respond. The reasons are not hard to discover. Descended of impoverished gentry, *streltsy*, and other petty service men, the homesteaders were relics of the age of Muscovite colonization beyond the Oka River, where they had been settled during the sixteenth and seventeenth centuries for defense against the Kalmyks and Tatars. In return for service, they had received, like the gentry, a plot of land and other privileges, including exemption from taxes and the right to own serfs. Additional homesteaders were settled on the northern Don and Donets by Peter the Great after Bulavin's insurrection in that region. By the end of his reign, however, Peter, hungry for recruits and taxpayers, reclassified them as state peasants, with all the obligations of that group, and ever since, they had been trying unsuccessfully to regain their former status.[94]

The *odnodvortsy*, then, occupied an anomalous position on the social ladder. An in-between class with features of both the peasantry and the lesser nobility, they aspired to the position of the latter while sinking to the level of the former. Like the gentry, they held their own land in return for service, and some continued to own a few serfs, though they were now prohibited by law from purchasing more. But, like the peasantry, they were liable to the poll tax and *obrok* and to regular military service. Caught in a squeeze between the peasantry and the gentry, distrusted by the one and despised by the other, the homesteaders suffered a kind of social schizophrenia from which they desperately tried to escape. Many became Old Believers, in quest of a happier past. Some worked as bailiffs for the nobility, others as merchants in the provincial towns, but the majority carried on their traditional occupations of cattle breeding, sheep herding, and agriculture, while being victimized by their gentry neighbors, who coveted their land and livestock, and who prevented them from entering their ranks. Again and again the homesteaders petitioned Catherine to recognize them as petty noblemen, but their appeals went unanswered. Small wonder, given their blurred identity and uncertain position, that they were susceptible to the blandishments of a pretender. Like the Cossacks and tribesmen, they were victims of an order in which they held no secure place, and they dreamed of a bygone age when they were distinguishable from the common herd of peasants.

Thus Pugachev's following was a varied lot, ranging from serfs and tribesmen to small landholders and petty merchants. What held them together was a common hatred of the nobility and of the existing social order. Whether prosperous or impoverished, all were victims of the so-called aristocratic reaction which followed the emancipation of the gentry from obligatory service. For serfs this had meant closer supervision and heavier exactions, for state peasants the threat of conversion to serfs, for Cossacks and *odnodvortsy* the barring of their ascent to the nobility, for tribesmen further encroachments on their shrinking domains. All had been overtaken by the juggernaut of modernization, by the growth of the centralized state and of a more sophisticated economy of which they were not the beneficiaries. All had suffered a loss of autonomy and status as well as of economic prosperity. And all, as a result, looked back to a lost past which they yearned to recapture.

Pugachev was fully alive to their grievances; indeed, he himself shared them. And in a language they dreamed of hearing he put forward a program which played on each group's aspirations while promising land, liberty, and equality to all. But the aims of his followers were not always egalitarian. Said one captured rebel: "Who Pugachev was did not trouble us, nor did we even care to know. We rose in order to come out on top and take the place of those who had tormented us. We wanted to be masters and to choose our own faith. But we lost. What's to be done? Their luck is our misfortune. Had we won, we would have had our own tsar and occupied whatever rank and station we desired." Another said he knew Pugachev was a simple Cossack but "served him faithfully, hoping that when he conquered the state, he, Ulianov, would become a great man." [95] Such sentiments, however, were strongest among the Cossacks and *odnodvortsy*, whose chief aim was to raise their status. Among the rural and

urban poor, by contrast, social equality remained an instinctive
and deeply rooted virtue.

It was a diverse and loose-knit movement that Pugachev inspired during his five-week sweep down the Volga. From Kazan
to Cherny Yar hundreds of bands sprang up, with little or no
central control, a *"Pugachevshchina* without Pugachev," as several historians have described it. Ranging in size from a handful to
several hundred (twenty or thirty was considered quite large),
they were led by self-styled *"atamans"* or "colonels" who acted
independently but invoked Peter III's name. Some of the leaders
went so far as to call themselves the emperor. In a Penza village,
for instance, "Peter Fyodorovich" was a local peasant named
Ivanov, a fact of which his followers were aware, but so desperately did they crave a deliverer that they "fell on their knees and
swore an oath of loyalty to the sovereign." [96] Little effort was
made by the scattered contingents to consolidate their forces or
to coordinate their operations. Nor did they attempt to secure
a territorial base from which to extend their movement into the
center. The rebellion, rather, remained splintered in hundreds
of local risings in which the overriding object was plunder.
Peasants normally confined their activity to their own villages,
settling old scores with the landlords or bailiffs, but sometimes
they went to the larger towns to join the marauding "Cossacks,"
and in a few cases they were recruited by forced levy into the
roving partisan detachments. In every Volga district granaries
were pillaged, livestock confiscated, timber felled, and manor
houses burned. In the towns treasuries were emptied and the
houses of the wealthy sacked and burned. "You cannot imagine
the intensity with which the whole population of this region are
rebelling," reported one government commander.[97]

Acts of violence occurred on an unparalleled scale. For the
growth of serfdom, now at its apogee, had sharpened class
antagonisms, and hatred of the nobility was never so strong.
Where Bolotnikov, Razin, and Bulavin could invite the gentry to
join them, for Pugachev this was quite unthinkable. His one
conciliatory gesture came at the start of the rebellion when,
surprisingly, he considered compensating landowners for the
seizure of their estates.[98] But such generosity was short-lived. By
the time the revolt reached the Volga, the gateway to peasant

Russia, it had changed to bitter hostility, sending the gentry fleeing from their homes in terror. Besides the development of serfdom, the widening cultural gap between master and serf played
a part, not to mention the traditional hatred of boyars and officials, so that any significant collaboration, as had occurred in the
past, was out of the question. Few nobles, then, could be found
among the insurgents. In one band, captured in September 1774,
only three of a hundred were from the gentry, and even this was
exceptional.[99] Those who did join came mostly from the lower
ranks, and though one can only speculate about their motives,
few if any were prototypes of the "conscience-stricken" noblemen of the following century, moved by compassion for the poor
and by a need for personal repentance. On the contrary, some
were clearly tempted by material gain, some (like the villain of
The Captain's Daughter) were paying off private grudges, while
others served under duress: Ensign Mikhail Shvanovich, a captured grenadier who drafted a letter in German to the governor
of Orenburg, apparently did so to save his own neck.[100]

Pugachev's own hatred of the gentry was unbridled. As he
moved down the Volga he issued numerous appeals to exterminate the landlords, which helps account for the violence committed against them. His famous July manifesto called on the
peasants to "seize them, punish them, hang them, treat them in the
same way as they, having no Christian feeling, oppressed you."
Bounties were promised for their scalps, and serfs were told to
"take their homes and estates as your reward." [101] Thus, with the
"emperor's" seal of approval, a great manhunt took place, and
gentry blood was spilled as never before. Landlords and their
families were tortured, strangled, drowned, impaled, set aflame,
beaten to death, or conveyed to rebel headquarters for execution
by hanging. In the towns of the Volga hundreds of officers and
bureaucrats were seized and executed. Occasionally Pugachev
himself held court, sitting on a portable throne guarded by
Cossacks with axes. All told, several thousand landlords, officials,
merchants, and priests lost their lives during the terrible summer
of 1774. The figures given by General P. I. Panin were 1572
gentry (including many wives and children), 1037 officers and
officials, and 237 clergymen. Other sources reckoned the total
at 2791, among them a scattering of peasants who were com-

paratively well off or who were loyal to their masters, though
such cases were not numerous. None of the available estimates
is complete, however, and the actual figure probably exceeded
3000. Startling though this is, during the same period, according
to Panin, 10,000 rebels were killed and almost as many captured.[102]

What stands out regarding the gentry victims is that most of
them were small landholders. Of the 392 estates attacked in
Voronezh province (which included the large districts of Tambov
and Shatsk) more than half had less than 50 male serfs; and,
even more significant, of the 54 proprietors who were killed only
three owned more than 100 serfs.[103] This was partly because the
larger estates were better defended—in some cases even with
light artillery—and partly because their owners were often ab-
sentees who lived in the cities or on other estates in the central
provinces which the rebellion failed to reach. Another reason was
simply that the number of small estates in the Volga region, indeed
throughout the country, was very large. The majority of landowners in Penza province, for instance, owned fewer than 20
male serfs, and a third of all the proprietors of European Russia
as a whole had no more than half that number.[104] But the character of the petty nobility also played a part. Like their counterparts in France, the so-called sparrow hawks, they were usually
more grasping and made heavier demands on their peasants than
the larger proprietors. This was especially true in the black-soil
districts, where the small landlords were heavily in debt and where
barshchina was emerging as the chief peasant obligation. For all
these reasons the minor nobility became the objects of the
strongest animosity and the most horrifying acts of revenge.

In its cyclonic fury the *Pugachevshchina* surpassed the most
terrible scenes of Razin's revolt a century before. "Everyone was
gripped with fear," wrote an eyewitness. "Death hung contin-
ually over the heads of the landowners. All of them fled their
estates, and the estates were laid waste." [105] The worst violence
occurred in such areas as Alatyr, Saransk, Penza, Tambov, and
Kerensk, where memories of Razin were still alive. In these
districts, observed General Golitsyn, the destruction was immense
and a "large number of gentry perished." Another officer reported seeing "countless bodies" everywhere—hanged, decapitated, mutilated.[106] In Penza province alone there were 600 vic-

tims, while more than 300 were massacred in Saransk. On July 27 a rebel mob attacked the provincial seat of Saransk and in a drunken spree—alcohol often magnified the violence—hanged the town's leading aristrocrat, a retired general named Sipiagin, along with 62 others. In the province of Alatyr a resourceful officer was able to save a few lives only by telling the peasants that it was forbidden to kill their masters themselves but that they should bring them into town, where Pugachev would pay them ten rubles for each male and five for each female. Since the pretender was indeed known to offer such bounties, this advice was accepted, giving some of the landlords a chance to flee. Elsewhere local peasants and tribesmen used the opportunity to settle old accounts, however petty, with the most brutal methods. In one town, for instance, a rebel party invaded a government distillery and hanged its manager on the complaint of local Mordva that he had refused to pay for wood which they had delivered. After consuming a quantity of wine the raiders proceeded to slaughter three more employees, an example of how alcohol increased the violence.

Apart from the killing, the plunder and destruction of property were more extensive than ever. Whole herds of cattle were seized or driven off, stores of grain confiscated, and money, clothing, and valuables taken in large quantities. At one estate the peasants unearthed a cache of 10,000 rubles, which they divided in equal shares. But manor houses were attacked for more than booty. Title deeds, account books, and tax rolls went up in smoke, and gentry factories were torn down with the same destructive passion with which the Bashkirs had wrecked the enterprises of the Urals. The smashing of dishes, porcelain, and statuary, moreover, bespoke not only the rage of the peasants but their determination to drive their oppressors from their lives with all their alien works.

Unfortunately for the victims, there were few government troops to stop the devastation and slaughter. And those who were available often were local tribesmen or state peasants of poor quality and dubious loyalty. In only a few districts, such as Shatsk, for example, were self-defense units formed, with gentry or Tatar *murzy* as cavalry and their peasants as infantry armed with axes and pikes. Most landowners fled to the towns, spreading panic with tales of the horrors they had witnessed. In Saransk, a

province which experienced heavy destruction, "not one nobleman thought of self-defense," complained Mikhelson, "but all
of them scattered like sheep into the woods." [107] Many were
afraid to arm their serfs, warning that it was a dangerous practice which might backfire. "They will be the first to go over,"
wrote Andrei Bolotov, "and turn their weapons against us." The
whole nobility was gripped with terror: "Thoughts about Pugachev never left our heads, and we were all convinced that all the
vulgar rabble, and especially our own bondsmen and servants,
secretly sympathized with the scoundrel and in their hearts were
all in revolt and ready at the tiniest spark to burst into flames." [108]
The rebels showed no mercy for peasants who aided their master. They threatened to impale even those who continued to pay
him dues or till his fields, let alone take up arms in his defense.
Following a raid on his estate, one landowner lamented that he
had lost not only his family and possessions but all his peasants
who showed him the least compassion.[109]

Yet some humane landlords were protected by their serfs, the
Radishchev estate near Penza being a case in point. Though Alexander Radishchev, the "Russian *philosophe*" whom Catherine was
to banish to Siberia for favoring the abolition of serfdom, was
away at the time, the serfs concealed his father in the woods and
disguised his younger brothers and sisters as peasant children
until the danger had passed. But few families were so fortunate.
Landlords found on their estates, however well liked by their
serfs, were seldom spared. "I cannot adequately express to your
excellency," wrote Mikhelson to General Panin, "how much
hatred lies rooted in the hearts of these people. All the barbarities
in these villages against the gentry and other worthy men have
been committed with the aid of the peasants, who try by every
means to catch the masters and bailiffs hiding in the forests and
to convey them to Pugachev to be hanged." [110] More typical
than the case of the Radishchevs was that of the Mertvago family
of Alatyr province, one of whom, a boy of fourteen, survived
to describe the nightmare he experienced. In July 1774 the peasants of the district, aroused by news of Pugachev's coming, went
on a rampage of burning and looting and hanged the bailiff of
an adjoining estate. Fleeing to the woods, the Mertvagos sent
a servant to the village for supplies, which only brought a posse

in pursuit. Shouts of hostile voices and the whistling of bullets sent the family scurrying for safety. The boy, separated from the rest, lay silent, terrified, till finally caught by a peasant. He promised a reward for his release when order should be restored. "Liar!" the peasant snarled. "That will never be—your time is past." Brought to Alatyr, he was rescued from death by the arrival of government forces. Though reunited with his mother, brothers, and sisters, he learned that his father had been overtaken in the forest and hanged. A similar account was left by a German tutor on a large estate near Arzamas: murder of a neighboring landowner with his wife and daughter, headlong flight into the forest, terror, near capture, and ultimate rescue.[111]

While similar scenes were being repeated up and down the Volga valley, Pugachev continued on his southerly trek, encountering few government troops and little resistance from the local populace. Everywhere he went he received the same enthusiastic reception. Innumerable processions greeted him with bread and salt, icons and crosses, and the jubilant clanging of church bells. Most of the larger towns opened their gates at his approach and surrendered without a struggle. Those that chose to resist—and even some that did not—were given over to plunder. Jails were thrown open, treasuries pillaged, officials hanged, houses ransacked, warehouses emptied, and wine and salt distributed free to the poor. As he went from town to town Pugachev gathered adherents. His own detachment, which numbered 800 at Saransk, swelled to 2000 at Penza and more than 4000 at Saratov, where he rejoined the path of the river. In the meantime, his agents fanned out toward the central provinces in an effort to extend the rebellion. In the district of Kaluga, not far from Moscow, the gentry were put on the alert against possible outbreaks. Serpukhov and Kolomna redoubled their watch for rebel agitators, and roadblocks were set up throughout the area at which all strangers and transients, all "lower types of men" and all "who shout and sing songs," were stopped for questioning. At the same time Catherine ordered 70,000 rifles from the factories at Tula to keep the gunsmiths busy so that "for four years or more they will not raise a rumpus."[112]

Penza and Saratov were the last major towns that Pugachev entered unopposed. For lack of adequate defenses and fear of

their lives and possessions the merchants at both places decided
not to resist. Some, in fact, especially those who were of Old
Believer or *odnodvortsy* background, gave the rebels a warm
reception. At Penza a lavish banquet was held in Pugachev's
honor, attended by many merchants and town officials, including
the mayor. Those who refused to cooperate met a violent end.
A dozen loyal noblemen and the military commander barricaded
themselves in the latter's house but were smoked out and executed. In Saratov a bitter dispute broke out over whether to
resist or surrender. The town had been largely destroyed in a
fire a few months before, leaving the inhabitants virtually defenseless. The argument, at any rate, ended abruptly with the
first rebel volley. On August 6 the gates were thrown open and
there began a three-day orgy of drinking and looting in which
an enormous treasury was seized, as well as large stores of flour
and oats, much of which was distributed free to the lower classes.

It was at Saratov that Pugachev publicly recognized his first
wife, a sign that, for all his success on the Volga, the pretender's
powers were waning. In just a few days, in fact, catastrophe
would overtake him. Meanwhile, however, at Dmitrievsk na
Kamyshinke, which he occupied on August 11, a small incident
occurred which typified the nature of the rebellion. Pugachev
learned that a member of the Imperial Academy of Sciences, an
astronomer named Löwitz, was taking levels nearby for the projected canal between the Volga and the Don which Peter the
Great had begun earlier in the century. Unfortunately for Löwitz, a scientist from St. Petersburg with a German name, he
represented everything the rebels loathed and distrusted. Pugachev had him brought before him and, informed that he was an
astronomer, ordered his men to lift him up on their pikes "in
order that he may be nearer the stars," in which position he was
cut to pieces.[113] Soon afterward the insurgents raided a neighboring colony of German settlers, whose presence the local peasantry had resented ever since Catherine invited them into the
area.[114] This, however, was Pugachev's last successful venture.
When he reached Tsaritsyn and the portage to the Don, his days
were already numbered. The final act of the rising was about to
begin.

7. Defeat

As he neared his home territory, Pugachev's hopes of winning the support of his fellow Don Cossacks, as Razin and Bulavin had done, ran high. From Dmitrievsk he ordered three detachments to sweep down the Medveditsa, the Ilovlia, and the Khoper, the main tributaries of the upper Don, in an effort to ignite the area, while the bulk of his army continued down the Volga toward Tsaritsyn. At the same time he appealed to the Don Cossacks to join his movement, promising to eliminate "German" customs and to restore their autonomy, subsidies, and old ritual. In a few upstream settlements his emissaries were met "not only with bread and salt but also with flags." [115] But the participation of the Host failed to materialize. In the first place, peace with Turkey was concluded on July 10, and seasoned regiments—one of them led by Colonel Ilya Denisov, who during the Seven Years' War had had Pugachev flogged for losing his horse— were rushed to the Don to form a barrier against the rebels. Furthermore, owing to bad harvests and to the demands of the war, food on the Don was extremely scarce, and the Cossacks were reluctant to share what little they had with the insurgents. But the underlying reason was a transformation in the character of the Host. Over the past century, although divisions between the oligarchy and the rank and file persisted, the Don community had gradually evolved from its former turbulence to a more settled life with substantial agricultural and commercial interests. Indeed, it was because of this change that the torch of rebellion had passed to the volatile Yaik Cossacks, whose frontier existence resembled that of their Don cousins three or four generations earlier. For all these reasons few Don Cossacks responded to Pugachev's appeal for help. The overwhelming majority, following their *ataman* and elders, remained loyal to the government, and some actually joined in suppressing the revolt, for which they received an appreciative letter from the empress.[116]

Meanwhile the peasants too were losing their taste for rebellion. For one thing, the conclusion of peace with the Turks took the edge off popular discontent. But more important was the lack of grain and livestock created in large measure by the general pandemonium. By the middle of August famine on the

Volga had sapped the strength and enthusiasm of the rebel bands.
The population of the area, reported Count Pavel Panin, Catherine's new commander-in-chief, was reduced to eating shrubs,
acorns, and moss.[117]

At the same time, victory over the Turks gave the government new confidence in dealing with the insurrection. It was
on July 29 that General Panin, the victor of Bender and younger
brother of Catherine's foreign minister, was put in charge of
the suppression. Shortly thereafter, experienced troops were
transferred from the front "to wipe out the villainous insurgents." [118] In the middle of August Panin issued a manifesto
denouncing Pugachev as a "man of Hell in whom, without doubt,
there lies the spirit of evil that is inimical to human nature." [119]
Panin promised amnesty to rebels who laid down their arms,
and he offered money and exemption from taxes and recruitment to whoever turned in the pretender either dead or alive. As
in the past, moreover, the church was called into service against
the rebels. Pugachev and his accomplices were anathematized
by the Holy Synod and condemned to "eternal damnation." A
circular went out to parish priests reminding them of their sacred
duty to oppose the insurgents. Pugachev, it read, was a chosen
instrument of the Devil, "a wolf who falls upon the sheep of
Christ's flock." A second proclamation warned that only damnation awaited the imposter's supporters: "He is the scourge of
humanity. He is an enemy of God and the Church and the
fatherland. Pay him no heed if you wish to hold the keys to
the Kingdom of Heaven and eternal salvation." [120]

Meanwhile Pugachev experienced the first serious setback of
his Volga campaign. Arriving at Tsaritsyn on August 21, he expected it to follow the example of the upstream towns and yield
without resistance. But the garrison, reinforced by a contingent
of Don Cossacks, launched a heavy bombardment which compelled him to withdraw. While he regrouped his forces for a
second attack, a message arrived with news of Mikhelson's approach. Breaking off his maneuvers, Pugachev fled down the
Volga toward Cherny Yar, with the Muscovites in pursuit.
Though he outnumbered his adversary by more than six to one,
his men were hungry and exhausted, and their quality was
never poorer. Of some 6000 adherents only 300 were Cossacks

and even fewer were Bashkir horsemen or Urals workers with mortars and cannon. The majority were poorly armed peasants, some traveling with their families in slow-moving wagons. As for the rest—tribesmen, convicts, boatmen, "and other scum," in the description of a hostile observer [121]—their military capacity was scarcely any better; indeed, their hopeless inefficiency against a disciplined army would soon make itself felt.

Mikhelson was clearly the pretender's most formidable opponent. With his small regiment he dogged the insurgents relentlessly, allowing them no respite. "From January 1774," in the words of a French contemporary,

> he pursued the rebels without intermission, how numerous soever their swarms, how remote the expedition, and whatever fortune attended his enterprise. It almost exceeds belief with what toilsome perseverance Mikhelson pursued his march over the deserts of trackless snow, without a guide, without succours, at times almost without food; how his company, always small, and often spent with fatigue, whenever they met with the great host of the rebels, always attacked, and always beat them: only by the prudence and the bravery of the colonel, and the confidence he had acquired from his troops. [122]

That this tribute was well deserved Mikhelson now showed in his last and most decisive victory. On August 24, after a three-day forced march, he caught up with the rebels a dozen miles above Cherny Yar. In a desperate maneuver Pugachev turned on his pursuer and charged in full strength. But Mikhelson stood his ground and, mounting a fierce counterattack, sent his opponent reeling. After a brief struggle Pugachev was completely routed. His motley army had been cut to pieces, with thousands killed or captured and all their cannon taken. What was left of his following, except for a battered remnant, quickly melted away. But the pretender again escaped, driven into the Urals, from which, rumor had it, he intended to follow the path of Nekrasov and flee to Persia or Turkey.

For his triumph over the rebels Mikhelson was lavishly rewarded, receiving a large estate near Vitebsk with a thousand serfs, as well as the Order of St. George and promotion to full colonel. Like Bibikov before him, he was the hero of the aristocracy, lionized for his courage and for the efficiency with which he had defeated the enemy. In glowing terms the German tutor from Arzamas paid tribute to Mikhelson's achievement. "I must confess," he wrote of the victory, "that this piece of news brought me greater joy than I had ever experienced in my life. Proud of the German name of our deliverer, my heart overflowed with admiration for his character, and as long as I live I shall pronounce the name of Mikhelson with the utmost respect." [123]

But Pugachev was still at large, having disappeared into the no-man's-land east of the Volga. To his fellow survivors he proposed fleeing south to Turkey or west to Zaporozhie or across the Urals into Siberia. But all such thoughts were rejected. Tired and hungry and embittered by their defeat, his confederates fell to quarreling. Some said it was "better to abandon our lawlessness and transgressions and to accept our well-earned execution rather than perish unrepentant on the steppe like wild animals." [124] Disillusioned with their leader, they began to question his identity before the others. If he is the true sovereign, they asked, why did he suffer defeat? Why is he unable to write his name? And why do the Don Cossacks call him Emelian Ivanovich? Having raised these doubts, they decided it was better not to die at all for a false messiah. Instead they would turn him in and save their own necks.

Thus it was that Pugachev, like Razin and Bulavin before him, was betrayed by his fellow Cossacks. He was seized with his wife and children and brought to Yaitsk and put in irons. From Yaitsk he was taken under heavy guard to Simbirsk, where Panin was anxious to question him. There, after preliminary interrogation, he was put in an iron cage specially built for the occasion and carried like a wild beast to Moscow. The cage being too small, Pugachev was forced to crouch throughout the long journey; and in this position, clothed in rags and inspiring more pity than awe, he arrived in the old capital. All Moscow went out to have a look at him, recalled Andrei Bolotov, and gaped "as at some sort of monster." [125] In government circles his capture was greeted with jubilation. "The marquis," wrote Catherine sardonically, "has been caught, shackled, and imprisoned"; he is "trussed and bound like a bear, and in Moscow a scaffold awaits him." In a letter to Voltaire, however, she conceded that Pugachev was "an uncommonly brave and resourceful person," though illiterate and as destructive as Tamerlane.[126] The poet Sumarokov composed a special ode on the occasion of his capture, and in Kazan portraits of the pretender were burned in a triumphant celebration.

Meanwhile General Panin had been given unlimited powers of repression, and he was using them to the hilt. Lest severity should touch off fresh outbursts, Catherine entered a mild plea for clemency, directing that "executions not take place save in extreme circumstances." [127] But her halfhearted recommendation did not weigh heavily, given the mood of revenge which gripped the nobility after the massacres on the Volga. In a fury of reprisal whole villages were leveled and, in addition to gibbets and breakwheels, wooden *glagoli* were erected, special devices in the shape of the Russian "G" with metal hooks for hanging victims by the rib. Cossacks, tribesmen, and peasants were flogged and tortured; their nostrils were slit and their ears torn off; their foreheads were branded and their hair and beards shorn. The fortunate got off with beatings and fines. In a typical case from the files of the secret police, a peasant named Rodion Loshkarev was sentenced to fifty strokes of the knout and exile at forced labor "because he willingly joined the rebel mob, received the rank of *ataman*, and returned to his village of Baikalovskoe with a copy of a sham manifesto from which he proclaimed the monster Pugachev to be Emperor Peter III; and he incited the peasants to steal money and wine and to pillage the home of Assessor Bryzgalov, whose books and papers they burned." [128] It was several months before the whirlwind of punishment had spent itself, during which tens of thousands were killed or banished at hard labor. In Bashkiria the revolt continued long after Pugachev's capture. General Suvorov, who arrived on the scene after the pretender's defeat, was sent to pacify the tribesmen. A determined effort was made to track down the principal leaders, notably Kinzia and Salavat. The former vanished without a trace, but Salavat was not so fortunate. At the end of November he was surrounded and captured in the woods and taken to Ufa, where he was branded, beaten with the knout, and sent in chains with his father to Rogervik, a traditional place of deportation for rebellious Bashkirs. As late as 1797 both were still alive, according to a recently discovered list of prisoners, as was Pugachev's secretary Ivan Pochitalin.[129]

At the end of December Pugachev was tried in the Kremlin by a court of landowners, officials, and high-ranking clergy. The outcome was hardly in doubt. "In a few days the farce of the Marquis de Pugachev will be over," wrote Catherine on December 21. "His sentence is already prepared—only a few formalities must be observed." [130] The pretender's sole defense was to try to shift the blame to the Yaik Cossacks who, so he claimed, had made a pawn of him and now sought to use him as a scapegoat. Whatever truth lay in these charges, they were of no avail. The court announced the anticipated sentence: "Emelian Pugachev will be quartered, his head mounted on a stake, the parts of his body carried to the four quarters of the city and put on wheels and then burned." [131]

There was one small concession, however. The empress, who had already refused to allow torture at Pugachev's interrogation and trial, directed the executioner to decapitate him first rather than quarter him alive, lest he should become, like Razin, too much of a popular martyr. Some influential aristocrats, by contrast, wanted to make an example of the pretender and to strike terror in the lower classes by administering the severest punishment. Prince A. A. Viazemsky, the procurator of the Senate, wrote Catherine that even quartering was not enough. He urged her to break Pugachev on the wheel "and thereby distinguish him from the others," namely the four Yaik Cossacks—Shigaev, Perfiliev, Padurov, and Tornov—who were to be executed with him.[132] But her orders were carried out. On January 10, 1775, Pugachev was taken to a square on the banks of the Moscow River below the Kremlin walls. There he was beheaded at a blow and then quartered. His head was mounted on a pike and the sections of his body put on wheels and exposed in different parts of Moscow for all to see. The next day the scaffold and the wheels were burned. The execution was witnessed by a large crowd. So many noblemen attended that Andrei Bolotov, noting that Pugachev had revolted chiefly against that class, called the spectacle "the true triumph of the gentry over this their common foe and villain." [133]

It remains to describe the fate of Pugachev's accomplices. Apart from the four who were executed with him, Zarubin was beheaded in Ufa and Beloborodov in Moscow. Lesser figures, such as Miasnikov and Kozhevnikov, were exiled to Siberia or the far north, while the nine Cossacks who had betrayed the impostor were pardoned. Pugachev's three children and both his wives were imprisoned in the fortress of Keksgolm, which they were never to leave. They were still listed on prison records as late as 1796, the year that Catherine died. One daughter survived until 1834. That year Tsar Nicholas I, hearing that Pushkin was writing a history of Pugachev, informed him that the pretender's sister had just died, meaning, of course, his daughter, who had languished in the Keksgolm dungeons for sixty years.[134]

Catherine, by a series of edicts, vainly sought to erase the memory of the pretender. On January 15, 1775, five days after his execution, she decreed that the Yaik River be renamed the Ural, the Yaik Cossacks the Ural Cossacks, and their capital city Uralsk. Zimoveiskaya Stanitsa, the birthplace of both Pugachev and Razin, was moved to the other side of the Don and renamed Potemkinskaya after the empress's favorite. What remained of Cossack independence was largely destroyed. The Zaporozhian and Volga Cossacks were transferred to the Kuban and the Caucasus, and a permanent garrison was installed in Uralsk, where the Cossacks were reorganized and henceforth kept under tight government control. Finally, by an edict of March 15, 1775, all matters concerning the rebellion were consigned to "eternal oblivion and profound silence." [135]

Yet, for all these measures, traces of the rising remained long after. Though an amnesty was granted at the end of 1775, sporadic flare-ups occurred on the Volga the following spring and summer. As late as 1778 Sir James Harris, the new British ambassador, warned that the sparks of discontent "are not yet extinguished; and it is much to be apprehended, that, in case of any national calamity, they would blow out afresh." [136] For the remainder of Catherine's reign the peasants were fairly quiet, but the three-year rule of her son Paul saw nearly 300 disturb-ances in 32 provinces, often requiring stringent repressions to put them down. The memory of Pugachev and his forerunners could not be eradicated. It was to survive not only in the scattered out-bursts of the nineteenth century but in the great upheavals of 1905 and 1917, and even beyond, as the next chapter of this work will attempt to show.

8. Conclusion

The revolt of Pugachev was the last and the most famous of the Cossack and peasant risings which shook the Russian state during the seventeenth and eighteenth centuries. It was, indeed, the most formidable mass upheaval in all of Europe between the Puritan and French revolutions, and the largest in Russia prior to the revolutions of 1905 and 1917, surpassing its predecessors in scope and violence, claiming the greatest number of gentry victims, and leaving a specter to haunt future generations of landlords and officials. In most respects, however, Pugachev's rising conformed to the pattern of its forerunners. It was an extremely complex affair, combining a Cossack mutiny with social rebellion, religious protest, and anticolonial resistance. Its imme-diate cause, the dispute on the Yaik, was of course unique; but its long-range causes—the rise of serfdom and autocracy, the heavy burdens of war, the loss of land and freedom and of former habits and customs—were the same as in the past. Once again, it was a sectional as well as a social conflict, pitting the expand-ing center against the vanishing frontier. In geographical terms the *Pugachevshchina* was probably the most extensive rising Rus-sia had ever known, engulfing the whole basin of the middle Volga together with the Yaik valley and the southern and central Urals, an eruption vaster than even Razin's a century before. Pugachev's greatest strength lay in the newly colonized region east of the Volga and Kama, where government conquest had been too recent and too rapid to be secure. The pretender's pledge to make Yaitsk his capital was a token of the sectional nature of the conflict. But his failure to penetrate the center, the territory within the

Oka perimeter, spelled the downfall of his movement. As a result, regional autonomy continued to decline under the weight of the expanding autocracy, and by the end of the eighteenth century there was no more "untamed steppe" except in central Asia or the remote stretches of Siberia.

The extension of the Russian frontier heralded the final destruction of Cossack independence. By the middle of the eighteenth century, after the defeats of Razin and Bulavin, the Don community had fallen within the orbit of government control. Now the Yaik Host met the same fate. The failure of Pugachev's revolt sounded the death knell of Cossack autonomy. In the aftermath the Cossacks were transplanted to remote corners of the empire or reduced to loyal instruments of the central government. The Cossack oligarchies came more and more to resemble their former gentry rivals, while the rank and file were gradually deprived of much that distinguished them from ordinary peasants. Flight beyond the Caucasus, following Nekrasov's example, became the only means of escape, but few were attracted by the prospect of starting life anew in an alien land and subject to the whims of an alien monarch. Henceforth the Cossacks ceased to be the catalysts of social rebellion. The wind from the steppe, as a modern historian has noted, would carry no more firebrands to the towns and villages farther north.[137] On the contrary, the Cossacks became a pillar of the autocracy, a praetorian guard to quell popular disturbances, a symbol of imperial authority rather than of freedom and independence as before. In the future the prophets of revolt would spring from a new class of radical intellectuals, "Pugachevs of the university," as Joseph de Maistre dubbed them.[138]

Yet, for all these similarities with the revolts of the past, there were a number of significant differences. For one thing the element of banditry was less conspicuous, especially in comparison with Razin's movement, though the looting of towns and estates took place on a wide scale. For another—and this is perhaps the most striking difference—the *Pugachevshchina* failed to take firm root in the towns, where Bolotnikov and Razin had won their greatest support. Of the more important Urals cities only Cheliabinsk was occupied by the insurgents, and even that for a short period. The same was true on the Volga, where rebel detachments moved swiftly from one town to the next, never establishing a solid territorial base from which to extend their activities into the heartland. The reasons for this have already been noted, the most important being that with the passage of time the frontier towns had lost much of their turbulent character and had evolved a more settled population with a larger stake in social stability. Moreover, with the rise of trade and manufacture and the emergence of a nationwide market, merchants and craftsmen developed stronger ties with the center, such as the commercial towns of northern Russia had enjoyed since the sixteenth century, making them bulwarks of the Muscovite order.

The social composition of the revolt was much the same as in the past, with Cossacks, peasants, and tribesmen constituting the bulk of the adherents. Yet here too there were noticeable differences. To begin with, Pugachev's was the first of the mass revolts to include a significant proletarian element, foreshadowing, however dimly, the revolutions of the twentieth century. The ascribed workers of the Urals, it is true, retained their peasant identity and outlook; but they were early prototypes of the future industrial workers. Moreover, by manufacturing arms for the rebels without the help of factory administrators, they not only played a key role in the rebellion but inaugurated a primitive form of workers' control which anticipated the more sophisticated experiments of 1917. The Bashkirs, too, took part in unprecedented numbers, continuing their century-long revolt against Russian colonization. Bulavin's outbreak, it will be recalled, had coincided with a large-scale Bashkir rising. But now the two movements —Russian and Bashkir—were combined under a single banner. It was the first time that such an alliance had been concluded— and also the last. The defeat of Pugachev marked an important step in Russia's eastward expansion at the expense of the semi-nomadic tribes beyond the Volga.

Another group which joined forces with the Cossacks for both the first and last time were the *odnodvortsy* homesteaders, whose participation in the *Pugachevshchina* was a last-ditch effort to recover their independence. They failed, however, and over the next few decades they rapidly faded from view, merging by and large with the state peasantry or the petty tradesmen of the provincial towns. A large proportion of the *odnodvortsy*, as well as of the Yaik Cossacks, were Old Believers, who occupied a prominent place in a mass uprising for the second time in the century. Yet the extent of their participation must not be exaggerated. Most schismatics, apart from Cossacks and homesteaders, preferred nonviolent methods of protest against government persecution. They shrank from open rebellion not only on religious grounds but also out of concern for their own possessions, many of them enjoying considerable prosperity as merchants and tradesmen. In some cases, potential supporters were alienated by the excesses of Pugachev's followers, by their indiscriminate killing and destruction, or they were mollified by Catherine's comparatively enlightened attitude toward religious nonconformity, and therefore maintained a passive stance throughout the revolt. As for Pugachev himself, he was probably not an Old Believer but merely exploited religious grievances as a means of drawing adherents into his camp. He issued appeals to the Old Believers, as he did to Moslems and Orthodox Christians, to broaden his base of support.

Whatever their religious affiliation, disaffected elements in the empire shared a common desire to recapture an idyllic past. They looked back with nostalgic yearning to a Garden of Eden before the emergence of centralized autocracy. More than anything else, it was this desire that Pugachev attempted to satisfy. His program, though somewhat more elaborate than those of his predecessors, was still rather vague and primitive. As Catherine put it, he promised his followers "castles in the air." [139] He was not opposed to tsardom itself but to the unbearable shape it had recently assumed. Like Razin before him, he aimed to inaugurate a popular government with a popular tsar. Above all, this meant eliminating the tyrannical landlords and officials, converting the serfs into state peasants with free use of the land, and replacing the autocracy with local self-rule in the Cossack manner. His propaganda, however, seemed better calculated to arouse a thirst for revenge than to present a clear vision of the future society. Serfdom being further developed, class antagonisms were correspondingly sharper; and his leaflets and manifestoes inspired a greater destructive passion, particularly among the peasantry, than ever before. At the same time, his was a cultural protest as well as a Cossack mutiny and a peasant jacquerie. His program, like those of Razin and Bulavin, was a reflection of growing nativist resentment against foreign innovations and the modernization of

Russian life, resentment which found expression in popular hatred of German officers and bureaucrats—the Traubenbergs and Freimans, the Reinsdorps and Brandts—not to speak of the murder of the astronomer Löwitz or the raiding of German settlements on the lower Volga. But cultural antagonisms took a back place to economic and social grievances and must not be given undue emphasis.

As before, myths and rumors occupied a central place in the rebellion. What is remarkable, however, is that the same myth —of a just tsar whom the aristocracy had conspired to eliminate in order to oppress the people—should have dominated all four upheavals spanning nearly two centuries. It was the persistence of this legend that paved the way for the appearance of a pretender—indeed, as in the Time of Troubles, a whole series of pretenders—which attests to the people's faith in a messianic ruler who would rescue them from their tormentors. But this time there was a difference, for Pugachev, unlike his forerunners, did not claim merely to represent the legitimate sovereign; instead he cast himself in the role, which may help to account for his large following.

Yet he never stirred the popular imagination as much as Razin had. Nor did he command the same devotion or acquire so exalted a place in folklore and legend. This is not easy to explain. Men were perhaps more deeply impressed by Razin's swashbuckling adventures or moved to greater compassion by his more terrible death. Moreover, with none of Pugachev's imperial trappings to taint his image, Razin perhaps seemed a truer "peasant tsar," even if he himself never claimed the role. Pugachev, some may have felt, was animated as much by personal ambition as by compassion for the oppressed. Indeed, the followers of Bakunin in the 1870s sometimes distinguished between the two great rebels, criticizing Pugachev's statist pretensions while praising Razin's selfless devotion to the poor. Yet the "third emperor" was, after all, a product of his times. Coming a century after Razin, he reflected the values of imperial rather than of Muscovite Russia, and behaved as he thought "Peter Fyodorovich" himself would have done.

This, however, is by no means to suggest that Pugachev was not a popular figure. On the contrary, he was widely regarded as Razin's legitimate heir. When he appeared among the Yaik Cossacks, noted a contemporary observer, he "renewed to their imagination the transactions of the Don Cossack Stenka Razin." Nor was the parallel lost on the empress. "His history," she wrote of the pretender, "corresponded exactly to the history of the brigand Stenka Razin." [140] For the lower classes the analogy went even further: he was nothing less than a reincarnation of his predecessor, "the second coming of Razin after a hundred years." [141] The progression from Razin to Pugachev, as has been noted, was a kind of apostolic succession in which the myth of the Christ-like rebel, martyred for the sake of the people, passed from one century to the next. Legend attributes to Pugachev some of the same magical powers which Razin had supposedly possessed—for instance, by drawing a horse on his prison wall he might escape from his enemies.[142] The peasants saw him as their returned messiah and called him (as they had called Razin) their "resplendent sun," a symbol of good against evil, of life against death, of renewal and resurrection. A lament sung in the Urals after Pugachev's execution is a striking illustration of this point:

> Emelian, our own dear father,
> Wherefore have you forsaken us?
> Our resplendent sun has gone down.

In the same spirit, for many years after his death the peasants of Saratov reckoned the date as before or after Pugachev in place of Christ.[143]

Yet, for all his charismatic qualities, Pugachev went down in defeat. And his failure was all too predictable, the reasons being much the same as in the rebellions of the past. Most important, perhaps, was a lamentable absence of unity in the rebel camp. Once again it was a heterogeneous assortment of Cossacks, peasants, and tribesmen that made common cause against the authorities. Although their weapons and organization were somewhat better than before, they were still no match for the trained and disciplined army at the government's disposal. Moreover, the insurgents were plagued by chronic internal rivalries. In the Urals it was a division of interests between the skilled and unskilled workers that prevented unity of action, in addition to which the ascribed peasants were more bent on settling private scores with their employers or on returning to their native villages than on undertaking the broader task of defeating the government. At the same time, both national and religious differences hampered effective collaboration between Pugachev's Russian and Bashkir followers. At one point tensions ran so high that Salavat was moved to appeal for unity: "In our hearts there is no malice toward Russians. There is no reason for Bashkirs and Russians to quarrel and to destroy each other." [144] But his plea fell on deaf ears. Throughout the rebellion real harmony was never achieved.

Nor was there effective coordination among the scattered rebel detachments. And considerable energy was wasted in pillage and destruction, which reached such a pitch that some of the more prosperous adherents—Bashkir elders, petty merchants, independent peasants—turned in fear against their allies and passed to the government side. Beyond all this, the disappointing response in the towns and the lack of a constructive program have already been noted. Finally, like his predecessors, Pugachev chose to remain in the peripheries rather than attack the vital core of the empire. On this last point Sir Robert Gunning laid special emphasis to account for the pretender's failure:

> the miscreant who was lately the author of so much confusion and devastation was, for want of common understanding, incapable of forming any plan; for had that of marching hither, either occurred, or been suggested to him, and that he had executed it, there is not the least doubt that he would have been joined here by the whole of the populace . . . in which case the flames must have spread through the whole Empire.[145]

For all these reasons Pugachev met the same end as his forerunners. But he, by contrast, had no successors. He was the last of the great Cossack rebels. And for 130 years, though there were numerous local disturbances, the military–bureaucratic state remained sufficiently strong to forestall another general outbreak.

Despite the immense shock of the *Pugachevshchina*, the autocracy emerged unimpaired. To the upper classes, in fact, the traditional justification of absolute rule seemed more persuasive than ever. The urge of the masses for spontaneous rebellion, it was argued, required a strong centralized government to maintain domestic order, not to speak of defending the empire against its foreign enemies. Thus the revolt buttressed the shaky alliance between crown and gentry against the lower orders of society. Pugachev's appeal for a class war against the nobility led to a healing of the frictions which had plagued the empress throughout the first decade of her reign. Instead of seeking to limit her powers, the aristocracy looked to Catherine for protection against the rebellion. Catherine, in turn, declaring herself the "first landowner" of Russia, relied more heavily on the nobility, who received a corporate status and a wide range of authority in matters of local government.

Pugachev's revolt, coming at the height of the Turkish War, was the most critical moment of Catherine's reign. Afterward she took an increasingly dim view of popular movements wherever they occurred, denouncing the American and French revolutions and describing the deputies of the National Assembly as so many Pugachevs.[146] At the same time, however, the rising brought home to her the need for reform. In a series of measures she lowered the price of salt, eliminated wartime taxes, and amnestied debtors, military deserters, and fugitive state peasants. Already in 1773, the year of Pugachev's outbreak, she had begun to soften government policy toward non-Russian peoples. The revolt gave further impetus to this trend. For the conversion of Moslem tribesmen the authorities relied increasingly on persuasion and incentives. Baptisms were rewarded by exemptions from taxes and conscription, and the construction of mosques and of Moslem schools was permitted over a broad area. The revolt also stimulated reform in the Urals metal factories, where fines and punishments were curtailed, hours reduced, and wages substantially increased. In 1807 the whole system of ascribed labor was finally scrapped.

But above all, the revolt paved the way for the reform of local administration. Under the impact of mass insurrection the inefficiency of the provincial authorities had been glaringly exposed. Officials had panicked and even abandoned their posts, leaving the populace defenseless before the rebel onslaught. Wherever the pretender had encountered firmness, Catherine noted, he had achieved little success, but "weakness, indolence, dereliction of duty, idleness, bribery, disagreements, extortions, and injustice on the part of individual officials" had facilitated the spread of rebellion in many areas.[147] Appalled by the behavior of her administrators, the empress introduced a comprehensive reform in the Statute of Provinces of 1775, which aimed at placing the management of local affairs in the hands of the nobility under the general supervision of government representatives.

For the peasantry, however, there was no fundamental relief. On the contrary, their lot became harder than ever. Owing to the extension of serfdom to the Ukraine and to Catherine's grants of state peasants to her favorites, the number of private bondsmen sharply increased. Moreover, the powers of the nobility over their serfs were in no way diminished. Indeed, the bloodshed of 1774 led some to favor even further restrictions on the lower classes. On the other hand there were a few who, either from sympathy or fear, called for the immediate alleviation of the peasantry's plight. Radishchev was the most celebrated case in point. "Enticed by a crude pretender," he wrote in his *Journey from St. Petersburg to Moscow,*

> they hastened to follow him, and wished only to free themselves from the yoke of their masters and in their ignorance they could think of no other means to do this than to kill their masters. They spared neither sex nor age. They sought more the joy of vengeance than the benefit of broken shackles. This is what awaits us, this is what we must expect. Danger is steadily mounting, peril is already hovering over our heads. Time has already raised its scythe and is only awaiting an opportunity. The first demagogue or humanitarian who rises up to awaken the unfortunate will hasten the scythe's fierce sweep. Beware! [148]

But Radishchev's call went unheeded. He himself was arrested and sent into exile. Catherine, in the end, confined herself to limited measures of reform, and even these were carried through to strengthen her administration in the face of popular discontent. In the long run, perhaps, the fear of another Pugachev revolt helped to bring about the emancipation of the peasantry. But for the time being, autocracy and serfdom remained intact. Indeed, the whole question of fundamental reform was postponed for nearly a century. And by then, it would seem, it was already too late to prevent another popular outbreak on a scale unimagined in the past.

Although the revolts of Pugachev and his predecessors anticipated the great social upheavals of the twentieth century, they
belong to an earlier period of Russian history. During the seventeenth and eighteenth centuries Russia saw the rapid growth of
the state, which imposed new ideas and institutions upon a reluctant people who remained deeply conservative and steadfast in
their resistance to change. At the same time, the monarchy was
strengthened and consolidated at the expense of local and regional
autonomy. By sheer force and terror the governing elite drove
the masses forward, harnessed to the needs of the state.

The result was a civil war between the government and the
people, a war in which the victims of triumphant progress—Cossacks, tribesmen, peasants, and other declining groups—sought to
regain their former independence. As a rule they limited themselves to passive methods, especially flight, to which Russian
geography presented few natural barriers. But in moments of
abnormal hardship, such as famine or war, they erupted into open
violence which threatened to rend the fabric of society. Perhaps
some unusual calamity might furnish the spark, perhaps some
new exaction imposed on the peasants or Cossacks, or a sudden
change in their status—a transfer to private ownership, a shift
from *obrok* to *barshchina*, assignment to factory labor—which
broke with established traditions. But the underlying cause, the
rise of autocracy and serfdom, was always the same. The state
swelled up, as Kliuchevsky put it, while the people shrank.

The state, in the eyes of the people, became an alien and evil
tyranny, extorting taxes, exacting military service, and trampling
on native customs and traditions. It neither ministered to their
welfare nor defended their concept of justice; nor did it perform
any other function which seemed vital, or even relevant, to their
way of life. Rather, it was an agent of oppressive innovation, a
giant octopus, as they saw it, which stifled their independence
and squeezed out their life's breath. Yet they always distinguished
sharply between the tsar and his advisers. The tsar was their
benevolent father, the bearer of justice and mercy, while the
boyars were wicked usurpers, demons in human form who throve
on the people's enslavement. To eliminate them—to "cleanse" or
"remove" them from the land, as rebel propaganda put it—was
their devout wish, for only by demolishing the wall of nobles

and bureaucrats, they felt, could the ancient bond with the sovereign, on which their salvation depended, be restored.

Myths of this type, above all the myth of a returning deliverer, played a major part in nearly every popular rebellion from Bolotnikov to Pugachev. For throughout the seventeenth and eighteenth centuries the lower classes were hungry for a messiah who would purge the land of suffering and usher in a golden age of abundance and tranquillity that would last forever. To fill this demand there appeared a series of impostors who combined a capacity for military leadership with the qualities of a prophet. The charismatic appeal of a Razin or Pugachev was essential to their gaining a mass following, and long after their death they continued to be regarded as the "good tsar" who, in imitation of Christ, had sacrificed his life to save the poor. Thus when Pushkin asked an old Ural Cossack what he remembered of Pugachev he angrily replied: "For you he is Pugachev, but for me he was the great sovereign, Peter Fyodorovich." [1] Similarly, as we have seen, an ancient Volga peasant in the mid-nineteenth century remained convinced that Pugachev had been the "second coming of Razin after a hundred years." Although Soviet scholars tend to discount the myth of the "good tsar" as the "naive monarchism" of a superstitious peasantry, the rebel leaders themselves (with the exception of Bulavin) considered the presence in their camp of a people's tsar indispensable for winning mass support. Bolotnikov, it will be recalled, went so far as to claim that the dead daughter of Tsar Fyodor was in fact a boy, who having miraculously survived, had joined his campaign against the boyars.

In every case, however, the risings were doomed to defeat. Although rebel propaganda could rouse the heterogeneous masses to revolt, it was incapable of uniting them into a coherent movement. Moreover, for all their mobility and tactics of surprise, the insurgents were joined in an unequal struggle with the expanding military state. Thus each successive rebellion was drowned in blood, the leaders invariably being betrayed by their own followers and turned over to the government to be executed. Nor could the outcome have been different. By resisting the centralization of power the rebels were opposing one of the overriding trends of modern history. They could not reverse a process whose roots ran far deeper than the aristocratic conspiracy to which they

attributed their declining fortunes. And even if they had succeeded in toppling the government, their program of Cossack
democracy, the survival of a vanishing age, would have condemned them to destruction by some outside aggressor with a
modern military–bureaucratic machine.

What then did the risings accomplish? Spontaneous and ill-
organized, they set out with millennial visions and ended in failure
and death. Indeed, like all unsuccessful revolts against authoritarian regimes, they achieved the very opposite of their hopes.
Each new revolt only carried the government forward and hastened the decline of the old life. Instead of a return to a golden
past, to an era of justice and tranquillity, autocracy and serfdom
were fastened upon the country more firmly than ever.

Yet the revolts must not be dismissed as mere reactionary outbursts, full of sound and fury but accomplishing nothing. Despite
their traditionalist framework and backward-looking orientation,
in their determination to sweep away the existing order they were
profoundly revolutionary. And though they failed to achieve
their goals, they shook the state, terrified the nobility, and ultimately convinced the authorities of the necessity for reform. At
the same time, they awakened the revolutionary consciousness
of the lower classes and left them with a thirst for vengeance
which no conciliatory measure or partial improvement could
eliminate. "God save us from a Russian revolt, senseless and
merciless." Pushkin's plea was an eloquent testimony to the legacy
of the four revolts which—particularly the *Pugachevshchina*, the
last and most formidable of the risings—were to serve as an inspiration for future opponents of the autocracy.

Long after Pugachev's death rumors continued to circulate
among the Cossacks, peasants, and tribesmen that "Peter Fyodorovich" was still alive, hiding, it was said, in the forests of the Volga
valley or the remote hills of Bashkiria or on the Don in the guise
of a simple oxherd, and preparing to raise a new army to liberate
the poor. Between the time of his execution and the end of
Catherine's reign, more than forty cases of rumors of his imminent return—some of which touched off local disturbances—
were reported by the secret police. "They caught the fish," as a
soldier remarked, "but his teeth still remain." [2]

These rumors, in turn, spawned a rich crop of pretenders, who called themselves Peter III or the Tsarevich Paul. An interesting case occurred in Samara when a Don Cossack spoke about "Pugachev and his mob" to a veteran of the revolt. "Why do you call him Pugachev and his army a mob?" the latter replied. "He was not Pugachev but the third emperor, Peter Fyodorovich. [In fact] he looked very like you." [3] With these words a new impostor was launched on his brief career, which ended in torture and death. But there were others to take his place. Another false Peter III appeared in Kiev in 1787, and in 1800 a Don Cossack was beaten with the knout for boasting that "Pugachev rose up for his homeland but was defeated. I shall do better. When I take up the sword all Russia will tremble." [4]

Nor did the legend die out as the new century unfolded. When Napoleon invaded Russia in 1812, religious sectarians in Tambov province, a stronghold of agrarian discontent, sent a delegation to greet him, convinced that he had come to "overthrow the false tsar." Some peasants, in fact, saw Napoleon himself as the pretender, who had returned to liberate them; and the Soviet historian Eugene Tarlé suggests that Napoleon might have triumphed had he followed Pugachev's example and proclaimed a general emancipation.[5] In 1825, on the other hand, when Alexander I died in mysterious circumstances, it was rumored that the tsar himself had been the true liberator, who, like Peter III, was about to free the serfs when the gentry decided to get rid of him. His coffin, it was said, contained the body of an ordinary soldier, for the tsar, having escaped his assassins, had gone to wander over the land and share the people's suffering. Similar legends arose during the Decembrist revolt, which was precipitated by Alexander's death. Pavel Pestel, the foremost leader of the rebellion, invoked the old myth that the aristocracy formed "a wall standing between the monarch and the people, hiding from the monarch the true condition of the people for the sake of selfish advantages," [6] and one of the rebel officers could get his troops to move only by claiming that Nicholas I was not the "true tsar."

The crushing of the revolt did not end the rumors of a returning deliverer. In 1827 the head of the secret police reported widespread unrest among the peasantry, who "await their liberator, whom they call Metelkin, as the Jews await their Messiah. They say: 'Pugachev frightened the masters, but Metelkin will sweep them away.'" [7] Millenarian expectations were particularly strong among sectarians and Old Believers. The Skoptsy, who adopted Peter III as their messiah, displayed portraits of the late emperor with dark hair and beard and dressed in a kaftan trimmed with fur—that is, as Pugachev, whose return, they said, would be heralded by the bells of the Uspensky Cathedral in Moscow.

The passage of time did little to erode the Pugachev legend. Throughout the nineteenth century Pugachev, in the eyes of the faithful, remained the "resplendent sun," a flaming symbol of revolt which having set must rise again. To this familiar image Pushkin, in his history of the rebellion, added the figure of a soaring bird which symbolized the coming revolution. According to Pushkin's account, the following dialogue took place between Pugachev and General Panin after the pretender's capture:

> PANIN: "Exactly who are you?"
> PUGACHEV: "Emelian Ivanovich Pugachev."
> PANIN: "Then how dare you, a brigand [*vor*], call yourself the Sovereign?"
> PUGACHEV: "I am not the raven [*voron*] but his offspring. The raven himself is still flying." [8]

That Pugachev had in fact uttered these words is doubtful. What Pushkin recorded, rather, was one of the legends he had unearthed during his research on the uprising. But the story, as we shall see, caught on and would be repeated many times in the future, especially by revolutionary populists trying to inspire the peasants with Pugachev's example.

The authorities, meanwhile, used every means of repression to prevent a new upheaval. Nicholas I himself admitted that serfdom was "a palpable evil," but to touch it, he said, would only stir up the peasants, and "the Pugachev rebellion proved how far popular rage can go." [9] Reform was thus postponed until the Crimean War, which saw a rising number of peasant outbreaks, centering as before along the middle Volga. Rumor once again played an important role in the disturbances. Some said that an emancipation edict had been drafted by the tsar but suppressed by the nobility, others that peasants who volunteered for the army would be given their freedom. As a result, whole villages were set in

motion to secure their birthright. The south, as before, continued
to beckon, where "the leaves never fall from the trees and all
men live in joy and righteousness," to quote Turgenev's *Sports-
man's Sketches*, a work which helped awaken society to the need
for reform. In a similar vein, a group of religious dissenters, the
Brothers of Zion, were convinced that a savior would come to
lead them to a millennial kingdom in Israel, where "all sorts of
blessings are to be heaped like mountains on us—woods, green
fields, gardens, honeycomb and fruit, gold, bronze, silver, gems.
There will be no barbaric studies, no schools for recruits, no violence, no tricks, no reports, no flattery of the authorities. All will
be equal and of one rank, no police, no judges, everywhere sanc-
tity and common people." [10]

With the death of Nicholas I in 1855 fresh rumors of liberation
swept the countryside. His successor, it was said, was sitting in
the Crimea "with a golden cap," granting land and freedom to all
who approached him. For the nobility, however, the tsar's death
was a moment of apprehension and suspense. Peter Kropotkin,
the future anarchist leader, noted a "real terror" among his aristocratic relatives, who, like their fellow landlords, dreaded "a
new uprising of Pugachev." [11] In radical circles, by contrast, the
prospect of mass rebellion was a source of hope, in spite of the
death and destruction it would inevitably entail. "If the liberation
of the peasants cannot be achieved in any other way," wrote
Alexander Herzen, "then even that would not be too great a
price. Terrible crimes bring with them terrible consequences."
Pugachev, he added echoing Pushkin, was "only a small crow.
The real one is still flying high in the sky." [12]

The authorities, however, remained alert for signs of a general
rising. More than any constitutionalist demands or Jacobin conspiracy, it was the nightmare of a spontaneous revolt that filled
them with alarm. "We are not afraid of Mirabeau," declared a
government spokesman, "but we are frightened by Emelka Pugachev. Ledru-Rollin and his Communists will find no sympathizers
here, but any village will goggle at Nikita Pustosviat. No one
will side with Mazzini, but Stenka Razin has only to say the
word. That is where our revolution is lurking, that is where our
danger lies." The peasants continued to set their hopes on a good
tsar, "a simple mortal, a man of the soil who understands the life

of the people and is chosen by the people," as a revolutionary leaflet put it in 1861. "Admittedly," wrote Yuri Samarin the same year, "an image of the remote tsar floats before their eyes, but it is not of the tsar who lives in St. Petersburg, who appoints governors, issues decrees, and moves armies; it is a wholly different, primeval, half-mythical tsar who might rise suddenly from nowhere in the shape of a drunken deacon or a peasant soldier on permanent leave." [13]

As in Pugachev's time, most serfs still thought of liberation as conversion to state peasants, but by the 1850s the new idea of total freedom was beginning to emerge. Witness the following conversation recorded by the secret police:

FIRST PEASANT: "They say that we will soon be free."
SECOND PEASANT: "Probably like the state peasants."
FIRST PEASANT: "No, that's just it—completely free. They won't demand either recruits or taxes and there won't be any kind of authorities. We will run things ourselves." [14]

Among the nobility, meanwhile, both the supporters and the opponents of emancipation evoked the specter of Pugachev to strengthen their case. Some saw the handwriting on the wall and called for immediate reform to forestall a new uprising. Alexander II himself, in a famous speech of 1856, declared that "it is better to abolish serfdom from above than to wait until the peasants begin to liberate themselves spontaneously from below." Others, on the contrary, fearing that emancipation might unleash rather than avert a general outbreak, warned that the day serfdom was abolished "the peasants would begin to kill the landlords wholesale, and Russia would witness a new Pugachev uprising, far more terrible than that of 1773." [15]

When the emancipation was granted in February 1861, a new *Pugachevshchina* failed to materialize. But sporadic outbreaks occurred over a wide area. Profoundly disillusioned, the serfs refused to believe that so much land would be retained by the nobility, still less that they must pay for their own allotments and meantime remain obligated to their masters and the state. At once it was whispered that the real emancipation, providing a total distribution of the land as well as the cancellation of all payments, had been suppressed by the gentry, or that a second manifesto ("in letters of gold") would grant them the genuine freedom they desired. Scattered risings broke out in the rural districts, especially along the Volga, where they threatened to assume the proportions of a general upheaval. During 1861 alone more than 500 outbreaks occurred in which troops had to be used. But without the Cossacks to lead them, and without a simultaneous war to divert the attention of the government, they were destined to remain fragmented and localized and were put down with little difficulty.

The most serious incident, however, vividly evoked the risings of the past. Erupting at the village of Bezdna in Kazan province, the heart of Pugachev country, it was led by an Old Believer named Anton Petrov, who declared the emancipation a forgery and advised his fellow villagers to stop working for the gentry, paying their dues, and obeying the authorities. Before long peasants from the surrounding area flocked to hear him say that they were free, that the land was theirs, and that they should remove the officials and elect their own elders. The villagers ceased carrying out their obligations and seized the landlords' fields and forests. The disturbances quickly spread to the adjoining provinces of Simbirsk and Samara, where memories of Razin and Pugachev were still alive. Troops were called to the scene and opened fire, killing or wounding several hundred, when the peasants refused to surrender their leader. After the first volley the peasants stood their ground, shouting "Freedom, freedom! We obey only God and the tsar. You are shooting at the tsar." In the end, however, Petrov was arrested and shot in the presence of his fellow villagers, who were forced to attend the execution. Like Razin and Pugachev, he came to be regarded as a Christ-like martyr who had sacrificed his life to save the poor. After his death, it was said, a fire sprang up on his tomb and an angel in white appeared and announced his imminent resurrection. For years to come the gentry of the area compared him to Pugachev and dreaded a repetition of his rising.[16]

"The present situation," noted a former Decembrist after the Bezdna massacre, "shows that Pugachev is a greater danger to the government than a Pestel or Ryleev." But a greater danger still was an alliance of the radical .intelligentsia with the spontaneous rebellion of the dispossessed. Joseph de Maistre understood this when he forecast a new upheaval led by "some university Pugachev." Similarly, the historian Shchapov foresaw a time when "Pugachev, mover of the popular masses, will extend his hand to Muraviev, Pestel, or Petrashevsky, when the mournful sounds and thoughts of popular ballad will mingle with the thoughts of Ryleev." [17]

The first serious attempt to forge such an alliance was made by the revolutionary populists, who emerged in the aftermath of the emancipation. Nikolai Chernyshevsky, a founding father of their movement, believed that only through a new *Pugachev-shchina*, led this time by the revolutionary intelligentsia, could socialism be achieved in Russia. In 1862 P. G. Zaichnevsky, a student at Moscow University, called for a "bloody and pitiless" revolt modeled on the risings of the past. The following year a group of students in Kazan, a traditional center of peasant rebellion, tried to incite a new uprising "to repeat the one led by Pugachev." In 1870, the bicentennial of Razin's rebellion, Sergei Nechaev predicted that before long popular fury would again "burst like a storm on the nobility, which wallows in vice and luxury." And in 1873 Peter Lavrov hailed the centennial of Pugachev as the signal for a new upheaval more powerful than those of the past. "*You* celebrate the memory of Catherine," he declared to the Russian nobility. "*You* celebrate the memory of Bibikov. *We*, however, honor Pugachev." Pugachev, he added, repeating Pushkin's legend, was only a small raven, but the raven of today will shape the "future destiny of the Russian people." [18]

When the populists went "to the people" in the 1870s, they consciously linked their efforts to the anniversaries of Razin and Pugachev. Some deliberately used the seventeenth-century term *shaika* (gang of brigands) to describe their clandestine circles, and called for the seizure of gentry land as well as the removal of local officials and the election of *atamans* and elders in their place. "Such was the invariable 'program' of the popular revolutionary socialists, Pugachev, Razin, and their associates," ran one of their leaflets, "and such it doubtless remains for the overwhelming majority of the Russian people. Therefore we revolutionary populists accept it." [19] Nor was it accidental that they should concentrate their efforts in the regions of the great jacqueries of the past or, mindful of their role in the earlier risings, seek to attract the Old Believers to their cause. "We believe that the greatest revolutionary traditions are preserved among the people of the Volga, Don, and Dnieper," said one populist militant, "for the largest popular movements originated in these borderlands. Pugachev's revolt was on the Volga, Razin's on the Don . . . and so we have decided not to scatter our forces over the whole of Russia but to concentrate them in these areas." Similarly, Kropotkin, who helped draft a popular history of the *Pugachevshchina* for propaganda purposes, urged his comrades of the Chaikovsky circle to "choose some district where memories of Razin and Pugachev are still alive, and move towards Moscow, on the way stirring up the peasants against the gentry and local authorities." [20]

The most successful populist venture in the countryside, at the southern village of Chigirin in 1877, revived the myth of the good tsar deceived by the wicked aristocracy. The agitators brought a manifesto with a large gold seal in which the tsar gave the peasants all the land without payment, "like the light of the sun and all God's other gifts." This old device of Pugachev, repeated by Anton Petrov, proved once again effective. The Chigirin villagers elected their own *ataman* and elders and were about to evict the landlords and officials when the authorities, learning of their plans from a drunken peasant, stepped in and crushed the rising.

The Chigirin episode was engineered by followers of Michael Bakunin, the famous Russian anarchist, who has aptly been described as "a Stenka Razin of the Russian gentry." [21] Of all the revolutionary leaders none drew more inspiration from the spontaneous upheavals of the past. For Bakunin, indeed, the revolts of Razin and Pugachev were prototypes of the coming social revolution, "not the first peasant revolutions in Russia, and not the last." Razin and Pugachev, he said, were model rebels, indomitable, indefatigable, and outside the pale of law, courageous popular avengers and irreconcilable enemies of the state. "We must ally ourselves with the doughty world of the brigands, who are the only real revolutionaries," he wrote with Nechaev in 1869. "The anniversaries of Stenka Razin and Pugachev are approaching. Let us prepare for the feast." [22]

Bakunin placed his faith not only in brigands but in all uprooted segments of society. Inspired by Razin and Pugachev, he saw the salvation of mankind in the destructive yet creative turbulence of the dispossessed. His, like theirs, was an apocalyptic vision, a dream of immediate and universal rebellion, of the leveling of all existing values and institutions and the creation of a free society on their ashes. He envisioned, moreover, a revolt of the backlands against the center, of the primitive against the advanced regions of the empire, indeed, of Europe as a whole, an all-embracing upheaval in both town and country, including the darkest elements of society—the landless peasants, the *Lumpenproletariat*, the unemployed—pitted against their wealthy and privileged oppressors. He called for an alliance of the déclassé intellectuals with the urban and rural poor into "a single calculated and ruthless popular revolution" to bring about a "new and genuine liberty which will no longer come from above but from below."

Against this must be set the view of the Russian Marxists, who began to emerge as a movement during the 1880s. Inheriting their mentor's scorn for the "idiocy of rural life," they saw the rural population as backward and superstitious and, though prone to sporadic rioting, incapable of posing a real threat to the existing order. Even when aroused, they thought, the peasantry would only dissipate their strength in wild and undisciplined violence. Their defeat was inevitable, moreover, since their backward-looking aspirations were incompatible with the emerging industrial system. For all their popular heroism, the peasant revolts represented nihilistic outbursts against the ineluctable process of modernization, desperate but futile protests against the unfamiliar forces that threatened on every side. In their quest for a pastoral utopia, according to this view, Razin and Pugachev were seeking to turn back the clock, to re-create a decentralized, agrarian, and economically stagnant society, a moribund primitive world which history had doomed to oblivion. Razin, wrote Plekhanov, the father of Russian Marxism, aimed to "replace the new order with the old," and Pugachev "looked backward into the dark recesses of bygone years." [23]

Not that the Marxists were completely blind to the revolutionary potential of the peasantry. Indeed Marx himself, for all his reservations about the rural folk, once wrote of the necessity to back "the proletarian revolution by some second edition of the Peasants' War." This remark, in turn, made a deep impression on

Lenin, who, echoing Marx's words, was to call the Russian Revolution the "union of a 'peasant war' with the working class movement." [24] Lenin was fully alive to the revolutionary implications of the peasantry's desire for land. He understood, moreover, that given Russia's backwardness a tactical alliance between the proletariat and peasantry was necessary for a successful revolution. His greatest achievement, in fact, was to return to the anarcho-populist roots of the Russian revolutionary tradition, to adapt his Marxist theories to suit the conditions of an underdeveloped country in which a proletarian revolution alone made little sense. As Zinoviev remarked in 1924, "the joining of the workers' revolution with the peasant war is the most basic feature of Leninism, Vladimir Ilyich's most important discovery." Trotsky put it in a similar way in his history of the revolution: "In order to realize the Soviet state, there was required a drawing together of two factors belonging to completely different historic species: a peasant war—that is, a movement characteristic of the dawn of bourgeois development—and a proletarian insurrection, the movement signalizing its decline. That is the essence of 1917." [25]

But this was hardly Lenin's "discovery," nor even Marx's. For Marx, on the contrary, the socialist revolution required the emergence of a well-organized and class-conscious proletariat, something to be expected in highly industrialized countries like Germany or England. It was Bakunin, rather, who saw that modern revolutions, like the Russian rebellions of the past, would emerge from the lower depths of society, and he therefore pinned his hopes on a peasant jacquerie and a simultaneous rising of the infuriated urban mobs, "solid and barbarian elements" which, having been the least exposed to the corrupting influences of bourgeois civilization, retained their primitive vigor and instincts for revolt. The real proletariat, he said, consisted of the great mass of "uncivilized, disinherited, and illiterate millions" who truly had nothing to lose. And his prophecy was fulfilled. For the three greatest revolutions of the twentieth century—in Russia, in Spain, and in China—have all occurred in relatively backward countries and have largely been "peasant wars" linked with outbreaks of the urban poor and a militant elite of déclassé intellectuals who, in Russia at least, replaced the Cossacks and schismatics of the past.

To what extent, then, did the revolts of the seventeenth and eighteenth centuries foreshadow the revolutions of 1905 and 1917? Clearly they had a deep influence on revolutionary thought in the nineteenth century and did much to shape the character of the Russian revolutionary movement. Yet 130 years elapsed between Pugachev's rising and the 1905 Revolution, during which profound and irrevocable changes occurred in the nature of Russian society. In particular, Russia saw the emergence of a labor movement and a radical intelligentsia, and new ideas and aspirations began to capture the popular imagination, replacing, at least in part, old beliefs and traditions. The beginnings of industrialization, moreover, created new pressures that helped to undermine the tsarist order, which in the days of Pugachev had been at the height of its strength. By the end of the nineteenth century, when the last of the Romanovs ascended the throne, the autocracy was a mere shadow of its former self, supported by a declining nobility and unable to withstand the mounting pressures from below. In its weakened condition, moreover, the old regime ˌsuffered humiliating defeats at the hands of external enemies. The Russo-Japanese War and the First World War, unlike those of the eighteenth century, went badly from the start, shattering the prestige of the ruling elite, undermining the discipline of the armed forces, and opening the way for the government's overthrow, which earlier rebellions had been unable to accomplish.

In their historical setting, then, the revolutions of 1905 and 1917 differed markedly from those of the past. More than that, they gathered around no dramatic personal symbols of leadership, they flared up in the heartland as well as the peripheries, and they led to political and economic changes that were far more sweeping than those which had followed the earlier upheavals. Yet the similarities are even more striking than the differences. For Russia remained a backward country with an antiquated social structure, so that old forms of rebellion persisted alongside the new. Like the risings of the past, the revolutions of 1905 and 1917 were explosions of mass discontent—elemental, unpremeditated, and unorganized—in which diverse social and national groups pursued disparate and often conflicting objectives. Triggered by unpopular wars, with their burdens of taxation and recruitment, the lower orders exhibited the same fierce hostility toward privilege and authority, the same destructive fury, compounded of envy, hatred, and mistrust, which they had previously directed against the wealthy and powerful. Furthermore, many of the same social elements—peasants, artisans, national minorities—were involved, including even the Cossacks (at least the poorer or "naked" segment), who reverted to their former insurrectionary role and sided with the people against the government. In February 1917, indeed, it was the Cossacks who, by refusing to fire on the Petrograd crowds, sealed the fate of the autocracy. The modern revolutions, moreover, were sectional as well as social conflicts, with the peripheries rising against the center as in the past, though for the first time the risings in the outlying rural districts coincided with outbreaks in Petrograd and Moscow, as well as other cities of the industrial heartland, and brought about the collapse of the autocracy.

The revolutions of 1905 and 1917 saw the same ideological simplicity, the same lack of a well-defined program, as before. For the peasants and for many workers the prototype of the new society remained a decentralized pastoral paradise in which they might live in peace and contentment with full economic and political freedom organized from below. Fired by simple slogans, the laboring classes aimed at a direct plebeian democracy through local councils and communes akin to the Cossack *krugs* of the past. Their frame of mind, moreover, remained passionately apocalyptic. They showed the same millennial drive, the same yearning for redemption, for a drastic renovation of society, as before. Many Russian peasants, as a contemporary observed, hailed the 1917 Revolution as "the direct realization of their religious hopes." [26] One finds the same faith in regeneration through destruction, which had made so strong an impression on Bakunin. One finds, too, the same popular legends which had been so conspicuous in earlier upheavals. The myth of the good tsar, for instance, was still widely accepted among artisans and peasants. During the rural outbreaks of 1905 and 1917, the villagers often claimed to be acting in the name of a popular ruler who had authorized the distribution of the gentry estates. "It was not so much the Emperor as the regime of which the nation as a whole was weary," noted the British ambassador in 1917. "As a soldier remarked, 'Oh yes, we must have a Republic, but we must have a good tsar at the head.' " [27]

Oral tradition, of course, played a key role in perpetuating these legends. When the writer Korolenko, following in Pushkin's footsteps, went to the Volga and Urals at the turn of the century to collect materials about Pugachev, he found the myth of "Peter Fyodorovich" still flourishing. What was more, following the great famine of 1891, pretenders again appeared in the byways of rural Russia, one of whom (typically, a former soldier) was said to bear the "marks of the tsar" on his chest, like Pugachev. About the same time, moreover, though over a century had passed since Pugachev's rebellion, a Bashkir was arrested in the Urals for singing a song about Salavat Yulaev at a village celebration. And in the mines and foundries of the Urals during the 1905 Revolution it was said that if a new *ataman* should appear he would find "hundreds or even thousands ready to follow him." [28]

Nor was this danger lost on the authorities, who often compared the rioting of 1905 and 1917 to that of Razin and Pugachev. In 1905, for instance, Prime Minister Witte raised the specter of Pugachev to persuade the tsar to sign the October Manifesto, lest "a Russian revolt, senseless and merciless, should sweep all before it and turn everything to dust." Using the same phrase from Pushkin, the head of the Kadet party, Pavel Miliukov, warned on the eve of 1917 that unless reforms were granted rebellion would engulf the whole country. "And God save us from this fire. It would not be a revolution. It would be that terrible 'Russian revolt, senseless and merciless' . . . an orgy of the mob." [29] But the Minister of the Interior, Durnovo, saw things in a different light. If reforms were in fact introduced, he said, as the Kadets demanded, they would undermine the whole social order, claiming the Kadets themselves among the victims, "and afterwards would come the revolutionary mob, the Commune, the destruction of the dynasty, pogroms of the possessing classes, and finally the peasant-brigand." As Trotsky commented: "It is impossible to deny that the police anger here rises to a certain kind of historic vision." [30]

Clearly, then, the Russian revolutions of the twentieth century were deeply rooted in the risings of the past. Traditional forms

and patterns, rather than vanishing, either persisted or were transformed and adapted to new conditions. Moreover, the urban and
rural poor continued to play a key revolutionary role, furnishing
the explosive that demolished the old order. But the makers of
the revolution were to become its chief victims, crushed by the
new regime which they helped into power. For the Bolsheviks
proceeded to erect a new centralized order that was stronger
than the one that it replaced. After a brief interval of freedom,
a new bureaucracy resumed the revolution from above begun
under the tsars, harnessing a reluctant population to the needs
of the state. For Bolshevism, as for tsarism, autonomy and spon-
taneity were evil words, evoking the stormy, ungovernable passions of the lower classes, which the governing elite was anxious
to control. According to Marxist theory, the peasant had to
be broken if the revolution was to be "progressive." Thus the
Bolsheviks turned on the very groups which had brought them
to power, putting an end to their rural and handicrafts world
and making them, in Barrington Moore's words, the main
"victims   of   the   socialist   version   of   primary   capitalist
accumulation." [31]

The result was a resumption of civil war between the state
and the people. As early as 1918 a peasant congress declared that
the organs of local self-government must defend themselves once
more against the usurpations of the center. There was no end to
it—tsars, landlords, bureaucrats, and now Bolsheviks—"all have
scoffed and mocked at us." [32] Among the political parties the
anarchists and Socialist Revolutionaries defended the popular
revolution against the new autocracy, opposing the "Communists
and commissars" as Razin and Pugachev had opposed the "boyars
and officials." In this sense the anarchist Makhno, the ex–Socialist
Revolutionary Antonov, and the sailors of Kronstadt were the
final echoes of the earlier mass protests against centralized bureaucratic despotism.

As in the past, the government's opponents were concentrated
in the peripheries, particularly in the Urals and along the Don
and Volga. For the Socialist Revolutionaries the nerve center was
the middle Volga, for Makhno the lower Dnieper. Among the
Don Cossacks, interestingly enough, the old slogan that "fugitives
are not handed over" was revived against the new Muscovite

government. In the eyes of the peasantry, moreover, the state remained a predator, while Makhno and Antonov were new Razins or Pugachevs come to rescue them from oppression and to grant them land and freedom. Makhno, wrote a fellow anarchist, "became the avenging angel of the lowly, and presently he was looked upon as the great liberator whose coming had been prophesied by Pugachev in his dying moments," [33] a reference to the "raven" legend from Pushkin. Following the example of his precursors, Makhno expropriated the gentry, removed the officials, established a Cossack-style "republic" in the steppe, and was revered by his followers as their *batko*. The government, for its part, denounced him and Antonov as "bandits"—the epithet with which Moscow had maligned its guerrilla opponents since the seventeenth century—and used draconian measures to suppress them. Antonov, by an odd coincidence, met the same fate as Bulavin, being shot while fleeing from a house that his pursuers had set ablaze. What is more, the same legends arose about them after their defeat. As Makhno's wife told Emma Goldman, "there grew up among the country folk the belief that Makhno was invincible because he had never been wounded during all the years of warfare in spite of his practice of always personally leading every charge." [34]

The myth of the good tsar was also long in dying. Accordingly, the peasants tended to blame not Lenin himself for their suffering, but rather his corrupt and scheming advisors, who kept the ruler in ignorance while robbing the people of their freedom. The rebels of Kronstadt, while denouncing Trotsky and Zinoviev for their treachery, treated Lenin with a certain respect and distinguished him sharply from his associates. The Bolshevik leader, they said, was actually fed up with government affairs and wanted only to escape. "But Lenin's cohorts would not let him flee. He is their prisoner and must utter slanders just as they do." [35] Thus as late as 1921 the ancient legend of the benevolent tsar as a helpless captive of his underlings had lost none of its vitality. But even that was not all. When Lenin died in 1924 it was rumored that he was still alive, awaiting the proper moment to rescue the people from their new masters. Lenin, according to one legend, had sent for his doctor a year or two before and asked if he could make him appear dead. "I want to see what becomes of

Russia if they think me dead," he explained. "At present they put everything on my shoulders and make me responsible." Only the doctor and Lenin's wife knew the secret. Lenin's death was announced, everyone mourned, and he was put in a mausoleum in Red Square. But at night he walks about in the Kremlin, in the factories, in the villages. "No one knows how long Lenin will lie in his glass case pretending to be dead." [36]

Notes

INTRODUCTION

1. V. V. Mavrodin *et al.*, *Krest'ianskaia voina v Rossii v 1773–1775 godakh*, 3 vols., Leningrad, 1961–1970, I, 41.
2. See Anatole G. Mazour, *Modern Russian Historiography*, 2nd edn., Princeton, N.J., 1958, pp. 152–53.
3. Quoted in Mavrodin, *Krest'ianskaia voina v Rossii*, I, 55.
4. V. O. Kliuchevsky, *A History of Russia*, 5 vols., New York, 1911–1931, III, 46.
5. N. N. Firsov, *Razinovshchina*, St. Petersburg, 1906, p. 3.
6. Mavrodin, *Krest'ianskaia voina v Rossii*, I, 180.
7. A. L. Shapiro, "Ob istoricheskoi roli krest'ianskikh voin XVII–XVIII vv. v Rossii," *Istoriia SSSR*, 1965, No. 5, p. 63.
8. Eric Hobsbawm, *Primitive Rebels*, Manchester, England, 1959, p. 2.

CHAPTER I: BOLOTNIKOV, 1606–1607

1. *Russia at the Close of the Sixteenth Century*, ed. Sir Edward Bond, London, 1856, p. 206.
2. *Ibid.*, p. 163.
3. Giles Fletcher, *Of the Russe Common Wealth*, London, 1591, p. 26.
4. *Ibid.*, p. 46.
5. V. I. Koretskii, "Iz istorii krest'ianskoi voiny v Rossii nachala XVII veka," *Voprosy Istorii*, 1959, No. 3, pp. 119–22.
6. Kliuchevsky, *A History of Russia*, II, 89.
7. See Iu. V. Got'e, *Zamoskovnyi krai v XVII veke*, Moscow, 1937, pp. 138–48.
8. Michael Cherniavsky, *Tsar and People*, New Haven, Conn., 1961, pp. 42–44.
9. Kliuchevsky, *History*, III, 50–51.
10. I. I. Smirnov, *Vosstanie Bolotnikova, 1606–1607*, 2nd. edn., Moscow, 1951, p. 63.
11. P. I. Lyashchenko, *History of the National Economy of Russia*, New York, 1949, p. 198.
12. *Polnoe sobranie russkikh letopisei*, XIV, part 1, St. Petersburg, 1910, 58, hereafter cited as *PSRL*; *Skazanie Avraamiia Palitsyna*, Moscow, 1955, pp. 107–8.

13. See *Voprosy Istorii*, 1958, No. 3, pp. 97–113; 1960, No. 6, pp. 90–101; and *Istoriia SSSR*, 1962, No. 4, pp. 112–18.

14. George Vernadsky, "The Death of the Tsarevich Dimitry: A Reconsideration of the Case," *Oxford Slavonic Papers*, V, 1954, 1–19.

15. Kliuchevsky, *History*, III, 24. See also A. H. Thompson, "The Legend of Tsarevich Dimitriy: Some Evidence of an Oral Tradition," *Slavonic and East European Review*, XLVI, January 1968, 45–59.

16. V. N. Aleksandrenko, "Materialy po Smutnomu vremeni na Rusi XVII v.," *Starina i Novizna*, XIV, 1911, 262.

17. Kliuchevsky, *History*, III, 32; Aleksandrenko, "Materialy po Smutnomu vremeni," p. 254. For an absorbing account of Dmitri's meteoric career, see Philip L. Barbour, *Dimitry, Called the Pretender*, Boston, 1966.

18. George Vernadsky, *A History of Russia*, New Haven, Conn., 1961, p. 117.

19. A. Hirschberg, ed., *Polska a Moskwa w perwszej polowie wieku XVII*, Lwow, 1901, p. 75.

20. *Akty, sobrannye v bibliotekakh i arkhivakh Rossiiskoi imperii Arkheograficheskoiu ekspeditsieiu Imperatorskoi akademii nauk*, 4 vols., St. Petersburg, 1836, II, 111–12, hereafter *AAE*; *PSRL*, XIV, part 1, 70; *Rerum rossicarum scriptores exteri*, II, St. Petersburg, 1868, 110–11.

21. "Yaroslav's daughter early weeps / in Putivl on the rampart." *The Song of Igor's Campaign*, tr. Vladimir Nabokov, New York, 1960, pp. 64–65.

22. N. G. Ustrialov, ed., *Skazaniia sovremennikov o Dimitrii Samozvantse*, 3rd edn., 2 vols., St. Petersburg, 1859, I, 79.

23. *Vosstanie I. Bolotnikova: dokumenty i materialy*, Moscow, 1959, p. 373; *PSRL*, XIV, part 1, 70.

24. Aleksandrenko, "Materialy po Smutnomu vremeni," p. 262. The author of this anonymous English report, which constitutes one of the most valuable sources on Bolotnikov's revolt, was in all probability John Merick (or Meyrick), a successor of Jerome Horsey, who spent many years in Moscow as chief agent of the Russia Company. In the words of an associate, he acquitted his duties "with wonderful judgment and discretion, with such credit with the Emperor [Boris] as never any Englishman had the like, both for honest pleasing of him and provident care of his own country's profit." Knighted by James I, Merick returned to Russia in 1615 as ambassador to the court of Tsar Michael. *Dictionary of National Biography*, XIII, 319–20; T. S. Willan, *The Early History of the Russia Company 1553–1603*, Manchester, England, 1956, p. 240; *Russia at the Close of the Sixteenth Century*, p. 265n; *Istoricheskie Zapiski*, XIII, 1942, 291–302.

25. Aleksandrenko, "Materialy po Smutnomu vremeni," p. 263.

26. Fletcher, *Of the Russe Common Wealth*, p. 67.

27. *Rerum rossicarum scriptores exteri*, I, 1851, 70; II, 107–8, 119, 154; *Vosstanie I. Bolotnikova*, pp. 186–87.

28. *Rerum rossicarum*, I, 71.

29. *PSRL*, XIV, part 1, 71.

30. N. I. Kostomarov, *Smutnoe vremia Moskovskogo gosudarstva v nachale XVII stoletiia*, 3 vols. in 1, St. Petersburg, 1868, II, 50; S. M. Solov'ev, *Istoriia Rossii s drevneishikh vremen*, 15 vols., Moscow, 1959–1966, IV, 468; *Rerum rossicarum*, II, 106.

31. S. A. Belokurov, ed., *Razriadnye zapisi za Smutnoe vremia (7113–7121 gg.)*, Moscow, 1907, p. 156.

32. Smirnov, *Vosstanie Bolotnikova*, pp. 194–200; *Rerum rossicarum*, II, 116; S. F. Platonov, *Ocherki po istorii smuty v Moskovskom gosudarstve XVI–XVII vv.*, St. Petersburg, 1899, pp. 327–29.

33. P. P. Smirnov, *Goroda Moskovskogo gosudarstva v pervoi polovine XVII veke*, 2 vols., Kiev, 1917–1919, I, part 1, 16–59.

34. According to the late Professor Smirnov, the leading authority on Bolotnikov, no less than 20,000 runaway slaves thronged the southern border towns. Some of them (including Bolotnikov himself) had been military servitors in their masters' private retinues and thus were of particular importance in the motley rebel army. *Vosstanie Bolotnikova*, pp. 107–9. See also V. I. Koretskii, "Letopisets s novymi izvestiiami o vosstanii Bolotnikova," *Istoriia SSSR*, 1968, No. 4, pp. 120–30.

35. "Piskarevskii letopisets," *Materialy po istorii SSSR*, II, 1955, 131.

36. *AAE*, II, 132.

37. Kostomarov, *Smutnoe vremia*, II, 44; Smirnov, *Vosstanie Bolotnikova*, p. 70. Pashkov's role at Elets, however, has been questioned by other specialists. See *Voprosy Istorii*, 1958, No. 3, pp. 97–113; and 1959, No. 7, pp. 72–75.

38. Platonov, *Ocherki po istorii smuty*, p. 334.

39. *AAE*, II, 137.

40. *Vosstanie I. Bolotnikova*, p. 175.

41. Belokurov, *Razriadnye zapisi*, p. 10.

42. *PSRL*, XIV, part 1, 71.

43. Kliuchevsky, *History*, III, 32.

44. Hirschberg, *Polska a Moskwa*, p. 81; *Vosstanie I. Bolotnikova*, p. 177.

45. Solov'ev, *Istoriia Rossii*, IV, 470.

46. M. N. Tikhomirov, "Novyi istochnik po istorii vosstaniia Bolotnikova," *Istoricheskii Arkhiv*, VI, 1951, 116.

47. *AAE*, II, 129. Compare Merick's account: "They continued the siege and writ letters to the slaves within the town, to take arms against their masters and possess themselves of their goods and substance. . . ." Aleksandrenko, "Materialy po Smutnomu vremeni," p. 262.

48. *Vosstanie I. Bolotnikova*, p. 184; Smirnov, *Vosstanie Bolotnikova*, pp. 289–91.

49. *AAE*, II, 131.

50. *Rerum rossicarum*, I, 71. Cf. Ustrialov, *Skazaniia souvremennikov*, I, 83.

51. *Vosstanie I. Bolotnikova*, pp. 175–77.

52. Aleksandrenko, "Materialy po Smutnomu vremeni," p. 263.

53. Platonov, *Ocherki po istorii smuty*, pp. 334–35.

54. Aleksandrenko, "Materialy po Smutnomu vremeni," p. 262.

55. *PSRL*, XIV, part 1, 72; *Istoricheskii Arkhiv*, I, 1936, 6–7, VIII, 1953, 32, 70.

56. *PSRL*, XIV, part 1, 73; *AAE*, II, 138.

57. *Rerum rossicarum*, I, 71.

58. Aleksandrenko, "Materialy po Smutnomu vremeni," p. 263.

59. Notably Yushka Bezzubtsev, a Cossack officer from Putivl, who previously had fought for Dmitri the Pretender and now, apparently, stood by Bolotnikov to the end. G. N. Anpilogov, "Novye materialy o krest'ianskoi voine pod rukovodstvom I. Bolotnikova," *Voprosy Istorii*, 1966, No. 12, pp. 199–202. Kostomarov and Platonov, however, say that Bezzubtsev defected on December 2, 1606.

60. *Rerum rossicarum*, II, 113.

61. Hirschberg, *Polska a Moskwa*, p. 86.

62. Smirnov, *Vosstanie Bolotnikova*, pp. 201–7.

63. Solov'ev, *Istoriia Rossii*, IV, 472; *PSRL*, XIV, part 1, 72.

64. L. M. Sukhotin, ed., *Chetvertchiki Smutnogo vremeni (1604–1617)*, Moscow, 1912, pp. 202–38; *Vosstanie I. Bolotnikova*, pp. 263–72.

65. "Piskarevskii letopisets," p. 125.

66. *Rerum rossicarum*, I, 74.

67. A. N. Popov, *Izbornik slavianskikh i russkikh sochinenii i statei*, Moscow, 1869, p. 332.

68. *Vosstanie I. Bolotnikova*, pp. 109–10, 223–26; *Skazanie Avraamiia Palitsyna*, p. 116; Belokurov, *Razriadnye zapisi*, p. 10; *PSRL*, XIV, part 1, 71.

69. *PSRL*, XIV, part 1, 74. Cf. *Vosstanie I. Bolotnikova*, p. 110.

70. "Smutnoe vremia Moskovskogo gosudarstva," ed. A. M. Gnevushev, *Chteniia*, 1915, II, p. 262.

71. *PSRL*, XIV, part 1, 74; *Rerum rossicarum*, II, 115–16.

72. Kostomarov, *Smutnoe vremia*, II, 41–42; Solov'ev, *Istoriia Rossii*, IV, 466.

73. *Vosstanie I. Bolotnikova*, pp. 117, 178–79.

74. *AAE*, II, 164.

75. *Rerum rossicarum*, II, 155.

76. *Ibid.*, I, 76; *Vosstanie I. Bolotnikova*, p. 118.

77. Kliuchevsky, *History*, III, 37.

78. *Rerum rossicarum*, I, 73; II, 156.

79. "Smutnoe vremia," *Chteniia*, 1915, book 2, pp. 171–72.

80. *Rerun rossicarum*, I, 79; II, 156–57.

81. Hirschberg, *Polska a Moskwa*, p. 128.

82. Solov'ev, *Istoriia Rossii*, IV, 703–4.

83. *Rerum rossicarum*, I, 80; *Vosstanie I. Bolotnikova*, p. 348.

CHAPTER II: RAZIN, 1670-1671

1. See J. L. H. Keep, "Bandits and the Law in Muscovy," *Slavonic and East European Review*, XXXV, December 1956, 201-22; and Denise Eeckaute, "Les brigands en Russie du XVIIe siècle," *Revue D'Histoire Moderne et Contemporaine*, XII, July–September 1965, 161-202.

2. N. I. Kostomarov, *Bunt Sten'ki Razina*, in his *Istoricheskie monografii i issledovaniia*, 2nd edn., St. Petersburg, 1872, II, 204.

3. Iu. M. Sokolov, *Russian Folklore*, New York, 1950, p. 264.

4. "Nechem platit' dolgu—stupai na Volgu, libo v razboiniki, libo v burlaki," in I. V. Stepanov, *Krest'ianskaia voina pod predvoditel'stvom S. T. Razina (1670–1671 gg.)*, Moscow, 1957, p. 24.

5. T. I. Smirnova, "Pobegi krest'ian nakanune vystupleniia S. Razina," *Voprosy Istorii*, 1956, No. 6, pp. 129–30.

6. I. V. Stepanov, *Krest'ianskaia voina v Rossii v 1670–1671 gg.: vosstanie Stepana Razina*, Leningrad, 1966, I, 256. See also A. G. Man'kov, *Razvitie krepostnogo prava v Rossii vo vtoroi polovine XVII veka*, Moscow, 1962, pp. 22ff.

7. See, for instance, R. B. Merriman, *Six Contemporaneous Revolutions*, Oxford, 1938; Trevor Aston, ed., *Crisis in Europe, 1560–1660*, New York, 1965; and Robert Forster and J. P. Greene, eds., *Preconditions of Revolution in Early Modern Europe*, Baltimore, 1971.

8. Aston, *Crisis in Europe*, p. 59; S. F. Platonov, *Lektsii po russkoi istorii*, 7th edn., St. Petersburg, 1910, p. 339; S. P. Mel'gunov, *Religiozno-obshchestvennye dvizheniia XVI–XVIII vv. v Rossii*, Moscow, 1922, p. 44.

9. See Michael Cherniavsky, "The Old Believers and the New Religion," *Slavic Review*, XXV, March 1966, 1–39.

10. Platonov, *Lektsii*, p. 344; Kliuchevsky, *History*, III, 136.

11. Leo Loewenson, "The Moscow Rising of 1648," *Slavonic and East European Review*, XXVII, December 1948, 153. See also S. B. Bakhrushin, "Moskovskii miatezh 1648 g.," in *Sbornik statei v chesti prof. M. K. Liubavskogo*, Petrograd, 1917, pp. 709–74.

12. George V. Lantzeff, *Siberia in the Seventeenth Century*, Berkeley, Calif., 1943, p. 85; Platonov, *Lektsii*, p. 344.

13. G. K. Kotoshikhin, *O Rossii v tsarstvovanii Alekseia Mikhailovicha*, 3rd edn., St. Petersburg, 1884, pp. 114–18.

14. Quoted in I. I. Smirnov *et al.*, *Krest'ianskie voiny v Rossii XVII–XVIII vv.*, Moscow, 1966, p. 209.

15. Lists of *zhalovanie* supplied by Moscow to the Don Cossacks from 1651 to 1692 are to be found in V. G. Druzhinin, *Raskol na Donu v kontse XVII veka*, St. Petersburg, 1889, pp. 229–32.

16. N. N. Firsov, *Krest'ianskaia revoliutsiia na Rusi v XVII veke*, Moscow, 1927, pp. 74–75.

17. Druzhinin, *Raskol na Donu*, p. 43.

18. *Donskie dela,* 5 vols., St. Petersburg, 1898–1917, V, 709–13, 765–66.

19. Adam Olearius, *Voyages and Travels,* 2nd edn., London, 1669, p. 112; A. I. Rigel'man, *Istoriia ili povestvovanie o donskikh kazakakh,* Moscow, 1846, VII, part 2, 11.

20. *Akty istoricheskie,* 5 vols., St. Petersburg, 1841–1842, IV, 374.

21. E. V. Chistiakova, *Vasilii Us—spodvizhnik Stepana Razina,* Moscow, 1963, pp. 12–40.

22. *Krest'ianskaia voina pod predvoditel'stvom Stepana Razina: sbornik dokumentov,* 3 vols. in 4, Moscow, 1954–1962, I, 70.

23. *Donskie dela,* IV, 551–52; V, 846, 922–25; *Krest'ianskaia voina,* I, 28–30, 261. There is evidence, however, that Razin did not make the second trip to Solovki, for in February 1662 he was already back in Astrakhan on another mission to the Kalmyks.

24. *Krest'ianskaia voina,* I, 30–31; V. I. Lebedev, *Krest'ianskaia voina pod predvoditel'stvom Stepana Razina, 1667–1671 gg.,* Moscow, 1955, p. 46.

25. For example, Jan Struys, *The Voyages and Travels of John Struys,* London, 1684, p. 184; and *A Relation Concerning the Particulars of the Rebellion Lately Raised in Muscovy by Stenko Razin,* London, 1672, p. 4.

26. See, for instance, *Donskie dela,* IV, 168.

27. Struys, *Voyages,* p. 186.

28. *A Relation,* pp. 4–5.

29. Kostomarov, *Bunt Sten'ki Razina,* pp. 228–29.

30. *Akty istoricheskie,* IV, 376–77.

31. *Krest'ianskaia voina,* I, 135–36; Kostomarov, *Bunt Sten'ki Razina,* p. 235.

32. Stepanov, *Krest'ianskaia voina v Rossii,* I, 328.

33. *Polnoe sobranie zakonov Rossiiskoi Imperii,* 234 vols., St. Petersburg, 1830–1916, I, 845; *Krest'ianskaia voina,* I, 134–56. Taking a town by guile is an important motif of Cossack folklore.

34. Jean Chardin, *The Travels of Sir John Chardin into Persia and the East Indies,* London, 1691, part 2, p. 141.

35. Struys, *Voyages,* p. 184.

36. Chardin, *Travels,* part 2, pp. 144–45; A. N. Popov, *Materialy dlia istorii vozmushcheniia Sten'ki Razina,* Moscow, 1857, p. 31.

37. *A Relation,* p. 6.

38. *Dopolneniia k aktam istoricheskim,* 12 vols., St. Petersburg, 1846–1875, VI, 15.

39. "Anonymous Narrative," in Struys, *Voyages,* p. 362.

40. Struys, *Voyages,* p. 187.

41. Ludwig Fabritius, another contemporary observer, gives a variant of Struys's tale, stating that Razin in 1668 threw a captured Tatar girl into the Yaik. Of the principal authorities on Razin, Kostomarov, Soloviev, and Firsov all accept the existence of the princess, while Tkhorzhevsky—probably correctly—rejects it.

42. *Dopolneniia k aktam istoricheskim,* VI, 161.

43. Firsov, *Razinovshchina,* p. 45.

44. "Anonymous Narrative," in Struys, *Voyages*, p. 362.

45. *A Relation*, p. 6; Popov, *Materialy*, p. 192.

46. Stepanov, *Krest'ianskaia voina v Rossii*, I, 14; *Krest'ianskaia voina*, I, 99–101.

47. *Dopolneniia k aktam istoricheskim*, VI, 57; *Polnoe sobranie zakonov*, I, 846; *Krest'ianskaia voina*, I, 163–65. Drowning was a traditional Cossack method of execution, the victim being placed in a sack filled with sand and stones, to prevent his body from rising to the surface. A pagan survival, this practice was intended to propitiate the water spirits, on which the Cossacks counted during fishing and maritime expeditions.

48. *Krest'ianskaia voina*, I, 235–36, 253.

49. Quoted in Kostomarov, *Bunt Sten'ki Razina*, p. 271.

50. *Krest'ianskaia voina*, I, 195–96, 221; *Polnoe sobranie zakonov*, I, 846.

51. A. N. Popov, *Istoriia vozmushcheniia Sten'ki Razina*, Moscow, 1857, pp. 67–69.

52. *Krest'ianskaia voina*, I, 163.

53. Quoted in R. Nesbit Bain, *The First Romanovs (1613–1725)*, London, 1905, pp. 55–57.

54. Popov, *Istoriia*, p. 69; *Krest'ianskaia voina*, I, 183.

55. S. Konovalov, "Ludwig Fabritius's Account of the Razin Rebellion," *Oxford Slavonic Papers*, VI, 1955, 81-83; *Dopolneniia k aktam istoricheskim*, VI, 58. On Fabritius see also *Voprosy Istorii*, 1966, No. 5, pp. 202–6.

56. Struys, *Voyages*, p. 177; Olearius, *Voyages*, pp. 65, 127; *Krest'ianskaia voina*, I, 244.

57. "David Butler's Narrative," in Struys, *Voyages*, p. 368.

58. *A Relation*, p. 8.

59. "David Butler's Narrative," in Struys, *Voyages*, p. 366.

60. Struys, *Voyages*, p. 196.

61. Konovalov, "Ludwig Fabritius's Account," *Oxford Slavonic Papers*, VI, 84.

62. *Krest'ianskaia voina*, III, 183.

63. *Ibid.*, I, 250; *AAE*, IV, 228–29.

64. "David Butler's Narrative," in Struys, *Voyages*, p. 373.

65. *Ibid.*, pp. 373–78. See also Popov, *Istoriia*, pp. 75–76; and *Sobranie gosudarstvennykh gramot i dogovorov*, 5 vols., Moscow, 1813–1894, IV, 253–54.

66. Konovalov, "Ludwig Fabritius's Account," *Oxford Slavonic Papers*, VI, 85.

67. *Krest'ianskaia voina*, I, 252.

68. Firsov, *Razinovshchina*, pp. 38–39.

69. S. G. Tomsinskii, ed., *Krest'ianstvo i natsionaly v revoliutsionnom dvizhenii i razinshchina*, Moscow, 1931, p. 309; *Krest'ianskaia voina*, II, part 1, 65.

70. Popov, *Istoriia*, p. 116.

71. Struys, *Voyages*, p. 192.

72. Stepanov, *Krest'ianskaia voina*, p. 14.

73. S. I. Porfir'ev, "Razinshchina v Kazanskom krae," *Izvestiia Obsh-chestva Arkheologii, istorii i etnografii pri Imperatorskom Kazanskom universitete*, XXIX, 1916, No. 5–6, p. 313.

74. Sokolov, *Russian Folklore*, p. 371. See also *Voprosy Istorii*, 1969, No. 4, pp. 138–47.

75. *A Relation*, p. 14. Cf. Tomsinskii, *Krest'ianstvo i natsionaly*, p. 63; Firsov, *Krest'ianskaia revoliutsiia*, p. 106; V. A. Nikol'skii, *Sten'ka Razin i razinovshchina*, St. Petersburg, n.d., p. 52; and *Istoricheskii Arkhiv*, I, 1936, 78.

76. *Krest'ianskaia voina*, II, part 1, 79.

77. See, for example, *ibid.*, II, part 1, 141; Tomsinskii, *Krest'ianstvo i natsionaly*, pp. 289–94; *Istoricheskii Arkhiv*, I, 79; and A. A. Geraklitov, *Istoriia Saratovskogo kraia v XVI–XVII vv.*, Saratov, 1923, p 215.

78. Popov, *Istoriia*, p. 81; Tomsinskii, *Krest'ianstvo i natsionaly*, p. 312.

79. *A Relation*, p. 10.

80. *Ibid.*

81. "Pis'mo Sten'ki Razina k Kazanskim tataram," *Izvestiia Obshchestva Arkheologii, istorii i etnografii pri Imperatorskom Kazanskom universitete*, VIII, No. 3, 44–45.

82. Tomsinskii, *Krest'ianstvo i natsionaly*, pp. 282–84; *Krest'ianskaia voina*, II, part 1, 78–79.

83. B. N. Tikhomirov, *Razinshchina*, Moscow, 1930, p. 105.

84. *A Relation*, pp. 11–12; *Krest'ianskaia voina*, I, 235, 279–80.

85. *A Relation*, p. 12; *Krest'ianskaia voina*, II, part 1, 203.

86. *Krest'ianskaia voina*, II, part 1, 31, 552; Tomsinskii, *Krest'ianstvo i natsionaly*, p. 63.

87. See N. A. Barsukov, *Solovetskoe vosstanie (1668–1676 gg.)*, Petro-zavodsk, 1954, pp. 49–50; M. I. Fenomenov, *Razinovshchina i pugachevsh-china*, Moscow, 1923, p. 15; and Tikhomirov, *Razinshchina*, p. 106.

88. Tomsinskii, *Krest'ianstvo i natsionaly* p. 19.

89. D. F. Karzhavin, *Stepan Razin v Simbirske*, Ulyanovsk, 1947, p. 34.

90. *Krest'ianskaia voina*, II, part 1, 69; A. I. Solov'ev, *Sten'ka Razin i ego soobshchniki v predelakh nyneshnei Simbirskoi gubernii*, Simbirsk, 1907, pp. 31–34.

91. *A Relation*, pp. 9–10.

92. Quoted in Lebedev, *Krest'ianskaia voina*, p. 105.

93. B. D. Grekov, *Novye materialy o dvizhenii Stepana Razina*, Lenin-grad, 1927, p. 208; *Krest'ianskaia voina*, III, 40.

94. *Krest'ianskaia voina*, II, part 1, 114; Tikhomirov, *Razinshchina*, pp. 116–17.

95. See, for example, *Krest'ianskaia voina*, II, part 1, 83, 172, 266.

96. See Fenomenov, *Razinovshchina i pugachevshchina*, p. 112n.

97. *Akty otnosiashchiesia k istorii iuzhnoi i zapadnoi Rossii*, 15 vols., St. Petersburg, 1863–1892, IX, 266–93; D. E. Kravtsov, "Otgoloski razinsh-chiny na Ukraine," *Trudy instituta slavianovedeniia Akademii nauk SSSR*,

II, 1934, 77–99; K. I. Stetsiuk, *Vpliv povstannia Stepana Razina na Ukraine*, Kiev, 1947, pp. 72–92.

98. *Krest'ianskaia voina*, II, part 2, 36, 58–61.

99. See, for instance, *ibid.*, II, part 1, 183–84; part 2, 199–200.

100. I. V. Stepanov, "K istorii krest'ianskoi voiny pod predvoditel'stvom Stepana Razina," *Vestnik Leningradskogo universiteta (seriia istorii, iazyka i literatury)*, 1961, No. 2, pp. 68–76.

101. *Krest'ianskaia voina*, II, part 1, 32.

102. *Ibid.*, II, part 1, 177.

103. A. K. Kabanov, "Razintsy v Nizhegorodskom krae," in *Sbornik statei v chesti M. K. Liubavskogo*, p. 414.

104. *Razgrom razinshchiny*, Leningrad, 1934, p. xiii.

105. Popov, *Istoriia*, p. 100; Solov'ev, *Sten'ka Razin i ego soobshchniki*, pp. 41–42.

106. Popov, *Materialy*, p. 30; *Krest'ianskaia voina*, II, part 1, 317.

107. Tomsinskii, *Krest'ianstvo i natsionaly*, p. 309; *Krest'ianskaia voina*, II, part 2, 74–75.

108. *A Relation*, p. 15.

109. *Razgrom razinshchiny*, p. 281; N. S. Chaev, "K istorii razinovshchiny," *Vestnik Akademii Nauk SSSR*, 1933, No. 4, pp. 32–37.

110. *A Relation*, p. 13.

111. A. A. Golubev, ed., "K istorii bunta Sten'ki Razina v Zavolzh'i," *Chteniia*, CLXX, part 1, p. 5; Popov, *Materialy*, p. 79.

112. Porfir'ev, "Razinshchina v Kazanskom krae," *Izvestiia Obshchestva Arkheologii*, XXIX, No. 5–6, 336–37.

113. *Krest'ianskaia voina*, III, 27–29.

114. *Dopolneniia k aktam istoricheskim*, V, 64, 71.

115. *A Relation*, p. 16.

116. *Ibid.*, pp. 16–17.

117. *Ibid.*, p. 17.

118. Tomsinskii, *Krest'ianstvo i natsionaly*, pp. 252–59; J. Reitenfels, in *Chteniia*, CCXIV, part 2, 119; *A Relation*, p. 18. There are many accounts of Razin's execution. See, for instance, S. Konovalov, "Razin's Execution: Two Contemporary Documents," *Oxford Slavonic Papers*, XII, 1965, 94–98; J. J. Martius, *Stephanus Razin Cossacus Perduellis*, Wittenberg, 1674, p. 30; *Katorga i Ssylka*, 1932, No. 3, pp. 128–36; and *Voprosy Istorii*, 1961, No. 8, pp. 208–12.

119. B. N. Tikhomirov, "Istochniki po istorii Razinshchiny," *Problemy Istochnikovedeniia*, 1933, No. 1, pp. 50–69; *Posol'stvo Kunraada fan-Klenka k tsariam Alekseiu Mikhailovichu i Fedoru Alekseevichu*, St. Petersburg, 1900, p. 210.

120. *AAE*, IV, 234; S. G. Svatikov, *Rossiia i Don (1549–1917)*, Belgrade, 1924, pp. 97–98.

121. *Krest'ianskaia voina*, III, 184.

122. Popov, *Istoriia*, 127–28.

123. *Krest'ianskaia voina*, III, 136, 183.

124. *Ibid.*, III, 184.

125. E. V. Chistiakova, "Astrakhan' v period vosstaniia Stepana Razina," *Istoriia SSSR*, 1957, No. 5, p. 199.

126. *Krest'ianskaia voina*, III, 185.

127. *Ibid.*, III, 184.

128. *Ibid.*, III, 344–45; Z. I. Mikhailovicheva, *Stepan Razin*, Moscow, 1939, p. 48.

129. Firsov, *Razinovshchina*, p. 4.

130. Kostomarov, *Bunt Sten'ki Razina*, p. 198. The *veche* was the local town assembly in medieval Russia.

131. S. I. Tkhorzhevskii, *Sten'ka Razin*, Petrograd, 1923, p. 120.

132. *A Relation*, p. 13.

133. S. G. Tomsinskii, *Ocherki istorii feodal'no-krepostnoi Rossii*, Moscow, 1934, p. 183; N. K. Firsov, *Narodnye dvizheniia v Rossii do XIX veka*, Moscow, 1924, p. 46.

134. M. N. Smentsovskii, "St. Razin v nauke, literature i iskusstve," *Katorga i Ssylka*, 1932, No. 7, p. 193; Sokolov, *Russian Folklore*, p. 358.

135. M. A. Iakovlev, *Narodnoe pesnotvorchestvo ob atamane Stepane Razine*, Leningrad, 1924, pp. 34, 40; T. A. Martem'ianov, "Iz predanii o Sten'ke Razine," *Istoricheskii Vestnik*, CIX, 1907, 850–60; Bernard Pares, *A History of Russia*, New York, 1965, p. 161.

136. Tomsinskii, *Krest'ianstvo i natsionaly*, p. xvi.

137. A. N. Lozanova, *Pesni i skazaniia o Razine i Pugacheve*, Moscow, 1935, p. 53.

138. Kostomarov, *Bunt Sten'ki Razina*, p. 356.

139. V. I. Lenin, *Polnoe sobranie sochineniia*, 5th edn., 55 vols., Moscow, 1958–1965, XXXVIII, 326.

140. *Sobranie gosudarstvennykh gramot*, IV, 292–94, 323–26; Svatikov, *Rossiia i Don*, p. 124.

141. *Krest'ianskaia voina*, III, 376–77, 387.

142. *Krest'ianskie i natsional'nye dvizheniia nakanune obrazovaniia Rossiiskoi Imperii: Bulavinskoe vosstanie (1707–1708 gg.)*, Moscow, 1935, p. 130.

CHAPTER III: BULAVIN, 1707-1708

1. Quoted in B. H. Sumner, *Peter the Great and the Emergence of Russia*, London, 1951, p. 45.

2. John Perry, *The State of Russia Under the Present Czar*, London, 1716, p. 96.

3. V. O. Kliuchevsky, *Peter the Great*, New York, 1961, pp. 77, 81–84.

4. *Ibid.*, pp. 6–7; P. K. Shchebal'skii, *Pravlenie tsarevna Sofii*, Moscow, 1856, pp. 49–67; C. Bickford O'Brien, *Russia Under Two Tsars, 1682–1689*, Berkeley, Calif., 1952, pp. 22–39. The most recent study of the *streltsy*

revolts is V. I. Buganov, *Moskovskie vosstaniia konsta XVII veka*, Moscow, 1969.

5. Quoted in B. H. Sumner, *Peter the Great and the Ottoman Empire*, Oxford, 1949, p. 9.

6. Whitworth to Harley, March 14, 1705, *Sbornik Imperatorskogo Russkogo istoricheskogo obshchestva*, 127 vols., St. Petersburg, 1867–1916, XXXIX, 53. Cited hereafter as *SIRIO*.

7. Sumner, *Peter the Great and the Emergence of Russia*, pp. 42–43.

8. Svatikov, *Rossiia i Don*, p. 130.

9. N. B. Golikova, *Politicheskie protsessy pri Petre I*, Moscow, 1957, pp. 112–19; M. D. Rabinovich, "Strel'tsy v pervoi chetverti XVIII v.," *Istoricheskie Zapiski*, LVIII, 1956, 277.

10. Sumner, *Peter the Great and the Emergence of Russia*, p. 47; Kliuchevsky, *Peter the Great*, pp. 157, 163, 178.

11. N. S. Chaev, *Bulavinskoe vosstanie (1707–1708 gg.)*, Moscow, 1934, p. 11.

12. Christopher Marsden, *Palmyra of the North: The First Days of St. Petersburg*, London, 1942, pp. 45–79.

13. Golikova, *Politicheskie protsessy*, p. 167.

14. Sumner, *Peter the Great and the Ottoman Empire*, pp. 22–23; Chaev, *Bulavinskoe vosstanie*, p. 13.

15. Solov'ev, *Istoriia Rossii*, VIII, 98.

16. Cherniavsky, "The Old Believers and the New Religion," *Slavic Review*, XXV, 28–29; Golikova, *Politicheskie protsessy*, pp. 123–24, 167–69; A. P. Shchapov, *Sochineniia*, 3 vols., St. Petersburg, 1906–1908, I, 472ff.

17. B. H. Sumner, *Survey of Russian History*, 2nd edn., London, 1947, p. 147.

18. Solov'ev, *Istoriia Rossii*, VIII, 122; Mel'gunov, *Religiozno-obshchestvennye dvizheniia*, p. 131.

19. Avvakum, *The Life of Archpriest Avvakum*, London, 1924, p. 121.

20. II Samuel, 24:1–10.

21. Stephen Marshall in 1644, quoted in Michael Walzer, *The Revolution of the Saints*, Cambridge, Mass., 1965, p. 295.

22. Cf. D. S. Mirsky, *Russia: A Social History*, London, 1931, pp. 176–77, 212–213.

23. P. N. Miliukov, *Outline of Russian Culture*, Philadelphia, 1948, part 1, pp. 43, 58–59.

24. Solov'ev, *Istoriia Rossii*, VIII, 108.

25. *Ibid.*, VIII, 117–18; Mel'gunov, *Religiozno-obshchestvennye dvizheniia*, p. 130.

26. Rabinovich, "Strel'tsy v pervoi chetverti XVIII v.," *Istoricheskie Zapiski*, LVIII, 289–90; V. I. Lebedev, "Astrakhan'skoe vosstanie 1705–1706 gg.," *Istorik-Marksist*, 1935, No. 4, p. 78.

27. Perry, *The State of Russia*, p. 96.

28. Golikova, *Politicheskie protsessy*, pp. 225–28; Svatikov, *Rossiia i Don*, p. 119.

29. S. V. Boldyrev, *Ataman K. A. Bulavin*, New York, 1957, p. 44.

30. *Krest'ianskie i natsional'nye dvizheniia nakanune obrazovaniia Rossiiskoi imperii: Bulavinskoe vosstanie (1707–1708 gg.)*, Moscow, 1935, pp. 83–87. Hereafter, *Bulavinskoe vosstanie*.

31. *Ibid.*, pp. 77–79; *Pis'ma i bumagi imperatora Petra Velikogo*, 11 vols. in 16, Moscow, 1887–1964, VI, 210.

32. Boldyrev, *Ataman K. A. Bulavin*, p. 1.

33. *Ibid.*

34. *Pis'ma i bumagi*, VI, 9–10.

35. *Ibid.*, VII, part 1, 160. On Dolgoruky's expedition see also Solov'ev, *Istoriia Rossii*, VIII, 177–78; and A. P. Pronshtein, *Zemlia Donskaia v XVIII veke*, Rostov-on-Don, 1961, pp. 201–2.

36. F. C. Weber, *The Present State of Russia*, 2 vols., London, 1723, I, 142.

37. A. Karasev, "Bumagi otnosiashchiesia k Bulavinskomu buntu," *Russkii Arkhiv*, XXXII, 1894, part 3, 301; V. I. Lebedev, *Bulavinskoe vosstanie, 1704–1708*, Moscow, 1934, pp. 88–90.

38. *Bulavinskoe vosstanie*, p. 130; Solov'ev, *Istoriia Rossii*, VIII, 179.

39. Whitworth to Harley, December 17, 1707, *SIRIO*, XXXIX, 437.

40. *Pis'ma i bumagi*, VII, part 1, 611; Whitworth to Harley, October 29, 1707, *SIRIO*, XXXIX, 428–29.

41. *Bulavinskoe vosstanie*, p. 368.

42. *Ibid.*, pp. 450–51; *Pis'ma i bumagi*, VII, part 1, 600–1.

43. Lebedev, *Bulavinskoe vosstanie*, p. 95.

44. *Bulavinskoe vosstanie*, p. 452.

45. *Ibid.*, p. 213.

46. *Ibid.*, pp. 182–83, 196.

47. *Ibid.*, p. 295.

48. *Ibid.*, p. 64; Lebedev, *Bulavinskoe vosstanie*, pp. 53–56.

49. *Bulavinskoe vosstanie*, p. 230.

50. E. P. Pod"iapol'skaia, *Vosstanie Bulavina, 1707–1709*, Moscow, 1962, pp. 104–6.

51. *Bulavinskoe vosstanie*, p. 466.

52. *Ibid.*, p. 129.

53 For example, by Charles Whitworth, *SIRIO*, L, 16.

54. Sumner, *Peter the Great and the Ottoman Empire*, pp. 50–51; *Materialy po istorii Bashkirskoi ASSR*, 5 vols., Moscow, 1936–1960, I, 236.

55. Lebedev, *Bulavinskoe vosstanie*, p. 35; *Bulavinskoe vosstanie*, p. 206; *Pis'ma i bumagi*, VII, part 1, 555, 599.

56. Solov'ev, *Istoriia Rossii*, VIII, 183; V. I. Lebedev, "O podavlenii narodnogo vosstaniia 1707–1708 gg.," *Istoricheskii Arkhiv*, 1955, No. 4, pp. 182–83.

57. Lebedev, *Bulavinskoe vosstanie*, p. 38.

58. Solov'ev, *Istoriia Rossii*, VIII, 185–86; *Bulavinskoe vosstanie*, pp. 230–38; E. P. Pod"iapol'skaia, "Novye materialy o vosstanii na Donu i v tsentral'noi Rossii v 1707–1709 gg.," *Materialy po istorii SSSR*, V, 1957, 122–23.

59. Whitworth to Harley, June 2, 1708, *SIRIO*, L, 16; Karasev, "Bumagi," *Russkii Arkhiv*, XXXII, 301; *Pis'ma i bumagi*, VII, part 2, 659–60.

60. *Bulavinskoe vosstanie*, pp. 453–56.

61. *Ibid.*, pp. 244, 270.

62. *Pis'ma i bumagi*, VII, part 2, 751–52; Pod"iapol'skaia, *Vosstanie Bulavina*, pp. 52–53.

63. "Podmetnoe vozzvanie Levengaupta 1708 g.," *Russkaia Starina*, XVI, 1876, 173.

64. Pod"iapol'skaia, *Vosstanie Bulavina*, pp. 109–10; "Novye materialy," *Materialy po istorii SSSR*, V, 140–41.

65. *Pis'ma i bumagi*, VII, part 1, 154; Solov'ev, *Istoriia Rossii*, VIII, 185.

66. Whitworth to Boyle, July 7, 1708, *SIRIO*, L, 25.

67. Tolstoy to Peter, *Bulavinskoe vosstanie*, pp. 359–60. See also Pod"iapol'skaia, "Novye materialy," *Materialy po istorii SSSR*, V, 126–29.

68. Pod"iapol'skaia, *Vosstanie Bulavina*, pp. 168–69; *Pis'ma i bumagi*, VII, part 2, 892.

69. "Ivan Andreevich Tolstoi: Pis'ma k nemu Petra Velikogo," *Russkaia Starina*, XXV, 1879, 146.

70. Whitworth to Boyle, July 21, 1708, *SIRIO*, L, 30-31.

71. Pod"iapol'skaia, "Novye materialy," *Materialy po istorii SSSR*, V, 524–26.

72. *Bulavinskoe vosstanie*, p. 360; *Pis'ma i bumagi*, VIII, part 1, 378; Sumner, *Peter the Great and the Ottoman Empire*, p. 54. Nekrasov died in 1737.

73. *Bulavinskoe vosstanie*, p. 466; Sumner, *Survey of Russian History*, p. 146.

74. Solov'ev, *Istoriia Rossii*, VIII, 196. See also *Bulavinskoe vosstanie*, pp. 336–38, 347.

75. Charles Whitworth, *An Account of Russia as It Was in the Year 1710*, London, 1758, p. 180.

76. Report of Brigadier Shidlovsky, October 15, 1708, *Bulavinskoe vosstanie*, p. 344.

77. Perry, *The State of Russia*, pp. 27–28.

78. See Boldyrev, *Ataman K. A. Bulavin*, pp. 37–41.

79. On Loskut's role in the rebellion see *Voprosy Istorii*, 1969, No. 8, pp. 187–89.

80. Lebedev, *Bulavinskoe vosstanie*, p. 38; *Pis'ma i bumagi*, VIII, part 2, 480.

81. W. R. Ralston, *Songs of the Russian People*, London, 1872, p. 42.

82. V. I. Lebedev, "Neizvestnye volneniia pri Petre I (1722-1724 gg.)," *Istoriia SSSR*, 1961, No. 1, pp. 159–62.

CHAPTER IV: PUGACHEV, 1773-1774

1. A. Riabnin, *Ural'skoe kazach'e voisko*, St. Petersburg, 1866, part 1, p. 15.

2. A. Gaisinovich, *Pugachev*, Moscow, 1937, p. 63. See also P. S. Pallas, *Reise durch verschiedene Provinzen des russischen Reichs*, 3 vols., St. Petersburg, 1771, I, 274–305.

3. N. F. Dubrovin, *Pugachev i ego soobshchniki*, 3 vols., St. Petersburg, 1884, I, 38; William Coxe, *Travels into Poland, Russia, Sweden and Denmark*, 2 vols., London, 1784, II, 67.

4. P. K. Shchebal'skii, *Nachalo i kharakter pugachevshchiny*, Moscow, 1865, p. 28.

5. On the events on the Yaik before Pugachev's rising see I. G. Rozner, *Kazachestvo v Krest'ianskoi voine, 1773–1775 gg.*, Lvov, 1966; Rozner, *Iaik pered burei*, Moscow, 1966; and V. N. Vitevskii, "Iaitskoe voisko do poiavleniia Pugacheva," *Russkii Arkhiv*, 1879, Nos. 3–12.

6. R. Nisbet Bain, *Peter III, Emperor of Russia*, Westminster, 1902, p. 46. For a recent appraisal of Peter III's brief reign see Marc Raeff, "The Domestic Policies of Peter III and His Overthrow," *American Historical Review*, LXXV, June 1970, 1289–1310.

7. "Otgoloski pugachevskogo bunta," *Russkaia Starina*, 1905, II, 664.

8. K. V. Sivkov, "Samozvanchestvo v Rossii v poslednei treti XVIII v.," *Istoricheskie Zapiski*, XXXI, 1950, 88–135.

9. V. I. Semevskii, *Krest'iane v tsarstvovanii imperatritsy Ekateriny II*, 2 vols., St. Petersburg, 1901–1903, I, 356–57.

10. Michael B. Petrovich, "Catherine II and a False Peter III in Montenegro," *American Slavic and East European Review*, XIV, April 1955, 169–94; D. L. Mordovtsev, *Samozvantsy i ponizovaia vol'nitsa*, 2 vols. in 1, St. Petersburg, I, 1–71.

11. Dubrovin, *Pugachev i ego soobshchniki*, I, 107.

12. R. V. Ovchinnikov, ed., "Sledstvie i sud nad E. I. Pugachevym," *Voprosy Istorii*, 1966, No. 3, pp. 131–38.

13. N. N. Firsov, *Pugachevshchina*, St. Petersburg, 1908, p. 61.

14. *Pugachevshchina*, 3 vols., Moscow, 1926–1931, II, 194–95; Sumner, *Survey of Russian History*, p. 148.

15. Coxe, *Travels*, II, 67.

16. *SIRIO*, XIX, 385; A. S. Pushkin, *Istoriia Pugachevskogo bunta*, 2 vols., St. Petersburg, 1834, I, 14.

17. *Voprosy Istorii*, 1966, No. 7, pp. 96–97.

18. Dubrovin, *Pugachev i ego soobshchniki*, I, 218–21. "Out of mud you can make a prince" is a Russian proverb which, says Trotsky, Stalin was fond of quoting. See Isaac Deutscher, *The Prophet Unarmed*, New York, 1959, p. 458.

19. *Pugachevshchina*, I, 25. For a photocopy of the original manifesto see *Krasnyi Arkhiv*, 1925, No. 1, p. 194.

20. Rozner, *Kazachestvo v Krest'ianskoi voine*, p. 54; Dubrovin, *Pugachev i ego soobshchniki*, II, 16–18.

21. N. A. Sereda, "Pugachevskii bunt po zapiskam sovremennika i ochevidtsa," *Vestnik Evropy*, 1870, III, 632–33.

22. Dubrovin, *Pugachev i ego soobshchniki*, II, 33.

23. *Ibid.*, II, 73.

24. *Ibid.*, II, 181; D. L. Mordovtsev, "Pugachevshchina," *Vestnik Evropy*, 1866, I, 327.

25. *Pugachevshchina*, III, 8, 11.

26. "Glavnye posobniki Pugacheva," *Russkaia Starina*, 1876, II, 483.

27. *Pugachevshchina*, I, 33.

28. See Roger Portal, "Les Bachkirs et le gouvernement russe au XVIIIe siècle," *Revue des Études Slaves*, XXII, 1946, 82–104; F. Nefedov, "Dvizhenie sredi bashkir pered pugachevskim buntom," *Russkoe Bogatstvo*, 1880, No. 10, pp. 83–96; and N. A. Firsov, *Inorodcheskoe naselenie prezhnego Kazanskogo tsarstva*, Kazan, 1869, pp. 211ff.

29. Solov'ev, *Istoriia Rossii*, X, 594.

30. *Ocherki po istorii Bashkirskoi ASSR*, 2 vols., Ufa, 1956–1959, I, 173.

31. Dubrovin, *Pugachev i ego soobshchniki*, I, 272; Lozanova, *Pesni i skazaniia o Razine i Pugacheve*, p. 212.

32. *Pugachevshchina*, I, 28.

33. Roger Portal, *L'Oural au XVIIIe siècle*, Paris, 1950, pp. 131–74; D. Kashintsev, *Istoriia metallurgii Urala*, Moscow, 1939, pp. 117–34. See also B. B. Kafengauz, *Istoriia khoziaistva Demidovykh v XVIII-XIX vv.*, Moscow, 1949. It is worth noting that some of the largest enterprises, such as the Avziano-Petrovsk works of Evdokim Demidov, were erected in Bashkir lands and that this figured prominently in Batyrsha's rising of 1755.

34. S. G. Tomsinskii, "Rol' rabochikh v Pugachevskom vosstanii," *Krasnaia Nov'*, 1925, No. 2, pp. 172–74; M. N. Martynov, "Pugachevskoe dvizhenie na zavodakh iuzhnogo Urala," *Zapiski Nauchnogo Obshchestva Marksistov*, 1928, No. 1, p. 45; Iu. Gessen, *Istoriia gornorabochikh v SSSR*, 2 vols., Moscow, 1926–1929, I, 71–129.

35. *SIRIO*, CXV, 264; *Pugachevshchina*, II, 435; Dubrovin, *Pugachev i ego soobshchniki*, I, 356.

36. *Velikaia reforma*, 6 vols., Moscow, 1911, II, 37.

37. Semevskii, *Krest'iane v tsarstvovanii Ekateriny II*, II, 335.

38. *Pugachevshchina*, II, 348–49.

39. A. V. Prussak, "Zavody rabotavshie na Pugacheva," *Istoricheskie Zapiski*, VIII, 1940, 178.

40. *Pugachevshchina*, I, 200.

41. François Auguste Thesby de Belcour, *Relation ou journal d'un officier françois au service de la Confédération de Pologne*, Amsterdam, 1776, p. 208.

42. *Pugachevshchina*, II, 188, 194.

43. Dubrovin, *Pugachev i ego soobshchniki*, II, 195.

44. Gunning to Suffolk, October 22, 1773, *SIRIO*, XIX, 380–81. Cf. O. E. Kornilovich, "Obshchestvennoe mnenie Zapadnoi Evropy o pugachevskom bunte," *Annaly*, III, 1923, 152.

45. M. M. Freidenberg, "Novaia publikatsiia o pugachevskom vosstanii," *Istoriia SSSR*, 1965, No. 1, p. 209.

46. *Pugachevshchina*, II, 134; III, 209–10.

47. Thesby de Belcour, *Relation*, pp. 197–98; *Krasnyi Arkhiv*, 1935, No. 2–3, p. 231.

48. Jean Henri Castéra, *The Life of Catharine II*, 3 vols., London, 1799, II, 221; *Osmnadtsatyi vek*, 4 vols., Moscow, 1869, I, 128.

49. Gunning to Suffolk, April 26, 1774, *SIRIO*, XIX, 411.

50. Dubrovin, *Pugachev i ego soobshchniki*, II, 174.

51. *Ibid., II*, 168–69; "Podlinnye bumagi, do bunta Pugachova otnosiashchiesia," *Chteniia*, 1860, II, 72–77.

52. Castéra, *The Life of Catharine II*, II, 221–22; Dubrovin, *Pugachev i ego soobshchniki*, II, 388.

53. Freidenberg, "Novaia publikatsiia," *Istoriia SSSR*, 1965, No. 1, p. 210.

54. *Pugachevshchina*, I, 74–75; "Pugachevskie listy 1774 g.," *Russkaia Starina*, XIII, 1875, 274–75.

55. *Salavat Iulaev*, Ufa, 1952, pp. 14–19; R. G. Ignat'ev, "Bashkir Salavat Iulaev," *Izvestiia Obshchestva arkheologii . . . pri Kazanskom universitete*, XI, 1893, 327–28. For a list of Bashkir elders who sided with the rebels see *Materialy po istorii SSSR*, V, 1957, 576-78.

56. A. A. Bibikov, *Zapiski o zhizni i sluzhbe Aleksandra Il'icha Bibikova*, Moscow, 1865, pp. 132–35; Mordovtsev, "Pugashevshchina," *Vestnik Evropy*, 1866, I, 333.

57. S. P. Petrov, *Pugachev v Penzenskom krae*, Penza, 1950, p. 50; Pushkin, *Istoriia Pugachevskogo bunta*, II, 65. Cf. Bibikov to Chernyshev, January 24, 1774: "It is not the enemy who is dangerous but the unrest of the people, the spirit of commotion and revolt." Bibikov, *Zapiski*, pp. 85–86.

58. G. R. Derzhavin, "Zapiski," *Sochineniia Derzhavina*, 7 vols., St. Petersburg, 1871–1876, VI, 465.

59. "Podlinnye bumagi," *Chtenniia*, 1860, II, 65; "Pis'ma imperatritsy Ekateriny II k A. I. Bibikovu vo vremia pugachevskogo bunta," *Russkii Arkhiv*, 1866, p. 393.

60. "Pis'ma A. I. Bibikova k A. M. Luninu," *Russkii Arkhiv*, 1866, p. 385.

61. Dubrovin, *Pugachev i ego soobshchniki*, II, 305.

62. *Pugachevshchina*, II, 347; Gunning to Suffolk, April 26, 1774, *SIRIO*, XIX, 411. Derzhavin wrote a moving ode on Bibikov's death: Bibikov, *Zapiski*, appendix, pp. 60–63.

63. Kornilovich, "Obshchestvennoe mnenie," *Annaly*, III, 165.

64. A. I. Dmitriev-Mamonov, *Pugachevshchina v Sibiri*, Moscow, 1898, p. 110.

65. Dubrovin, *Pugachev i ego soobshchniki*, III, 26; I. Z. Kadson, "Vosstanie Pugacheva i raskol," *Ezhegodnik Muzeia istorii religii i ateizma*, IV, 1960, 227.

66. *Pugachevshchina*, II, 319; N. I. Pavlenko, *Istoriia metallurgii v Rossii XVIII veka*, Moscow, 1962, p. 110.

67. Gessen, *Istoriia gornorabochikh*, I, 134; Kashintsev, *Istoriia metallurgii*

Urala, pp. 149–55, 252–81; I. F. Ushakov, "Rabotnye liudi Beloretskogo zavoda v krest'ianskoi voine," *Istoriia SSSR*, 1960, No. 6, pp. 131–35.

68. Prussak, "Zavody rabotavshie na Pugacheva," *Istoricheskie Zapiski*, VIII, 181.

69. D. A. Anuchin, "Vtoroe poiavlenie Pugacheva i razorenie Kazani," *Voennyi Sbornik*, XIV, April 1871, 228.

70. Portal, "Les Bachkirs," *Revue des Études Slaves*, XXII, 91. Cf. M. N. Martynov, "Satkinskii zavod vo vremia vosstaniia Emel'iana Pugacheva," *Istoricheskie Zapiski*, LXIII, 1956, 241.

71. Gunning to Suffolk, July 15, 1774, *SIRIO*, XIX, 421–22.

72. Dubrovin, *Pugachev i ego soobshchniki*, III, 44–52.

73. Mavrodin *et al.*, *Krest'ianskaia voina v Rossii*, II, 438.

74. "P. S. Potemkin vo vremia pugachevshchiny," *Russkaia Starina*, 1870, II, 492.

75. Dubrovin, *Pugachev i ego soobshchniki*, III, 94.

76. "P. S. Potemkin," *Russkaia Starina*, 1870, II, 494.

77. Dubrovin, *Pugachev i ego soobshchniki*, III, 98.

78. James Harris, *Diaries and Correspondence*, 2nd edn., 4 vols., London, 1845, I, 177.

79. *SIRIO*, XIX, 431–33.

80. S. A. Piontkovskii, "Arkhiv Tainoi ekspeditsii o krest'ianskikh nastroeniiakh v 1774 g.," *Istorik-Marksist*, 1935, No. 7, p. 96.

81. Mavrodin *et al.*, *Krest'ianskaia voina v Rossii*, I, 266; John T. Alexander, *Autocratic Politics in a National Crisis*, Bloomington, Ind., 1969, p. 141.

82. Pushkin, *Istoriia Pugachevskogo bunta*, I, 141.

83. Dubrovin, *Pugachev i ego soobshchniki*, III, 104.

84. Geroid T. Robinson, *Rural Russia Under the Old Regime*, New York, 1932, p. 29.

85. In Voronezh province, to cite an extreme case, 384 of the 393 estates attacked by the rebels were on *barshchina*. S. I. Tkhorzhevskii, *Pugachevshchina v pomeshchich'ei Rossii*, Moscow, 1930, p. 36.

86. *SIRIO*, XIII, 381.

87. *Russkaia Starina*, 1875, p. 441; Sumner, *Survey of Russian History*, p. 146.

88. Derzhavin, *Sochineniia*, V, 140; *Russkaia Starina*, 1896, p. 118; *Pugachevshchina*, III, 110, 286; E. S. Kogan, "Volneniia krest'ian Penzenskoi votchiny A. B. Kurakina vo vremia dvizheniia Pugacheva," *Istoricheskie Zapiski*, XXXVII, 1951, 109.

89. P. D'iakonov, "Bedstviia Shatskoi provintsii v 1774 godu," *Russkoe Obozrenie*, 1892, No. 7, p. 150.

90. *Pugachevshchina*, III, 83.

91. E. I. Glazatova, "Vosstanie krest'ian Kazanskogo kraia na pervom etape krest'ianskoi voiny," *Uchenye zapiski Chitinskogo pedagogicheskoga instituta*, 1957, No. 1, p. 105.

92. Dubrovin, *Pugachev i ego soobshchniki*, III, 113.

292 NOTES

93. V. D. Dimitriev, *Istoriia Chuvashii XVIII veka*, Cheboksary, 1959, p. 171; Iu. A. Limonov *et al.*, *Pugachev i ego spodvizhniki*, Moscow, 1965, p. 133.

94. On the *odnodvortsy* see Semevskii, *Krest'iane v tsarstvovanii Ekateriny II*, II, 721–75; and Thomas Esper, "The Odnodvortsy and the Russian Nobility," *Slavonic and East European Review*, XLV, January 1967, 124–34.

95. A. A. Kondrashenkov, "Krest'ianstvo Isetskoi provintsii v Krest'ianskoi voine 1773–1775 gg.," *Uchenye zapiski Kurganskogo pedagogicheskogo instituta*, 1958, No. 1, pp. 121–22; *Pugachevshchina*, II, 127.

96. Tomsinskii, "Rol' rabochikh v Pugachevskom vosstanii," *Krasnaia Nov'*, 1925, No. 2, p. 180. Cf. L. D. Ryslaev, "Pugachev v Saratove," *Vestnik Leningradskogo universiteta*, 1962, No. 8, pp. 58–60.

97. Kh. I. Muratov, *Krest'ianskaia voina 1773–1775 gg. v Rossii*, Moscow, 1954, p. 162.

98. *Voprosy Istorii*, 1966, No. 4, p. 115.

99. Tkhorzhevskii, *Pugachevshchina v pomeshchich'ei Rossii*, pp. 129–30.

100. Mavrodin *et al.*, *Krest'ianskaia voina v Rossii*, III, 339–43; R. V. Ovchinnikov, "Nemetskii ukaz E. I. Pugacheva," *Voprosy Istorii*, 1969, No. 12, pp. 133–41.

101. *Pugachevshchina*, I, 36; III, 7.

102. Ia. K. Grot, ed., *Materialy dlia istorii pugachevskogo bunta*, St. Petersburg, 1876, pp. 141–42; Pushkin, *Istoriia Pugachevskogo bunta*, I, Notes, 61–105; Tkhorzhevskii, *Pugachevshchina v pomeshchich'ei Rossii*, pp. 182–83; V. I. Nedosekin, "Popytka E. I. Pugacheva podniat' vosstanie na Donu, Ukraine i v Chernozemnom Tsentre Rossii v iiule–sentiabre 1774 goda," *Trudy Voronezhskogo universiteta*, 1960, No. 1, pp. 80–81.

103. Tkhorzhevskii, *Pugachevshchina v pomeshchich'ei Rossii*, pp. 115–16, 125–26.

104. *Ibid.*, pp. 34–36.

105. V. F. Zheludkov, "Krest'ianskaia voina pod predvoditel'stvom E. I. Pugacheva i podgotovka gubernskoi reformy 1775 g.," *Vestnik Leningradskogo universiteta*, 1963, No. 8, p. 56.

106. D. Anuchin, "Graf Panin, usmiritel' Pugachevshchiny," *Russkii Vestnik*, 1869, No. 3–4, p. 38; *Pugachevshchina*, III, 286.

107. Dubrovin, *Pugachev i ego soobshchniki*, III, 121.

108. A. T. Bolotov, *Zhizn' i prikliucheniia Andreia Bolotova*, 4 vols., St. Petersburg, 1870–1873, III, 377.

109. *Pugachevshchina*, III, vi, 8, 12.

110. *Ibid.*, III, 79.

111. D. B. Mertvago, "Zapiski D. B. Mertvago," *Russkii Arkhiv*, 1867, Supplement, pp. 4–37; *Bemerkungen über Esthland, Liefland, Russland, nebst einigen Beiträgen zur Empörungs-Geschichte Pugatschews*, Prague and Leipzig, 1792, pp. 186–210.

112. Gaisinovich, *Pugachev*, pp. 201–2.

113. Coxe, *Travels*, II, 74.

114. E. I. Indova, "Bor'ba privolzhskikh dvortsovykh krest'ian," *Istoricheskii Arkhiv*, VIII, 1953, 301–6; Gottlieb Bauer, *Geschichte der deutschen Ansiedler an der Wolga*, Saratov, 1908, pp. 29–41. Contrast D. Schmidt, *Studien über die Geschichte der Wolgadeutschen*, Kharkov, 1930, pp. 95–107, who says that the colonists supported the rebels. The evidence, however, indicates that most were victims rather than participants.

115. "Iz arkhiva Saratovskogo gubernskogo pravleniia," *Russkii Arkhiv*, 1873, I, 451–52; *Pugachevshchina*, I, 41–42; II, 238.

116. M. Seniutkin, *Dontsy*, Moscow, 1866, part 1, pp. 37–88.

117. Grot, *Materialy dlia istorii pugachevskogo bunta*, p. 111.

118. *Pugachevshchina*, III, 277.

119. Anuchin, "Graf Panin," *Russkii Vestnik*, 1869, No. 3–4, p. 25; "Podlinnye bumagi," *Chteniia*, 1860, II, 53–56.

120. *Vosstanie Emel'iana Pugacheva*, Leningrad, 1935, p. 197; Dubrovin, *Pugachev i ego soobshchniki*, III, 53–54.

121. Quoted in Tkhorzhevskii, *Pugachevshchina v pomeshchich'ei Rossii*, p. 100.

122. Castéra, *The Life of Catharine II*, II, 237.

123. *Bemerkungen über Esthland, Liefland, Russland*, p. 205. In the battle near Cherny Yar, Andrei Ovchinnikov was killed and Pugachev's two daughters were captured.

124. *Pugachevshchina*, II, 151–58, 171–72.

125. Bolotov, *Zhizn' i prikliucheniia*, III, 486. Pugachev's cage has been preserved and is now on display at the State Historical Museum in Red Square.

126. "Pis'ma Ekateriny Vtoroi k baronu Gimmu," *Russkii Arkhiv*, 1878, III, 10; *SIRIO*, XXIII, 9; XXVII, 2–3.

127. "Pis'mo imperatritsy Ekateriny II k grafu P. I. Paninu," *Chteniia*, 1858, II, 54.

128. *Pugachevshchina*, III, 46.

129. A. N. Usmanov, "Kinzia Arslanov," *Istoricheskie Zapiski*, LXXI, 1962, 133; P. L. Iudin, "Sud i kazn' Salavatki," *Istoricheskii Vestnik*, LXXIII, August 1898, 584–86; *Voprosy Istorii*, 1958, No. 8, pp. 221–22.

130. Catherine to Grimm, December 21, 1774, *SIRIO*, XXIII, 11.

131. *Voprosy Istorii*, 1966, No. 3, p. 129; Pushkin, *Istoriia Pugachevskogo bunta*, II, 22–53.

132. *Vosstanie Emel'iana Pugacheva*, p. 199.

133. Bolotov, *Zhizn' i prikliucheniia*, III, 488.

134. A. V. Arsen'ev, "Zhenshchiny pugachevskogo vosstaniia," *Istoricheskii Vestnik*, XVI, June 1884, 625; L. B. Svetlov, "Sud'ba sem'i E. I. Pugacheva," *Voprosy Istorii*, 1968, No. 12, pp. 204–5.

135. *SIRIO*, XXVII, 1; *Polnoe sobranie zakonov*, XX, 85.

136. Harris, *Diaries and Correspondence*, I, 177.

137. Robinson, *Rural Russia*, p. 32.

138. Joseph de Maistre, *Quatre chapitres inédits sur la Russie*, Paris, 1859, p. 27.

139. *Voprosy Istorii,* 1966, No. 3, p. 129.

140. *Osmnadtsatyi vek,* III, 232.

141. Kostomarov, *Bunt Sten'ki Razina,* II, 356.

142. P. G. Bogatyrev, "Obraz narodnogo geroia v slavianskikh predaniiakh i skazochnaia traditsiia," *Russkii Fol'klor,* VIII, 1963, 53–55.

143. A. N. Lozanova, ed., *Pugachev v Srednem Povolzh'e i Zavolzh'e,* Kuibyshev, 1947, pp. 26, 35; Petrov, *Pugachev v Penzenskom krae,* p. 135.

144. *Salavat Iulaev,* p. 24.

145. Gunning to Suffolk, January 26, 1775, *SIRIO,* XIX, 449.

146. G. P. Gooch, *Catherine the Great and Other Studies,* London, 1954, p. 99.

147. *SIRIO,* XXVII, 9–10.

148. A. N. Radishchev, *A Journey from St. Petersburg to Moscow,* Cambridge, Mass., 1958, p. 153.

CHAPTER V: THE LEGACY

1. A. S. Pushkin, *Polnoe sobranie sochinenii,* 17 vols., Moscow, 1937–1959, IX, part 1, 373.

2. K. V. Sivkov, "Podpol'naia politicheskaia literatura v Rossii v poslednei treti XVIII veka," *Istoricheskie Zapiski,* XIX, 1946, 73.

3. D. L. Mordovtsev, "Samozvanets Khanin," *Russkii Vestnik,* 1860, II, 325.

4. E. Al'bovskii, "Otgolosok Pugachevshchiny na Ukraine," *Russkii Arkhiv,* 1898, III, 297–308; Svatikov, *Rossiia i Don,* p. 251.

5. August von Haxthausen, *The Russian Empire,* 2 vols., London, 1856, I, 287–88; *Rewriting Russian History,* ed. C. E. Black, New York, 1962, p. 371.

6. Cherniavsky, *Tsar and People,* pp. 147–48; Marc Raeff, *The Decembrist Movement,* Englewood Cliffs, N.J., 1966, pp. 53–54.

7. Chistov, *Russkie narodnye sotsial'no-utopicheskie legendy,* p. 178; Hugh Seton-Watson, *The Russian Empire, 1801–1917,* Oxford, 1967, p. 227. The names Pugachev and Metelkin involve a pun on the words "frighten" and "sweep" (in Russian: "Pugachev popugal gospod, a Metelkin pometet ikh").

8. Pushkin, *Istoriia pugachevskogo bunta,* I, 162–63.

9. *SIRIO,* XCVIII, 114–15.

10. F. C. Conybeare, *Russian Dissenters,* Cambridge, Mass., 1921, p. 331; A. S. Prugavin, *Religioznye otshchepentsy,* 2 vols., St. Petersburg, 1904, I, 238–52.

11. Peter Kropotkin, *Memoirs of a Revolutionist,* Boston, 1899, pp. 64–65.

12. P. Péchoux, "L'ombre de Pugačev," in *Le Statut des paysans libérés du servage, 1861–1961,* ed. R. Portal, Paris, 1963, p. 153; Franco Venturi, *Roots of Revolution,* New York, 1960, pp. 93–94.

13. E. Lampert, *Sons Against Fathers,* Oxford, 1965, pp. 8, 39; M. K.

Lemke, *Politicheskie protsessy v Rossii 1860-kh gg.*, Moscow, 1923, pp. 63–64.

14. *The Peasant in Nineteenth-Century Russia,* ed. Wayne S. Vucinich, Stanford, 1968, pp. 51–52.

15. Kropotkin, *Memoirs of a Revolutionist,* p. 131.

16. S. G. Pushkarev, "The Russian Peasants' Reaction to the Emancipation of 1861," *The Russian Review,* XXVII, April 1968, 201–7; Venturi, *Roots of Revolution,* pp. 214–17; Lampert, *Sons Against Fathers,* pp. 40–43.

17. Mavrodin, *Krest'ianskaia voina v Rossii,* I, 28, 66. "Thoughts" (*Dumy*) was the title of Ryleev's poems.

18. Venturi, *Roots of Revolution,* pp. 310–12, 372–73; P. L. Lavrov, *1773–1873: v pamiat' stoletiia pugachevshchiny,* London, 1874, pp. 4, 40.

19. V. Bogucharskii, *Aktivnoe narodnichestvo vo semidesiatykh godakh,* Moscow, 1912, p. 347.

20. Stepanov, *Krest'ianskaia voina v Rossii,* I, 140; Venturi, *Roots of Revolution,* p. 484.

21. N. Berdiaev, *The Origin of Russian Communism,* London, 1937, p. 74.

22. E. H. Carr, *Michael Bakunin,* New York, 1961, p. 395; Venturi, *Roots of Revolution,* pp. 367–69.

23. G. V. Plekhanov, *Sochineniia,* 24 vols., Moscow, 1923–1927, XX, 362; XXI, 296.

24. Karl Marx and Frederick Engels, *Selected Works,* 2 vols., Moscow, 1962, II, 454; Lenin, *Polnoe sobranie sochinenii,* XLV, 380.

25. L. Trotsky, *The History of the Russian Revolution,* 3 vols. in 1, Ann Arbor, Mich., 1957, I, 51.

26. *Ibid.,* III, 30.

27. Sir George Buchanan, *My Mission to Russia,* 2 vols., London, 1923, II, 86.

28. V. Korolenko, "Sovremennaia samozvanshchina," *Russkoe Bogatstvo,* 1896, No. 8, p. 131; *Salavat Iulaev,* p. 32; James Mavor, *Economic History of Russia,* 2 vols., New York, 1914, II, 569–71.

29. Alexander Kerensky, *Russia and History's Turning Point,* New York, 1965, p. 54; B. B. Grave, ed., *Burzhuaziia nakanune Fevral'skoi revoliutsii,* Moscow, 1927, p. 62.

30. Trotsky, *History,* I, 31.

31. Barrington Moore, Jr., *Social Origins of Dictatorship and Democracy,* Boston, 1966, p. 481.

32. Oliver H. Radkey, *The Sickle Under the Hammer,* New York, 1963, p. 443.

33. Alexander Berkman, *The Bolshevik Myth,* New York, 1925, p. 191.

34. Emma Goldman, *My Disillusionment in Russia,* London, 1925, pp. 148–49.

35. Paul Avrich, *Kronstadt 1921,* Princeton, 1970, p. 177.

36. Lydia Seifulina, "A Peasant Legend of Lenin," *Labour Literature,* March–April 1924; quoted in Walter Laqueur, *The Fate of the Revolution,* New York, 1967, p. 62.

Bibliography

The literature on the four rebellions, particularly on those of Razin and Pugachev, is so immense that a comprehensive list of sources would require a sizable volume in itself. What follows makes no attempt to be an exhaustive bibliography. The emphasis, rather, is on works of basic importance and on recent studies, both Soviet and Western, that may not be included in existing bibliographies. Some of the more specialized literature is cited in the reference notes.

The first section of the bibliography contains works of a general nature, while the succeeding sections list, in turn, studies of each particular revolt. For fuller listings see the items marked by an asterisk, which provide useful bibliographies. These should be supplemented by the bibliographical articles in *Istorik-Marksist*, 1933, No. 6, pp. 80–119; and *Voprosy Istorii*, 1957, No. 12, pp. 135–60; 1961, No. 5, pp. 24–47; and 1965, No. 3, pp. 127–40.

General Works

* Billington, James H. *The Icon and the Axe*. New York, 1966. A cultural history of Russia with many provocative suggestions.
* Blum, Jerome. *Lord and Peasant in Russia*. Princeton, 1961. A useful history from the ninth to the nineteenth century.

Cherniavsky, Michael. *Tsar and People*. New Haven, Conn., 1961. A pioneering work.

———. "The Old Believers and the New Religion," *Slavic Review*, XXV, March 1966, 1–39. A fascinating article.

Chistov, K. V. *Russkie narodnye sotsial'no-utopicheskie legendy XVII-XIX vv*. Moscow, 1967. A valuable study of the folk myths which figured prominently in the risings.

Cohn, Norman. *The Pursuit of the Millennium*. Rev. edn. New York, 1970. An immensely stimulating work.

Eeckaute, Denise. "Les brigands en Russie du XVIIe au XIXe siècle," *Revue d'Histoire Moderne et Contemporaine*, XII, July–September 1965, 161–202.

Firsov, N. K. *Narodnye dvizheniia v Rossii do XIX veka.* Moscow, 1924.

Florinsky, Michael T. *Russia: A History and an Interpretation.* 2 vols. New York, 1953.

Forster, Robert, and Jack P. Greene, eds. *Preconditions of Revolution in Early Modern Europe.* Baltimore, 1971. A valuable symposium with a chapter on Pugachev by Marc Raeff.

Hobsbawm, Eric. *Bandits.* London, 1970.

————. *Primitive Rebels.* Manchester, 1959. Stimulating books, full of original ideas.

Keep, J. L. H. "Bandits and the Law in Muscovy," *Slavonic and East European Review,* XXXV, December 1956, 201–22.

Kliuchevsky, V. O. *A History of Russia.* 5 vols. New York, 1911–1931. Volumes III and IV have recently appeared in new and improved translations, New York, 1961 and 1969.

Lanternari, Vittorio. *The Religions of the Oppressed.* New York, 1963.

* Longworth, Philip. *The Cossacks.* London, 1969. The most up-to-date and readable history in English.

Mavrodin, V. V., *et al.* "Ob osobennostiakh krest'ianskikh voin v Rossii," *Voprosy Istorii,* 1956, No. 2, pp. 69–79.

Mel'gunov, S. P. *Religiozno-obshchestvennye dvizheniia XVI–XVIII vv. v Rossii.* Moscow, 1922.

Mirsky, D. S. *Russia: A Social History.* London, 1931.

Moore, Barrington, Jr. *Social Origins of Dictatorship and Democracy.* Boston, 1966. A thoughtful and illuminating study.

Mousnier, Roland. *Peasant Uprisings of the Seventeenth Century.* New York, 1971. Compares revolts in France, Russia and China.

* Robinson, Geroid T. *Rural Russia Under the Old Regime.* New York, 1932. The standard work in English.

Rudé, George. *The Crowd in History, 1770–1848.* New York, 1964. One of several pioneering studies of the preindustrial crowd by a first-rate historian.

Shapiro, A. L. "Ob istoricheskoi roli krest'ianskikh voin XVII–XVIII vv. v Rossii," *Istoriia SSSR,* 1965, No. 5, pp. 61–80.

Shchapov, A. P. *Zemstvo i raskol.* St. Petersburg, 1862.

* Smirnov, I. I., *et al., Krest'ianskie voiny v Rossii XVII–XVIII vv.* Moscow, 1966. The best general survey in Russian.

Solov'ev, S. M. *Istoriia Rossii s drevneishikh vremen.* 15 vols. Moscow, 1959–1966.

————. "Zametki o samozvantsakh v Rossii," *Russkii Arkhiv,* 1868, VI, 265–81.

Sumner, B. H. *Survey of Russian History*. 2nd edn. London, 1947. An outstanding book.

Svatikov, S. G. *Rossiia i Don (1549–1917)*. Belgrade, 1924.

Tkhorzhevskii, S. I. *Narodnye vosstaniia pri pervykh Romanovykh*. Petrograd, 1924.

Tomsinskii, S. G. *Krest'ianskie dvizheniia v feodal'no-krepostnoi Rossii*. Moscow, 1932.

Troitskii, S. M. "Samozvantsy v Rossii XVII–XVIII vekov," *Voprosy Istorii*, 1969, No. 3, pp. 134–46.

* Venturi, Franco. *Roots of Revolution*. New York, 1960. A monumental history of Russian populism.

Yaresh, Leo. "The 'Peasant Wars' in Soviet Historiography," *American Slavic and East European Review*, XVI, October 1957, pp. 241–59.

Bolotnikov

Firsov, N. N. *Krest'ianskaia revoliutsiia na Rusi v XVII veke*. Moscow, 1927. Discusses both Bolotnikov and Razin.

* Makovskii, D. P. *Pervaia krest'ianskaia voina v Rossii*. Smolensk, 1967. The most recent history of the revolt, but does not supersede Smirnov.

Ovchinnikov, R. V. "Nekotorye voprosy Krest'ianskoi voiny nachala XVII veka v Rossii," *Voprosy Istorii*, 1959, No. 7, pp. 69–83.

Platonov, S. F. *Ocherki po istorii smuty v Moskovskom gosudarstve XVI–XVII vv*. St. Petersburg, 1899. The classic history of the Time of Troubles.

Smirnov, I. I. "O nekotorykh voprosakh istorii bor'by klassov v russkom gosudarstve nachala XVII veka," *Voprosy Istorii*, 1958, No. 12, pp. 116–31.

* ———. *Vosstanie Bolotnikova, 1606–1607*. 2nd edn. Moscow, 1951. The best study of the revolt by its foremost historian.

Zimin, A. A. "Nekotorye voprosy istorii krest'ianskoi voiny v Rossii v nachale XVII veka," *Voprosy Istorii*, 1958, No. 3, pp. 97–113.

Razin

Buganov, V. I., and E. V. Chistiakova. "O nekotorykh voprosakh istorii Vtoroi Krest'ianskoi voiny v Rossii," *Voprosy Istorii*, 1968, No. 7, pp. 36–51.

Chistiakova, E. V. "Astrakhan' v period vosstaniia Stepana Razina," *Istoriia SSSR*, 1957, No. 5, pp. 188–202.

———. *Vasilii Us—spodvizhnik Stepana Razina*. Moscow, 1963.

Druzhinin, V. G. *Raskol na Donu v kontse XVII veka*. St. Petersburg, 1889.

Fenomenov, M. I. *Razinovshchina i pugachevshchina*. Moscow, 1923.

Field, Cecil. *The Great Cossack*. London, 1947.

Firsov, N. N. *Razin i razinovshchina; Pugachev i pugachevshchina*. Kazan, 1930.

———. *Razinovshchina*. St. Petersburg, 1906. A social and psychological analysis of the revolt.

Iakovlev, M. A. *Narodnoe pesnotvorchestvo ob atamane Stepane Razine*. Leningrad, 1924. A good collection of folksongs with valuable commentary.

Karzhavin, D. F. *Stepan Razin v Simbirske*. Ulyanovsk, 1947.

Kataev, I. M. *Sten'ka Razin*. Moscow, 1906.

Kostomarov, N. I. *Bunt Sten'ki Razina*. 2nd edn. St. Petersburg, 1872. The most imaginative history of the revolt.

Krest'ianskaia voina pod predvoditel'stvom Stepana Razina. 3 vols. in 4. Moscow, 1954–1962. A basic collection of documents on the rising.

Lebedev, V. I. *Krest'ianskaia voina pod predvoditel'stvom Stepana Razina, 1667–1671 gg.* Moscow, 1955.

* Lozanova, A. N. "K bibliografii o Stepane Razine," *Uchenye zapiski Saratovskogo universiteta*, VI, 1927, 279–89.

———. *Pesni i skazaniia o Razine i Pugacheve*. Moscow, 1935. A good collection of songs and legends about Razin and Pugachev.

Lunin, B. V. *Stepan Razin*. Rostov-on-Don, 1960.

Man'kov, A. G. *Razvitie krepostnogo prava v Rossii vo vtoroi polovine XVII veka*. Moscow, 1962.

Popov, A. N. *Istoriia vozmushcheniia Sten'ki Razina*. Moscow, 1857.

Porfir'ev, S. I. "Razinshchina v Kazanskom krae," *Izvestiia Obshchestva Arkheologii, istorii i etnografii pri Kazanskom universitete*, XXIX, 1916, 289–366.

Razgrom razinshchiny. Leningrad, 1934. A valuable collection of documents relating to the suppression of the revolt.

* Smentsovskii, M. N. "St. Razin v nauke, literature i iskusstve," *Katorga i Ssylka*, 1932, No. 7, pp. 193–239; Nos. 8–9, pp. 309–66.

Solov'ev, A. I. *Sten'ka Razin i ego soobshchniki v predelakh nyneshnei Simbirskoi gubernii*. Simbirsk, 1907.

* Stepanov, I. V. *Krest'ianskaia voina v Rossii v 1670–1671 gg.* Leningrad, 1966. The first of two volumes which will constitute the

fullest history of the revolt. See also Stepanov's survey of archival materials on Razin in *Vestnik Leningradskogo universiteta*, seriia istorii, 1969, No. 4.

Terpigorev, S. N. "Raskaty Sten'kina groma v Tambovskoi zemle," *Istoricheskii Vestnik*, XL, 1890, 560–84; XLI, 49–70.

* Tikhomirov, B. N. "Istochniki po istorii Razinshchiny," *Problemy Istochnikovedeniia*, 1933, No. 1, pp. 50–69.

———. *Razinshchina*. Moscow, 1930.

Tkhorzhevskii, S. I. *Sten'ka Razin*. Petrograd, 1923. A good brief account.

Tomsinskii, S. G., ed. *Krest'ianstvo i natsionaly v revoliutsionnom dvizhenii: Razinshchina*. Moscow, 1931. An important collection of documents.

Bulavin

Chaev, N. S. *Bulavinskoe vosstanie (1707–1708 gg.)*. Moscow, 1934.

Golikova, N. B. *Politicheskie protsessy pri Petre I*. Moscow, 1957.

Krest'ianskie i natsional'nye dvizheniia nakanune obrazovaniia Rossiiskoi imperii: Bulavinskoe vosstanie (1707–1708 gg.). Moscow, 1935. The most important collection of source materials on the rising.

Lebedev, V. I. *Bulavinskoe vosstanie, 1707–1708*. Moscow, 1934. A good short history. The appendix has interesting rebel manifestoes.

* Pod"iapol'skaia, E. P. *Vosstanie Bulavina, 1707–1709*. Moscow, 1962. The fullest history of the revolt, based on a firm command of the sources.

Pronshtein, A. P. *Zemlia Donskaia v XVIII veke*. Rostov-on-Don, 1961. Has useful material on both Bulavin and Pugachev.

Sumner, B. H. *Peter the Great and the Emergence of Russia*. London, 1951. An excellent concise study.

Pugachev

* Alexander, John T. *Autocratic Politics in a National Crisis: The Imperial Russian Government and Pugachev's Revolt, 1773–1775*. Bloomington, Ind., 1969. A well-written study, with a useful bibliography, stressing the impact of the revolt on the Russian government.

————. "Western Views on the Pugachov Rebellion," *Slavonic and East European Review*, XLVIII, October 1970, 520–36.

Andrushchenko, A. I. *Krest'ianskaia voina 1773–1775 gg. na Iaike, v Priural'e, na Urale i v Sibiri*. Moscow, 1969. A detailed account of Pugachev's operations in the Urals and Siberia, based largely on archival sources.

Beliavskii, M. T. *Krest'ianskii vopros v Rossii nakanune vosstaniia E. I. Pugacheva*. Moscow, 1965.

Chuzhak, N. *Pravda o Pugacheve*. Moscow, 1926.

Confino, Michael. *Domaines et seigneurs en Russie vers la fin du XVIIIe siècle*. Paris, 1963. An intelligent study.

————. "Maîtres de forges et ouvriers dans les usines métallurgiques de l'Oural aux XVIIIe–XIXe siècles," *Cahiers du Monde Russe et Soviétique*, I, 1959, 239–84.

Dubrovin, N. F. *Pugachev i ego soobshchniki*. 3 vols. St. Petersburg, 1884. Though somewhat dated, contains a mine of information on the rebellion.

Esper, Thomas. "The Odnodvortsy and the Russian Nobility," *Slavonic and East European Review*, XLV, January 1967, 124–34.

Firsov, N. N. *Pugachevshchina*. St. Petersburg, 1908.

Gaisinovich, A. *Pugachev*. Moscow, 1937. A good popular history.

Kizevetter, A. A. *Posadskaia obshchina v Rossii XVIII st.* Moscow, 1903.

Limonov, Iu. A., *et al. Pugachev i ego spodvizhniki*. Moscow, 1965.

Martynov, M. N. *Pugachevskii ataman Ivan Beloborodov*. Perm, 1958.

* Mavrodin, V. V., *et al. Krest'ianskaia voina v Rossii v 1773–1775 godakh*. 3 vols. Leningrad, 1961–1970. The most recent and comprehensive history, with an excellent survey of the sources.

Mordovtsev, D. L. *Samozvantsy i ponizovaia vol'nitsa*. 2 vols. in 1. St. Petersburg, 1867.

Muratov, Kh. I. *Krest'ianskaia voina 1773–1775 gg. v Rossii*. Moscow, 1954.

Ovchinnikov, R. V., ed. "Sledstvie i sud nad E. I. Pugachevym," *Voprosy Istorii*, 1966, Nos. 3–9.

Pascal, Pierre. *La révolte de Pougatchëv*. Paris, 1971. A readable new history by a respected French scholar.

Petrov, S. P. *Pugachev v Penzenskom krae*. Penza, 1950.

Portal, Roger. *L'Oural au XVIIIe siècle*. Paris, 1958. An important study.

————. "Pugačev: une révolution manquée," *Études d'Histoire Moderne et Contemporaine*, I, 1947, 68–98. A good brief account of the revolt and its participants.

Pugachevshchina. 3 vols. Moscow, 1926–1931. An indispensable collection of documents.

Pushkin, A. S. *Istoriia Pugachevskogo bunta.* 2 vols. St. Petersburg, 1834. The starting point for all subsequent research.

Raeff, Marc. "Pugachev's Rebellion," in *Preconditions of Revolution in Early Modern Europe,* ed. by Robert Forster and J. P. Greene. Baltimore, 1971, pp. 161–202. A stimulating essay.

* Rozner, I. G. *Kazachestvo v Krest'ianskoi voine, 1773–1775 gg.* Lvov, 1966.

Rubinshtein, N. L. *Sel'skoe khoziaistvo Rossii vo vtoroi polovine XVIII v.* Moscow, 1957.

Semevskii, V. I. *Krest'iane v tsarstvovanii imperatritsy Ekateriny II.* 2 vols. St. Petersburg, 1901–1903. Essential for the situation of the peasantry under Catherine.

Simonov, S. *Pugachevshchina.* Kharkov, 1931.

Sivkov, K. V. "Samozvanchestvo v Rossii v poslednei treti XVIII v.," *Istoricheskie Zapiski,* XXXI, 1950, 88–135.

Tkhorzhevskii, S. I. *Pugachevshchina v pomeshchich'ei Rossii.* Moscow, 1930. An excellent work.

Tomsinskii, S. G. "O kharaktere Pugachevshchiny," *Istorik-Marksist,* 1927, No. 6, pp. 48–78.

Index

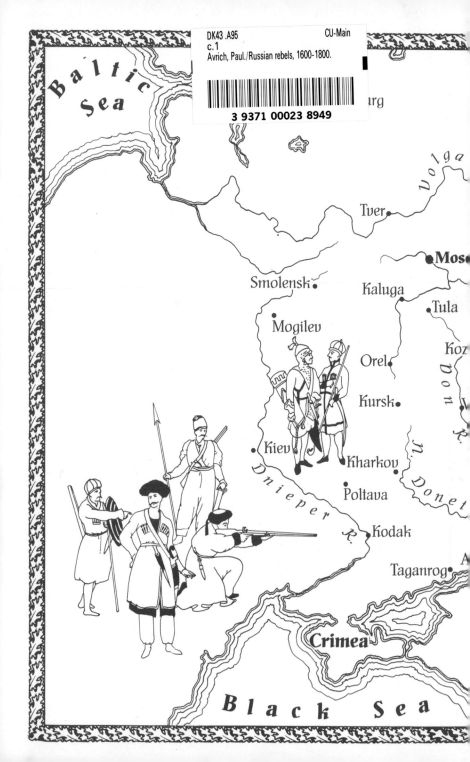

Baltic Sea

Volga

Tver

urg

Mos

Smolensk

Kaluga

Tula

Mogilev

Koz

Orel

Don R.

Kursk

Kiev

Kharkov

N. Donet

Dnieper R.

Poltava

Kodak

Taganrog

A

Crimea

Black Sea